SELF-INTEREST BEFORE ADAM SMITH
A Genealogy of Economic Science

Self-Interest before Adam Smith inquires into the foundations of economic theory. It is generally assumed that the birth of modern economic science, marked by the publication of *The Wealth of Nations* in 1776, was the triumph of the "selfish hypothesis" (the idea that self-interest is the motive of human action). Yet, as a neo-Epicurean idea, this hypothesis had been a matter of controversy for over a century and Smith opposed it from a neo-Stoic point of view. But how can the Epicurean principles of orthodox economic theory be reconciled with the Stoic principles of Adam Smith's philosophy? Pierre Force shows how Smith's theory refutes the "selfish hypothesis" and integrates it at the same time. He also explains how Smith appropriated Rousseau's "republican" critique of modern commercial society, and makes the case that the autonomy of economic science is an unintended consequence of Smith's "republican" principles. This book sheds light on some classic puzzles of economic theory and is a major work from an outstanding scholar.

PIERRE FORCE, Nell and Herbert M. Singer Professor of Contemporary Civilization and Professor of French at Columbia University in New York, is the author of *Le Problème herméneutique chez Pascal* (1989) and *Molière ou Le Prix des choses* (1994).

T0381563

IDEAS IN CONTEXT

Edited by Quentin Skinner (*General Editor*), Lorraine Daston,
Dorothy Ross and James Tully

The books in this series will discuss the emergence of intellectual traditions and of related new disciplines. The procedures, aims and vocabularies that were generated will be set in the context of the alternatives available within the contemporary frameworks of ideas and institutions. Through detailed studies of the evolution of such traditions, and their modification by different audiences, it is hoped that a new picture will form of the development of ideas in their concrete contexts. By this means, artificial distinctions between the history of philosophy, of the various sciences, of society and politics, and of literature may be seen to dissolve.

The series is published with the support of the Exxon Foundation.

A list of books in the series will be found at the end of the volume.

SELF-INTEREST BEFORE ADAM SMITH

A Genealogy of Economic Science

PIERRE FORCE

Columbia University

CAMBRIDGE UNIVERSITY PRESS

CAMBRIDGE UNIVERSITY PRESS
Cambridge, New York, Melbourne, Madrid, Cape Town, Singapore, São Paulo

Cambridge University Press
The Edinburgh Building, Cambridge CB2 8RU, UK

Published in the United States of America by Cambridge University Press, New York

www.cambridge.org
Information on this title: www.cambridge.org/9780521830607

First published 2003
Third printing 2006
This digitally printed version 2007

A catalogue record for this publication is available from the British Library

Library of Congress Cataloguing in Publication data
Force, Pierre.
Self-interest before Adam Smith: a genealogy of economic science / Pierre Force.
p.   cm. – (Ideas in context; 68)
Includes bibliographical references and index.
ISBN 0 521 83060 5
1. Economics – History. I. Title. II. Series.
HB75.F67   2003
330.15 – dc21   2003043590

ISBN 978-0-521-83060-7 hardback
ISBN 978-0-521-03619-1 paperback

Contents

Acknowledgments

The topic of this book has been with me for a long time. I first touched upon it in a 1989 article.[1] It was in the background of my 1994 book on Molière.[2] The colloquium I organized at the Maison Française of Columbia University in 1994 was dedicated in great part to these issues.[3] Some of the arguments developed in chapter 1 were presented in a *Yale French Studies* article in 1997.[4] Many of the ideas present in this book were tested in the seminar I taught in 1996, "The Commerce of the Self from Montaigne to Adam Smith," and in the seminar I co-taught with Allan Silver in 2000, "Self-Interest before Capitalism in Literature and Social Theory." The questions and comments from students in these seminars greatly helped me to clarify my thinking. This work owes a lot to the many conversations I had with Allan Silver, a colleague who is also a true friend. I thank another friend, Kathy Eden, for helping me find my way in the complete works of Augustine. Thanks are also due to Charles Larmore for several useful suggestions, and to Knud Haakonssen for his generous advice on how to navigate the waters of Smith scholarship. I also wish to acknowledge the comments, suggestions and criticisms from colleagues and friends who read parts of the manuscript. I had the opportunity to discuss chapter 1 with the members of the Chicago Group on Modern France. Chapter 2 has benefited from Jean Lafond's unmatched expertise on the Augustinian tradition in the early modern period. Incisive comments by Jon Elster and John D. Collins have led me to reformulate some key passages in chapter 3.

[1] "What Is a Man Worth? Ethics and Economics in Molière and Rousseau," *Romanic Review* 1 (1989), pp. 18–29.

[2] *Molière ou Le Prix des choses. Morale, économie et comédie*, Paris: Nathan, 1994.

[3] *De la morale à l'économie politique. Dialogue franco-américain sur les moralistes français*, edited by Pierre Force and David Morgan, introduction by Pierre Force, Pau: Publications de l'Université de Pau, 1996.

[4] "Self-Love, Identification, and the Origin of Political Economy," in *Exploring the Convertible World: Text and Sociability from the Classical Age to the Enlightenment*, edited by Elena Russo, *Yale French Studies* 92 (1997), pp. 46–64.

Chapter 4 was discussed at a session of Columbia's Early Modern Salon. It incorporates many helpful suggestions I received from Katherine Almquist, James Helgeson, and Gita May. Chapter 6 was almost entirely re-written in response to the criticisms and suggestions I received from two anonymous readers at Cambridge University Press. I thank my colleagues and students in Contemporary Civilization at Columbia for providing the intellectual environment that made this book possible. Special thanks are also due to the staff of the Columbia French Department, Isabelle Chagnon, Benita Dace, and Meritza Moss, for providing the administrative environment that allowed me to write this book while chairing an academic department. Last but not least, I would like to express my gratitude to my research assistant, Julia Chamberlin, who has been an example of efficiency and thoughtfulness.

My wife Christel Hollevoet was completing a book of her own when this one was being written. Being able to share the toils and the joys of scholarship has strengthened our love. I dedicate this book to our beloved children Charlotte and Eliot.

Introduction

In an eloquent formula manifesting the reverence economists have for the founder of their discipline, George Stigler characterizes Adam Smith's *Wealth of Nations* as "a stupendous palace erected upon the granite of self-interest."[1] The meaning of the metaphor is clear. Self-interest provides a rock-solid foundation for the theory developed in *The Wealth of Nations*. Furthermore, since Adam Smith's work is itself the foundation of modern economic science, self-interest is the first principle of economics. Because self-interest is a concept of such fundamental importance, one would expect Adam Smith to mention it quite often. Yet the term "self-interest" is remarkably rare in *The Wealth of Nations*. It appears only once, in the context of a discussion of religion. Smith explains that in the Catholic Church, "the industry and zeal of the inferior clergy are kept more alive by the powerful motive of self-interest than perhaps in any established Protestant church."[2] Catholic priests work harder than the established Protestant clergy because, instead of being salaried, they depend upon voluntary gifts from their parishioners. In the famous passage analyzing the motives "the butcher, the brewer, or the baker" may have for providing our dinner, Smith does not refer to *self-interest* but rather to *self-love*: "We address ourselves, not to their humanity but to their self-love, and never talk to them of our own necessities but of their advantages."[3] One may be tempted to brush the difference aside, and argue that *self-love* and *self-interest* are synonyms. I contend, however, that Smith's choice of terms is significant, especially in a passage that lays out the theoretical foundations for the rest of the book. *Self-love* is a term used by moral philosophers throughout the seventeenth and eighteenth centuries, from Hobbes to Shaftesbury, Mandeville,

---

[1] George J. Stigler, "Smith's Travels on the Ship of State," *History of Political Economy* 3 (1971), p. 265.

[2] Adam Smith, *An Inquiry into the Nature and Causes of the Wealth of Nations, The Glasgow Edition of the Works and Correspondence of Adam Smith*, vol. 2, Oxford: Oxford University Press, 1976 [London: Strahan and Cadell, 1776], v.i.g.2.

[3] *The Wealth of Nations*, I.ii.2.

and Hume. It is the translation of a technical term used by Renaissance humanists, *philautia*.[4] The French translation of the term, used by Pascal, La Rochefoucauld, Nicole, and Rousseau among many others, is *amour-propre*. The choice of the term *self-love* carries with it an entire philosophical and literary tradition.

The purpose of this book is to study the history of the concepts of self-love and self-interest before Adam Smith, in order to understand what these concepts meant when Adam Smith decided to use them as foundation for the system he constructed in *The Wealth of Nations*. Some important work has been done (especially by late-nineteenth-century German scholars) on the connections between Smith and the philosophical tradition exemplified by La Rochefoucauld in France and Mandeville in England.[5] A lot of excellent work exists on the intellectual origins of modern economics.[6] My purpose in this book is narrower. I dedicate all my attention to first principles. I ask what the first principles of Smith's system are, and what the previous history of these first principles is. My goal is to place Adam Smith's axiomatic choices in their historical and philological context.

My greatest intellectual debt is to Albert Hirschman's work, *The Passions and the Interests*.[7] Hirschman has shown many essential connections between the rise of the modern concept of self-interest and the development of moral philosophy and reason of State theory in the seventeenth century. This book brings a lot of additional evidence in support of Hirschman's insights, and it takes them further on some key points. For instance, I show that in collapsing all the passions into the drive for the "augmentation of fortune," Smith was appropriating Rousseau's psychology. As to

---

[4] *Philautia* is itself the transliteration of a term used by Plato and neo-Platonic philosophers. On the history of the words *philautia* and *amour-propre*, see Hans-Jürgen Fuchs, *Entfremdung und Narzißmus. Semantische Untersuchungen zur Geschichte der "Selbstbezogenheit" als Vorgeschichte von französisch "amour-propre"*, Stuttgart: Metzler, 1977.

[5] See Wilhelm Hasbach, "Larochefoucault und Mandeville," *Jahrbuch für Gesetzgebung und Volkswirtschaft im Deutschen Reich*, Leipzig, 1890, pp. 1–43 and *Untersuchungen über Adam Smith und die Entwicklung der Politischen Ökonomie*, Leipzig, 1891; Albert Schatz, "Bernard de Mandeville. Contribution à l'étude des origines du libéralisme économique," *Vierteljahrschrift für Social- und Wirtschaftgeschichte*, Leipzig, 1903.

[6] James Bonar, *Philosophy and Political Economy in Some of Their Historical Relations*, New Brunswick, NJ: Transaction Books, 1992 [New York: Macmillan, 1893]; Karl Pribram, *A History of Economic Reasoning*, Baltimore: Johns Hopkins University Press, 1983; Louis Dumont, *From Mandeville to Marx. The Genesis and Triumph of Economic Ideology*, Chicago: University of Chicago Press, 1977; Jean-Claude Perrot, *Une histoire intellectuelle de l'économie politique*, Paris: Editions de l'Ecole des Hautes Etudes en Sciences Sociales, 1992.

[7] *The Passions and the Interests. Political Arguments for Capitalism before its Triumph*, Princeton: Princeton University Press, 1997 [1977].

Hirschman's main thesis (that Smith sided with the "republican" critique of modern commercial society in rejecting the Montesquieu–Steuart doctrine on the political benefits of commerce), I qualify it by showing that a limited endorsement of the Montesquieu–Steuart doctrine was compatible with a "republican" point of view.

My training as a literary scholar makes me especially sensitive to issues of consistency and inconsistency in discourse. I attempt to withhold judgment about the meaning of a text until all of its aspects have been accounted for. In some instances, Smith contradicts himself. This, I argue, should not be interpreted as a shortcoming in his doctrine, or as an apparent contradiction that should be resolved in favor of one's favorite interpretation of Smith. Like his classical models, Cicero and Carneades, Smith believes that one gets closer to the truth by arguing both sides of an issue. This is particularly clear in *The Theory of Moral Sentiments*, where Smith develops Rousseau's arguments on the corrupting influence of commerce, and subsequently refutes them as "splenetic philosophy."[8] In Smith's view, Rousseau's critique of commerce and the critique of Rousseau's critique were equally true. I read *The Wealth of Nations* as an attempt by Smith to reconcile Hume's views on the social and political benefits of commerce with Rousseau's republican critique of commercial society.

Smith scholars rarely mention Rousseau as an important interlocutor for Smith.[9] Charles Griswold wrote recently that "a comparative work on Smith and Rousseau holds tremendous interest."[10] This book does more than a comparison. It makes the case that Rousseau is an essential interlocutor for Smith. There has been a good deal of debate in the past twenty years on Smith's place within the traditions of civic humanism and natural jurisprudence. The interpretation I propose here emphasizes the connections with the civic humanist tradition, and it agrees in some respects with Emma Rothschild's recent parallel of Smith and Condorcet,[11] where Smith appears as a fervent republican. What I argue, however, following

[8] Adam Smith, *The Theory of Moral Sentiments* (sixth edition), *The Glasgow Edition of the Works and Correspondence of Adam Smith*, vol. 1, edited by D.D. Raphael and A.L. Macfie, Oxford: Oxford University Press, 1976 [London and Edinburgh, 1790; first edition 1759], IV.1.

[9] The most notable exceptions are Donald Winch, *Riches and Poverty. An Intellectual History of Political Economy in Britain, 1750–1834*, Cambridge: Cambridge University Press, 1996, pp. 66–76, and Michael Ignatieff, *The Needs of Strangers*, London: Chatto & Windus, 1984. Also see Ignatieff's "Smith, Rousseau and the Republic of Needs," in *Scotland and Europe, 1200–1850*, edited by T.C. Smout, Edinburgh: J. Donald, 1986, pp. 187–206.

[10] Charles Griswold, *Adam Smith and the Virtues of Enlightenment*, Cambridge: Cambridge University Press, 1999, p. 25.

[11] Emma Rothschild, *Economic Sentiments. Adam Smith, Condorcet, and the Enlightenment*, Cambridge, MA: Harvard University Press, 2001.

Hirschman's suggestion, is that Smith's republican leanings are the paradoxical cause of the advent of economics as an autonomous science.

The current fashion among historians is to dismiss as teleological any interpretive scheme that reads past events and past ideas as a foreshadowing of the present. Donald Winch argues, correctly, that the historical Smith has little to do with the image today's economists have of the founding father of their discipline.[12] This does not mean, however, that we should not approach Smith with today's questions. My goal is not to describe a historical Smith or a historical Rousseau as objects of knowledge that would themselves be abstracted from history. We could read authors from the past as if there were no historical distance, and blindly project our own concerns onto them. We would gain nothing from this experience because we would learn nothing that we did not know in the first place. On the other hand, we could make the historical distance so great that authors from the past would appear as radically strange and foreign to us. This also would teach us little, and the study of the past would be a matter of mere intellectual curiosity. I agree with Gadamer that the locus of hermeneutics is somewhere between complete strangeness and the complete absence of strangeness. As Gadamer puts it, "the call to leave aside the concepts of the present does not mean a naïve transposition into the past. It is, rather, an essentially relative demand that has meaning only in relation to one's own concepts."[13] A hermeneutic approach to Rousseau and Smith should start with the familiar image we have of these authors; it should then seek to question this image by making them strange and unfamiliar; in the end, we should gain a better knowledge of Smith and Rousseau, but, more importantly, this process should make us more aware of the pre-conceptions that had defined and structured our understanding of these authors. These pre-conceptions do not need to be discarded. In fact, they cannot be discarded because they form the core of what we are as historical beings. We can simply gain a greater awareness of them. The ultimate purpose of a hermeneutic approach is self-knowledge.

The main characters in this story are La Rochefoucauld, Bayle, Mandeville, Hume, Montesquieu, Rousseau, and Smith. I attempt to explain how one goes from the interest doctrine (selfish motives are behind all human actions) to economic science (self-interest explains *economic* behavior, but not all types of human behavior). All the authors mentioned here did position themselves strategically with respect to their predecessors and

[12] Donald Winch, *Adam Smith's Politics. An Essay in Historiographic Revision*, Cambridge: Cambridge University Press, 1978.

[13] Hans-Georg Gadamer, *Truth and Method*, translation revised by Joel Weinsheimer and Donald G. Marshall, New York: Crossroad, 1992, p. 397 [*Wahrheit und Methode*, Tübingen: J.C.B. Mohr, 1960].

contemporaries, sometimes explicitly, sometimes implicitly. I focus on the way in which authors construct their own systems by adopting or rejecting the first principles used by other authors. In all cases, I try to show what authors *do* as much as what they *say*. Throughout this book, I show how each author uses, rejects, or transforms what Hume calls "the selfish hypothesis," i.e. the idea that all human conduct can be explained in terms of self-interest. This exclusive focus on the "selfish hypothesis" is what gives my story its unity.

Instead of trying to construct a grand narrative that would take us step by step from the middle of the seventeenth century to the end of the eighteenth century, I have chosen to approach the same problem from several angles. Each chapter discusses a distinct question. In the first chapter, I ask: "Is self-interest the engine of human behavior?" In the second chapter, I establish an important distinction, used in the rest of the book, between two main traditions: an Epicurean/Augustinian tradition, which uses self-interest as its sole principle, and a neo-Stoic tradition, which uses self-interest as one among other principles. The third chapter discusses the meaning of the expression: "rational pursuit of self-interest." In the fourth chapter, I revisit the topic of Hirschman's book on the passions and the interests, and I discuss the ways in which passions and interests can be either opposed or identified. The fifth chapter studies the rise of the concept of disinterestedness, in theology first, and subsequently in moral philosophy. I argue that the novel concept of disinterestedness is fundamental to the establishment of economics as a distinct field of knowledge. In the sixth and last chapter, I examine the relationship between private interests and the public interest, and I trace the genealogy of Jean-Baptiste Say's affirmation of the autonomy of economics with respect to politics.

This narrative includes works like La Rochefoucauld's *Maxims*, which have most often been studied as "literature." Yet the subject matter of the *Maxims* would probably now go under the rubric of "psychology" or "social theory." Conversely, in spite of many efforts to come up with a language free of connotations, social scientists continue to use words like utility, preference, rationality, which are loaded with history – a history that is the philologist's province. This book tries to look at the issue from both ends. It approaches the works of seventeenth- and eighteenth-century moral philosophers with today's questions. At the same time, it seeks to illuminate today's questions by reconstructing the intellectual tradition that has made them possible. Some of the puzzles for social theory can find the beginning of an explanation if one looks at economic science at the moment of its coming into being. It is my hope that this book can do its bit to help rediscover the common ground shared by the social sciences and the humanities.

Since this investigation is taking place "under the guidance of language" (to use Gadamer's expression) I systematically give the original language (French or Latin) in the footnote for every excerpt I quote. Whenever possible, I use translations from the period of the work quoted, because they usually provide a better rendition of the terminology. Seventeenth- and eighteenth-century translations always render *amour-propre* by *self-love*, while many modern translations use anachronistic terms like *egoism* or *ego- centrism*. When using modern translations, I have systematically made the changes necessary to keep the terminology consistent. In some instances, I have made the translation myself. Whenever I speak in my own name, I follow the now-prevailing custom of using gender-neutral language. How- ever, I follow the usage of the authors I study when I paraphrase or analyze them.

As far as editions are concerned, I refer to the standard *Glasgow Edition of the Works and Correspondence of Adam Smith*. For *The Wealth of Na- tions* and *The Theory of Moral Sentiments*, I refer to the book, chapter, and paragraph number rather than to the page number. I quote the original text of Rousseau from the *Œuvres complètes* (Gallimard, Bibliothèque de la Pléiade) with the volume number and the page number. English trans- lations come from the excellent but still incomplete *Collected Writings of Rousseau* (University Press of New England). I quote *Émile* in Allan Bloom's translation. For every work I quote in an edition other than the original, I give, where known, the date, place and publisher of the original edition between square brackets. Spelling in all quotes has been modernized.

Self-interest as a first principle

Self-interest is the only motive of human actions.

P. H. d'Holbach, *A Treatise on Man* (1773)

In his classic work, *The Passions and the Interests*, Albert Hirschman describes the rise of the concept of interest in the seventeenth and eighteenth centuries. He shows how this concept, originally linked to statecraft and *raison d'État* theory, was so successful that it soon became a tool for interpreting not only the behavior of rulers, but also the totality of human conduct. "Once the idea of interest had appeared," Hirschman remarks, "it became a real fad as well as a paradigm (à la Kuhn) and most of human action was suddenly explained by self-interest, sometimes to the point of tautology."[1] It is generally assumed that the birth of modern economic science, conventionally marked by the publication of *The Wealth of Nations* in 1776, was one of the most significant manifestations of the triumph of the "interest paradigm." According to this view, self-interest provided the axiom upon which Adam Smith constructed his political economy. After the marginalist revolution in the second half of the nineteenth century, when economics became a highly formalized and mathematical discipline, self-interest was enshrined as the first principle that made all theoretical constructions possible. As F. Y. Edgeworth put it in 1881, "the first principle of Economics is that every agent is actuated only by self-interest."[2] More recently, Kenneth Arrow traced back to Adam Smith the idea that "a decentralized economy motivated by self-interest and guided by price signals would be compatible with a coherent disposition of economic resources that could be regarded, in a well defined sense, as superior to a large class of possible alternative dispositions."[3]

---

[1] Albert O. Hirschman, *The Passions and the Interests. Political Arguments for Capitalism before its Triumph*, Princeton: Princeton University Press, 1997 [1977], p. 42.
[2] Francis Y. Edgeworth, *Mathematical Psychics. An Essay on the Application of Mathematics to the Moral Sciences*, London: C. Kegan Paul, 1881, p. 16.
[3] Kenneth Arrow and F. H. Hahn, *General Competitive Analysis*, San Francisco: Holden Day, 1971, p. vi.

Traditionally, economists have maintained that the assumption of self-interested behavior holds only for economic activity (as well as the business of warfare, according to Edgeworth). There have been attempts, however, to generalize the scope of self-interest (or its more abstract synonym, *utility maximizing behavior*) as a first principle in the analysis of all human conduct. Gary Becker claims that "the economic approach is a comprehensive one that is applicable to all human behavior, be it behavior involving money prices or imputed shadow prices, repeated or infrequent decisions, large or minor decisions, emotional or mechanical ends, rich or poor persons, men or women, adults or children, brilliant or stupid persons, patients or therapists, businessmen or politicians, teachers or students."[4] Becker too ascribes a long ancestry to his axiomatic choices. "The economic approach to human behavior is not new," he writes, "even outside the market sector. Adam Smith often (but not always!) used this approach to understand political behavior."[5] Becker could have added other moral philosophers of the same period, who are probably better examples of the "interest paradigm." In 1758, Claude-Adrien Helvétius asserted that "if the physical universe be subject to the laws of motion, the moral universe is equally so to those of interest."[6] In the same spirit, d'Holbach, a major contributor to the *Encyclopédie*, wrote: "Self-interest is the only motive of human actions."[7] Incomparably more famous, however, is Adam Smith's pronouncement: "It is not from the benevolence of the butcher, the brewer, or the baker, that we expect our dinner, but from their regard to their own interest."[8] George Stigler expresses a view shared by the vast majority of economists when he says that the inevitable quote about the butcher, the brewer and the baker, constitutes the first principle not only of Smith's doctrine, but also of modern economic science:

Smith had one overwhelmingly important triumph: he put into the center of economics the systematic analysis of the behavior of individuals pursuing their self-interest under conditions of competition. This theory was the crown jewel of

[4] Gary Becker, "The Economic Approach to Human Behavior," in *Rational Choice*, edited by Jon Elster, New York: New York University Press, 1986, p. 112.

[5] Ibid., p. 119.

[6] Claude-Adrien Helvétius, *Essays on the Mind*, London: Albion Press, 1810, II, 2, p. 42. "Si l'univers physique est soumis aux lois du mouvement, l'univers moral ne l'est pas moins à celle de l'intérêt." *De l'Esprit*, Paris: Durand 1758, vol. I, p. 53.

[7] "L'intérêt est l'unique mobile des actions humaines." Paul Henri Thiry, baron d'Holbach, *Système de la nature, ou des lois du monde physique et du monde moral*, Geneva: Slatkine Reprints, 1973 (2 vols.) [London, 1770], I, xv, p. 312.

[8] Adam Smith, *An Inquiry into the Nature and Causes of the Wealth of Nations*, The Glasgow Edition of the Works and Correspondence of Adam Smith, vol. 2, Oxford: Oxford University Press, 1976 [London: Strahan and Cadell, 1776], I.ii.

The Wealth of Nations and it became, and remains to this day, the foundation of the theory of the allocation of resources.[9]

ONE OR SEVERAL PRINCIPLES?

The fact that interest-based interpretations come to mind so easily, even in popular consciousness, testifies to the power of the "interest paradigm." Originally, the idea that the pursuit of self-interest by independent agents would result in some kind of order or equilibrium was a paradox. Arrow and Hahn rightly notice that the most surprising thing about the interest paradigm is that it is no longer seen as a paradox:

> The immediate "common sense" answer to the question "What will an economy motivated by individual greed and controlled by a very large number of different agents look like?" is probably: There will be chaos. That quite a different answer has long been claimed true and has indeed permeated the economic thinking of a large number of people who are in no way economists is itself sufficient grounds for investigating it seriously.[10]

For social scientists, the principle of self-interest complies with the injunction that one should not needlessly generate assumptions. Between two explanations, the one that relies on the smallest number of first principles is to be preferred. That certainly is Gary Becker's view. Whenever human behavior seems to contradict the assumption that self-interest is the motive, the theorist must stick to the axiom, and assume that an explanation based on self-interest is possible, even if it cannot be provided immediately:

> When an apparently profitable opportunity to a firm, worker, or household is not exploited, the economic approach does not take refuge in assertions about irrationality, contentment with wealth already acquired, or convenient *ad hoc* shifts in values (that is, preferences). Rather it postulates the existence of costs, monetary or psychic, of taking advantage of these opportunities that eliminate their profitability – costs that may not be easily "seen" by outside observers. Of course, postulating the existence of costs closes or "completes" the economic approach in the same, almost tautological, way that postulating the existence of (sometimes unobserved) uses of energy completes the energy system, and preserves the law of energy... The critical question is whether a system is completed in a useful way.[11]

Alternatively, one may decide to deprive self-interest of its pre-eminent status, and assume that motives other than self-interest are at work. For

[9] George J. Stigler, "The Successes and Failures of Professor Smith," Selected Papers no. 50, Graduate School of Business, University of Chicago, 1976, p. 3.
[10] Arrow and Hahn, *General Competitive Analysis*, p. vii.
[11] Becker, "The Economic Approach to Human Behavior," p. 112.

instance, Jon Elster, while acknowledging the appeal of interest-based explanations, dismisses them as being contrary to experience:

The assumption that all behavior is selfish is the most parsimonious we can make, and scientists always like to explain much with little. But we cannot conclude, neither in general nor on any given occasion, that selfishness is the more widespread motivation. Sometimes the world is messy, and the most parsimonious explanation is wrong.

The idea that self-interest makes the world go round is refuted by a few familiar facts. Some forms of helping behavior are not reciprocated and so cannot be explained by long-term self-interest. Parents have a selfish interest in helping their children, assuming that children will care for parents in their old age – but it is not in the selfish interest of children to provide such care. And many still do. Some contributors to charities give anonymously and hence cannot be motivated by prestige.[12]

Another type of argument is invoked by Hirschman, who recalls Macaulay's critique of an attempt by James Mill to construct a theory of politics on the axiom of self-interest. Simply put, if self-interest explains everything, it explains nothing. In that sense, the interest doctrine is "essentially tautological."[13] For Hirschman, parsimony is certainly a virtue when it comes to positing first principles, but like any virtue, it can be overdone. Consequently, Hirschman proposes to complicate economic discourse by assuming that "benevolence" may be just as important as self-interest in explaining economic behavior.[14] In so doing, he implicitly goes against Smith's famous statement dismissing "the benevolence of the butcher, the brewer, or the baker" as a motive for trade.

Along the same lines, Amartya Sen questions the wisdom of limiting the first principles of economics to self-interest, and notices that, according to Edgeworth himself, pure egoism could not explain the behavior of real people: "I should mention that Edgeworth himself was quite aware that his so-called first principle of Economics was not a particularly realistic one."[15] Indeed, Edgeworth added a caveat to the assertion that self-interest is the first principle of economic science. His system is based on a dichotomy between economics and ethics. Each domain has its own species of agents.

---

[12] Jon Elster, *Nuts and Bolts for the Social Sciences*, Cambridge: Cambridge University Press, 1989, p. 54.
[13] Albert O. Hirschman, "The Concept of Interest: From Euphemism to Tautology," in *Rival Views of Market Society*, Cambridge, MA: Harvard University Press, 1992 [1986], p. 48.
[14] Albert O. Hirschman, "Against Parsimony: Three Easy Ways of Complicating Some Categories of Economic Discourse," in *Rival Views of Market Society*, Cambridge, MA: Harvard University Press, 1992 [1986], p. 159.
[15] Amartya Sen, "Rational Fools: A Critique of the Behavioral Foundations of Economic Theory," *Philosophy and Public Affairs* 6 (1977), pp. 317–344.

The "Egoist" (driven only by self-interest) operates in the economic sphere. The "Utilitarian" (who cares only about the interest of all) operates in the ethical sphere. That is the theoretical construction. However, Edgeworth adds, "it is possible that the moral constitution of the concrete agent would be neither Pure Utilitarian nor Pure Egoistic, but "μικτη τις [some combination of both] . . . For between the two extremes Pure Egoistic and Pure Universalistic, there may be an indefinite number of impure methods."[16] For his part, in an attempt to come up with a more realistic set of first principles, Sen proposes to add "commitment" to self-interest in the analysis of human behavior.[17]

While Gary Becker quotes Smith as the founder of the "economic approach" to explaining all human behavior, Amartya Sen refers to the founding father in order to prove the opposite.[18] He mentions Part VII of *The Theory of Moral Sentiments*, where Smith criticizes Epicurus for building his ethical system on a single principle:

By running up all the different virtues too to this one species of propriety, Epicurus indulged a propensity, which is natural to all men, but which philosophers in particular are apt to cultivate with a peculiar fondness, as the great means of displaying their ingenuity, the propensity to account for all appearances from as few principles as possible. And he, no doubt, indulged this propensity still further, when he referred all the primary objects of natural desire and aversion to the pleasures and pains of the body. The great patron of the atomical philosophy, who took so much pleasure in deducing all the powers and qualities of bodies from the most obvious and familiar, the figure, motion, and arrangement of the small parts of matter, felt no doubt a similar satisfaction, when he accounted, in the same manner, for all the sentiments and passions of the mind from those which are most obvious and familiar.[19]

According to Smith, Epicurus showed the same parsimony in his physics as in his ethics. In physics, he derived all explanations from the fall and combination of atoms. In ethics, "prudence" was "the source and principle of all the virtues."[20] Prudence itself was based solely on self-interest. Smith believes that parsimony is no virtue here, but rather a vain display of theoretical prowess.

A few years before Adam Smith wrote these lines, his friend David Hume criticized the propensity of Epicureans to "explain every affection to be

---

[16] Edgeworth, *Mathematical Psychics*, p. 15.   [17] Sen, "Rational Fools," p. 344.
[18] Amartya Sen, *On Ethics and Economics*, Oxford: Blackwell, 1987, p. 24.
[19] Adam Smith, *The Theory of Moral Sentiments* (sixth edition), in *The Glasgow Edition of the Works and Correspondence of Adam Smith*, vol. 1, Oxford: Oxford University Press, 1976 [London and Edinburgh, 1790; first edition 1759], VII.ii.2.14.
[20] Ibid., VII.ii.2.8.

self-love, twisted and molded, by a particular turn of imagination, into a variety of appearances."[21] For Hume, "the selfish hypothesis" is so counter-intuitive that "there is required the highest stretch of philosophy to establish so extraordinary a paradox."[22] Epicurean philosophers have erred in their search for theoretical simplicity at any cost:

> To the most careless observer, there appear to be such dispositions as benevolence and generosity; such affections as love, friendship, compassion, gratitude. These sentiments have their causes, effects, objects, and operations, marked by common language and observation, and plainly distinguished from those of the selfish passions. And as this is the obvious appearance of things, it must be admitted; till some hypothesis be discovered, which, by penetrating deeper into human nature, may prove the former affections to be nothing but modifications of the latter. All attempts of this kind have hitherto proved fruitless, and seem to have proceeded entirely, from that love of *simplicity*, which has been the source of much false reasoning in philosophy.[23]

In many ways, Hirschman's critique of Becker's "economic approach" is a modern continuation of Hume's critique of the neo-Epicurean philosophers of his age. The arguments and counter-arguments remain very much the same. The Epicureans posit interest as the one and only first principle, and assume that an interest-based explanation is always possible. In that sense, says d'Holbach, "no man can be called disinterested. We call a man disinterested only when we do not know his motives, or when we approve of them."[24] Of course, countless observations seem to contradict the self-interest doctrine, and the theorist does not claim to be able to solve them all to the interlocutor's satisfaction. All that is needed, according to Stigler and Becker, is an overall confidence in the explanatory power of the theory:

> It is a thesis that does not permit of direct proof because it is an assertion about the world, not a proposition in logic. Moreover, it is possible almost at random to throw up examples of phenomena that presently defy explanation by this hypothesis: Why do we have inflation? Why are there few Jews in farming? Why are societies with polygynous families so rare in the modern era? Why aren't blood banks responsible for the quality of their product? If we could answer these questions to your satisfaction, you would quickly produce a dozen more.
>
> What we assert is not that we are clever enough to make illuminating applications of utility-maximization theory to all important phenomena – not even our entire generation of economists is clever enough to do that. Rather, we assert

---

[21] David Hume, *Enquiry Concerning the Principles of Morals*, edited by J. B. Schneewind, Indianapolis: Hackett, 1983 [London, 1777; first edition 1751], Appendix II, p. 89.

[22] *Enquiry Concerning the Principles of Morals*, Appendix II, p. 90.   [23] Ibid.

[24] D'Holbach, *Système de la nature*, I, XV, p. 321.

that this traditional approach of the economist offers guidance in tackling these problems – and that no other approach of remotely comparable generality and power is available.[25]

In a footnote to the foregoing passage, Stigler and Becker humorously give an example of the *regressus ad infinitum* that characterizes the conflict between interest-based interpretations and interpretations that allow for a multiplicity of motives. If there are few Jews in farming, they hypothesize, it may be that "since Jews have been persecuted so often and forced to flee to other countries, they have not invested in immobile land, but in mobile human capital – business skills, education, etc. – that would automatically go with them."[26] This argument invites a counter-argument: "Of course, someone might counter with the more basic query: but why are they Jews, and not Christians or Moslems?"[27]

One could make similar arguments with the examples provided by Jon Elster in his refutation of interest-based theories. For instance, Elster observes that "parents have a selfish interest in helping their children, assuming that children will care for parents in their old age – but it is not in the selfish interest of children to provide such care. And many still do."[28] Economist Oded Stark proposes a selfish interpretation for this apparently disinterested behavior. Children take care of their aging parents because, anticipating their own physical decline, they want to instill a similar behavior in their own children. If this theory is correct, people with children would be more likely to let their aging parents move in with them than people without children, even though the burden of child-raising makes this living arrangement less attractive. Empirical evidence seems to indicate that it is the case.[29] Of course, one could counter that, no matter what their motives are, parents are simply teaching altruism.

Not much seems to have changed since the eighteenth-century disputes between neo-Epicureans and their critics, except for the highly mathematical form assumed by the interest doctrine in the twentieth century. All these disputes, then and now, seem to have one common feature. First comes the self-interest theorist, who examines an apparently innocent conduct and claims that, beneath the surface, lies a self-interested motive. Then come the critics, who say that the selfish interpretation is intellectually attractive but factually incorrect. However schematic this presentation may appear,

---

[25] George J. Stigler and Gary S. Becker, "De Gustibus Non Est Disputandum," *American Economic Review* 67:2 (1977), p. 76.
[26] Ibid.   [27] Ibid.   [28] Elster *Nuts and Bolts*, p. 54.
[29] Oded Stark, *Altruism and Beyond. An Economic Analysis of Transfers and Exchanges within Families and Groups*, Cambridge: Cambridge University Press, 1995, pp. 59–64.

it pretty much describes the historical development of the debate in the eighteenth century. We shall see that, surprisingly, Adam Smith sides for the most part with those who believe that interest-based explanations are too clever to be true.

THE PRINCIPLE OF PITY

We started this discussion with Hirschman's account of the extraordinary success of the doctrine of interest in the eighteenth century. This must be kept in mind in order to fully understand the opening lines of *The Theory of Moral Sentiments*:

How selfish soever man may be supposed, there are evidently some principles in his nature, which interest him in the fortune of others, and render their happiness necessary to him, though he derives nothing from it except the pleasure of seeing it. Of this kind is pity or compassion, the emotion which we feel for the misery of others, when we either see it, or are made to conceive it in a very lively manner. That we often derive sorrow from the sorrow of others, is a matter of fact too obvious to require any instances to prove it; for this sentiment, like all the other original passions of human nature, is by no means confined to the virtuous and humane, though they perhaps may feel it with the most exquisite sensibility. The greatest ruffian, the most hardened violator of the laws of society, is not altogether without it.[30]

By the middle of the eighteenth century, any attempt to give a reasoned account of human behavior must start with the examination of the hypothesis that all behavior might be driven by self-interest. Hence the beginning: "How selfish soever man may be supposed..." The clearest, most univocal, and most famous presentation of the doctrine of self-interest is Mandeville's *Fable of the Bees*.[31] Bert Kerkhof[32] sees in the first paragraph of *The Theory of Moral Sentiments* an allusion to a graphic passage in *The Fable of the Bees*, where Mandeville describes the passion of pity. The scene that causes pity is the dismemberment of a two-year-old child by a mad sow:

To see her widely open her destructive jaws, and the poor lamb beat down with greedy haste; to look on the defenseless posture of tender limbs first trampled on, then tore asunder; to see the filthy snout digging in the yet living entrails suck up

---

[30] Smith, *The Theory of Moral Sentiments*, I.i.1.1.

[31] Bernard Mandeville, *The Fable of the Bees*, edited by F.B. Kaye, Oxford: Clarendon Press, 1924, 2 vols. [*The Fable of the Bees, or Private Vices, Public Benefits*, sixth edition, London: J. Tonson, 1732].

[32] Bert Kerkhof, "A Fatal Attraction? Smith's *Theory of Moral Sentiments* and Mandeville's *Fable*," *History of Political Thought* 16:2 (Summer 1995), pp. 219–233.

the smoking blood, and now and then to hear the cracking bones, and the cruel animal with savage pleasure grunt over the horrid banquet; to hear and see all this, what tortures would give it the soul beyond expression![33]

Such a scene, says Mandeville, would provoke pure, unadulterated feelings of pity in any human being:

There would be no need of virtue or self-denial to be moved at such a scene; and not only a man of humanity, of good morals and commiseration, but likewise an highwayman, an house-breaker, or a murderer could feel anxieties on such an occasion; how calamitous soever a man's circumstances might be, he would forget his misfortunes for the time, and the most troublesome passion would give way to pity.[34]

To Mandeville's "house-breaker" or "murderer" who is taken by pity, corresponds Smith's "greatest ruffian," or "most hardened violator of the laws of society," who is "not altogether without it." Mandeville's purpose in presenting this vision of horror is to demonstrate that the virtue of charity "is often counterfeited by a passion of ours called pity or compassion, which consists in a fellow-feeling and condolence for the misfortune and calamities of others."[35] This fits within Mandeville's general argument that virtues are nothing but the manifestation of various passions. Smith, however, makes his own use of the reference. He seems to be saying: if the greatest advocate of the interest doctrine acknowledges that pure pity is possible, we can take this as proof that there is such a thing as pure pity. Indeed, Mandeville insists that in this case, the feeling of pity is not tainted with any other passions:

Let me see courage, or the love of one's country so apparent without any mixture, cleared and distinct, the first from pride and anger, the other from the love of glory, and every shadow of self-interest, as this pity would be clear and distinct from all other passions.[36]

Because Smith operates *more geometrico* in *The Theory of Moral Sentiments* (he starts from first principles, and gradually derives the consequences of the first principles),[37] the beginning of the book is of the utmost importance. The remark concerning pity is an empirical illustration (not a proof, since first principles cannot be proven — and if they could, they would not be first principles) of the psychological phenomenon that Smith

[33] Mandeville, *The Fable of the Bees*, vol. 1, p. 255.   [34] Ibid., p. 256.
[35] Ibid., p. 254.   [36] Ibid., p. 255.
[37] Unlike *The Wealth of Nations*, where the order is the reverse, i.e. analytical: gradual resolution of a problem posed in the introduction.

subsequently proposes to call sympathy. If it is true that the first sentence of *The Theory of Moral Sentiments* refers to *The Fable of the Bees*, then the doctrine of sympathy, which forms the core of Smith's first book, must be regarded as a response to Mandeville's "licentious system," as Smith labels it in Part VII.[38]

In order to discover further evidence in support of this hypothesis, it will be useful to examine a book published four years before *The Theory of Moral Sentiments*: Rousseau's *Discourse on the Origin of Inequality*. Rousseau's book happens to include an explicit reference to Mandeville's pathetic description of the dismemberment of a child:

One sees with pleasure the author of the Fable of the Bees, forced to recognize man as a compassionate and sensitive Being, departing from his cold and subtle style in the example he gives in order to offer us the pathetic image of an imprisoned man who sees outside a wild Beast tearing a Child from his Mother's breast, breaking his weal limbs in its murderous teeth, and ripping apart with its claws the palpitating entrails of this Child.[39]

Rousseau's purpose in bringing up this scene is strikingly similar to the point made by Smith at the beginning of *The Theory of Moral Sentiments*. Talking about man in general, Smith asserts that "there are evidently some principles in his nature, which interest him in the fortune of others, and render their happiness necessary to him, though he derives nothing from it except the pleasure of seeing it."[40] In other words, pity is an entirely disinterested feeling. Similarly, in his analysis of the spectator's feelings regarding the slaughter of a child, Rousseau notices that the witness has "no personal interest"[41] in what is happening. This is a crucial point for Rousseau: pity cannot be derived from, or explained by self-interest.

---

[38] For a full account of sympathy in Smith's doctrine, see T.D. Campbell, *Adam Smith's Science of Morals*, London: George Allen & Unwin, 1971, pp. 94–106; David Marshall, *The Figure of Theater. Shaftesbury, Defoe, Adam Smith, and George Eliot*, New York: Columbia University Press, 1986, pp. 167–192; Eugene Heath, "The Commerce of Sympathy: Adam Smith on the Emergence of Morals," *Journal of the History of Philosophy* 33:3 (July 1995), pp. 447–466.

[39] Jean-Jacques Rousseau, *Discourse on the Origin of Inequality*, in *The Collected Writings of Rousseau*, vol. 3, edited by Roger D. Masters and Christopher Kelly, translated by Judith R. Bush, Roger D. Masters, Christopher Kelly, and Terence Marshall, Hanover, NH: University Press of New England, 1992, p. 36. "On voit avec plaisir l'auteur de la *Fable des Abeilles*, forcé de reconnaître l'homme pour un être compatissant et sensible, sortir, dans l'exemple qu'il en donne, de son style froid et subtil, pour nous offrir la pathétique image d'un homme enfermé qui aperçoit au-dehors une bête féroce arrachant un enfant du sein de sa mère, brisant sous sa dent meurtrière les faibles membres, et déchirant de ses ongles les entrailles palpitantes de cet enfant." *Discours sur l'origine et les fondements de l'inégalité parmi les hommes*, in *Œuvres complètes*, Paris: Gallimard, 1964 [Amsterdam: Marc Michel Rey, 1755], vol. 3, p. 154.

[40] Smith, *The Theory of Moral Sentiments*, I.i.1.1.

[41] Rousseau, *Discourse on the Origin of Inequality*, p. 36.

Rhetorically, Rousseau's reference to Mandeville is, in the technical sense, an *ad hominem* argument. Not a personal attack against Mandeville (that would be an argument *ad personam*) but a way of refuting Mandeville's theory on the basis of premises that Mandeville himself accepts as true.[42] The reference to *The Fable of the Bees* comes in the context of a discussion of Hobbes. Rousseau seeks to refute Hobbes's assertion that self-interest is the engine of all human behavior:

There is, besides, another principle which Hobbes did not notice, and which – having been given to man in order to soften, under certain circumstances, the ferocity of his amour-propre or the desire for self-preservation before the birth of this love – tempers the ardor he has for his own well-being by an innate repugnance to see his fellow suffer.[43]

What better way to refute an advocate of self-interest than to invoke another leading exponent of the interest doctrine? This argument, Rousseau believes, is absolutely compelling:

I do not believe I have any contradiction to fear in granting man the sole Natural virtue that the most excessive Detractor of human virtues was forced to recognize. I speak of Pity, a disposition that is appropriate to beings as weak and subject to as many ills as we are.[44]

If Mandeville, "the most excessive detractor of human virtues," the one who sees selfish motives behind all virtuous conduct, has acknowledged the reality of pity, that is proof enough of the existence and authenticity of this feeling.

Affirming the authenticity of pity is a primary concern for Smith as well. After stating it in the opening lines of *The Theory of Moral Sentiments*, he comes back to this issue in his examination of systems of moral philosophy. "Sympathy," he writes, "cannot, in any sense, be regarded as a selfish principle."[45] Although sympathy proceeds from "an imaginary change of

---

[42] See Gabriël Nuchelmans, "On the Fourfold Root of the *Argumentum ad Hominem*," in *Empirical Logic and Public Debate*, Amsterdam, 1993, pp. 37–47, and Pierre Force, "*Ad Hominem* Arguments in Pascal's *Pensées*," in *Classical Unities: Place, Time, Action*, Tübingen: Gunter Narr, 2001, pp. 393–403.

[43] Rousseau, *Discourse on the Origin of Inequality*, p. 36. "Il y a d'ailleurs un autre principe que Hobbes n'a point aperçu, et qui, ayant été donné à l'homme pour adoucir, en certaines circonstances, la férocité de son amour-propre, ou le désir de se conserver avant la naissance de cet amour, tempère l'ardeur qu'il a pour son bien-être par une répugnance innée à voir souffrir son semblable." *Discours sur l'origine de l'inégalité*, p. 154.

[44] *Discourse on the Origin of Inequality*, p. 36. "Je ne crois pas avoir aucune contradiction à craindre, en accordant à l'homme la seule vertu naturelle, qu'ait été forcé de reconnaître le détracteur le plus outré des vertus humaines. Je parle de la pitié, disposition convenable à des êtres aussi faibles, et sujets à autant de maux que nous sommes." *Discours sur l'origine de l'inégalité*, p. 154.

[45] Smith, *The Theory of Moral Sentiments*, VII.iii.1.4.

situations with the person principally concerned," if I sympathize with you, I don't imagine myself suffering from the same ills you are suffering. I imagine that I have become you:

> When I condole with you for the loss of your only son, in order to enter into your grief I do not consider what I, a person of such a character and profession, should suffer, if I had a son, and if that son was unfortunately to die: but I consider what I should suffer if I was really you, and I not only change circumstances with you, but I change persons and characters. My grief, therefore, is entirely upon your account, and not in the least upon my own. It is not, therefore, in the least selfish.[46]

It is clear from the order of *The Theory of Moral Sentiments* that sympathy is the cornerstone of Smith's system. It is also widely acknowledged that pity has a central role in Rousseau's philosophy. It is the foundation of all natural virtues. One of the first critics to have noticed the centrality of pity in Rousseau's system is Adam Smith himself. In March 1756, just a few months after the publication of Rousseau's *Second Discourse*, Smith, who was then thirty-three years old and a professor of moral philosophy at the University of Glasgow, reviewed Rousseau's latest book in the *Edinburgh Review*. In his review, Smith hailed Rousseau as the most important and original French philosopher since Descartes, and presented him as the worthy continuator of a philosophical tradition that used to thrive in England, with authors like Hobbes, Locke, Mandeville, Shaftesbury, Butler, Clarke, and Hutcheson. "This branch of the English philosophy," he added, "which seems to be now entirely neglected by the English themselves, has of late been transported into France."[47] Consistent with his claim that Rousseau was a continuator of the English philosophical tradition, Smith asserted that Rousseau's main source of inspiration in the *Discourse on the Origin of Inequality* was none other than Mandeville's *Fable of the Bees*:

> Whoever reads this last work with attention, will observe, that the second volume of the Fable of the Bees has given occasion to the system of Mr. Rousseau, in whom however the principles of the English author are softened, improved, and embellished, and stripped of all that tendency to corruption and licentiousness which has disgraced them in their original author.[48]

Following this initial statement is a detailed parallel between Mandeville and Rousseau, where Smith analyzes the similarities and differences between the two authors, in order to show how Rousseau has adapted and

---

[46] Ibid.
[47] Adam Smith, "Letter to the *Edinburgh Review*," in *Essays on Philosophical Subjects*, *The Glasgow Edition of the Works and Correspondence of Adam Smith*, vol. 3, Oxford: Oxford University Press, 1980, p. 250.
[48] Ibid.

transformed Mandeville's work in order to build his own system. A crucial point is the role of pity:

Mr. Rousseau however criticizes upon Dr. Mandeville: he observes that pity, the only amiable principle which the English author allows to be natural to man, is capable of producing all those virtues, whose reality Dr. Mandeville denies. Mr. Rousseau at the same time seems to think, that this principle is in itself no virtue, but that it is possessed by savages and by the most profligate of the vulgar, in a greater degree of perfection than by those of the most polished and cultivated manners; in which he agrees perfectly with the English author.[49]

As we have seen above, when Rousseau refers to the passage in *The Fable of the Bees* where a small child is dismembered by a mad sow, he makes an *ad hominem* argument. He starts by agreeing with Mandeville in order to refute him. However, as Smith's reading of Rousseau and Mandeville shows us, the purpose of Rousseau's argument is not exclusively polemical. Rousseau subscribes entirely to Mandeville's psychological analysis of pity. Here, the only change he brings to Mandeville's doctrine consists in positing pity as the first principle and the foundation of natural virtues:

Mandeville sensed very well that even with all their morality men would never have been anything but monsters if Nature had not given them pity in support of reason; but he did not see that from this quality alone flow all the social virtues he wants to question in men. In fact, what are Generosity, Clemency, Humanity, if not Pity applied to the weak, to the guilty, or to the human species in general? Benevolence and even friendship are, rightly understood, the products of a constant pity fixed on a particular object.[50]

From what we have seen so far, two preliminary conclusions and one hypothesis can be made. Firstly, as Adam Smith himself suggests, reading Rousseau's *Second Discourse* as an appropriation of *The Fable of the Bees* will yield some important insights. Secondly, the similarities we have seen between Rousseau's analysis of pity and Smith's account of sympathy indicate that they are both taking Mandeville's description of pity as their starting point. Thirdly, the similarities between Rousseau's pity and Smith's sympathy would appear to indicate that, when Smith talks about Rousseau's work

---

[49] Ibid., p. 251.
[50] Rousseau, *Discourse on the Origin of Inequality*, p. 37. "Mandeville a bien senti qu'avec toute leur morale les hommes n'eussent jamais été que des monstres, si la nature ne leur eût donné la pitié à l'appui de la raison: mais il n'a pas vu que de cette seule qualité découlent toutes les vertus sociales qu'il veut disputer aux hommes. En effet, qu'est-ce que la générosité, la clémence, l'humanité, sinon la pitié appliquée aux faibles, aux coupables, ou à l'espèce humaine en général? La bienveillance et l'amitié même sont, à le bien prendre, des productions d'une pitié constante, fixée sur un objet particulier." *Discours sur l'origine de l'inégalité*, p. 154.

as an appropriation of *The Fable of the Bees*, he is also thinking about his own work in progress, *The Theory of Moral Sentiments*, as an appropriation of Mandeville's book, and acknowledging Rousseau as a philosopher who shares many of his concerns.

SMITH'S "REAL SENTIMENTS" ON ROUSSEAU

Each of the three points mentioned above goes against the conventional wisdom regarding Mandeville, Rousseau and Smith. Rousseau's reference to Mandeville is explicit and therefore well known, but it is generally assumed that Mandeville is a polemical target, not a worthy interlocutor. Since Rousseau is usually seen as a fierce critic of trade and commerce as foundations of civil society, one wonders how he could build his system on the work of an author who extols the public benefits of greed. It is also surprising to see the author of *The Wealth of Nations* and the author of the *Discourse on the Origin of Inequality* together as readers of Mandeville. Finally, is would seem implausible that *The Theory of Moral Sentiments* could share some of the premises of the *Discourse on the Origin of Inequality*. Few Smith scholars would be inclined to see the author of *The Theory of Moral Sentiments* as a secret admirer of Rousseau.[51] This view is not shared by many Rousseau scholars either, but it was proposed by a Rousseau scholar of the *Quellen-Kritik* period who stated that, although Adam Smith "was suspicious of Rousseau's sentimental picture of the state of nature, there was much in the *Discourse* that he found to praise and even to make use of in future publications of his own."[52] The same critic added that the first paragraph of *The Theory of Moral Sentiments* "is little more than a restatement of Rousseau's conception of pity."[53] More recently, Donald Winch suggested that "Smith's theory of sympathy, as expounded in the *Theory*

---

[51] For an insightful discussion of Smith's position with respect to Rousseau, see Donald Winch, *Riches and Poverty. An Intellectual History of Political Economy in Britain, 1750–1834*, Cambridge: Cambridge University Press, 1996, pp. 57–89, as well as Michael Ignatieff, *The Needs of Strangers*, London: Chatto & Windus, 1984, pp. 107–131, and "Smith, Rousseau and the Republic of Needs," in *Scotland and Europe, 1200–1850*, edited by T.C. Smout, Edinburgh: J. Donald, 1986, pp. 187–206. Also see A.L. Macfie, *The Individual in Society. Papers on Adam Smith*, London: Allen & Unwin, 1967, p. 44 and D.D. Raphael, *Adam Smith*, Oxford: Oxford University Press, 1985, pp. 71–72 and 79–80. The relatively small number of critics who mention Rousseau as an important interlocutor for Smith tend to agree that Smith is only interested in refuting Rousseau's theories. I'm arguing here and will argue again in chapters 4 and 6 that the ambiguities in *The Theory of Moral Sentiments* and *The Wealth of Nations* can be traced in no small part to Smith's ambivalent assessment of Rousseau's philosophy.

[52] Richard B. Sewall, "Rousseau's Second Discourse in England from 1755 to 1762," *Philological Quarterly* 17:2 (April 1938), p. 98.

[53] Ibid.

of Moral Sentiments, is an augmented version of Rousseau's conception of *pitié*."⁵⁴

On the other hand, in another recent study of the Mandeville–Rousseau–Smith triangle, E.J. Hundert argued that Smith's review of the *Second Discourse* in the *Edinburgh Review* was an "attack upon Rousseau."⁵⁵ This view is consistent with the prevailing opinion on the Rousseau–Smith connection, and it is based on a plausible reading of the review. Smith's final assessment of the *Second Discourse* is that it "consists almost entirely of rhetoric and description."⁵⁶ In his essay on the imitative arts, Smith characterized Rousseau as "an author more capable of feeling strongly than of analyzing accurately."⁵⁷ We also know that in a letter to Hume, Smith called Rousseau a "hypocritical pedant."⁵⁸

At first sight, these quotes seem totally inconsistent with the notion that Smith might have been an admirer of Rousseau. However, the language Smith uses in his letter to Hume must be put in the context of the Hume–Rousseau quarrel. That Smith should side with his close friend Hume is to be expected. The Hume–Smith correspondence reveals at the same time that Smith was eager to hear the latest news about Rousseau.⁵⁹ In response, Hume provided a lot of details, including Davenport's prognostication that Rousseau's *Confessions* (still unpublished at that time) would be "the most taking of all his works."⁶⁰ We also know that Smith possessed most of the books that Rousseau published during his lifetime.⁶¹ As we have seen above, in the *Edinburgh Review* article, Smith presented

---

⁵⁴ Winch, *Riches and Poverty*, p. 72. Winch qualifies his judgment by mentioning the fact that Rousseau thinks *pitié* diminishes with civilization, while Smith sees civil society as the vehicle for the perfection of sympathy. This is certainly true but, as I argue later in this chapter, the pertinent concept for this discussion is not *pity* but *identification* (a concept that is very close to Smith's *sympathy*). In Rousseau's narrative, natural pity diminishes with civilization, but the capacity for identification increases with it.

⁵⁵ E.J. Hundert, *The Enlightenment's Fable. Bernard Mandeville and the Discovery of Society*, Cambridge: Cambridge University Press, 1994, p. 220. This is an old debate. Sewall's 1938 article takes issue with an earlier critic who was reading Smith's 1755 review of the *Second Discourse* as an attack on Rousseau.

⁵⁶ Smith, "Letter to the *Edinburgh Review*," p. 251.

⁵⁷ Adam Smith, "Of the Imitative Arts," in *Essays on Philosophical Subjects, The Glasgow Edition of the Works and Correspondence of Adam Smith*, vol. 3, Oxford: Oxford University Press, 1980, p. 198.

⁵⁸ Letter 92 to David Hume (March 13, 1766) in *Correspondence of Adam Smith, The Glasgow Edition of the Works and Correspondence of Adam Smith*, vol. 6, Oxford: Oxford University Press, 1985, p. 113.

⁵⁹ Letter 109 to David Hume (September 13, 1767), ibid., p. 132.

⁶⁰ Letter 112 from David Hume to Adam Smith (October 17, 1767), ibid., p. 137.

⁶¹ *Lettre à d'Alembert* (Amsterdam, 1758); *La Nouvelle Héloïse* (Amsterdam, 1761); *Émile* (Frankfurt, 1762); *Lettres écrites de la montagne* (Amsterdam, 1764); *Dictionnaire de musique* (vols. 10 and 11 of *Œuvres de M. Rousseau de Genève*, Amsterdam: Marc Michel Rey, 1769). See James Bonar, *A Catalogue of the Library of Adam Smith*, New York: Augustus M. Kelley, 1966 [first edition 1894] and Hiroshi Mizuta, *Adam Smith's Library. A Supplement to Bonar's Catalogue with a Checklist of the Whole Library*, Cambridge: Cambridge University Press, 1967.

Rousseau as the most important and original philosopher writing in French since Descartes, in a field ("morals" and "metaphysics") where improving upon the doctrines of the Ancients was much more difficult than in natural science.[62] According to Smith, English moral philosophy, from Hobbes to Mandeville and Hutcheson, had made genuine attempts to bring something new to the field (it "endeavored at least, to be, in some measure, original")[63] but it was now quiescent. Because he based his *Second Discourse* on Mandeville's *Fable of the Bees*, Rousseau was, in Smith's eyes, the worthy continuator of a philosophical tradition that the English had developed and then neglected.

Evidence and testimony regarding Smith's personal views (aside from what we can infer from his writings) is scarce. As Donald Winch puts it, "if behind those publications to which he attached his name, Smith often appears private and aloof, that is how he wished it to be."[64] Smith's review of the *Second Discourse* is difficult to interpret because in this text, as in many other instances, Smith is ironic, elusive, and almost impossible to identify univocally with a particular opinion or position.[65] As a result, the few anecdotes we have on Smith's private sentiments carry much more weight than they would for another author (and should accordingly be treated with an abundance of caution). There is a least one testimony regarding Smith's private views on Rousseau. In October 1782, Barthélémy Faujas de Saint-Fond, a French geologist, had several conversations with "that venerable philosopher" Adam Smith in Edinburgh. Saint-Fond describes Smith's admiration for Rousseau in the strongest possible terms:

One evening while I was at tea with him he spoke of Rousseau with a kind of religious respect: "Voltaire sought to correct the vices and the follies of mankind by laughing at them, and sometimes by treating them with severity: Rousseau conducts the reader to reason and truth, by the attraction of sentiment, and the force of conviction. His *Social Compact* will one day avenge all the persecutions he experienced."[66]

This testimony is consistent with Emma Rothschild's recent speculation on "Smith's real sentiments,"[67] which, according to many of his French

---

[62] Smith, "Letter to the *Edinburgh Review*," p. 249.   [63] Ibid., p. 250.

[64] Winch, *Riches and Poverty*, p. 35.

[65] The practice of concealing one's "real" sentiments, especially on political and religious issues, is characteristic of many Enlightenment thinkers. Smith is an extreme case, however, because, unlike Voltaire for instance, his correspondence reveals little about his private views.

[66] Barthélémy Faujas de Saint-Fond, *Travels in England, Scotland and the Hebrides, undertaken for the purpose of examining the state of the arts, the sciences, natural history and manners, in Great Britain*, London: James Ridgway, 1799 [Paris: H.-J. Jansen, 1797], vol. 2, p. 242.

[67] Emma Rothschild, *Economic Sentiments. Adam Smith, Condorcet, and the Enlightenment*, Cambridge, MA: Harvard University Press, 2001, p. 66. Rothschild makes a brief reference to this anecdote (p. 54) but she takes it only as a proof of Smith's republican sentiments.

friends, were considerably more radical in private than they were in public. As we shall see, it can also be reconciled with Smith's apparently negative assessments of Rousseau's work. What is remarkable about Saint-Fond's testimony is that Smith judges Voltaire and Rousseau less on the intellectual validity of their doctrines than on their ability to change the hearts and minds of their readers. Voltaire is presented as a satirist and a moralist who "sought to correct the vices and the follies of mankind" through mockery and blame. Rousseau's effectiveness, on the other hand, is based on "the attraction of sentiment" and "the force of conviction." In the comparison, Rousseau appears therefore as a more profound philosopher than Voltaire. This is particularly significant if we recall that Smith's admiration for Voltaire was immense.

As Hadot and Davidson have shown,[68] the ancient tradition of "philosophy as a way of life" made a strong comeback during the early modern period. That explains the profound interest in Hellenistic philosophy (Stoicism, Epicureanism, Skepticism) that characterizes many philosophers from Erasmus to Kant. In this tradition, intellectual speculation is not an end in itself (as it is in the institutional practice of philosophy), but rather a tool for moral and personal reformation. Smith's deep interest in Stoicism and other Hellenistic doctrines must be understood in this context. If one believes, as Smith probably did, that the ultimate purpose of philosophy is the moral progress of the philosopher and his disciples, the *rhetorical* dimension of philosophy must be acknowledged as fundamental. Constructing a solid and coherent doctrine is not enough. The philosopher's task is to change and reform some of his reader's most deeply held beliefs. In this enterprise, rational argumentation plays of course an important role, but feelings and sentiment are also essential. The interlocutor will not change his fundamental beliefs if he is not moved by a profound *desire* to achieve a greater degree of wisdom. This ability to appeal to feelings and sentiment is what Smith admires most in Rousseau. The philosopher from Geneva may be wrong on some particulars in his doctrine, but he is a great philosopher because he inspires his readers, and he leads them to change some of their core beliefs through "the attraction of sentiment" and "the force of conviction."

It appears therefore that when Smith characterizes Rousseau as "an author more capable of feeling strongly than of analyzing accurately," he criticizes him and pays him a compliment at the same time. As to the characterization of the *Second Discourse* as consisting "almost entirely of rhetoric and

[68] Pierre Hadot and Arnold Davidson, *Philosophy as a Way of Life. Spiritual Exercises from Socrates to Foucault*, Oxford: Blackwell, 1995.

description" it is much less critical than it sounds. "Rhetoric" in modern parlance is often a pejorative term. For Smith, however, the "rhetorical" is simply a type of discourse to be distinguished from the "didactic":

> Every discourse proposes either barely to relate some fact, or to prove some proposition. In the first ... the discourse is called a narrative one. The latter is the foundation of two sorts of discourse: the didactic and the rhetorical. The former proposes to put before us the arguments on both sides of the question in their true light ... The rhetorical again endeavors by all means to persuade us.[69]

The goal of both the didactic and the rhetorical discourses is to "prove some proposition." In didactic discourse, reasoning is primary, persuasion secondary. In rhetorical discourse it is the opposite. As to "description," it is, for Smith, the main characteristic of "narrative" discourse. Smith talks about Milton's "description of Paradise,"[70] and he dedicates four lectures to the various modes of description in poetry and prose.[71] When Smith refers to the *Second Discourse* as consisting "almost entirely of rhetoric and description," he is simply stating a fact. Rousseau's work consists of "rhetoric" because its primary goal is to *persuade*. It consists of "description" because it is mostly a *narrative*. Smith's own way of philosophizing was of course much more "didactic" than "rhetorical." This does not diminish (and it may even explain) Smith's admiration and respect for Rousseau's rhetorical abilities.

PITY AS A MANIFESTATION OF SELF-INTEREST

Both Rousseau and Smith seek to build systems on principles other than the "selfish hypothesis." In order to do so, they must respond to the account of pity that can be found in the proponents of the interest doctrine. Augustinians and Epicureans agree that pity is a manifestation of self-interest. Among the Augustinians, one may quote La Rochefoucauld, whose maxim 264 reads:

> Pity is often a way of feeling our own misfortunes in those of other people; it is a clever foretaste of the unhappiness we may some day encounter. We help others to make sure they will help us under similar circumstances, and the services we render them are, properly speaking, benefits we store up for ourselves in advance.[72]

---

[69] Adam Smith, *Lectures on Rhetoric and Belles Lettres, The Glasgow Edition of the Works and Correspondence of Adam Smith*, vol. 4, Oxford: Oxford University Press, 1983, p. 62.

[70] Ibid., p. 64. [71] Ibid., Lectures 12 to 15.

[72] François de La Rochefoucauld, *The Maxims*, translated by Louis Kronenberger, New York: Stackpole, 1936. "La pitié est souvent un sentiment de nos propres maux dans les maux d'autrui. C'est une

As an Augustinian, La Rochefoucauld assumes that all human behavior, except when God's grace is at work, is driven by self-love (Augustine's *amor sui*). This particular maxim proposes an interest-based interpretation of pity. When we feel pity, La Rochefoucauld explains, the feeling is apparently directed towards the persons who feel pain, but in reality, it goes back to ourselves. We only see our interests in the sufferings of others. We help those who suffer in the hope that they will help us if we suffer in the future.

For an Epicurean account of pity, we may turn to Helvétius, in a text that is posterior to the *Second Discourse* and *The Theory of Moral Sentiments*, but nonetheless illuminating, because it is a response to Rousseau's refutation of the interest-based interpretation of pity. Helvétius endeavors to prove that "compassion is neither a moral sense, or an innate sentiment, but the pure effect of self-love":[73]

My affliction for the miseries of an unhappy person, is always in proportion to the fear I have of being afflicted of the same miseries. I would, if it were possible, destroy in him the very root of his misfortune, and thereby free myself at the same time from the fear of suffering in the same manner. The love of others is therefore never any thing else in man than an effect of the love of himself.[74]

Helvétius goes on to say that compassion is only a product of education. Consequently, the only way of rendering a child "humane and compassionate" is "to habituate him from his most tender age to put himself in the place of the miserable."[75] The expression used by Helvétius in the original French (*s'identifier avec les malheureux*) is worth mentioning. Literally, it means "to identify with the miserable." In modern English or French, the word *identification* is commonly used by psychologists to describe a process whereby the subject puts himself or herself emotionally or mentally in the place of another person, real or imaginary. The first recorded use of the

---

habile prévoyance des malheurs où nous pouvons tomber; nous donnons du secours aux autres pour les engager à nous en donner en de semblables occasions; et ces services que nous leur rendons sont à proprement parler des biens que nous nous faisons à nous-mêmes par avance." *Maximes*, edited by Jean Lafond, Paris: Gallimard, 1976 [Paris: Barbin, 1678], maxim 264.

[73] Claude Adrien Helvétius, *A Treatise on Man*, translated by W. Hooper, New York: Burt Franklin, 1969, vol. 2, p. 18. "J'ai prouvé que la compassion n'est ni un sens moral, ni un sentiment inné, mais un pur effet de l'amour de soi." *De l'Homme. De ses facultés intellectuelles, et de son éducation*, London: Société Typographique, 1773, v.3.

[74] *A Treatise on Man*, vol. 2, p. 16. "Mon attendrissement pour les douleurs d'un infortuné est toujours proportionné à la crainte que j'ai d'être affligé des mêmes douleurs. Je voudrais, s'il était possible, en anéantir en lui jusqu'au germe: je m'affranchirais en même temps de la crainte d'en éprouver de pareilles. L'amour des autres ne sera jamais dans l'homme qu'un effet de l'amour de lui-même." *De l'Homme*, v.3.

[75] *A Treatise on Man*, vol. 2, p. 18. "...l'habituer dès sa plus tendre jeunesse à s'identifier avec les malheureux et à se voir en eux." *De l'Homme*, v.3.

term *identification* in French goes back to Rousseau's *Second Discourse*[76] (which gives Rousseau a plausible claim as inventor of this key concept in modern psychology). Rousseau uses the term in a passage dealing with La Rochefoucauld's conception of pity:

> Even should it be true that commiseration is only a feeling that puts us in the position of him who suffers – a feeling that is obscure and lively in Savage man, developed but weak in Civilized man – what would this idea matter to the truth of what I say, except to give it more force? In fact, commiseration will be all the more energetic as the Observing animal identifies himself more intimately with the suffering animal. Now it is evident that this identification must have been infinitely closer in the state of Nature than in the state of reasoning.[77]

Rousseau coins the neologism *identification* in response to La Rochefoucauld's Augustinian interpretation of pity.[78] As we have seen above, La Rochefoucauld claims that we feel pity because we put ourselves in the position of the person who is suffering ("Pity is often a way of feeling our own misfortunes in those of other people"). As a consequence, we see what it would be like to suffer, and we decide to help sufferers in order to get help from them in case we would need it in the future. Rousseau decides to retain the premise of La Rochefoucauld's analysis: we put ourselves in the place of the person who is suffering. He also gives a name to the psychological phenomenon described by La Rochefoucauld: *identification*. Then comes the *ad hominem* argument. La Rochefoucauld, a classic defender of the interest doctrine, agrees that pity is based on identification. For La Rochefoucauld, pity causes us to see that it is in our best interest to help others, with the understanding that favors will be reciprocated. In other words, a consequence of pity is *commerce*, in the classical sense: the exchange of services or goods, which may or may not involve money. These inferences, Rousseau claims, are false. If we really understand the psychological phenomenon of identification, we must agree that the capacity for pity was far stronger in the state of nature than it is in the state of civilization. If La

---

[76] I base this claim on a search of the University of Chicago ARTFL database. The *Oxford English Dictionary* mentions *identification* as a term of logic as early as the seventeenth century. *Identification* in the modern sense (identification with a fictional character) does not occur until 1857.

[77] Rousseau, *Discourse on the Origin of Inequality*, p. 37. "Quand il serait vrai que la commisération ne serait qu'un sentiment qui nous met à la place de celui qui souffre, sentiment obscur et vif dans l'homme sauvage, développé mais faible dans l'homme civil, qu'importerait cette idée à la vérité de ce que je dis, sinon de lui donner plus de force? En effet, la commisération sera d'autant plus énergique que l'animal spectateur s'identifiera plus intimement avec l'animal souffrant: or il est évident que cette identification a dû être infiniment plus étroite dans l'état de nature que dans l'état de raisonnement." *Discours sur l'origine de l'inégalité*, p. 155.

[78] There is no explicit reference to La Rochefoucauld in the quoted passage, but most Rousseau scholars believe that the author of the *Second Discourse* has the *Maxims* in mind here. The Gagnebin and Raymond edition gives maxim 264 as Rousseau's most likely reference.

Rochefoucauld were correct in saying that commerce is a consequence of pity, then commerce would have existed – and in fact thrived – in the state of nature. We know that, on the contrary, commerce has thrived in the state of civilization. La Rochefoucauld is drawing false consequences from a true premise. Pity, Rousseau claims, is a pre-rational faculty, made weaker by the full use of human reason. In other words, in the pre-rational state of nature, the capacity for pity was strong, and reason was undeveloped. In the state of civilization, reason is fully developed, and with it the understanding of what we deem to be our interests. This understanding of our interests stands in the way of our natural propensity to identify with sufferers. In Rousseau's vocabulary, the rational understanding of our interests is *self-love* (*amour-propre*) as opposed to the primitive *love of oneself* (*amour de soi*, i.e. instinct of self-preservation). For Rousseau, "reason engenders *amour-propre* and reflection fortifies it."[79] The philosopher, rational man *par excellence*, says at the sight of a sufferer: "Perish if you will; I am safe."[80] On the contrary, Rousseau says ironically, "savage man does not have this admirable talent, and for want of wisdom and reason he is always seen heedlessly yielding to the first feeling of humanity."[81] With this demonstration, Rousseau means to destroy the causal link that La Rochefoucauld established between pity (based on identification) and commerce. In short, the argument is: La Rochefoucauld is right to say that pity is based on identification, but he errs in saying that commerce is a consequence of pity; pity, a primary human impulse, is strongest when no interests are at stake; it cannot possibly be the cause of trade and commerce. From La Rochefoucauld's own principles, it is thus demonstrated (as with Mandeville before) that there is no connection between pity and self-interest. Pity is an entirely disinterested feeling.

A similar demonstration can be found in *The Theory of Moral Sentiments*. Smith notices that, "whatever the cause of sympathy, or however it may be excited, nothing pleases us more than to observe in other men a fellow-feeling with all the emotions of our own breast; nor are we ever so much shocked as by the appearance of the contrary."[82] In other words, since we have a disagreement about first principles with the defenders of the interest doctrine, let's not assume anything about the causes of sympathy. Let us simply acknowledge that we all want sympathy from others. Of

---

[79] Rousseau, *Discourse on the Origin of Inequality*, p. 37. "C'est la raison qui engendre l'amour-propre, et c'est la réflexion qui le fortifie." *Discours sur l'origine de l'inégalité*, p. 156.

[80] Ibid. "Péris si tu veux. Je suis en sûreté." *Discours sur l'origine de l'inégalité*, p. 156.

[81] Ibid. "L'homme sauvage n'a point cet admirable talent; et faute de sagesse et de raison, on le voit toujours se livrer étourdiment au premier sentiment de l'humanité."

[82] Smith, *The Theory of Moral Sentiments*, I.i.2.1.

course, it is always possible to form a selfish hypothesis to account for this fact:

> Those who are fond of deducing all our sentiments from certain refinements of self-love, think themselves at no loss to account, according to their own principles, both for this pleasure and this pain. Man, say they, conscious of his own weakness, and of the need which he has for the assistance of others, rejoices whenever he observes that they adopt his own passions, because he is then assured of that assistance; and grieves whenever he observes the contrary, because he is then assured of their opposition.[83]

We want sympathy from others because a person who sympathizes with us will be inclined to serve our interests. This line of argument is reminiscent of La Rochefoucauld's maxim 264, which establishes a link between pity and self-interest via the trading of favors.[84] The only difference is that La Rochefoucauld stresses the sympathy we have for others while Smith emphasizes the sympathy others have for us. As Rousseau before, Smith is eager to show that sympathy has nothing to do with self-interest:

> But both the pleasure and the pain are always felt so instantaneously, and often upon such frivolous occasions, that it seems evident that neither of them can be derived from any such self-interested consideration.[85]

Experience shows that we want sympathy even when no real interests are at stake. When we tell a joke, we expect others to laugh, and we are mortified if they don't. According to Smith, it would be hard to argue in this case that the desire for sympathy is grounded in the expectation that members of the audience will come to our assistance in the future. The selfish hypothesis cannot explain sympathy. As Rousseau removed the connection between pity and self-interest, Smith dissociates self-interest from sympathy.

IDENTIFICATION AND SYMPATHY

Let us now pursue the comparison between Rousseau's concept of iden-tification and Smith's concept of sympathy. The point is not to ascertain

---

[83] Ibid.

[84] The editors of *The Theory of Moral Sentiments*, seeking to identify "those who are fond of deducing all our sentiments from certain refinements of self-love," claim that "Smith presumably has Hobbes and Mandeville in mind as the leading exponents of the view that all sentiments depend on self-love, but in fact neither of them gives this, or any account of the pleasure and pain felt on observing sympathy and antipathy." Therefore the editors suppose that "Smith may simply be making a reasonable conjecture of what an egoistic theorist would say" (Smith, *The Theory of Moral Sentiments*, p. 14, note 1). Although La Rochefoucauld's maxim 264 does not discuss the pain and pleasure associated with sympathy and antipathy, the analysis of the relationship between sympathy and the commerce of favors would seem to indicate that Smith is in fact referring to the French moralist.

[85] Smith, *The Theory of Moral Sentiments*, 1.i.2.1.

intellectual ownership, but rather to acknowledge that Rousseau and Smith do indeed agree on some key points, in order to show the fundamental differences between a novel concept of sympathy based on identification (shared by Rousseau and Smith), and the concept of sympathy prevailing at the time.

When, in the *Second Discourse*, Rousseau coins the term *identification* to refute La Rochefoucauld's analysis of pity, he lays the ground for a new and original theory of sympathy. According to the traditional conception (which can be traced back to Greek medicine), sympathy is a sort of emotional contagion whereby the feelings of one person affect one or several persons near by. Traditionally, sympathy is described as a physiological phenomenon. A modern form of the traditional conception can be found in Malebranche, who uses Cartesian vocabulary to explain how the feelings of one person can physiologically impact the feelings of another person. In Malebranche's theory, the brain communicates with the body by way of "animal spirits." In its communication with the body, the brain has two propensities: "imitation" and "compassion." When we see others, our natural tendency is either to imitate or to pity them:

We must therefore know that animal spirits not only flow towards our body parts in order to imitate the actions and movements we see in others; but also they in some way receive their wounds, and share in their misery. Experience tells us that when we attentively observe someone who is being beaten up violently, or is affected with some great wound, animal spirits flow painfully towards the parts of our body that correspond to those that are being hurt in the person before our eyes.[86]

It is essential to notice that, according to Malebranche's theory, we "feel the pain" of the sufferer quite literally. To the physical pain in the person we are looking at corresponds an identical sensation in our own body. For Malebranche, the propensity to sympathize with someone else's pain is a function of the plasticity of our brain's fibers. Since that plasticity is itself a function of age, children are naturally more sympathetic than older persons. The extreme case of brain plasticity is the child in the womb, who can be permanently wounded by a traumatic impression received by the mother.

---

[86] "Il faut donc savoir que non seulement les esprits animaux se portent naturellement dans les parties de notre corps pour faire les mêmes actions et les mêmes mouvements que nous voyons faire aux autres; mais encore pour recevoir en quelque manière leurs blessures, et pour prendre part à leurs misères. Car l'expérience nous apprend que lorsque nous considérons avec beaucoup d'attention quelqu'un qu'on frappe rudement, ou qui a quelque grande plaie, les esprits se transportent avec effort dans les parties de notre corps qui répondent à celles qu'on voit blesser dans un autre." Nicolas Malebranche, *De la Recherche de la vérité*, in *Œuvres complètes de Malebranche*, vol. 1, Paris: Vrin, 1962 [Paris: Pralard, 1674], p. 236 (II, I, VII, § II).

This, according to Malebranche, is the likely explanation of birthmarks and birth defects.[87] Malebranche's account of sympathy is entirely medical and physiological.

A somewhat different, but in part still traditional analysis of sympathy appears in Shaftesbury:

> It is impossible to suppose a mere sensible creature originally so ill-constituted and unnatural, as that from the moment he comes to be tried by sensible objects, he should have no one good passion towards his kind, no foundation either of pity, love, kindness, or social affection. It is full as impossible to conceive that a rational creature, coming first to be tried by rational objects, and receiving into his mind the images or representations of justice, generosity, gratitude, or other virtue, should have no liking of these, or dislike of the contraries, but be found absolutely indifferent towards whatsoever is presented to him of this sort.[88]

In this passage, Shaftesbury seeks to show that we have an innate sense of right and wrong, which he calls "moral sense." This sense operates both on a sub-rational level ("a mere sensible creature") and a rational level ("a rational creature"). According to Jean Morel's authoritative study of the sources of the *Second Discourse*, Rousseau's conception of pity is to some extent derived from Shaftesbury's. Discussing his use of the aforementioned passage, Morel claims that "Rousseau operated two reductions: 1. He eliminated the rational creature, and kept only the sensible creature. 2. He reduced social passions, from several in Shaftesbury, to one, from which all others spring."[89] This account of the genesis of Rousseau's doctrine is certainly appealing, especially since Rousseau was quite aware of Shaftesbury's work, which he read in Diderot's translation. Morel shows very well how Rousseau's focus on Shaftesbury's "sensible creature" corresponds to his own idea of pity as a pre-rational sentiment. He also rightly insists on Rousseau's decision to single out pity from Shaftesbury's list of social virtues ("pity, love, kindness, or social affection") and promote it to the status of a first principle. However, according to Morel himself, this interpretation leaves out one key aspect of Rousseau's innovativeness.[90] Shaftesbury describes "moral sense" as something analogous to the sense of sight or hearing. His

---

[87] *De la Recherche de la vérité*, II, I, VII, § III.

[88] Anthony Ashley Cooper, Third Earl of Shaftesbury, *An Inquiry Concerning Virtue*, in *Characteristics of Men, Manners, Opinions, Times*, Hildesheim: Georg Olms, 1978, Anglistica & Americana Series no. 123, vol. 2 [London: A. Bell, E. Castle, and S. Buckley, 1699], p. 43.

[89] Jean Morel, "Recherches sur les sources du *Discours de l'inégalité*," *Annales Jean-Jacques Rousseau*, vol. 5, Geneva, 1909, p. 128.

[90] "The theory of pity understood as identification with the suffering animal does not proceed from Diderot, who adopted Shaftesbury's – that the immediate sight of the suffering object in all its details causes us to feel pity. Diderot suspects the blind of being inhumane." Ibid., p. 125.

follower Diderot even suggests that the blind may be inhumane because they are deprived of the ability to perceive the suffering of others. For Shaftesbury, pity is a direct, immediate reaction to the sufferer's pain. On the contrary, in Rousseau's theory, we experience pity by putting ourselves mentally in the position of the sufferer. Rousseau's key innovation consists in basing pity on identification.

Hutcheson's moral philosophy includes another notable account of sympathy. Many aspects of this account are quite similar to Smith's analyses in *The Theory of Moral Sentiments*, including the naturalness of sympathy, and its disinterestedness:

> There are other still more noble senses and more useful: such is that *sympathy* or fellow-feeling, by which the state and fortunes of others affect us exceedingly, so that by the very power of nature, previous to any reasoning or meditation, we rejoice in the prosperity of others, and sorrow with them in their misfortunes, as we are disposed to mirth when we see others cheerful, and to weep with those that weep, without any consideration of our own interests.[91]

Since Hutcheson was Smith's teacher, the similarities are to be expected, and have been noticed often. However, just as the parallel between Rousseau and Shaftesbury shows that identification is the distinguishing feature of Rousseau's concept of pity, the comparison between Smith and Hutcheson reveals that Smith, unlike Hutcheson, bases sympathy on a psychological disposition that is very similar to what Rousseau calls identification.

As we have seen above, according to the traditional, medical account, sympathy is a sort of emotional contagion, whereby the feelings of one individual are transmitted to others. Hutcheson remains close to this traditional conception, when he describes sympathy as "a sort of contagion or infection."[92] Smith, on the other hand, insists that we cannot share the feelings of others. What we feel is a mental representation of what others are feeling. Since we have no access to the feelings of others, this mental representation can only be based upon our own feelings:

> Though our brother is upon the rack, as long as we ourselves are at our ease, our senses will never inform us of what he suffers. They never did, and never can, carry us beyond our own person, and it is by the imagination only that we can form any conception of what are his sensations. Neither can that faculty help us to this any other way, than by representing to us what would be our own, if we were in his case. It is the impressions of our own senses only, not those of his, which our imaginations copy.[93]

[91] Francis Hutcheson, *A Short Introduction to Moral Philosophy, translated from the Latin*, in *Collected Works*, Hildesheim: Georg Olms, 1990, vol. 4 [Glasgow: Robert Foulis, 1747], i.ix, p. 14.
[92] Ibid., i.ix, p. 14.   [93] Smith, *The Theory of Moral Sentiments*, I.i.1.1.

In this passage, Smith does away with pre-Cartesian doctrines of sympathy that described the "fellow-feeling" as a form of contagion, or subconscious communication whereby the feelings of others did make a direct imprint onto our own feelings. Here, sympathy operates within the Cartesian distinction between subject and object. By definition, we cannot have access to the feelings or mental representations of other subjects as subjects. To us, other subjects can only be objects.

A very revealing aspect of Smith's analysis of sympathy is the fact that he illustrates his point with examples taken from literature, and compares sympathy in social relations with the type of relationship we have with a character in a novel or a protagonist on the stage. For instance, it would be a mistake to believe that, when the hero of a novel is in love, we sympathize with the hero's passion. First of all, these feelings are too intense to be able to generate sympathy. Secondly, we could not sympathize with feelings that are directed towards a fictional character:

> But though we feel no proper sympathy with an attachment of this kind, though we never approach even in imagination towards conceiving a passion for that particular person, yet as we either have conceived, or may be disposed to conceive, passions of the same kind, we readily enter into those high hopes of happiness which are proposed from its gratification, as well as into that exquisite distress which is feared from its disappointment. It interests us not as a passion, but as a situation that gives occasion to other passions which interest us; to hope, to fear, and to distress of every kind: in the same manner as in a description of a sea voyage, it is not the hunger which interests us, but the distress which that hunger occasions. Though we do not properly enter into the attachment of the lover, we readily go along with those expectations of romantic happiness which he derives from it.[94]

The only feelings we can sympathize with are the feelings associated with the feeling of love: hope, fear, distress, etc. We can sympathize with these subsidiary feelings because they are weaker and, even more importantly because hope, fear, distress are familiar feelings. They interest us because they are familiar to us, because we already know them. It is on that basis only that we can sympathize with a fictional character. Similarly, in Racine's *Phèdre*, we cannot sympathize with the protagonist's incestuous love. We can, however, feel sympathy for the subsidiary feelings associated with Phèdre's passion: "her fear, her shame, her remorse, her horror, her despair."[95] Here again, "it is the impressions of our own senses only," not the fictional character's, "which our imaginations copy."

As David Marshall says judiciously, "for Smith, sympathy depends upon a theatrical relation between a spectator and a spectacle."[96] The omnipresence

[94] Ibid., I.ii.2.1.   [95] Ibid., I.ii.2.4.   [96] Marshall, *The Figure of Theater*, p. 190.

of theatrical metaphors in *The Theory of Moral Sentiments* suggests that social relations in general should be understood as something similar to the relationship between a spectator and a spectacle. At first sight, Smith is only reactivating the *topos* of the world as a stage. This is not surprising, given the Stoic origins of the theme, and Smith's neo-Stoicism. However, theatrical metaphors carry a much more specific meaning. Saying that social intercourse is like the relationship between a spectator and a spectacle means that the fellow-members of society with whom I sympathize could just as well be fictional characters. When I sympathize with a fictional character, I sympathize with feelings that do not exist. The feelings I experience come from within myself. When I sympathize with a fellow-member of society, I obviously sympathize with feelings that are real. But whether or not the object of my sympathy has real feelings makes no difference at all, since I can only have access to my own feelings. What makes "fellow-feeling" possible is an "imaginary change of situation," or, to borrow Rousseau's term again, an "identification" with the object of sympathy.

The parallel with Rousseau still holds when we examine the vocabulary of the *Second Discourse*. In his analysis of pity in the state of nature, Rousseau says that pity will be stronger when the "observing animal" (*animal spectateur*) identifies more closely with the "suffering animal" (*animal souffrant*).[97] The idea, which the translation fails to convey fully, is that the animal experiencing pity is a *spectator*, and the suffering animal is a *spectacle*. The reference to theater is not simply metaphorical. For Rousseau, the experience of the theater proves that the propensity to feel pity is an integral part of human nature:

Such is the force of natural pity, which the most depraved morals still have difficulty destroying, since daily in our theaters one sees, moved and crying for the troubles of an unfortunate person, a man who, if he were in the Tyrant's place, would aggravate his enemy's torment even more.[98]

When we see characters on the stage, we have no personal connection to them in the sense that no interests are at stake. We expect nothing from them, and they expect nothing from us. For all his misgiving about the theater as a source of corruption, Rousseau argues that the position of a spectator in front of a theatrical representation approximates the position of men vis-à-vis each other in the state of nature. Since no interests are at

---

[97] Rousseau, *Discourse on the Origin of Inequality*, p. 37.
[98] Ibid., p. 36. "Telle est la force de la pitié naturelle, que les mœurs les plus dépravées ont encore peine à détruire, puisqu'on voit tous les jours dans nos spectacles s'attendrir et pleurer aux malheurs d'un infortuné, tel, qui, s'il était à la place du tyran, aggraverait encore les tourments de son ennemi." *Discours sur l'origine de l'inégalité*, p. 155.

stake, the sight of suffering can trigger the full force of natural pity. It could be argued that, paradoxically, civil society is corrupt because it has drifted away from this theatrical model. Men are no longer simply looking at each other and feeling pity at the sight of suffering. Interest calculations stand in the way of the natural tendency to identify with the sufferer.

A RECONSTRUCTION OF MANDEVILLE'S ANTHROPOLOGY

As we have seen above, in his review of the *Second Discourse*, Smith claims that *The Fable of the Bees* has provided Rousseau with most of the materials he used for the construction of his own system. With the playful, tongue-in-cheek tone that characterizes the entire article, Smith adds that Rousseau has performed some sort of magic by transforming Mandeville's "licentious" doctrine into a system that seems "to have all the purity and sublimity of the morals of Plato."[99] Smith calls Rousseau's use of Mandeville an act of "philosophical chemistry." In other words, Rousseau is an alchemist who transformed Mandeville's vile metal into pure gold. Following Smith's suggestion, let us now analyze the way in which Rousseau appropriated and transformed Mandeville's work.

In his review, Smith specifically mentions "the second volume of the Fable of the Bees" as having "given occasion to the system of Mr. Rousseau."[100] The second volume appeared in 1728, fourteen years after the first volume. Smith mentions the second volume because, unlike the first, it contains a narrative of the evolution of humanity from the origins to the present.

Smith points out that both Mandeville and Rousseau propose a description of "the primitive state of mankind."[101] While Mandeville paints this state as a wretched one, Rousseau represents it as happy and most suited to man's nature. Both authors, however, assume that "there is in man no powerful instinct which necessarily determines him to seek society for its own sake."[102] Smith also notices that both thinkers "suppose the same slow progress and gradual development of all the talents, habits, and arts which fit men to live together in society, and they both describe this progress pretty much in the same manner."[103] Smith also mentions the passage in the *Second Discourse* where Rousseau criticizes Mandeville:

Mr. Rousseau however criticizes upon Dr. Mandeville: he observes that pity, the only amiable principle which the English author allows to be natural to man, is capable of producing all those virtues, whose reality Dr. Mandeville denies.

---

[99] Smith, "Letter to the *Edinburgh Review*," p. 251.   [100] Ibid., p. 250.
[101] Ibid.   [102] Ibid.   [103] Ibid.

Mr. Rousseau at the same time seems to think, that this principle is in itself no virtue, but that it is possessed by savages and by the most profligate of the vulgar, in a greater degree of perfection than by those of the most polished and cultivated manners; in which he perfectly agrees with the English author.[104]

This passage about pity is of fundamental importance. In his previous comments, Smith simply pointed out the similarities and differences between two narratives. Here, he puts his finger on the act of "philosophical chemistry." Rousseau's move is decisive because it deals with first principles. While Mandeville's work does not propose a fully formed philosophical system, it can be safely said that the first principles of *The Fable of the Bees* are Epicurean. Human behavior is driven by the pursuit of pleasure. Self-interest is the first principle. As we have seen before, Rousseau puts forward an *ad hominem* argument. If Mandeville, the most vocal advocate of the interest doctrine, acknowledges that human nature has a fundamental propensity to pity, we must admit that self-interest alone cannot explain human behavior. But the *ad hominem* argument goes beyond the refutation of Mandeville. It provides the cornerstone for Rousseau's own philosophical system.

If we now follow step by step the narrative of the *Second Discourse*, and focus on first principles, we shall see that Rousseau's main concern is to propose a coherent response to the interest doctrine. The response is a complicated one, because Rousseau does not simply aim at refuting the interest doctrine. His system has to fulfill two apparently incompatible objectives. On the one hand, the non-selfish tendencies of human nature must have the rank of a first principle. On the other hand, there must be room in the system for the "selfish hypothesis."

The *Second Discourse* is divided into two parts, but Rousseau's narrative contains three main episodes. The first part of the *Discourse* describes man in his *primitive* state. The second part narrates the passage from the *primitive* to the *savage* state, and from the *savage* to the *civilized* state. It is important to keep in mind that both the primitive and the savage state belong to the state of nature.

Man's behavior in the primitive state is driven by two principles: love of oneself (*amour de soi*) and pity:

Leaving aside therefore all the scientific books which teach us only to see men as they have made themselves, and meditating on the first and simplest operations of the human Soul, I believe I perceive in it two principles anterior to reason, of

---

[104] Ibid., p. 251.

which one interests us ardently in our well-being and our self-preservation, and the other inspires in us a natural repugnance to see any sensitive Being perish or suffer, especially those like ourselves.[105]

The love of oneself is pre-rational. Man shares it with the other animals. It is a survival instinct. Pity, also a pre-rational sentiment, "tempers the ardor [primitive man] has for his own well-being by an innate repugnance to seeing his fellow suffer."[106] We thus have not one, but two first principles, or perhaps, as Victor Goldschmidt suggests, one first principle with two faces, because pity could be seen not as an antagonistic principle, but rather simply as the limit that nature has set for the love of oneself.[107] In any case, Rousseau insists that *all* the behavior of primitive man can be derived from these two principles:

It is from the conjunction and combination that our mind is able to make of these two Principles, without the necessity of introducing that of Sociability, that all the rules of natural right appear to me to flow.[108]

The entire conduct of man in the state of nature can be explained as manifestations or combinations of the principle of *amour de soi* and the principle of pity. Rousseau's axiomatic choice could be described as a moderate form of theoretical parsimony: a middle ground between the neo-Epicureans, who explain everything with self-interest, and philosophers like Shaftesbury, who need yet another principle, sociability, in addition to self-love and sympathy, in order to explain human behavior.

The second episode in Rousseau's narrative focuses on the *savage*. The distinguishing feature of the savage is his ability to compare and reflect. Although he does not yet fully enjoy the use of reason, savage man is capable of making comparisons between the animals he sees, and soon between himself and the other animals:

---

[105] Rousseau, *Discourse on the Origin of Inequality*, p. 14. "Laissant donc tous les livres scientifiques qui ne nous apprennent qu'à voir les hommes tels qu'ils se sont faits, et méditant sur les premières et plus simples opérations de l'âme humaine, j'y crois apercevoir deux principes antérieurs à la raison, dont l'un nous intéresse ardemment à notre bien-être et à la conservation de nous-mêmes, et l'autre nous inspire une répugnance naturelle à voir périr ou souffrir tout être sensible et principalement nos semblables." *Discours sur l'origine de l'inégalité*, p. 125.

[106] Ibid., p. 36. "... tempère l'ardeur qu'il a pour son bien-être par une répugnance innée à voir souffrir son semblable." *Discours sur l'origine de l'inégalité*, p. 154.

[107] Victor Goldschmidt, *Anthropologie et politique. Les principes du système de Rousseau*, Paris: Vrin, 1974, p. 354.

[108] Rousseau, *Discourse on the Origin of Inequality*, p. 15. "C'est du concours et de la combinaison que notre esprit est en état de faire de ces deux principes, sans qu'il soit nécessaire d'y faire entrer celui de la sociabilité, que me paraissent découler toutes les règles du droit naturel." *Discours sur l'origine de l'inégalité*, p. 126.

This repeated utilization of various beings in relation to himself, and of some beings in relation to others, must naturally have engendered in man's mind perceptions of certain relations. Those relationships that we express by the words large, small, strong, weak, fast, slow, fearful, bold, and other similar ideas, compared when necessary and almost without thinking about it, finally produced in him some sort of reflection, or rather a mechanical prudence that indicated to him the precautions most necessary for his safety.[109]

This ability to compare led man to perceive in others a "way of thinking and feeling" that "conformed entirely to his own."[110] It also allowed him to understand that the "love of well-being is the sole motive of human actions."[111] The latter maxim is remarkable coming from Rousseau, because it seems to subscribe univocally to the interest doctrine. Quoted out of context, it could easily be attributed to Helvétius. However, for Rousseau, "love of well-being" is synonymous with "love of oneself" (*amour de soi*). Human desire is aimed only at the satisfaction of biological needs. Goldschmidt is quite right to point out that for Rousseau, the realization that love of wellbeing is the sole motive of human actions provides a solid foundation for the first social relations. In the state of civilization, the intricacy of motives makes human conduct dangerously unpredictable. In the state of nature, human behavior is always predictable.[112]

The ability to reflect has two decisive consequences: the rise of self-love, and the transformation of pity into a sentiment based on identification. Because he is able to make comparisons between himself and others, man becomes aware of the fact that others make comparisons between him and themselves. Hence a competition for attention and esteem:

Each one began to look at the others and to want to be looked at himself, and public esteem had a value. The one who sang or danced the best, the handsomest, the strongest, the most adroit or the most eloquent became the most highly considered.[113]

[109] Ibid., p. 44. "Cette application réitérée des êtres divers à lui-même, et les uns aux autres, dut naturellement engendrer dans l'esprit de l'homme les perceptions de certains rapports. Ces relations que nous exprimons par les mots de grand, de petit, de fort, de faible, de vite, de lent, de peureux, de hardi, et d'autres idées pareilles, comparées au besoin, et presque sans y songer, produisirent enfin chez lui quelque sorte de réflexion, ou plutôt une prudence machinale qui lui indiquait les précautions les plus nécessaires à sa sûreté." *Discours sur l'origine de l'inégalité*, p. 165.
[110] Ibid. "Il conclut que leur manière de penser et de sentir était entièrement conforme à la sienne." *Discours sur l'origine de l'inégalité*, p. 166.
[111] Ibid., p. 45. "L'amour du bien être est le seul motif des actions humaines." *Discours sur l'origine de l'inégalité*, p. 166.
[112] Goldschmidt, *Anthropologie et politique*, p. 412.
[113] Rousseau, *Discourse on the Origin of Inequality*, p. 47. "Chacun commença à regarder les autres et à vouloir être regardé soi-même, et l'estime publique eut un prix. Celui qui chantait ou dansait le mieux; le plus beau, le plus fort, le plus adroit ou le plus éloquent devint le plus considéré." *Discours sur l'origine de l'inégalité*, p. 169.

Goldschmidt argues that, although Rousseau does not use the term *amour-propre* to designate the savage man's desire for esteem and consideration, the concern for the opinion of others is an essential component of *amour-propre* as Rousseau describes it in the state of civilization. On the other hand, there is a crucial distinction between the savage man's desire for esteem and the civilized man's *amour-propre*. The savage man does not want any tangible goods. He is only interested in receiving praise and other marks of consideration:

As soon as men had begun to appreciate one another, and the idea of consideration was formed in their minds, each one claimed a right to it, and it was no longer possible to be disrespectful toward anyone with impunity. From this came the first duties of civility, even among Savages; and from this any voluntary wrong became an outrage, because along with the harm that resulted from the injury, the offended man saw in it contempt for his person which was often more unbearable than the harm itself. Thus, everyone punishing the contempt shown him by another in a manner proportionate to the importance he accorded himself, vengeances became terrible, and men bloodthirsty and cruel.[114]

With a complete lack of concern for the concrete and material consequences of his actions, savage man seeks to force others to give him the marks of esteem and consideration he thinks he deserves. This results in extreme violence and cruelty but, for Rousseau, the state of affairs described here is morally superior to the state of civilization. As Goldschmidt puts it very aptly, savage man's self-love is "disinterested."[115] Esteem is sought for its own sake, not as a means towards the acquisition of tangible goods.

The other consequence of man's ability to compare and reflect is the emergence of a modified form of pity, based on identification with the sufferer. It must be mentioned that there has been considerable debate about this among Rousseau scholars. Rousseau argues at the same time that pity is "prior to all reflection,"[116] and that pity is based on identification (which implies the ability to reflect). In addition, the *Essay on the Origin of Language* says explicitly that there can be no pity without identification:

[114] Ibid. "Sitôt que les hommes eurent commencé à s'apprécier mutuellement et que l'idée de la considération fut formée dans leur esprit, chacun prétendit y avoir droit, et il ne fut plus possible d'en manquer impunément pour personne. De là sortirent les premiers devoirs de la civilité, même parmi les sauvages, et de là tout tort volontaire devint un outrage, parce qu'avec le mal qui résultait de l'injure, l'offensé y voyait le mépris de sa personne souvent plus insupportable que le mal même. C'est ainsi que chacun punissant le mépris qu'on lui avait témoigné d'une manière proportionnée au cas qu'il faisait de lui-même, les vengeances devinrent terribles, et les hommes sanguinaires et cruels." *Discours sur l'origine de l'inégalité*, p. 170.

[115] Goldschmidt, *Anthropologie et politique*, p. 452.

[116] Rousseau, *Discourse on the Origin of Inequality*, p. 36. "Tel est le pur mouvement de la nature, antérieur à toute réflexion." *Discours sur l'origine de l'inégalité*, p. 155.

Pity, although natural to the heart of man, would remain eternally inactive without the imagination that puts it into play. How do we let ourselves be moved to pity? By transporting ourselves outside of ourselves; by identifying ourselves with the suffering being.[117]

The various strategies to deal with this contradiction have included attempts to reconcile the opposing statements, and claims that Rousseau had changed his mind between the *Discourse* and the *Essay* (there is also some disagreement as to which one was written first). David Marshall treats the contradiction from a deconstructionist point of view: by claiming at the same time that pity is prior to all reflection and that pity requires identification, Rousseau subverts his own quest for origins. For Marshall, this shows that reflection is always already there and that the state of nature is "always already theatrical."[118]

For the purposes of our analysis here, Goldschmidt's solution seems the most appropriate. The contradiction between Rousseau's statements is less striking when one recalls that Rousseau makes a distinction between the primitive man and the savage man, both of whom belong to the state of nature. The pity prior to all reflection pertains to the primitive man. The pity based on identification belongs to the savage man. In that sense, there exists a parallel evolution of the primitive sentiments of man. With the ability to reflect, love of oneself (*amour de soi*) evolves into disinterested self-love (*amour-propre désintéressé* – Goldschmidt's expression), while simple pity becomes identifying pity (*pitié identifiante* – Goldschmidt's expression again).[119]

The third stage in the evolution is marked by the full development of human reason, and with it the ability to perform interest calculations:

Behold all our faculties developed, memory and imagination in play, amour-propre aroused, reason rendered active, and the mind having almost reached the limit of the perfection of which it is susceptible.[120]

---

[117] Jean-Jacques Rousseau, *Essay on the Origin of Languages*, in *The Collected Writings of Rousseau*, vol. 7, translated and edited by John T. Scott, Hanover, NH: University Press of New England, 1998, p. 306. "La pitié, bien que naturelle au cœur de l'homme, resterait éternellement inactive sans l'imagination qui la met en jeu. Comment nous laissons nous émouvoir par la pitié? En nous transportant hors de nous-mêmes; en nous identifiant avec l'être souffrant." Rousseau, *Essai sur l'origine des langues*, edited by Charles Porset, Bordeaux: Ducros, 1970, p. 93.

[118] David Marshall, *The Surprising Effects of Sympathy: Marivaux, Diderot, Rousseau, and Mary Shelley*, Chicago: University of Chicago Press, 1988, p. 151. I follow this line of argument in "Self-Love, Identification, and the Origin of Political Economy," *Yale French Studies* 92 (1997) pp. 46–64. The present chapter proposes a different view.

[119] Goldschmidt, *Anthropologie et politique*, pp. 337–341.

[120] Rousseau, *Discourse on the Origin of Inequality*, p. 51. "Voilà donc toutes nos facultés développées, la mémoire et l'imagination en jeu, l'amour-propre intéressé, la raison rendue active et l'esprit arrivé presque au terme de la perfection, dont il est susceptible." *Discours sur l'origine de l'inégalité*, p. 174.

The ability to make rational evaluations of his interests transforms man's self-love. It is no longer disinterested. It has become *intéressé* ("aroused," in the translation above, or more precisely "looking out for its interests"). This is why Rousseau makes the claim (so counterintuitive for Augustinians and Epicureans) that self-love is a product of reason and reflection: "Reason engenders amour-propre and reflection fortifies it."[121] In Rousseau's narrative, the development of reason also affects the workings of identification. The "feeling that puts us in the position of him who suffers" is "obscure and lively in Savage man, developed but weak in Civilized man."[122] In other words, prior to the full development of human reason, the propensity to identify with the feelings of others always results in pity. When combined with reflection and reasoning, the capacity for identification is weaker (and therefore it does not result in pity). It is, however, more developed in the sense that we have a greater ability to see things through the eyes of others. In that sense, the capacity for identification increases with the development of reason and civilization, and it is an essential component in the development of *amour-propre* (a passion based on our desire to be seen favorably by others).

In the second stage of evolution (savage man) human needs belong to two distinct spheres. On the one hand, man has physical needs (love of well-being). On the other hand, he competes with other men for public esteem (disinterested self-love). There is no connection between these two classes of needs. With the full development of human reason, a contamination occurs. Access to material goods requires some measure of public esteem. Conversely, the possession of material goods is necessary to acquire and retain the esteem of others. In such a state, computing one's interests is a constant necessity. How much public esteem do I need to obtain a certain amount of material goods? What quantity of material goods do I need in order to acquire a certain degree of public esteem? How can I obtain the maximum degree of public esteem? Public esteem goes to tangible goods, but also to intangibles such as "mind, beauty, strength or skill... merit or talents." Since those intangible qualities can be real or simulated, everyone has an interest in pretending that he has them in the greatest degree possible:

Behold all our faculties developed, memory and imagination in play, amour-propre aroused, reason rendered active, and the mind having almost reached the limit of the perfection of which it is susceptible. Behold all the natural qualities put into

---

[121] Ibid., p. 37. "C'est la raison qui engendre l'amour-propre, et c'est la réflexion qui le fortifie." *Discours sur l'origine de l'inégalité*, p. 156.

[122] Ibid. "... un sentiment qui nous met à la place de celui qui souffre, sentiment obscur et vif dans l'homme sauvage, développé mais faible dans l'homme civil ..." *Discours sur l'origine de l'inégalité*, p. 155.

action, the rank and fate of each man established, not only upon the quantity of goods and the power to serve or harm, but also upon the mind, beauty, strength, or skill, upon merit or talents. And these qualities being the only ones which could attract consideration, it was soon necessary to have them or affect them; for one's own advantage, it was necessary to appear to be other than what one in fact was. To be and to seem to be became two altogether different things; and from this distinction came conspicuous ostentation, deceptive cunning, and all the vices that follow from them.[123]

Readers of this passage usually focus their attention on Rousseau's moral condemnation of civil society, and the pathetic description of human duplicity in the civilized state. For the purposes of our analysis, the most important aspect is Rousseau's insistence that deception is "necessary" to man because it is to "one's own advantage." In other words, deception is a compelling matter of self-interest. In the civilized state, the selfish hypothesis is fully operational. Self-interest is the only engine of human behavior. *As far as the civilized state is concerned, Rousseau subscribes entirely to the analyses of Hobbes and Mandeville.*

One could account for the whole story by showing how Rousseau uses and transforms La Rochefoucauld's analysis of pity. For La Rochefoucauld, self-love is the fundamental human impulse. Self-love results in identification with sufferers, which in turn triggers the trading of favors. In short, the causal chain is self-love → identification → commerce. Rousseau retains all the elements in La Rochefoucauld's analysis, but he complicates the categories and modifies the order. He splits La Rochefoucauld's self-love into love of oneself (*amour de soi*) and self-love (*amour-propre*). He then invokes Mandeville to claim that pity is a fundamental impulse, not a derivative manifestation of self-interest. The causal chain is: 1. Love of oneself + pity → 2. Disinterested self-love + strong identifying pity → 3. Self-love looking out for its interests + weak identifying pity. Or, to put it more simply: love of oneself → identification → self-love → commerce. The reference to Mandeville's analysis of pity is key because it provides Rousseau with a first principle for his system. Taking the interest doctrine (La Rochefoucauld, Mandeville) as his point of departure, Rousseau refutes it on its own terms. He singles out the analysis of pity (a subsidiary element

---

[123] Ibid., p. 51. "Voilà donc toutes nos facultés développées, la mémoire et l'imagination en jeu, l'amour-propre intéressé, la raison rendue active et l'esprit arrivé presque au terme de la perfection, dont il est susceptible. Voilà toutes les qualités naturelles mises en action, le rang et le sort de chaque homme établi, non seulement sur la quantité des biens et le pouvoir de servir ou de nuire, mais sur l'esprit, la beauté, la force ou l'adresse, sur le mérite ou les talents, et ces qualités étant les seules qui pouvaient attirer de la considération, il fallut bientôt les avoir ou les affecter, il fallut pour son avantage se montrer autre que ce qu'on était en effet. Etre et paraître devinrent deux choses tout à fait différentes, et de cette distinction sortirent le faste imposant, la ruse trompeuse, et tous les vices qui en sont le cortège." *Discours sur l'origine de l'inégalité*, p. 174.

in Mandeville's work) and posits it as a first principle for his own system. In that sense, Rousseau's *Second Discourse* is a *reconstruction of Mandeville's anthropology based on pity, not self-love*. This is how, according to Smith's analysis, "the principles and ideas of the profligate Mandeville seem in [Rousseau] to have all the purity and sublimity of the morals of Plato."[124]

SYMPATHY AND SELF-INTEREST IN SMITH AND ROUSSEAU

As we have seen before, Smith's analysis of the appropriation by Rousseau of *The Fable of the Bees* can tell us a lot about the genesis of Smith's own work. Smith performs his own act of philosophical chemistry by transforming Mandeville's "licentious system" into a *Theory of Moral Sentiments*. In addition, Smith's axiomatic choices bear a remarkable resemblance to Rousseau's. The author of the *Second Discourse*, taking the selfish hypothesis as his point of departure, complicates it by introducing the principle of pity. Rousseau's system has two first principles: love of oneself and pity. Starting from the same initial hypothesis ("How selfish soever man may be supposed"),[125] Smith complicates it by introducing the principle of sympathy. It is worth noticing that sympathy does not supersede love of oneself as a first principle. Smith does insist that "every man is, no doubt, by nature, first and principally recommended to his own care."[126] Therefore, Smith's system also has two first principles: self-love and sympathy.

A clarification concerning vocabulary is probably needed here. When Smith uses the term "self-love" in *The Theory of Moral Sentiments*, he means something similar to Rousseau's *amour de soi*, or self-love according to the Stoics: an instinct for self-preservation and immediate gratification. For instance, in his account of Stoicism, he states that "according to Zeno, the founder of the Stoical doctrine, every animal was by nature recommended to its own care, and was endowed with the principle of self-love."[127] This principle is in itself neither vicious nor virtuous. On the one hand, "the natural misrepresentations of self-love"[128] lead us to act in ways that are selfish and partial. On the other hand, according to Smith, it would be false to say that "self-love can never be the motive of a virtuous action."[129] At the same time, the conceptual equivalent of Rousseau's *amour-propre* does exist in the *Theory of Moral Sentiments*. Smith calls it "vanity." In his account of the various systems of moral philosophy, Smith alludes to "some splenetic philosophers" (i.e. La Rochefoucauld, Mandeville, and, to the

---

[124] Smith, "Letter to the *Edinburgh Review*," p. 251.
[125] Smith, *The Theory of Moral Sentiments*, I.i.1.1.   [126] Ibid., II.ii.2.1.
[127] Ibid., VII.ii.1.14.   [128] Ibid., III.3.4.   [129] Ibid., VII.ii.3.16.

extent that he follows Mandeville, Rousseau himself) who "have imputed to the love of praise, or to what they call vanity, every action which ought to be ascribed to that of praise-worthiness."[130] What distinguishes vanity from self-love is the fact that vanity is a *relative* feeling. Persons driven by self-love will be satisfied with getting the goods and advantages they desire. Persons driven by vanity are not primarily interested in the acquisition of goods and advantages. What they want is praise and approbation from other human beings. "What are the advantages," Smith asks, "which we propose by that great purpose of human life which we call bettering our condition?" And he responds: "To be observed, to be attended to, to be taken notice of with sympathy, complacency, and approbation, are all the advantages which we can propose to derive from it. It is the vanity, not the ease, or the pleasure, which interests us."[131] Rousseau makes the same distinction in the *Second Discourse*. In civilized society, instead of following the impulse of *amour de soi* and seeking immediate gratification (what Smith calls "the ease, or the pleasure"), man "cannot live but in the opinion of others."[132] Everything he does is aimed at securing marks of respect and admiration from others. This central concern for the opinion of others is precisely what Rousseau calls *amour-propre*.

There are strong axiomatic similarities between the system Smith develops in *The Theory of Moral Sentiments* and the one Rousseau proposes in the *Second Discourse*. In both cases, the system has two first principles. "Self-love" in Smith corresponds to *amour de soi* in Rousseau. "Sympathy" in *The Theory of Moral Sentiments* corresponds to *identification* in the *Second Discourse*. Even more importantly, Smith and Rousseau have in common the fact that their axiomatic choices constitute a deliberate response to the interest doctrine. One may wonder why Rousseau and Smith felt it necessary to take the interest doctrine as their starting point. The first reason has to do with issues of persuasion. As Hirschman reminds us, the interest doctrine had an extraordinary success, embodied by the *succès de scandale* of *The Fable of the Bees*. The interest doctrine also formed a wide ideological front. It had philosophical support in Epicureanism and Augustinianism (we will examine this in chapter 2). Almost everyone writing on issues of moral philosophy felt compelled to express an opinion on Mandeville's work. But the treatment of the *Fable* that we find in Rousseau and Smith is far cleverer than a simple censure. Rousseau and Smith argue *ad hominem*. They agree with Mandeville in order to refute him. Secondly,

---

[130] Ibid., III.2.27.   [131] Ibid., I.iii.2.1.
[132] Rousseau, *Discourse on the Origin of Inequality*, translated by Adam Smith in "Letter to the *Edinburgh Review*," p. 253.

Rousseau and Smith take Mandeville seriously because they actually agree with him on several points. In the *Second Discourse*, Rousseau does not reject the selfish hypothesis. Rather, he historicizes it. The main mistake of philosophers like "Hobbes and others" (for "others," read Mandeville) is that, having to explain "a fact of the state of Nature,... they did not think of carrying themselves back beyond the Centuries of Society."[133] As a result, they mistakenly assumed that self-interest had been the engine of human behavior since the birth of humanity. For Rousseau, the selfish hypothesis does not account for the nature of man in his original state. Human nature has changed, however, and the selfish hypothesis does explain the behavior of man in civilized society. Similarly, Smith does not reject Mandeville's doctrine altogether. "How destructive soever" Mandeville's system may appear, "it could never have imposed upon so great a number of persons, nor have occasioned so general an alarm among those who are friends of better principles, had it not in some respects bordered upon the truth."[134]

What is true then in Mandeville's system? It is the description of human behavior in civilized society, a behavior that is in large part driven by the desire to obtain marks of esteem and approbation from others. This is why the picture Smith paints bears a striking resemblance to the descriptions we find in both Mandeville and Rousseau:

> For to what purpose is all the toil and bustle of this world? What is the end of avarice and ambition, of the pursuit of wealth, of power, and pre-eminence? Is it to supply the necessities of nature? The wages of the meanest labourer can supply them. We see that they afford him food and clothing, the comfort of a house, and of a family... What then is the cause of our aversion to his situation, and why should those who have been educated in the higher ranks of life, regard it as worse than death, to be reduced to live, even without labor, upon the same simple fare with him, to dwell under the same roof, and to be clothed with the same humble attire? Do they imagine that their stomach is better, or their sleep sounder, in a palace than in a cottage? The contrary has been so often observed, and indeed, is so very obvious, though it had never been observed, that there is nobody ignorant of it... To be observed, to be attended to, to be taken notice of with sympathy, complacency, and approbation, are all the advantages which we can propose to derive from it. It is the vanity, not the ease, or the pleasure, which interests us. But vanity is always founded upon the belief of our being the object of attention and approbation.[135]

Just like Rousseau, Smith describes the contamination that occurs between the sphere of physical needs and the sphere of public esteem. Man no longer

---

[133] Rousseau, *Discourse on the Origin of Inequality*, p. 90, note 10. "Ils avaient à expliquer un fait de l'état de nature... et ils n'ont pas songé à se transporter au-delà des siècles de société." *Discours sur l'origine de l'inégalité*, p. 218, note XII.

[134] Smith, *The Theory of Moral Sentiments*, VII.ii.4.14.   [135] Ibid., I.iii.2.1.

seeks material goods in order to meet physical needs ("Do they imagine that their stomach is better?"). The material goods are a means toward the acquisition of public esteem ("It is the vanity, not the ease, or the pleasure, which interests us"). Smith's description resembles a passage of the *Second Discourse* he had translated for the readers of the *Edinburgh Review*:

> The savage breathes nothing but liberty and repose; he desires only to live and be at leisure; and the *ataraxia* of the Stoic does not approach his indifference for every other object. The citizen, on the contrary, toils, bestirs and torments himself without end, to obtain employments which are still more laborious; he labors on till his death, he even hastens it, in order to put himself in a condition to live, or renounces life to acquire immortality... For such in reality is the true cause of all those differences: the savage lives in himself; the man of society, always out of himself, cannot live but in the opinions of others, and it is, if I may say so, from their judgment alone that he derives the sentiment of his own existence.[136]

Smith's "belief of our being the object of attention and approbation" echoes Rousseau's "man of society" who "cannot live but in the opinion of others." For Smith, the need for attention and approbation is the cause of "the toil and bustle of this world." For Rousseau, the concern for the opinion of others is the reason why the citizen "toils, bestirs and torments himself without end." In both cases, civilized life has little to do with the satisfaction of natural needs, and almost everything to do with the search for esteem and approbation. Both Rousseau and Smith seem to say that if modern human beings were reasonable Epicureans, they would focus their attention on consumption and immediate gratification. Yet, driven as they are by *amour-propre* and vanity, they seek wealth and material goods only as a means towards an infinitely more elusive goal: praise and approbation from others. As Rousseau puts it in his *Project of Constitution for Corsica*, "upon close examination, the great motives that cause men to act can be reduced to two: pleasure and vanity."[137] Furthermore, in the final analysis, "almost everything can be reduced to vanity alone"[138] because those who claim to seek pleasure are more interested in making a display of that claim than they are in actually experiencing pleasure. As far as civilized man is concerned, vanity is the only motive.

Against the contention of economists like Stigler who claim that Smith used self-interest as a general explanatory principle in *The Wealth of Nations*, one may argue that Smith mentions several other motives of human

---

[136] Rousseau, *Discourse on the Origin of Inequality*, translated by Adam Smith in "Letter to the *Edinburgh Review*," p. 253.

[137] Rousseau, "Les grands mobiles qui font agir les hommes bien examinés se réduisent à deux, la volupté et la vanité." *Projet de constitution pour la Corse*, in *Œuvres complètes*, vol. 3, p. 937.

[138] "Tout se réduit à la presque seule vanité." Ibid.

behavior: examples include the landowners in medieval times who bartered away their immense political power "for trinkets and baubles,"[139] or the slave owners of the West Indies, who ignore the fact that "the work done by slaves . . . is in end the dearest of any"[140] because "the pride of man makes him love to domineer."[141] Clearly, neither type of behavior can be described as rational pursuit of self-interest. Nonetheless, both types of behavior can be analyzed on the basis of the two principles that Smith posits at the beginning of *The Theory of Moral Sentiments*: self-love and sympathy. In *The Wealth of Nations*, these same two principles manifest themselves as "the passion for present enjoyment" and "the desire of bettering our condition."[142] In Smith's historical scheme (which we will discuss at greater length in chapter 6) the passion for present enjoyment is dominant in the primitive stages of society. When a legal system is in place, which makes it possible to save one's earnings, the desire to better our condition (based on our desire to obtain the sympathy of others) overtakes the desire for instant gratification. In that sense, the behavior of the landowners is characteristic of the earliest stages of economic development. The legal and economic system of modern commercial society encourages the vanity of men to express itself as a "wish to better their condition," and "an augmentation of fortune is the means by which the greater part of men propose"[143] to satisfy this wish. As to the "love to domineer," it is also based on the principle of sympathy. As Smith puts it in *The Theory of Moral Sentiments*, "the desire of being believed, the desire of persuading, of leading and directing other people, seems to be one of the strongest of all our natural desires."[144] What is remarkable is that Smith does not ascribe the desire of "leading and directing other people" to self-love, or to some "selfish" tendency in human nature. In the final analysis, the "love to domineer" is a consequence of our desire to be seen favorably by others. As Thomas Lewis puts it, "domination is not an end in itself; it is a means to the end of recognition for being powerful."[145] The driving principle here is not self-love (in the sense of Rousseau's *amour de soi*) but sympathy and the desire for sympathy. Whether the desire for sympathy expresses itself as an impulse to dominate others or as a desire to better our condition is again dependent on the degree of legal and economic development. In Mandeville's narrative, the first principle of human behavior is a boundless and tyrannical desire for universal domination. This first principle is the root of the pride, or vanity, that characterizes human

[139] Smith, *The Wealth of Nations*, III.iv.15.   [140] Ibid., III.ii.9.   [141] Ibid., III.ii.10.
[142] Ibid., II.iii.28.   [143] Ibid.   [144] Smith, *The Theory of Moral Sentiments*, VII.iv.25.
[145] Thomas J. Lewis, "Persuasion, Domination and Exchange: Adam Smith on the Political Consequences of Markets," *Canadian Journal of Political Science* 33:2 (2000), p. 287.

behavior in civilized society: pride is a modified form of our desire to "lord it over the earth." In the reconstruction of Mandeville's anthropology that we find in Smith and Rousseau, vanity remains the main engine of civilized behavior, but instead of being founded on a desire for universal domination, it is derived from our capacity for identification (Rousseau) or from our desire for sympathy (Smith).

The notion that self-interest is a general explanatory principle in *The Wealth of Nations* must be doubly qualified. First, when we use the term self-interest as a synonym for the "desire to better our condition," we must remember that this desire is not grounded in natural selfishness (Smith's *self-love* or Rousseau's *amour de soi*) but rather in what Smith calls *vanity*, or what Rousseau calls *amour-propre*. Second, the nearly universal nature of *vanity* or *amour-propre* is a historical consequence of the development of commerce and the division of labor.

Having gone to the source of the debates regarding the first principles of economics, we are now in a better position to evaluate the contradictory claims of the authors we quoted at the beginning of this chapter. The findings are paradoxical. When authors like Hirschman or Sen propose to discard the theoretical parsimony advocated by their fellow economists, they follow the path opened by Rousseau and Smith, who both believed that the "selfish hypothesis" was too clever to be true, and proposed systems based on principles other than self-interest. On the other hand, we have seen that Rousseau and Smith shared another belief: although it is true that the "selfish hypothesis" cannot explain human nature, human behavior in civilized society can be described in very large part as a search for wealth and material goods. In other words, the ultimate goal of economic activity is something symbolic and intangible: approbation from others. At the same time, for historical reasons, the search for praise and approbation now manifests itself almost exclusively as a search for wealth. Regarding Smith, the conclusion that human behavior is driven by self-interest will appear trivial to most. In any case, it will justify the claims of those like Becker who see Adam Smith as the founder of the "economic approach." What is more surprising is that, when he enunciated this belief, Smith was appropriating the thought of someone who is remembered as the fiercest critic of modern commercial society: Jean-Jacques Rousseau.

2

Epicurean vs. Stoic schemes

*The Church fathers claimed to have much scorn for the virtues of the
ancient Pagans which – according to them – had no other principle than
vainglory. Nevertheless, I believe they might have been extremely perplexed
to prove such a reckless assertion solidly.*

Rousseau, *Political Fragments*

TRAHIT SUA QUEMQUE VOLUPTAS

Mandeville, the polemical target of Smith and Rousseau, defends a doctrine
that is highly ambiguous. Because Mandeville sees the quest for pleasure as
the source of human actions, he may be called an Epicurean. E.J. Hundert
reminds us that Mandeville was defending "an ancient insight into the fundamentally egoistic sources of human behavior – a thesis still associated in
the early eighteenth century with Lucretius (ca.94–ca.50 BC), whose epic *De
rerum natura* contained the most detailed classical exposition of the atom-
ist, hedonist and purportedly atheist doctrines of Epicurus (341–271 BC)."[1]
Others insist on the similarities between Mandeville's critique of human
virtues and La Rochefoucauld's *Maxims*. As the editor of *The Fable of the
Bees* puts it, "much of Mandeville's philosophy might be summarized as
an elaboration of La Rochefoucauld's maxim, '*Nos vertus ne sont le plus
souvent que des vices déguisés*', with *le plus souvent* changed to *toujours*."[2]
This would categorize Mandeville as a representative of the Augustinian
tradition. At first sight, these two interpretations are strictly incompatible. On the one hand, a doctrine that was famously hostile to religion.
On the other hand, a tradition that went back to a pre-eminent Father
of the Church. Yet, as far as our subject matter is concerned, the dividing

[1] E.J. Hundert, *The Enlightenment's Fable. Bernard Mandeville and the Discovery of Society*, Cambridge:
Cambridge University Press, 1994, p. 17. Hundert also mentions the role of Augustinian themes in
Mandeville, but he subordinates them to a neo-Epicurean interpretation of Mandeville's work.

[2] F.B. Kaye, introduction to Bernard Mandeville, *The Fable of the Bees*, Oxford: Clarendon Press, 1924
[London: J. Tonson, 1732], p. cv.

line is not between Epicureans and Augustinians. Most of the notions that Rousseau and Smith criticize in Mandeville could indifferently be called Epicurean or Augustinian. In particular, it is the Epicurean/Augustinian doctrine of self-interest that Rousseau and Smith attack from a Stoic point of view.

In order to understand this critique, it is necessary to draw a parallel between the Epicurean and Augustinian conceptions of self-interest. This must start with an examination of the first principle of Epicurean philosophy, namely that all human action tends to maximize pleasure. According to Gassendi, the chief exponent of Epicurean philosophy in the early modern period, the ends of human action are subordinated to the quest for pleasure:

It is generally assumed that there are three classes of goods, the honorable, the useful, and the pleasurable. However, the pleasurable is mixed with the other goods in such a way that it does not seem to constitute a distinct and specific category. Rather, it is the common genus, or common property that makes these goods good or desirable, as if what is honorable or useful was sought only because it is pleasurable.[3]

Gassendi refers to the classic Aristotelian distinction between three ends of human action: the honorable (*kalon*), the useful (*sympheron*), and the pleasurable (*hedu*).[4] He subverts the distinction by showing that the pleasurable is a category of a higher order than the other two. We seek things that are honorable or useful, not for their own sake, but because, in the final analysis, they give us pleasure. For Gassendi and the Epicureans, the universality of the quest for pleasure is an axiomatic, self-evident truth. As such, it requires no demonstration:

There is no need to reason, to dispute or to inquire about the reasons why pleasure must be sought and pain must be avoided. It is self-evident, like fire is hot, snow is white, and honey is sweet.[5]

---

[3] "Encore qu'on fasse ordinairement trois sortes de biens, l'honnête, l'utile, et l'agréable, l'agréable (qui n'est autre chose que la volupté même) est de telle manière mêlé avec les autres, qu'il ne semble point tant être une espèce particulière, et distincte des autres, que leur genre commun, ou une commune propriété qui fait qu'ils sont biens, ou désirables, comme si ce qui est honnête, et utile n'était désiré que parce qu'il est plaisant, et agréable." François Bernier, *Abrégé de la Philosophie de Gassendi*, Corpus des œuvres de philosophie en langue française, Paris: Fayard, 1992 [Lyon: Anisson, Posuel et Rigaud, 1684], vol. 7, p. 98.

[4] Aristotle, *Nicomachean Ethics*, translated by H. Rackham, Cambridge, MA: Harvard University Press, 1926, II.3.7.

[5] "Il n'est point besoin de raisonner, ni de disputer ou de chercher des raisons pourquoi la volupté soit à désirer, et la douleur à fuir; cela se sent de soi-même, et naturellement, comme le feu être chaud, la neige être blanche, le miel être doux." Cicero, quoted in Bernier, *Abrégé de la Philosophie de Gassendi*, vol. 7, p. 98.

The principle of pleasure is truly universal. It applies to religious matters. According to Gassendi, we love God because we find pleasure in it. This is Gassendi's response to those who claim that their love of God is entirely disinterested:

I will not attempt to test their consciences and ask what they would do if God, content of being loved and worshipped, did not care for those who love and worship him, granted no benefits to them, and left no reward to be hoped for in all eternity. I don't doubt that they would respond in good faith that they would love and worship God nonetheless. I hope they would not mind being asked why it is so sweet to love and worship God in this way. They say it is very sweet to get one's mind ready for God. By their own admission, this action is not being conducted for its own sake.[6]

Even if one refrains from an uncharitable interpretation of the declarations of those who claim to love God in a disinterested way, their admission that it is "sweet" to love God proves that the worship of God is not conducted for its own sake. For Gassendi, pleasure is the central element in the religious experience:

You cannot discount the pleasure involved in knowing him who says that his yoke is sweet. His yoke is the law, which says first and foremost that we should love God with all our heart, all our soul, all our mind, and all our strength. Certainly, there is no love of God without pleasure or feelings of joy, which are God's way of leading us into loving him.[7]

For such a claim, Gassendi invokes first the authority of Scripture, and then the authority of Augustine, whom he quotes at length:

It is thus written: *Lead us behind you; let us follow the sweet smell of your perfumes.* The Holy Doctor also says: *being led on by one's will is not much, if one is not also led on by pleasure. What is it to be led on by pleasure? It is finding one's pleasure in God.* And he adds: *If the poet could say,*

Each is led on by his own pleasure

---

[6] "Ac non testor quidem istorum conscientiam quid acturi essent, si Deus amari et coli contentus, nihil prorsus amatores, cultoresque sui curaret, nihil beneficii illis conferret, nullam tota aeternitate sperandum bonum faceret? Nimirum quasi agnituri, responsurique bona fide sint, nihilone minus amantes, venerantesque Dei forent. Velim solum grave non sit, si rogentur, id – ne saltem non faciant, quia Deum ea ratione amare, ipsique servire suavissimum sit; suavissimumque adeo ducant mentem sic habere in Deum comparatam, ut ob ipsum plane, nullo vero modo sui causa faciant." Pierre Gassendi, *Animadversiones in Decimum Librum Diogenis Laertii, qui est de vita, moribus, placitisque Epicuri*, Lyon: Guillaume Barbier, 1649, vol. 3, p. 1370.

[7] "Suavitas haec certe ab eo non excluditur, qui suave esse clamat jugum suum, hoc est legem suam, cujus caput est, ut ex toto corde, ex tota anima, ex tota mente, ex totis viribus diligamus deum. Et certe hujusmodi dilectio sine libentia, seu voluntate suaviter affecta, qua Deus ad se suave dilectionem nos trahit, non est." Ibid., p. 1371.

Not necessity, but pleasure, not obligation, but enjoyment; how much more strongly shall humans be led on towards Christ, in whom one enjoys truth, happiness, and justice? And further: Show a green branch to a sheep, and it will follow you; show walnuts to a child, and he will follow you. If it is true that everyone is led on by his own pleasure, won't they follow Christ revealed by the Father? And finally: *This is how the Father attracts us: his lessons are a pleasure to learn.*[8]

This quote from Augustine belongs to a chapter entitled "The good life consists in pleasure (*voluptas*), i.e. peace of the mind and absence of physical pain,"[9] which exposes the main thesis of Epicurean moral philosophy. Invoking Augustine is characteristic of Gassendi's overall intent, which is to propose a Christian interpretation of Epicurean thought. But more specifically, it reveals a convergence between Epicureans and Augustinians regarding the centrality of pleasure as a motive for human action. One finds the same quote from Augustine, interpreted in much the same way, in *bona fide* Augustinians of the same period. In his *Writings on Grace*, Pascal uses the Augustine quote to explain why God's grace never fails to move those who receive it. The power of grace is comparable, on a spiritual level, to the power a green branch exerts on a sheep, or a bunch of walnuts on a child. It is absolute, because we never fail to choose what pleases us most:

Is there anything more evident than the proposition that we always do what delights us most? In other words, we always do what we like best, or we always will what pleases us, or we always will what we will, and in the current, fallen state of our soul, it is inconceivable that the soul could will something other than what it likes to will, i.e. what delights it most.[10]

This passage is remarkable in the fact that it illustrates a point often made by the adversaries of the interest doctrine: that it is tautological (see chapter 1).

<hr/>

[8] "Juxta illud videlicet: *Trahe nos post te; curremus in odorem unguentorum tuorum.* Praeclare idem Doctor sanctus: *Parum est, inquit, voluntate trahi, etiam voluptate traheris. Quid est trahi voluptate? Delectari in Domino.* Et statim: *si Poeta licuit dicere:*

Trahit sua quemque voluptas

non necessitas, sed voluptas, non obligatio, sed delectatio, quanto fortius dicere debemus trahi hominem ad Christum, qui delectatur veritate, beatitudine, justitia? Et postea: Ramum viridem ostendis ovi, et trahis illam; nuces puero, et trahitur. Si ergo trahit sua quemque voluptas, non trahit revelatus Christus a Patre? Et mox: Ecce quomodo trahit pater: docendo delectat, etc." The quote is from Augustine, *Tractatus in Joannem*, 26.30, ibid.

[9] "Vitam beatam in voluptate, hoc est, tranquillitate mentis et indolentia corporis, sitam esse." Ibid., p. 1320.

[10] "Car qu'y a-t-il de plus clair que cette proposition qu'on fait toujours ce qui délecte le plus? Puisque ce n'est autre chose que de dire que l'on fait toujours ce qui plaît le mieux, c'est-à-dire que l'on veut toujours ce qui plaît, c'est-à-dire qu'on veut toujours ce que l'on veut, et que dans l'état où est aujourd'hui notre âme réduite, il est inconcevable qu'elle veuille autre chose que ce qu'il lui plaît de vouloir, c'est-à-dire ce qui la délecte le plus." Blaise Pascal, *Écrits sur la grâce*, in *Œuvres complètes*, edited by Jean Mesnard, Paris: Desclée de Brouwer, 1991, vol. 3, p. 704.

Pascal's claim is that "we always will what we will." The rule has no exceptions. Even when we choose something other than what pleases us most, our will is still following its own pleasure:

Do not think you can complicate the issue by saying that the will, in order to assert its power, sometimes chooses what it likes least, because it then likes asserting its power better than willing the good it gives up. So much so that when the will strives to avoid what it likes, it still seeks what it likes, because it can only will what it likes to will.[11]

In spite of its tautological appearance, the proposition that "we always will what we will" has a specific theological content, related to the dogma of the original sin. Before the Fall, the will was subordinated to reason, and reason itself was subordinated to the will of God. In that sense, every choice was by definition a rational choice, and the will was entirely in command of the body and of itself. The punishment subsequent to the Fall was that the will would no longer be in command of itself. It would, on the contrary, be subservient to pleasure. Augustine meditates about this point in the *Confessions*. I am not free to will what I will, he says, because I can only will what I like. My will stands in opposition to itself:

The mind commands the mind to will, and yet though it be itself it does not obey itself. Whence this strange anomaly and why should it be? I repeat: The will commands itself to will, and could not give the command unless it wills; yet what is commanded is not done. But actually the will does not will entirely; therefore it does not command entirely. For as far as it wills, it commands. And as far as it does not will, the thing commanded is not done. For the will commands that there be an act of will – not another, but itself. But it does not command entirely. Therefore, what is commanded does not happen; for if the will were whole and entire, it would not even command it to be, because it would already be.[12]

The proposition "we always will what we will" is therefore not a tautology because the will is divided against itself. We will (in the sense of issuing a command) only what we will (in the sense of wanting what pleases us). In Augustine's theology, salvation operates exactly where the original sin has occurred. Since the human will is now a slave to pleasure, God's grace manifests itself as something that the will wants absolutely because it brings an overwhelming joy. Without God's grace, the will commands itself to love

---

[11] "Et qu'on ne prétende pas subtiliser en disant que la volonté pour marquer sa puissance, choisira quelquefois ce qui lui plaît le moins; car alors il lui plaira davantage de marquer sa puissance que de vouloir le bien qu'elle quitte, de sorte que, quand elle s'efforce de fuir ce qu'il lui plaît, ce n'est que pour suivre ce qu'il lui plaît, étant impossible qu'elle veuille autre chose que ce qu'il lui plaît de vouloir." *Écrits sur la grâce*, p. 704.

[12] Augustine, *Confessions*, translated by Albert C. Outler, Philadelphia: Westminster Press, 1955, 8.9.21.

God and is unable to do so. With God's grace, the two wills become whole again, and we "will what we will" in the sense that the will is now identical with itself. For Pascal, quoting Augustine, the first and last word regarding the workings of the will in the fallen state is: "We can only do what pleases us most."[13]

A similar description of the human will can be found in an author who is generally seen as one of Mandeville's main sources of inspiration: Pierre Bayle. In true Augustinian fashion, Bayle asserts that an analysis of the human will must distinguish between the fallen state and the state of grace. In the fallen state, self-love is the sole engine of human conduct:

Only two things drive the human will: self-love, and the grace of the Holy Spirit. All those whom God does not lead by an effective grace conduct themselves according to the interests of self-love. They are slaves to the original sin and its consequences.[14]

Bayle's allegiance to the doctrine of the original sin does not prevent him from being a strong advocate of Epicureanism. The article on Epicurus in the *Dictionnaire historique et critique* affirms the Epicurean thesis that the chief good consists in pleasure:

As to the doctrine regarding the chief good, or happiness, it was likely to be misinterpreted, and it had adverse consequences that gave the [Epicurean] sect a bad reputation. But it was in fact very reasonable, and no one could deny that if we understand the word happiness as he did, the felicity of man consists in pleasure.[15]

For Bayle, the principle of pleasure explains the variations that may be observed in the behavior of atheists. At first sight, someone who does not believe in the rewards and punishments of eternal life would be inclined to indulge in every kind of physical pleasure. Yet we observe that some atheists are more restrained on that count than many Christians. Whether someone indulges in drunkenness is not a matter of opinion regarding the existence of a punishment for it in the afterlife. It is simply a difference in humor and temper. Some people love to drink, others don't:

---

[13] "Quod amplius delectat, secundum id operemur necesse est." Augustine, *Expositio in Epistolam ad Galatas*, § 49, quoted by Pascal in *Ecrits sur la grâce*, p. 704.

[14] "Il n'y a que deux mobiles de la volonté de l'homme, l'amour-propre et la grâce du Saint Esprit. Tous ceux que Dieu ne dirige point par une grâce efficace se conduisent par les intérêts de l'amour-propre: ils sont esclaves du péché originel et de ses suites." Pierre Bayle, *Continuation des pensées diverses*, in *Œuvres diverses*, vol. 3, The Hague: P. Husson, F. Boucquet et al., 1727 [Rotterdam: Reinier Leers, 1704], § 153, p. 411.

[15] "Quant à la doctrine touchant le souverain bien ou le bonheur, elle était fort propre à être mal interprétée, et il en résulta de mauvais effets qui décrièrent la secte. Mais au fond elle était très raisonnable, et l'on ne saurait nier qu'en prenant le mot de bonheur comme il le prenait, la félicité de l'homme ne consiste dans le plaisir." Pierre Bayle, "Épicure," in *Dictionnaire historique et critique*, Amsterdam: P. Brunel, 1740 [Rotterdam: Reinier Leers, 1697].

If you examine things in general, you suppose that, as soon as an atheist realizes that he can get drunk with impunity, he will get drunk every day. But those who know the maxim, *Trahit sua quemque voluptas*, and who have examined the heart of man more carefully, do not go so fast. Before judging the conduct of this atheist, they inquire about his taste. If they find that he likes to drink, that he is very sensitive to this pleasure, that he prefers it to his reputation as a good person, they conclude that he actually will drink as much as possible. But they do not conclude that he will drink more than countless Christians, who are drunk most of the time. If they find that he is somewhat indifferent to wine, they do him the justice of believing that he will drink only when thirsty.[16]

Bayle believes that, in general, differences in behavior cannot be explained by differences in belief. The adherence to such and such system of belief is irrelevant when it comes to explaining concrete human behavior. Preferences are not a matter of opinion. They are a matter of habit and custom, grounded in the body, not the mind:

The spirit of debauchery is not a function of the opinions one has, or does not have, concerning the nature of God. It is a function of a certain corruption coming from the body, which grows every day because of the pleasure one finds in indulging oneself.[17]

A similar allegiance to the Epicurean doctrine of pleasure can be found in *The Fable of the Bees*. In Remark (O), commenting the line "Real pleasures, comforts, ease," Mandeville mentions the name of Epicurus:

That the highest good consisted in pleasure was the doctrine of Epicurus, who yet led a life exemplary of continence, sobriety, and other virtues, which made people of the succeeding ages quarrel about the significance of pleasure.[18]

The quarrel is between philosophers like Erasmus, who argued that "the delight Epicurus meant was being virtuous," so much so that "there are no greater *Epicures* than pious Christians," and those who hold the more conventional view that "by pleasures he would have understood nothing

[16] "Mais ceux qui savent la maxime, *Trahit sua quemque voluptas*, et qui ont examiné plus exactement le cœur de l'homme, ne vont pas si vite. Ils s'informent, avant de juger de la conduite de cet athée, quel est son goût. S'ils trouvent qu'il aime à boire, qu'il est fort sensible à ce plaisir là, qu'il en est plus friand que de la réputation d'honnête homme, ils jugent qu'effectivement il boit autant qu'il peut. Mais ils ne jugent pas pour cela qu'il en fait plus qu'une infinité de chrétiens, qui sont saouls presque toute leur vie. S'ils trouvent qu'il a de l'indifférence pour le vin, ils lui font la justice de croire qu'il ne boit qu'à sa soif." Pierre Bayle, *Pensées diverses écrites à un docteur de Sorbonne à l'occasion de la comète qui parut au mois de décembre 1680*, in *Œuvres diverses*, vol. 3, The Hague: P. Husson, F. Boucquet et al., 1727 [Rotterdam: Reinier Leers, 1682], § 144.
[17] "L'esprit de débauche ne dépend pas des opinions que l'on a, ou que l'on n'a pas, touchant la nature de Dieu, mais d'une certaine corruption qui nous vient du corps, et qui se fortifie tous les jours par le plaisir qu'on trouve dans l'usage des voluptés." Ibid.
[18] Mandeville, *The Fable of the Bees*, vol. 1, p. 147.

but sensual ones, and the gratification of our passions."[19] Mandeville refuses to take sides in the dispute, but he, like Bayle, affirms the Epicurean belief that all human conduct, whether moral or immoral, is driven by the quest for pleasure:

I shall not decide their quarrel, but am of opinion, that whether men be good or bad, what they take delight in is their pleasure, and not to look out for any further etymology from the learned languages, I believe an Englishman may justly call every thing a pleasure that pleases him, and according to this definition we ought to dispute no more about men's pleasures than their tastes: *Trahit sua quemque voluptas.*[20]

The Latin sentence, *trahit sua quemque voluptas* ("Each is led on by his own pleasure") is a quote from Vergil's second *Eclogue*. We have already seen it in the passage from Augustine describing the pleasure involved in loving God. As we have seen above, this passage from Augustine is quoted by both Epicureans like Gassendi and Augustinians like Pascal. It is worth noting that the original context of *trahit sua quemque voluptas* (Vergil's second *Eclogue*) is Epicurean. Vergil's line takes on a Christian meaning when quoted by Augustine. It carries an Epicurean *and* Augustinian meaning when quoted, as we have just seen, by Gassendi, Pascal, Bayle, and Mandeville.

It is perhaps on the issue of suicide that the Epicurean/Augustinian theory of pleasure manifests itself in the most paradoxical way. In the second volume of *The Fable of the Bees*, Cleomenes argues that "no man can resolve upon suicide while self-liking lasts." However, "as soon as that is over, all hopes are extinct, and we can form no wishes but for the dissolution of our frame, till at last our being becomes so intolerable to us that self-love prompts us to make an end of it, and seek refuge in death."[21] The interlocutor, Horatius, objects that if self-love prompts us to commit suicide, it should not be called self-love, but rather self-hatred. Cleomenes acknowledges that it is a fair point, but it only proves that "man is made up of contrarieties."[22] It still remains that,

whoever kills himself by choice, must do it to avoid something which he dreads more than that death which he chooses. Therefore, how absurd soever a person's reasoning may be, there is in all suicide a palpable intention of kindness to one's self.[23]

The proposition that "man is made up of contrarieties" is reminiscent of an Augustinian author like Pascal (*Contrariétés* is the title of section VII

[19] Ibid.   [20] Ibid.   [21] *The Fable of the Bees*, vol. 2, p. 136.   [22] Ibid.   [23] Ibid.

of the *Pensées*). It refers ultimately to the Augustinian theory of the will
standing in opposition to itself. Mandeville makes an explicit reference to
it in the first volume of *The Fable of the Bees*: "It is impossible that man,
mere fallen man, should act with any other view but to please himself."[24]
In that sense, according to Mandeville, "there is no difference between will
and pleasure."[25] The notion that all suicide proceeds from an "intention
of kindness to one's self" is also Augustinian. In section X of the *Pensées*
entitled "The sovereign good," Pascal develops the proposition that, behind
the wide range of human choices and preferences, lies a single motivating
factor:

All men seek happiness. There are no exceptions. However different the means
they may employ, they all strive toward this goal. The reason why some go to war
and some do not is the same desire in both, but interpreted in two different ways.
The will never takes the least step except to that end. This is the motive of every
act of every man, including those who go and hang themselves.[26]

Elsewhere, Pascal claims that pleasure "is the coin for which we will give
others all they want."[27] These arguments come from Book XIV of *The
City of God*, where Augustine claims that "man has undoubtedly the will
to be happy, even when he pursues happiness by living in a way which
makes it impossible of attainment."[28] In that sense, "we commit sin to
promote our welfare, and the result is rather to increase our misfortune."[29]
Using an anachronistic language, we could say that Augustine describes
human behavior as self-seeking in its intent, and utility-minimizing in its
outcome. It appears from this that the two notions invoked by Cleomenes in
the passage quoted above are closely related in an Augustinian perspective:
everything we do proceeds from our desire to be happy (kindness to one's
self); yet, because we are sinners, we always set our desire on things that
make us unhappy (we are made up of contrarieties).

[24] Ibid., vol. 1, p. 348.   [25] Ibid.

[26] Blaise Pascal, *Pensées*, translated by A.J. Krailsheimer, London: Penguin Books, 1966, fragment 148.
"Tous les hommes recherchent d'être heureux. Cela est sans exception, quelques différents moyens
qu'ils y emploient. Ils tendent tous à ce but. Ce qui fait que les uns vont à la guerre et que les autres
n'y vont pas est ce même désir qui est dans tous les deux accompagné de différentes vues. La volonté
fait jamais la moindre démarche que vers cet objet. C'est le motif de toutes les actions de tous les
hommes, jusqu'à ceux qui vont se pendre." Blaise Pascal, *Pensées*, edited by Louis Lafuma, Paris:
Seuil, 1963, fragment 148 (*Pensées*, edited by Philippe Sellier, Paris: Bordas, 1991, fragment 181). On
Pascal's Augustinianism, see Philippe Sellier, *Pascal et saint Augustin*, second edition, Paris: Albin
Michel, 1995.

[27] "La monnaie pour laquelle nous donnons tout ce qu'on veut" (my translation). Pascal, *Pensées*,
fragment 710 (Sellier 588).

[28] Augustine, *The City of God*, translated by John O'Meara, London: Penguin Books, 1984, XIV, 4.

[29] Ibid.

Of course, there are fundamental differences between the Epicurean and Augustinian doctrines. Augustinians believe that lasting pleasure can only be found in loving God, while Epicureans (at least the ones who do not subscribe to Gassendi's Christian interpretation of Epicurus) recommend limiting oneself to the satisfaction of natural and necessary needs. However, as Lafond points out, the psychological analysis of pleasure is so similar on both sides that it is often difficult to decide whether an argument is Epicurean or Augustinian.[30] "Each is led on by his own pleasure" is the common motto of Epicureans and Augustinians, from Gassendi and Pascal to Bayle and Mandeville.

THE CRITIQUE OF VIRTUES

In Book XIX of *The City of God*, Augustine attacks the Stoics in a vehement diatribe. He takes issue with the idea that the various ills that affect our lives are not ills at all:

Yet so great is the stupefying arrogance of those people who imagine that they find the Ultimate Good in this life, and that they can attain happiness by their own efforts, that their "wise man" (that is, the wise man as described by them in their amazing idiocy), even if he goes blind, deaf, and dumb, even if enfeebled in limb and tormented with pain, and the victim of every other kind of ill that could be mentioned or imagined, and thus is driven to do himself to death – that such a man would not blush to call that life of his, in the setting of all those ills, a life of happiness![31]

For Augustine, this Stoic idea is a lie (pain and suffering are evil, no matter how one looks at them); it is also a manifestation of the "stiff-necked pride"[32] that characterizes Stoic philosophers. More generally, the virtues that philosophy has analyzed and advocated (temperance, prudence, justice, and fortitude) have consistently failed to make us happy. In that sense, the virtues advocated by philosophers are nothing but a proof of the wretchedness of our condition.

Written after the sack of Rome by a Barbarian army, *The City of God* is, in many ways, an inquiry into the nature and causes of the power of Rome. In other words, Augustine seeks to understand the reasons why Rome became so powerful, and subsequently went into decline. Augustine's analysis is relevant to early modern moral philosophers because, having started from

---

[30] Jean Lafond, "Augustinisme et épicurisme au XVIIe siècle," in *L'Homme et son image. Morales et littérature de Montaigne à Mandeville*, Paris: Champion, 1996, pp. 345–368.

[31] Augustine, *The City of God*, XIX, 4.   [32] Ibid.

a concrete situation, it gradually ascends to a consideration of the first principles of human behavior. At the center of Augustine's analysis is a critique of Roman virtues.

For Augustine, Rome became a great power because its citizens did not care about self-interest narrowly understood (monetary gain). Instead, they had a consuming passion for fame and glory. This passionate love of glory was the cause of great acts of courage and devotion to the cause of Rome. Divine providence rewarded the Romans by giving them a great empire and a universal fame. The current setbacks of the Empire should give one no reason to complain about the justice of God. The Romans "have received their reward in full."[33] From a Christian perspective, Roman virtues are admirable in a sense, but they are worthless in the final analysis because they have the sin of pride as their single source. Glory, Augustine says, "is puffed up with empty conceit." Consequently, "it is most improper that the Virtues, with their solidity and strength, should be her servants."[34] This applies even to those who "pay no heed to the opinions of others" and "esteem themselves as wise men and win their own approval," because "the man who wins his own approval, is still a man," and as such, his virtue is still "dependent on the praise of man."[35] Augustine's final word on the Roman Empire is the famous distinction between the earthly city, "created by self-love (*amor sui*)," and the Heavenly City, created "by the love of God."[36] The earthly city "looks for glory from men," while the Heavenly City "finds its highest glory in God."[37]

The critique of virtues is the dominant theme in the works of early modern Augustinian writers.[38] As we have seen above, La Rochefoucauld's *Maxims* begin with the epigraph "Our virtues are usually nothing but vices in disguise." In a sense, all 504 maxims repeat this initial assertion in various ways. Regarding the virtue of justice, La Rochefoucauld asserts that "love of justice, in most men, is only a fear of encountering injustice."[39] Temperance

[33] *The City of God*, v, 15.   [34] *The City of God*, v, 20.   [35] Ibid.
[36] *The City of God*, xiv, 28.   [37] Ibid.
[38] For a full account of the Augustinian tradition in seventeenth- and early eighteenth-century France and England, see Jean Lafond, *La Rochefoucauld. Augustinisme et littérature*, third edition, Paris: Klincksieck, 1986; Lafond, *L'Homme et son image*; Sellier, *Pascal et saint Augustin*; Philippe Sellier, *Port-Royal et la littérature*, vols. 1 and 2, Paris: Champion, 1999–2000; Antony McKenna, *De Pascal à Voltaire. Le rôle des Pensées de Pascal dans l'histoire des idées de 1670 à 1734*, Oxford: The Voltaire Foundation, 1990 (2 vols.); Antony McKenna and Jean Jehasse (eds.), *Religion et politique. Les avatars de l'augustinisme*, Saint-Etienne: Publications de l'Université de Saint-Etienne, 1998; Pierre Force and David Morgan (eds.), *De la morale à l'économie politique. Dialogue franco-américain sur les moralistes français*, introduction by Pierre Force, Pau: Publications de l'Université de Pau, 1996.
[39] François de la Rochefoucauld, *The Maxims*, translated by Louis Kronenberger, New York: Stackpole, 1936, maxim 78. "L'amour de la justice n'est en la plupart des hommes que la crainte de souffrir

"in men at the height of their careers is a desire to seem greater than their luck."[40] Prudence gets universal praise, yet the greatest prudence "cannot guarantee our smallest undertaking."[41] Finally, as to fortitude, "we all have strength enough to endure the misfortunes of others."[42]

La Rochefoucauld had a close relationship with Jacques Esprit, author of a book entitled *La Fausseté des vertus humaines* (*The Falsity of Human Virtues*),[43] which appeared at the same time as the fifth and last edition of the *Maxims*. By the end of the seventeenth century, the critique of virtues had become so commonplace that, in 1684, Jacques Abbadie could assert that "the falsity of human virtues is no longer in dispute."[44] For Abbadie, as for others in the Augustinian tradition, disinterestedness is "a subtle form of self-interest," generosity "a scheme in the service of pride," modesty "an artful dissimulation of our vanity," etc. Fundamentally, virtues are nothing but "safeguards" implanted by self-love in order to make sure that "the vices inside do not appear outside."[45]

The critique of virtues is also an important aspect of Epicurean moral philosophy. Augustinians and Epicureans have a common enemy, the Stoics, who claim that the chief good, achievable by all humans, resides in the practice of virtue. Gassendi follows Augustine in criticizing the Stoics for extolling the life of Regulus, who was tortured to death by the Carthaginians, as an example of perfect virtue and perfect happiness.[46] Regulus was not truly virtuous because he broke a promise made to the Carthaginians by advocating the pursuit of war before the Roman senate. In addition, it

---

l'injustice." *Maximes*, edited by Jean Lafond, Paris: Gallimard, 1976 [Paris: Barbin, 1678], maxim 78. On La Rochefoucauld's Augustinianism, see Lafond, *La Rochefoucauld*; also Philippe Sellier, "La Rochefoucauld, Pascal, saint Augustin," *Revue d'histoire littéraire de la France* (May–August 1969), pp. 551–575.

40 "La modération des hommes dans leur plus haute élévation est un désir de paraître plus grands que leur fortune." La Rochefoucauld, *The Maxims*, maxim 18.

41 "Il n'y a point d'éloges qu'on ne donne à la prudence. Cependant elle ne saurait nous assurer du moindre événement." La Rochefoucauld, maxim 65.

42 "Nous avons tous assez de force pour supporter les maux d'autrui." La Rochefoucauld, maxim 19.

43 Jacques Esprit, *La Fausseté des vertus humaines*, Paris: Desprez, 1677–1678 (2 vols.).

44 Jacques Abbadie, *Traité de la vérité de la religion chrétienne*, Rotterdam: Reinier Leers, 1684, p. 293.

45 "La fausseté des vertus humaines n'est plus une chose contestée. On sait que le désintéressement n'est qu'un intérêt délicat; la libéralité qu'un trafic de notre orgueil, qui préfère la gloire de donner à tout ce qu'il donne; la modestie, qu'un art de cacher sa vanité, la civilité, qu'une préférence affectée que nous faisons des autres à nous-mêmes, pour cacher la préférence véritable que nous faisons de nous-mêmes à tout le monde; la pudeur, qu'une affectation de ne point parler des mêmes choses auxquelles la luxure nous fait penser avec plaisir; le désir d'obliger les autres, qu'un secret désir de s'obliger soi-même en se les acquérant; comme l'impatience de s'acquitter n'est qu'une honte d'être trop longtemps redevable; et toutes ces vertus en général sont autant de gardes dont l'amour propre se sert pour empêcher que les vices qui sont au dedans ne paraissent au dehors." *Traité de la vérité de la religion chrétienne*, p. 294.

46 Bernier, *Abrégé de la Philosophie de Gassendi*, vol. 7, pp. 123–130.

is impossible to accept that someone who died in the most excruciating pain could be called happy. There are some differences between Augustine's critique and Gassendi's. They agree on the absurdity of claiming that happiness is possible in the face of physical pain. However, Augustine's most fundamental critique (absent in Gassendi) is that the virtue of Regulus had glory as its ultimate end.[47] It remains that, for Augustine as well as for Gassendi, Regulus, the Stoic hero, is an example of "false virtue" and "false happiness."[48]

It should not be surprising that in Bayle, an author who partakes of both the Epicurean and Augustinian traditions, the critique of virtues would play such an important role. For Bayle, chastity in women is a prime example of the falsity of human virtues:

> Do not think that, according to me, all women draw their virtue from their fear of ill repute. God forbid that I should make judgments so injurious to the grace of the Holy Spirit. I have already declared, and I declare once again, that I except from the general rule a good number of persons, who behave according to the true spirit of the Christian religion ... But after this declaration, I don't see anything surprising in the fact that I suspect most human virtues to be false, and especially the chastity of women. If those who comply with their duty in that regard examine themselves rigorously, they will find, I am sure, that fear of gossip contributed to it more than anything else.[49]

Bayle begins his analysis with a disclaimer that keeps him within Augustinian orthodoxy: the critique of virtues applies only to those who lack the assistance of the Holy Spirit. He goes on to criticize the virtue of chastity by showing that it has everything to do with a woman's concern for her own reputation. The words "I suspect most human virtues to be false" echo the title of Jacques Esprit's book, *The Falsity of Human Virtues*. Our virtues are an illusion because "we convince ourselves that God forgives everything while men forgive nothing; so that we should do everything for appearances' sake."[50]

---

[47] Augustine, *The City of God*, v, 18–20.

[48] Bernier, *Abrégé de la Philosophie de Gassendi*, vol. 7, p. 123.

[49] "N'allez pas vous imaginer, cependant, que selon moi, il n'y a point de femme qui n'emprunte sa vertu de la crainte de l'infamie. A Dieu ne plaise que je fasse des jugements si injurieux à la grâce du St. Esprit. J'ai déjà déclaré, et je déclare encore une fois, que j'excepte de la règle générale un bon nombre de personnes, qui se conduisent par le véritable esprit de la religion chrétienne ... Mais après cette déclaration, je ne vois pas qu'on doive trouver étrange que je soupçonne de fausseté la plupart des vertus humaines, et la chasteté des femmes nommément. Si celles qui ont fait leur devoir de ce côté-là s'examinent à la rigueur, elles trouveront, je m'assure, que la peur du qu'en dira-t-on y a plus contribué que tout autre chose." Bayle, *Pensées diverses*, § 164. On Bayle's position within the Augustinian tradition, see Antony McKenna, "Bayle, moraliste augustinien," in Force and Morgan (eds.), *De la morale à l'économie politique*, pp. 175–186.

[50] "On se persuade que Dieu pardonne tout, mais que les hommes ne pardonnent rien; et qu'ainsi tout consiste à bien sauver les apparences." Bayle, *Pensées diverses*, § 164.

Mandeville's critique of virtues is very close to Bayle's. In the second volume of *The Fable of the Bees*, Cleomenes and Horatius discuss the life of a "perfect gentleman," who seems to possess all imaginable virtues. Cleomenes starts by saying that it would be "ill-natured or uncharitable" to assume that the virtues of the perfect gentleman are not authentic. This disclaimer satisfies Augustinian orthodoxy, according to which only God can ultimately decide whether someone's inner motives are good or evil. Cleomenes limits his claim to saying that the selfish hypothesis can account for the apparently most perfect virtue:

> For I have not said, that if I found a gentleman in possession of all the things I mentioned, I would give his rare endowments this turn, and think all his perfections derived from no better stock than an extraordinary love of glory. What I argue for, and insist upon, is, the possibility that all these things might be performed by a man from no other views, and with no other helps, than those I have named.[51]

Like Bayle, Mandeville also discusses the virtues of women. Commenting on the rape and suicide of Lucretia, he argues that the famous Roman heroine had a passion for her good reputation, not for virtue itself:

> Lucretia held out bravely against the attacks of the ravisher, even when he threatened her life; which shows that she valued her virtue beyond it: but when he threatened her reputation with eternal infamy, she fairly surrendered, and then slew herself; a certain sign that she valued her virtue less than her glory, and her life less than either.[52]

As F.B. Kaye indicates in a footnote of this edition, Mandeville is following Bayle in his interpretation of the story. Indeed, Bayle concludes from Lucretia's behavior that "all she loved in virtue was the glory that came with it."[53] But the story of Lucretia is an arch-classical example in the Augustinian critique of virtues, starting with *The City of God*, where Augustine says that Lucretia decided to commit suicide after being raped by Tarquin's son because "as a Roman woman, excessively eager for honor, she was afraid that she should be thought, if she lived, to have willingly endured what, when she lived, she had violently suffered."[54]

Taking the Augustinian critique of virtues to its paradoxical extreme, Mandeville argues that a woman's concern for her own reputation can

---

[51] Mandeville, *The Fable of the Bees*, vol. 2, p. 77.   [52] Ibid., vol. 1, p. 210.

[53] "Elle n'aimait dans la vertu que la seule gloire qui l'accompagnait." Bayle, *Pensées diverses*, § 180.

[54] Augustine, *The City of God*, I, 19. On the connections between Mandeville, Bayle, La Rochefoucauld, and the Augustinian critique of virtues, see Wilhelm Hasbach, "La Rochefoucault und Mandeville," in *Jahrbuch für Gesetzgebung und Volkswirtschaft im Deutschen Reich*, Leipzig, 1890, pp. 1–43, and Jean Lafond, "Mandeville et La Rochefoucauld, ou des avatars de l'augustinisme," in *L'Homme et son image. Morales et littérature de Montaigne à Mandeville*, Paris: Champion, 1996, pp. 441–458.

have criminal consequences. A chambermaid who becomes pregnant will sometimes decide to kill her child rather than face the opprobrium of the family who has a great opinion of her virtue. Anyone who thinks this kind of behavior is monstrous or aberrant, Mandeville argues, does not understand the "nature and force of passions."[55] Maternal love is natural and universal, but "as this is a passion, and all passions center in self-love, so it may be subdued by any superior passion."[56] In this case, the needs of self-love are better satisfied by one passion (fear of shame) than they are by another passion (fondness for one's children). Modesty is based on fear of shame, which is itself based on self-love. Modesty is therefore a false virtue.

In Remark (O) of *The Fable of the Bees*, Mandeville, after so many others, draws a parallel between Epicureans and Stoics. We have already seen the passage where he praises the Epicurean theory of pleasure. This is how Mandeville describes the Stoic doctrine:

But on the other side, most of the ancient philosophers and grave moralists, especially the *Stoics*, would not allow anything to be a real good that was liable to be taken from them by others. They wisely considered the instability of fortune, and the favor of princes; the vanity of honor, and popular applause; the precariousness of riches, and all earthly possessions; and therefore placed true happiness in the calm serenity of a contented mind free from guilt and ambition; a mind, that, having subdued every sensual appetite, despises the smiles as well as frowns of fortune, and taking no delight but in contemplation, desires nothing but what everybody is able to give to himself.[57]

Mandeville acknowledges that among the Ancients, the Stoics "have always bore the greatest sway."[58] Yet "others that were no fools neither, have exploded those precepts as impracticable, called their notions romantic, and endeavored to prove that what these Stoics asserted of themselves exceeded all human force and possibility."[59] Consequently, "the virtues they boasted of could be nothing but haughty pretence, full of arrogance and hypocrisy."[60] This last sentence summarizes the meaning of the critique of virtues, for Epicureans as well as Augustinians. The critique of virtues is first and foremost a critique of the Stoic conception of virtue. The Stoic virtues are based on a passion for glory. They are virtues in name only, and they must be called fraudulent.

The alliance between Epicureans and Augustinians is more than a marriage of convenience for the sake of anti-Stoic polemic. As Olivier-René Bloch suggests, Gassendi believes that the truth of Epicureanism resides in the fallen nature of human beings. In this world, *voluptas* is the only

---

[55] Mandeville, *The Fable of the Bees*, vol. 1, p. 75.   [56] Ibid.   [57] Ibid., p. 150.
[58] Ibid.   [59] Ibid., p. 151.   [60] Ibid.

engine of human behavior because human nature makes it impossible to have access to higher truths.[61] In this respect, among philosophers, only Epicureans have spoken the truth about the nature of human beings in their fallen state. Gassendi himself is not an Augustinian, but it is not surprising to see this convergence between Epicurean themes and the Augustinian doctrine of the original sin in an author like Bayle. As to Mandeville, he mentions the original sin rarely,[62] but any Augustinian could subscribe to his description of "the natural instinct of sovereignty, which teaches man to look upon everything as centering in himself."[63] It may be that Mandeville, in spite of his declarations of allegiance to Augustinian orthodoxy, is, unlike Gassendi, a "pagan" Epicurean who does not believe in the Fall of man. It remains that his description of human nature is entirely compatible with the doctrine of the original sin. *Mandeville's anthropology is consistent with both the Epicurean and Augustinian accounts of human nature.*

THE NEO-STOIC REAPPRAISAL OF VIRTUE

In chapter 1, we presented the doctrines of Rousseau and Smith as a reconstruction of Mandeville's anthropology based on pity, not self-love. *This reconstruction presents itself as a neo-Stoic critique of the Epicurean/Augustinian critique of virtues.* Like most thinkers of the Enlightenment, Rousseau and Smith want to believe that the practice of virtue is within the reach of human power. In that respect, they find the doctrine of the original sin especially repugnant, because it assumes that only divine intervention (in the form of grace) can make virtue authentic. This is why Rousseau objects so strongly to Augustine's critique of Roman virtue, as he does in this passage on the virtue of Brutus:

I am annoyed by the jokes St. Augustine dared to make about this great and beautiful act of virtue. The Church Fathers were unable to see all the harm they did to their cause by thus tarnishing all the greatest things that courage and honor had produced. By dint of wanting to elevate the sublimity of Christianity, they taught Christians to be cowardly men...[64]

---

[61] Olivier-René Bloch, *La philosophie de Gassendi*, The Hague: Nijhoff, 1971, p. 470.
[62] See Mandeville, *The Fable of the Bees*, vol. 1, pp. 229 and 348.   [63] Ibid., vol. 2, p. 271.
[64] Jean-Jacques Rousseau, *Political Fragments*, in *The Collected Writings of Rousseau*, translated by Judith R. Bush, Roger D. Masters, and Christopher Kelly, Hanover, NH: University Press of New England, 1994, vol. 4, p. 38. "Je suis fâché pour St Augustin des plaisanteries qu'il a osé faire sur ce grand et bel acte de vertu. Les Pères de l'Eglise n'ont pas su voir le mal qu'ils faisaient à leur cause en flétrissant ainsi tout ce que le courage et l'honneur avaient produit de plus grand; à force de vouloir élever la sublimité du christianisme ils ont appris aux chrétiens à devenir des hommes lâches..." Rousseau, *Fragments politiques*, in *Œuvres complètes*, edited by Bernard Gagnebin and Marcel Raymond, vol. 3, Paris: Gallimard, 1964, p. 506.

This is a debate about first principles and fundamental assumptions. Because so much is at stake, the debate, as we shall see, often takes a violently polemical form.

To be sure, Rousseau's narrative in the *Second Discourse* retains some aspects of the story of the Fall of man in the Book of Genesis. The original nature of man was good. The present nature of man is corrupt. However, Rousseau ascribes the corruption of human nature not to the sin of Adam, but to a gradual, historical process. Because Mandeville thinks of self-love in Epicurean/Augustinian terms as "the natural instinct of sovereignty, which teaches man to look upon everything as centering in himself,"[65] it is important for Rousseau to show that the natural instinct of man is not what the Epicureans and Augustinians say it is. Rousseau agrees that the natural instinct of man is self-love, but it is self-love as the Stoics understand it: a moderate and legitimate concern for one's welfare. Self-love, as the Stoics see it, is natural, instinctive, and innocent. This is how Epictetus claims the right to have regard only to himself before a tyrant who wants the philosopher to show regard for him:

"So when you approach me, you have no regard to me?" No, but I have regard to myself; and if you wish me to say that I have regard to you also, I tell you that I have the same regard to you that I have to my pipkin.

This is not a perverse self-regard, for the animal is constituted so as to do all things for itself. For even the sun does all things for itself; nay, even Zeus himself.[66]

In order to avoid confusion with the Epicurean/Augustinian concept of self-love, Rousseau decides to give a new name to the natural and instinctive regard one has for one's own welfare. This name is *amour de soi* (love of oneself). This is the origin[67] of the famous distinction between love of oneself and self-love (*amour-propre*):

Amour-propre and love of oneself, two passions very different in their Nature and their effects, must not be confused. Love of oneself is a natural sentiment which inclines every animal to watch over his own preservation, and which, directed in man by reason and modified by pity, produces humanity and virtue.

[65] Mandeville, *The Fable of the Bees*, vol. 2, p. 271.

[66] Epictetus, *Discourses*, translated by George Long, London: George Bell, 1909, I, 19.

[67] Rousseau is remembered as the author of the distinction between *amour-propre* and *amour de soi* because he made it a cornerstone of his system. However, mentions of a legitimate *amour de soi* (distinguished from a sinful *amour-propre*) can be found as early as the 1640s in Jean-Pierre Camus and La Mothe le Vayer. See Hans-Jürgen Fuchs, *Entfremdung und Narzißmus. Semantische Untersuchungen zur Geschichte der "Selbstbezogenheit" als Vorgeschichte von französisch "amour-propre"*, Stuttgart: Metzler, 1977, p. 224. Rousseau had probably read the chapter "De l'amour-propre et de l'amour de nous-mêmes" in Vauvenargues' *Introduction à la connaissance de l'esprit humain*, Paris: Briasson, 1747, pp. 54–59.

Amour-propre is only a relative sentiment, artificial and born in Society, which inclines each individual to have a greater esteem for himself than for anyone else, inspires in men all the harm they do one another, and is the true source of honor.[68]

For Rousseau, love of oneself, far from being an obstacle to virtue, is the foundation, in association with reason and pity, of virtue itself. As to self-love, according to Rousseau, Mandeville gives an accurate description of it but he errs in assuming that it is the bedrock of an unchanging human nature. Self-love reigns supreme today because human nature has changed.

One might argue that the distinction between self-love and love of oneself is something that already exists in Mandeville. In the second volume of *The Fable of the Bees*, Mandeville draws a distinction between "self-love" and "self-liking." It is probable, as F.B. Kaye suggests, that Mandeville decided to draw this distinction in response to Butler, who criticized the assumptions of the first volume by arguing that self-love (in the sense of self-interest) could not possibly be the cause of all human conduct because our various passions cause us often to act against our best interests.[69] Mandeville thus distinguishes between an instinct for self-preservation, which he calls self-love, and an instinct "by which every individual values itself above its real worth."[70] He calls this other instinct "self-liking." For Mandeville, the concept of self-liking includes all the passions generated by our desire to be esteemed and considered by others. As such, it refutes Butler's idea that self-love had to exclude the passions. Rousseau's distinction between self-love (*amour-propre*) and love of oneself (*amour de soi*) is very close to Mandeville's distinction between self-liking and self-love. There is a fundamental difference, however. In Rousseau's system, only love of oneself has the status of a first principle. Self-love is a derivative and historically contingent feeling. For Mandeville, on the contrary, self-liking comes in addition to self-love as an instinct given by nature "to increase the care in creatures to preserve themselves."[71] Self-liking is just as natural and fundamental as self-love. It is a first principle.

---

[68] Jean-Jacques Rousseau, *Discourse on the Origin of Inequality* in *The Collected Writings of Rousseau*, vol. 3, p. 91, note 12. "Il ne faut pas confondre l'amour-propre et l'amour de soi-même; deux passions très différentes par leur nature et par leurs effets. L'amour de soi-même est un sentiment naturel qui porte tout animal à veiller à sa propre conservation et qui, dirigé dans l'homme par la raison et modifié par la pitié, produit l'humanité et la vertu. L'amour-propre n'est qu'un sentiment relatif, factice et né dans la société, qui porte chaque individu à faire plus cas de soi que de tout autre, qui inspire aux hommes tous les maux qu'ils se font mutuellement et qui est la véritable source de l'honneur." *Discours sur l'origine et les fondements de l'inégalité parmi les hommes* in *Œuvres complètes*, vol. 3, p. 219.

[69] Joseph Butler, Sermon I, "Upon the Social Nature of Man," in D.D. Raphael (ed.), *British Moralists 1650–1800*, Oxford: Clarendon Press, 1969, pp. 337–346.

[70] Mandeville, *The Fable of the Bees*, vol. 2, p. 130.   [71] Ibid.

Smith begins with the same assumption as Rousseau regarding the original instinct of human nature. He explicitly refers it to the Stoic tradition:

Every man, as the Stoics used to say, is first and principally recommended to his own care; and every man is certainly, in every respect, fitter and abler to care of himself than any other person.[72]

In his examination of the various systems of moral philosophy, Smith comes back to this original instinct when he explains the Stoic system. He refers to this instinct as self-love:

According to Zeno, the founder of the Stoical doctrine, every animal was by nature recommended to its own care, and was endowed with the principle of self-love, that it might endeavour to preserve, not only its existence, but all the different parts of its nature, in the best and most perfect state of which they were capable.[73]

Smith takes great pains to distinguish, like Mandeville and the Augustinians, between virtue and the appearance of virtue:

Man naturally desires, not only to be loved, but to be lovely; or to be that thing which is the natural and proper object of love. He naturally dreads, not only to be hated, but to be hateful; or to be that thing which is the natural and proper object of hatred. He desires, not only praise, but praiseworthiness; or to be that thing which, though it should be praised by nobody, is, however, the natural and proper object of praise. He dreads, not only blame, but blame-worthiness; or to be that thing which, though it should be blamed by nobody, is, however, the natural and proper object of blame.[74]

Smith is adamant that in spite of the similarities and connections between "the love of praise" and "the love of praiseworthiness"[75] these two notions are "distinct and independent of one another."[76] So much so that "so far is the love of praise-worthiness from being derived altogether from that of praise, that the love of praise seems, at least in a great measure, to be derived from that of praise-worthiness."[77] In other words, the existence of false virtues does not prove that genuine virtue does not exist. On the contrary, false virtues exist because they imitate true virtue. This critique strikes at the heart of the Augustinian argument. Love of praise, which Mandeville and the Augustinians posit as the first principle of human behavior, is but a derivative manifestation of a more fundamental desire, love of praiseworthiness. Smith's insistence on the difference between virtue and the

---

[72] Adam Smith, *The Theory of Moral Sentiments* (sixth edition), *The Glasgow Edition of the Works and Correspondence of Adam Smith*, vol. 1, edited by D.D. Raphael and A.L. Macfie, Oxford: Oxford University Press, 1976 [London and Edinburgh, 1790, first edition, 1759], VI.ii.1.1.
[73] Ibid., VII.ii.1.15.   [74] Ibid., III.2.1.   [75] Ibid.   [76] Ibid.   [77] Ibid., III.2.3.

appearance of virtue indicates that Mandeville and the Augustinians do set the terms of the debate. However, for Smith, the distinction between true and false virtue, far from casting a doubt on the authenticity of human virtues, proves the fact that genuine virtue is within the reach of human efforts.

PROVIDENCE AND THE INVISIBLE HAND

Against Hutcheson, who shares with Mandeville the assumption that a truly virtuous act ought to be disinterested, Smith assumes that genuinely virtuous actions can proceed from self-interest:

Regard to our own private happiness and interest, too, appear upon many occasions very laudable principles of action. The habits of œconomy, industry, discretion, attention, and application of thought, are generally supposed to be cultivated from self-interested motives, and at the same time are apprehended to be very praiseworthy qualities, which deserve the esteem and approbation of every body.[78]

More generally, Smith believes that selfish impulses play a fundamental role in the natural order as well as the social order. In his examination of justice, Smith argues that the "natural principles" that ensure the stability of the social order are "the terrors of merited punishment."[79] In that respect, a selfish impulse, like the fear of being sent to prison or put to death, brings about consequences that could just as well be interpreted as proceeding from a rational design:

When by natural principles we are led to advance those ends, which a refined and enlightened reason would recommend to us, we are very apt to impute to that reason, as to their efficient cause, the sentiments and actions by which we advance those ends, and to imagine that to be the wisdom of man, which in reality is the wisdom of God.[80]

The stability of society is not a consequence of human rational design. It is the consequence of "the wisdom of God." In God's design (or in nature's design – the two are nearly synonymous in Smith's Stoic perspective), the stability of society is ensured by something stronger and more reliable than human reason, namely human selfishness. Smith makes an explicit comparison between the order of society, ensured by fear of punishment, and "the œconomy of nature."[81] Nature, in order to achieve its "favorite ends," has endowed creatures not only with "an appetite for the ends she proposes," but also "with an appetite for the means by which alone this end

[78] Ibid., VII.ii.3.16. [79] Ibid., II.ii.3.5. [80] Ibid. [81] Ibid., II.i.5.10.

can be brought about."[82] An example of the favorite ends of nature is the propagation of the species. Our efforts at self-preservation are not primarily the consequence of a rational design of ours. They stem from instinctual forces like "hunger, thirst, the passion which unites the two sexes, the love of pleasure, and the dread of pain."[83] These forces "prompt us to apply those means for their own sakes, and without any consideration of their tendency to those beneficent ends which the great Director of nature intended to produce by them."[84] In other words, we eat because we are hungry, not because we intend to preserve our life. Yet, our behavior could just as well be described as a rational choice motivated by the intent to preserve our life.

This convergence between nature and reason, between instinctual tendencies and rational designs, is one of the most characteristically Stoic aspects of Smith's thought.[85] For Smith, a full understanding of this convergence is the supreme task of the philosopher, who seeks to discern God's wisdom in all natural and social phenomena:

The idea of that divine Being, whose benevolence and wisdom have, from all eternity, contrived and conducted the immense machine of the universe, so as at all times to produce the greatest possible quantity of happiness, is certainly of all the objects of human contemplation by far the most sublime. Every other thought necessarily appears mean in the comparison.[86]

Understanding "the œconomy of nature" means understanding the relationship between the whole, which God alone can fully see, and the parts, which humans mistake for the whole. This is the traditional sense of the word "economy" in philosophy and rhetoric: the economy of something is the relationship between the whole and its parts.[87] The proper understanding of the relationship between the whole and the parts is not simply a matter of speculation. In Stoic philosophy, speculations about the nature of the universe are closely related to moral concerns. A person who strives to understand God's design will never protest the dictates of Providence:

---

[82] Ibid.   [83] Ibid.   [84] Ibid.

[85] For a fuller account of Adam Smith's neo-Stoicism, see Gloria Vivenza, *Adam Smith and the Classics. The Classical Heritage in Adam Smith's Thought*, Oxford: Oxford University Press, 2001, esp. pp. 191–212; Norbert Waszek, "Two Concepts of Morality: A Distinction of Adam Smith's Ethics and its Stoic Origin," *Journal of the History of Ideas* 45 (1984), pp. 591–606; the introduction by D.D. Raphael and A.L. Macfie to *The Theory of Moral Sentiments*, pp. 5–10; T.D. Campbell, *Adam Smith's Science of Morals*, London: Allen & Unwin, 1971, pp. 217–220.

[86] Smith, *The Theory of Moral Sentiments*, VII.ii.3.5.

[87] See Kathy Eden, *Hermeneutics and the Rhetorical Tradition*, New Haven: Yale University Press, 1997, esp. chapter 2.

A wise man never complains of the destiny of Providence, nor thinks the universe in confusion when he is out of order. He does not look upon himself as a whole, separated and detached from every other part of nature, to be taken care of by itself and for itself. He regards himself in the light in which he imagines the great genius of human nature, and of the world, regards him. He enters, if I may say so, into the sentiments of that divine Being, and considers himself as an atom, a particle, of an immense and infinite system, which must and ought to be disposed of, according to the conveniency of the whole.[88]

Similarly, a truly wise person will overlook considerations of self-interest in order to embrace the interest of larger entities: a group rather than an individual, a country rather than a group, the world rather than one country:

The wise and virtuous man is at all times willing that his own private interest should be sacrificed to the public interest of his own particular order or society. He is at all times willing, too, that the interest of this order or society should be sacrificed to the greater interest of the state or sovereignty, of which it is only a subordinate part. He should, therefore, be equally willing that all those inferior interests should be sacrificed to the greater interest of the universe, to the interest of that great society of all sensible and intelligent beings, of which God himself is the immediate administrator and director.[89]

It would seem at first sight that there is a contradiction between the idea that the pursuit of individual interest will have beneficial consequences for the whole, and the view mentioned here, that the wise person must overlook self-interest in favor of the interest of the whole. In Smith's Stoic perspective, however, these two ideas, far from being contradictory, are complementary. Providence achieves its ends by giving incentives, as it were, to the vast majority of people who are driven by selfish motives. These people contribute to the common good unknowingly. On the other hand, a small number of people contribute to the common good by rational design. These happy few are capable of sacrificing their individual interest to larger entities, up to and including "the greater interest of the universe."

When Smith talks about "the œconomy of nature," he is referring to something that is quite remote from the object of today's economic science. On the other hand, Smith's views on "the œconomy of nature" cannot be entirely disconnected from the doctrine that is usually considered to be the foundation of modern economics. The famous "invisible hand," now associated with economic science, appears twice in the context of a providential interpretation of nature and society.

---

[88] Smith, *The Theory of Moral Sentiments*, VII.ii.1.20.   [89] Ibid., VI.ii.3.3.

In an article entitled "The Invisible Hand of Jupiter," Alec Macfie notices that the expression "invisible hand" appears only three times in the entire corpus of Smith's work.[90] The first occurrence is in the *History of Astronomy*, where Smith derides the mythological beliefs of the Ancients, who ascribed a divine origin to irregular events of nature, like thunder and lightning, but did not attribute the familiar properties of water and fire to the "invisible hand of Jupiter."[91] The second occurrence is in *The Theory of Moral Sentiments*, where Smith describes the "œconomy of greatness,"[92] i.e. the system that makes it possible to meet the basic needs of the large quantities of workers who produce luxury goods for the consumption of a small number of wealthy persons. For Smith, the rich "are led by an invisible hand to make nearly the same distribution of the necessities of life, which would have been made, had the earth been divided into equal portions among all its inhabitants."[93] The third occurrence is in *The Wealth of Nations*, where Smith explains that investors decide to put their money in a particular industry in order to maximize the return on their investment. In so doing, they unknowingly contribute to maximizing the "annual revenue of society."[94] Macfie notices that it seems hard to reconcile the meaning of the first occurrence (an expression mocking the mythological beliefs of the ancients) with the other two (the invisible hand made famous by modern economists).[95] Emma Rothschild, remarking that "the intellectual history of invisible hands" is "uniformly grim,"[96] suggests that Smith's intent might be ironic in all three occurrences.

There is no "*invisible* hand of Jupiter" in Latin literature. The "hand of Jupiter," however, is a poetic expression used to designate thunder. The most notable occurrence is in Horace's *Odes*,[97] a canonical text that Smith knew well.[98] If we keep this in mind, Smith's use of the expression in the

---

[90] Alec Macfie, "The Invisible Hand of Jupiter," *Journal of the History of Ideas* 32:4 (1971), pp. 595–599.

[91] Adam Smith, *History of Astronomy, The Glasgow Edition of the Works and Correspondence of Adam Smith*, vol. 3, Oxford: Oxford University Press, 1980, p. 49.

[92] Smith, *The Theory of Moral Sentiments*, IV.1.10.   [93] Ibid.

[94] Adam Smith, *An Inquiry into the Nature and Causes of the Wealth of Nations, The Glasgow Edition of the Works and Correspondence of Adam Smith*, vol. 2, Oxford: Oxford University Press, 1976 [London: Strahan and Cadell, 1776], IV.ii.9.

[95] See Robert Nozick, "Invisible Hand Explanations," *American Economic Review* 84:2 (May 1994), pp. 314–318.

[96] Emma Rothschild, "Adam Smith and the Invisible Hand," *American Economic Review* 84:2 (May 1994), p. 319. A much expanded version of this argument can be found in her *Economic Sentiments, Adam Smith, Condorcet, and the Enlightenment*, Cambridge, MA: Harvard University Press, 2001, pp. 116–156.

[97] "Fulminantis magna manus Jovis" (The mighty hand of thundering Jove), Horace, *Odes*, 3.3.6. Also see Valerius Flaccus, *Argonautica*, IV, 414.

[98] Smith quotes from Horace's *Odes* in Milton's unrhymed translation. See Adam Smith, *Lectures on Rhetoric and Belles Lettres, The Glasgow Edition of the Works and Correspondence of Adam Smith*, vol. 4, Oxford: Oxford University Press, 1983, p. 225.

History of Astronomy makes perfect sense: the Ancients ascribed a divine origin to irregular events like thunder or lightning (they saw the hand of Jupiter in thunder and lightning), but they did not attribute regular events to the "invisible hand of Jupiter." As to the invisible hand itself, it does not occur in pre-Christian Latin literature. However, there is a well-attested invisible hand in Christian literature: the invisible hand of God. The expression always occurs in the context of a discussion of the attributes of God according to Scripture. Augustine, for instance, notices that the Old Testament describes the creation of man and woman with terms reminiscent of human craftsmanship. He adds that these expressions should not be taken literally because God's hand is invisible: "God's 'hand' is his power, which moves visible things by invisible means."[99] It is particularly significant that, in Augustine's work, this analysis comes immediately after a paragraph on God's foreknowledge of man's sin and of the salvation of the elect. According to Augustine, when God created man, he knew that man would commit sin. He also knew that "by his grace a community of godly men was to be called to adoption as his sons, and these men, with their sins forgiven, were to be justified by the Holy Spirit and then enter into fellowship with the holy angels in eternal peace, when the 'last enemy', death, had been destroyed."[100] In that sense, the creation of man by God's invisible hand already includes God's providential design for the world, and the economy of salvation.

It appears therefore that the first occurrence of the "invisible hand" in Smith must be distinguished from the other two. The "invisible hand of Jupiter" is invisible in contradistinction to Jupiter's very visible hand: thunder and lightning. The other two mentions of the invisible hand bring up providential connotations. It is true, as Emma Rothschild points out, that the "invisible hand" sometimes had sinister or threatening connotations, but these instances are the exception, not the rule.[101] Most of the time, in early modern English and French literature, the phrase "invisible hand" is associated with divine providence.

For instance in Daniel Defoe's *Colonel Jack* (1723), the narrator, having reflected on the fact that his life has been miraculously saved several times, considers the hypothesis that "it has all been brought to pass by an invisible hand in mercy to [him]" and concludes that if the hypothesis is true, he is

---

[99] "Manus Dei potentia Dei est, qui etiam visibilia invisibiliter operatur." Augustine, *The City of God*, XII, 24. Also see *De Genesi ad litteram*, VI, 12, 22.
[100] Augustine, *The City of God*, XII, 23.
[101] Rothschild mentions three occurrences of the phrase "invisible hand" (in *Macbeth*, Voltaire's *Oedipe*, and Ovid's *Metamorphoses*) with sinister connotations. The rest of her demonstration is based on an analysis of the connotations of the words "hand" and "invisible" taken separately.

"the most thoughtless, and unthankful of all God's creatures!"[102] In 1735, Nicolas Lenglet Dufresnoy, discussing "the economy of the universe" and the meaning of history, asserted that an "invisible hand" has sole power over "what happens under our eyes."[103] Around the same time, Charles Rollin, a historian whose writings were very well known in English and Scottish universities, developed a providentialist interpretation of ancient history. Referring to the swift military successes of the kings of Israel, he claimed that "the rapidity of their conquests ought to have enabled them to discern the invisible hand which conducted them."[104] The expression "invisible hand" was also used in providentialist interpretations of nature. In 1761, Jean-Baptiste Robinet, a naturalist (and translator of Hume), in a description of the harmony of nature, referred to fresh water as "those basins of mineral water, prepared by an invisible hand."[105] In 1764, another naturalist, Charles Bonnet (whom Smith befriended when he stayed in Geneva in the autumn of 1765), in a discussion of "the economy of the animal," explained that what looks to us as rational behavior in animals is directed by an "invisible hand":

The wisdom that has built and arranged their organs with such art and made them work together for a common purpose is also at work in the various operations that result naturally from the economy of the animal. It is led towards its end by an invisible hand. To our surprise, it carries out tasks precisely and unfailingly. It is as if it acted rationally, as if it turned back on purpose or made a different move as needed. In all this the animal only obeys that secret mechanism that makes it move. It is but a blind instrument that would be incapable of judging its own actions. It has been built by this adorable intelligence that has drawn its own circle for each insect, as it has drawn its orbit for each planet.[106]

---

[102] Daniel Defoe, *Colonel Jack*, London, 1723, p. 215.
[103] "Il n'y a qu'une main invisible qui règle, qui arrange et qui détermine tout ce qui se passe à nos yeux. Il n'y a que cette main par conséquent qui soit grande parce qu'elle seule distribue les véritables grandeurs. Ce sont là les sages et utiles réflexions, où la lecture de l'histoire nous doit porter." Nicolas Lenglet Dufresnoy, *L'Histoire justifiée contre les romans*, Amsterdam, 1735.
[104] "La rapidité de leurs conquêtes aurait dû leur faire entrevoir la main invisible qui les conduisait; mais, dit l'un d'entre eux au nom de tous les autres: 'C'est par la force de mon bras que j'ai fait ces grandes choses, et c'est ma propre sagesse qui m'a éclairé.'" Charles Rollin, *Histoire ancienne des Égyptiens, des Carthaginois, des Assyriens, des Babyloniens, des Grecs*, in *Œuvres complètes*, Paris: Didot, 1821–1831 [Paris: Veuve Etienne, 1731–1738], vol. 1, p. L.
[105] "Ces bassins d'eaux minérales, préparés par une main invisible." Jean-Baptiste Robinet, *De la nature*, Amsterdam: Van Harrevelt, 1761, p. 46. Adam Smith owned a copy of this book in the 1766 edition.
[106] "La même sagesse qui a construit et arrangé avec tant d'art leurs divers organes, qui les a fait concourir à un but déterminé, a fait de même concourir à un but les diverses opérations qui sont les résultats naturels de l'économie de l'animal. Il est dirigé vers sa fin par une main invisible: il exécute avec précision et du premier coup, des ouvrages que nous admirons; il paraît agir comme s'il raisonnait, se retourner à propos, changer de manœuvre au besoin, et dans tout cela il ne fait qu'obéir aux ressorts secrets qui le poussent; il n'est qu'un instrument aveugle qui ne saurait juger de

Bonnet's neo-Stoic providentialism, as evidenced in this description of
"the economy of the animal," is very close to Smith's reflections on "the
œconomy of nature" and the "œconomy of greatness" as described in _The
Theory of Moral Sentiments._[107] Smith and Bonnet share the belief that there
is a convergence between nature and reason, and they both describe instinctual behavior "as if" it were rational. Also noticeable is the connection (found in Lenglet Dufresnoy, Bonnet, and Smith) between the term
"economy" and the phrase "invisible hand". As we have seen above, in the
rhetorical tradition, the economy of something is the relationship between
the whole and the parts. Understanding the economy of nature, the animal,
or the universe, means understanding the connection between individual
events and the harmony of the whole. To those who have gained this understanding, the invisible hand has become visible. In that sense, it can
be argued, against Rothschild's contention that the association between
economic theory and the invisible hand theme is accidental,[108] that the
modern concept of "economy" has its roots in neo-Stoic providentialism.

Two aspects of Smith's description of the "œconomy of greatness" are
particularly symptomatic. First, the idea that the "invisible hand" serves not
only "the interests of society" but also "affords means to the multiplication
of the species."[109] In Smith's Stoic perspective, the same Providence is at
work, and uses comparable means, in society and in nature. In that sense,
all the speculations regarding the ways in which nature brings about its
favorite ends apply directly to the understanding of what we now call "the
economy." Secondly, Smith remarks that, as far as basic needs are concerned
(in Smith's words, "the real happiness of human life") the poor "are in no
respect inferior to those who would seem so much above them."[110] The idea
that all human conditions are essentially equivalent and interchangeable is

sa propre action, mais qui est monté par cette intelligence adorable qui a tracé à chaque insecte son
petit cercle, comme elle a tracé à chaque planète son orbite." Charles Bonnet, _Contemplation de la
nature_, in _Œuvres_, Neuchâtel: S. Fauche, 1781 [Amsterdam, 1764], vol. 4, p. 443. Adam Smith owned
a copy of the original edition of this book. Bonnet called Adam Smith "the sage of Glasgow," and
Smith recommended Bonnet to Hume as "one of the worthiest, and best hearted men in Geneva
or indeed in the world; notwithstanding he is one of the most religious." See Letter 144, From
Patrick Clason to Adam Smith, 25 February, 1775, in _Correspondence of Adam Smith, The Glasgow
Edition of the Works and Correspondence of Adam Smith_, vol. 6, Oxford: Oxford University Press,
1977, p. 180, and Letter 146 to David Hume, 9 May, 1775 ibid., p. 181.
[107] The comparison between Smith and Bonnet is not aimed at suggesting that one influenced the
other (Bonnet's _Contemplation de la nature_ was published five years after _The Theory of Moral
Sentiments_). My purpose is to show that Smith and Bonnet (who knew and admired each other)
used the expression "invisible hand" in very similar contexts (neo-Stoic meditations on the harmony
of the universe). Bonnet's allegiance to a neo-Stoic form of providentialism is stated explicitly at
the beginning of his _Contemplation de la nature_.
[108] Rothschild, _Economic Sentiments_, pp. 116–156.
[109] Smith, _The Theory of Moral Sentiments_, IV.1.10.   [110] Ibid.

also characteristic of a Stoic conception of Providence. In his examination of the sense of duty in Book III of *The Theory of Moral Sentiments*, Smith notices that

The never-failing certainty with which all men, sooner or later, accommodate themselves to whatever becomes their permanent situation, may, perhaps, induce us to think that the Stoics were, at least, thus far very nearly in the right; that, between one permanent situation and another, there was, with regard to real happiness, no essential difference: or that, if there were any difference, it was no more than just sufficient to render some of them the objects of simple choice or preference; but not of any earnest or anxious desire: and others, of simple rejection, as being fit to be set aside or avoided; but not of any earnest or anxious aversion.[111]

Equally Stoic is the context of the occurrence of the invisible hand in *The Wealth of Nations*. The discussion is about "restraints upon the importation from foreign countries of such goods as can be produced at home,"[112] i.e. in our language, protectionism vs. free trade. Smith assumes, as we would expect, that the behavior of the industrialist is always self-interested. This applies to the behavior of the industrialist who prefers "the support of domestic to that of foreign industry." The expression implies two things: first of all, the industrialist supports domestic industry by investing in it. Secondly, he lobbies the government for protectionist measures in favor of the industry he has invested in. In order to obtain such measures, the industrialist will unfailingly invoke reasons of public interest, but of course he is promoting "partial interests," and not "the general good."[113] This is why Smith is skeptical of those industrialists who claim to have the public good in mind:

I have never known much good done by those who affected to trade for the public good. It is an affectation, indeed, not very common among merchants, and very few words need be employed in dissuading them from it.[114]

What we now call "the economy" obeys the same laws as the "œconomy of nature" as we have seen above. It is possible for a virtuous person to bring about the ends of nature through rational design: the path consists in broadening one's horizons from self-interest to the interest of a group, from a group to a country, and from a country to the entire world. The industrialist who solicits the legislature in order to obtain protective tariffs for his industry serves the interests of a group, but he harms the interests

---

[111] Ibid., III.3.30.   [112] Smith, *The Wealth of Nations*, IV.ii.1.
[113] Ibid., IV.ii.45.   [114] Ibid., IV.ii.9.

of the country. Therefore, in the best interest of the country, all pretense of rational design must be abandoned. The industrialist's actions will promote the public good only if they are restricted to self-interest in the narrowest sense:

He intends only his own gain, and he is in this, as in many other cases, led by an invisible hand to promote an end which was no part of his intention. Nor is it always the worse for the society that it was no part of it. By pursuing his own interest he frequently promotes that of the society more effectually than when he really intends to promote it.[115]

One can therefore say of self-interest with respect to the wealth of nations what Smith says of thirst, hunger, and sexual instinct with respect to "the œconomy of nature": they "prompt us to apply those means for their own sakes, and without any consideration of their tendency to those beneficent ends which the great Director of nature intended to produce by them."[116] Smith's opposition to government-granted monopolies and protective tariffs is grounded in Stoic assumptions about the relationship between nature and society. For Smith, there is a fundamental convergence between natural ends and rational designs. However, human reason can be led astray by erroneous conceptions. The safest way consists in letting nature achieve its ends through its own means. In fact, Smith believes that nature's power is often greater than the rational attempts to interfere with its course. Because it is a natural impulse, self-interest is sufficient to offset the misguided interventions of government in the natural harmony of the economy:

The uniform, constant, and uninterrupted effort of every man to better his condition, the principle from which public and national, as well as private opulence is originally derived, is frequently powerful enough to maintain the natural progress of things towards improvement, in spite both of the extravagance of government and of the greatest errors of administration. Like the unknown principle of animal life, it frequently restores health and vigour to the constitution, in spite, not only of the disease, but of the absurd prescriptions of the doctor.[117]

What is most remarkable in this passage is the comparison between the state of what we now call the economy and the health of a person. In both instances, a natural force ensures the harmony of the whole. The "effort of every man to better his condition" (i.e. the pursuit of self-interest) is nature's way of producing the wealth of nations.

[115] Ibid.   [116] Smith, *The Theory of Moral Sentiments*, ii.i.5.10.
[117] Smith, *The Wealth of Nations*, ii.iii.31.

NATURE, PROVIDENCE, AND THE ORIGINAL SIN

If there is a clear opposition between the Epicurean/Augustinian concept of self-love and the Stoic concept, it would seem, at first sight, that the lines are drawn differently when it comes to understanding Providence. Gassendi's interpretation of Epicureanism includes Providence, but classical Epicureanism excludes it. On the other hand, Augustinians and Stoics share the belief that the universe operates according to providential design. We shall see, however, that there are some fundamental differences between the Augustinian and the Stoic concepts of Providence. As with the concept of self-love, these differences revolve around the idea of original sin.

The clearest difference between Augustinians and Stoics appears in the providential account of the origin of society. Among Augustinians, Pierre Nicole is undoubtedly the one who gives the most detailed narrative of the role of self-love in the establishment of society. Nicole, starting of course from the assumption that man after the Fall is entirely driven by self-love, presents the existence of society as a puzzle. Since self-love is by nature a cause of dissension and war, it is hard to see how it could be the cause of social order:

It cannot possibly be imagined, how there can be formed societies, commonwealths, and kingdoms out of this multitude of people full of passions so contrary to union, and who only endeavor the ruin of one another.[118]

However, the suppression of the obstacle will come from the obstacle itself: "Self-love which is the cause of this war, will easily tell the way how to make them live in peace."[119] Self-love originally prompts us to satisfy its needs by making other people subservient to us. However, since everyone has the same impulse, we run into unavoidable difficulties:

Each man sees himself in an impossibility of succeeding by force into the designs which his ambition suggests to him, and apprehends likewise the losing by that violence of others of the essential goods he possesses. It is that which obliges at first to submit oneself to the care of his own preservation, and there is no other way found for that, but to unite oneself with others, to beat back by force those who undertake to deprive us of both our lives and fortunes. And to strengthen this

---

[118] Pierre Nicole, *Moral Essays*, London: Manship, 1696, p. 80. "On ne comprend pas d'abord comment il s'est pu former des sociétés, des républiques et des royaumes de gens pleins de passions si contraires à l'union, et qui ne tendent qu'à se détruire les uns les autres." *Essais de morale*, edited by Laurent Thirouin, Paris: PUF, 1999 [Paris: Desprez, 1675], p. 383.

[119] "Mais l'amour-propre qui est la cause de cette guerre, saura bien le moyen de les faire vivre en paix." Ibid.

union, laws are made, and punishment ordered for those who violate them. Thus by the means of tortures and gibbets set up in public, the thoughts and tyrannical designs of every particular man's self-love are withheld.[120]

Unchecked self-love puts everyone in mortal danger. It is therefore in everyone's interest to set up and enforce laws: "Fear of death is then the first tie of civil society, and the first check of self-love."[121] Nicole agrees entirely with Hobbes on the description of human nature, and the war of all against all. He disagrees only with Hobbes's characterization of the war of all against all in terms of natural law:

And if he who has said, that men are born in a state and condition of war, and that each man is naturally an enemy to all other men, had a mind only to represent by these words the disposition of the hearts of men, one towards another, without pretense of passing it for legitimate and just, he would have said a thing as conforms to truth and experience, as that which is maintained is contrary to reason and justice.[122]

After the establishment of laws, self-love can no longer manifest itself as a tyrannical impulse. Because force is excluded as a means to satisfy the needs of our self-love, we employ indirect means, like flattery and persuasion:

Thus seeing themselves excluded from the open violence, they are constrained to seek other ways, and to substitute craft for force, and they find therein no other means to endeavor to content the self-love of those whom they have need of, instead of tyrannizing over them.

Some endeavor to make it fit for their interests, others employ flattery to gain it. Gifts are bestowed to obtain it. This is the source and the foundation of all commerce practiced amongst men, and which is varied a thousand ways. For they do not truck merchandises for merchandises or for money, but they mutually traffic, I mean they make a trade also of labors and toils, of services done, of

---

[120] "Chacun se voit donc dans l'impuissance de réussir par la force dans les desseins que son ambition lui suggère, et appréhende même justement de perdre par la violence des autres les biens essentiels qu'il possède. C'est ce qui oblige d'abord à se réduire au soin de sa propre conservation, et l'on ne trouve d'autre moyen pour cela que de s'unir avec d'autres hommes pour repousser par la force ceux qui entreprendraient de nous ravir la vie ou les biens. Et pour affermir cette union, on fait des lois, et on ordonne les châtiments contre ceux qui les violent. Ainsi, par le moyen des roues et des gibets qu'on établit en commun, on réprime les pensées et les desseins tyranniques de l'amour-propre de chaque particulier." Ibid.

[121] "La crainte de la mort est donc le premier lien de la société civile, et le premier frein de l'amour-propre." Ibid., p. 81/384.

[122] "Et si celui qui a dit qu'ils naissent dans un état de guerre, et que chaque homme est naturellement ennemi de tous les autres hommes, eût voulu seulement représenter par ces paroles la disposition du cœur des hommes les uns envers les autres, sans prétendre la faire passer pour légitime et juste, il aurait dit une chose aussi conforme à la vérité et à l'expérience, que celle qu'il soutient est contraire à la raison et à la justice." Ibid., p. 80/382. On the connection between Hobbes and Nicole, see E.D. James, *Pierre Nicole, Jansenist and Humanist*, The Hague: Nijhoff, 1972.

diligence and assiduity, of civility; and men exchange all that, either for things of the same nature, or for real goods, as when by vain complacencies we obtain effective commodities.[123]

Nicole's narrative is exemplary in the sense that it gives a full account of the origins of civil society. In true Augustinian fashion, the account is entirely based on the assumption that man's behavior in the fallen state is driven by self-love. Each step in the narrative (fear of death, establishment of laws, establishment of commerce) is explicitly tied to the initial assumption. We must specify that Nicole views self-love as the cause of commerce in the broad sense the word has in the early modern period: an exchange of goods or services that may or may not involve money. Nicole's account ends with a paradox that caught Bayle's attention: a society based on self-love functions just as effectively as a society entirely driven by charity:

It is thus, that by the means and help of this commerce, all necessaries for this life are in some sort supplied without intermixing charity with it. So that in estates where charity has no admittance, because true religion is banished from thence, men do not cease to live with as much peace, safety, and commodiousness, as if they were in a republic of saints.[124]

A contemporary of Nicole, Malebranche, who attempted to reconcile the Augustinian and Cartesian traditions, made a similar point regarding the providential effects of self-love:

The desire all men have for greatness, tends, in and of itself, to destroy all societies. Nevertheless, the order of nature tempers this desire in such a way that it serves the good of the state much better than other inclinations that are languishing and weak . . . Similarly, those who make up armies may work for their particular interests, but they do not fail to bring about the good of the country as a whole.[125]

---

[123] Nicole, *Moral Essays*, p. 81. "Ainsi se voyant exclus de la violence ouverte, ils sont réduits à chercher d'autres voies et à substituer l'artifice à la force, et ils n'en trouvent point d'autres que de tâcher de contenter l'amour-propre de ceux dont ils ont besoin, au lieu de le tyranniser.
    Les uns tâchent de se rendre utiles à ses intérêts, les autres emploient la flatterie pour le gagner. On donne pour obtenir. C'est la source et le fondement de tout le commerce qui se pratique entre les hommes, et qui se diversifie en mille manières. Car on ne fait pas seulement trafic de marchandises qu'on donne pour d'autres marchandises ou pour de l'argent, mais on fait aussi trafic de travaux, de services, d'assiduités, de civilités; et l'on échange tout cela, ou contre des choses de même nature, ou contre des biens plus réels, comme quand par de vaines complaisances on obtient des commodités effectives." *Essais de morale*, p. 384.

[124] "C'est ainsi que par le moyen de ce commerce tous les besoins de la vie sont en quelque sorte remplis, sans que la charité s'en mêle. De sorte que dans les États où elle n'a point d'entrée, parce que la vraie Religion en est bannie, on ne laisse pas de vivre avec autant de paix, de sûreté et de commodité, que si l'on était dans une république de saints." Ibid.

[125] "Le désir, par exemple, que tous les hommes ont pour la grandeur tend par lui-même à la dissolution de toutes les sociétés. Néanmoins ce désir est tempéré de telle manière par l'ordre de la nature, qu'il sert davantage au bien de l'état, que beaucoup d'autres inclinations faibles et languissantes . . . Ainsi ceux qui composent les armées, ne travaillant que pour leurs intérêts particuliers, ne laissent pas

The most forceful expression of the paradoxical effects of self-love is to be found in another Augustinian thinker, Blaise Pascal. In the first sections of the *Pensées*, Pascal seeks to present human nature as a living paradox: we are inexplicably great and wretched at the same time. A prime example of this contradiction is the existence of society itself. The fact that civil society exists testifies to the greatness of human nature, but the social order is based on self-love, an evil impulse. If we look at the foundations of the social order, we must admit that human nature is wretched:

Man's greatness even in his concupiscence. He has managed to produce such a remarkable system from it and make it the image of true charity.[126]

Another way of expressing the paradox consists in saying that self-love makes people foolish and weak. As a consequence, the power of government is based not on the wisdom but on the folly and the weakness of the people:

The power of kings is founded on the reason and the folly of the people, but especially on their folly. The greatest and most important thing in the world is founded on weakness. This is a remarkably sure foundation, for nothing is surer than that the people will be weak. Anything founded on sound reason is very ill-founded, like respect for wisdom.[127]

As often in Pascal, the paradox is not exactly where you would expect to find it. It is remarkable, says Pascal, that power should be grounded in weakness. What is truly paradoxical is that weakness should be the surest possible foundation for power. The paradox reveals a providential design: in the fallen state of humanity, reason is not a reliable foundation for government. Folly and weakness, being much more *predictable* (to borrow a term from social scientists), constitute a solid foundation. That is a manifestation of God's wisdom.

This type of reasoning occurs frequently in *The Fable of the Bees*. Like Nicole and Hobbes, Mandeville assumes that self-love makes man essentially unfit for society, or rather that man seeks the company of others only "for his own sake, in hopes of being the better for it."[128] Government is what makes society possible, and government is itself based on fear of death:

de procurer le bien de tout le pays." Nicolas Malebranche, *De la Recherche de la vérité*, in *Œuvres complètes de Malebranche*, Paris: Vrin, 1962, vol. 2 [Paris: Pralard, 1674], IV, XIII, § 1, p. 118.

[126] "Grandeur de l'homme dans sa concupiscence même, d'en avoir su tirer un règlement admirable et en avoir fait un tableau de charité." Pascal, *Pensées*, fragment 118 (Sellier 150).

[127] "La puissance des rois est fondée sur la raison et sur la folie du peuple, et bien plus sur la folie. La plus grande et importante chose du monde a pour fondement la faiblesse. Et ce fondement est admirablement sûr, car il n'y a rien de plus sûr que cela, que le peuple sera faible. Ce qui est fondé sur la saine raison est bien mal fondé, comme l'estime de la sagesse." Ibid., fragment 26 (Sellier 60).

[128] Mandeville, *The Fable of the Bees*, vol. 2, p. 183.

The undoubted basis of all societies is government. This truth, well examined into, will furnish us with all the reasons of man's excellency, as to sociableness. It is evident from it, that creatures, to be raised into a community, must, in the first place, be governable. This is a qualification that requires fear, and some degree of understanding; for a creature not susceptible of fear is never to be governed.[129]

In their dialogue, Cleomenes and Horatius explore the paradox of the origin of government. Starting from first principles, Cleomenes asserts that "the desire of dominion is a never-failing consequence of the pride that is common to all men."[130] It is of course in the nature of things that our self-love should be frustrated in its attempts to rule others. No one is in a position to lord it over the earth. Horatius then asks: "Is it not strange, that Nature should send us all into the world with a visible desire after government, and no capacity for it at all?"[131] Cleomenes responds by invoking a providential design:

What seems strange to you is an undeniable instance of divine wisdom. For if all had not been born with this desire, all must have been destitute of it, and multitudes could never have been formed into societies, if some of them had not been possessed of this thirst of dominion. Creatures may commit force upon themselves, they may learn to warp their natural appetites, and divert them from their proper objects, but peculiar instincts that belong to a whole species are never to be acquired by art of discipline, and those that are born without them, must remain destitute of them forever.[132]

To be sure, many passages in *The Fable of the Bees* are ironic, and one may be tempted to dismiss the reference to divine wisdom as a mere token of allegiance to religious orthodoxy. Whatever Mandeville's personal beliefs may have been, ignoring the reference to Providence would cause us to overlook an essential aspect of Mandeville's understanding of the workings of self-love. For Mandeville, the desire for domination is providential because it works in a paradoxical way. At first sight, it does not bring order, but chaos. But in the final analysis, it is a solid foundation for government because it is instinctual and universal.

Adam Smith's understanding of Providence is noticeably different. The emphasis is on the harmony of society and the universe. In particular, the order of society is based upon the fact that there exists a harmony between the interests of the individual and the interests of society. This neo-Stoic conception of Providence can be found in early eighteenth-century authors like Shaftesbury and Butler.

---

[129] Ibid.   [130] Ibid., p. 204.   [131] Ibid.   [132] Ibid., p. 205.

Shaftesbury begins by refuting the interest doctrine. Characteristically, he lumps Epicureans and Augustinians together as advocates of the notion that "interest governs the world."[133] He expresses special scorn for La Rochefoucauld and his followers, authors of "yet an inferior kind" [than the Epicureans]: "a sort of distributors and petty retailers of this [Epicurean] wit who have run changes, and divisions, without end, upon this article of *self-love*."[134]

Shaftesbury assumes that nature prompts us to seek our own good. Certain passions are contrary to this end. It is remarkable, according to Shaftesbury, that the passions that are harmful to us are also harmful to others. On the other hand, the passions and appetites that are good for us happen to be good for others as well. Therefore, the pursuit of private interest is consistent with the pursuit of the interest of all:

Now if, by the natural constitution of any rational creature, the same irregularities of appetite which make him ill to *others*, make him ill also *to himself*, and if the same regularity of affections, which causes him to be good in *one* sense, causes him to be good also *in the other*, then is that goodness by which he is thus useful to others a real good and advantage to himself. And thus *virtue* and *interest* may be found at last to agree.[135]

This convergence between virtue and interest is typically Stoic. The ends of nature can be achieved through either reason (virtue) or instinct (self-interest). The sub-rational pursuit of self-interest produces the same results as the rational pursuit of the public good.

Butler offers a similar argument. He makes a distinction between "the nature of man as respecting self, and tending to private good" and "the nature of man as having respect to society, and tending to promote public good."[136] Contrary to the belief of interest theorists, "these ends do indeed perfectly coincide; and to aim at public and private good are so far from being inconsistent, that they mutually promote each other."[137] The convergence between private and public good is ensured by rational behavior. It is also a providential consequence of instinct:

---

[133] Anthony Ashley Cooper, Third Earl of Shaftesbury, *Sensus Communis, viz. An Essay on the Freedom of Wit and Humor*, in *Characteristics of Men, Manners, Opinions, Times*, Anglistica & Americana Series no. 123, vol. 1, Hildesheim: Georg Olms, 1978 [London, 1709], p. 115.

[134] Ibid., p. 120. Although Shaftesbury, following the custom of the time, does not mention La Rochefoucauld by name, the reference is clear. An editor's note in the 1711 edition confirms that La Rochefoucauld is Shaftesbury's target here.

[135] Anthony Ashley Cooper, Third Earl of Shaftesbury, *An Inquiry Concerning Virtue*, in *Characteristics of Men, Manners, Opinions, Times*, Anglistica & Americana Series no. 123, vol. 2, Hildesheim: Georg Olms, 1978 [London: A. Bell, E. Castle, and S. Buckley, 1699], p. 15.

[136] Butler, Sermon I, in Raphael (ed.), *British Moralists, 1650–1800*, p. 337.   [137] Ibid.

It may be added, that as persons without any conviction from reason of the desirableness of life, would yet of course preserve it merely from the appetite of hunger; so by acting merely from regard (suppose) to reputation, without any consideration of the good of others, men often contribute to the public good. In both these instances they are plainly instruments in the hands of another, in the hands of Providence, to carry on ends, the preservation of the individual and good of society, which they themselves have not in their view or intention.[138]

Butler's language is remarkably similar to the words Adam Smith will use in *The Theory of Moral Sentiments* and *The Wealth of Nations*. Smith's industrialist, "led by an invisible hand to promote an end which was no part of his intention,"[139] echoes Butler's egoists who are "plainly instruments... in the hands of Providence, to carry on ends... which they themselves have not in their view or intention." Also typically Stoic is the comparison between the providential consequences of a natural instinct like hunger, and the providential consequences of self-interest behavior in social intercourse.

Like Shaftesbury and Butler, Smith insists on the convergence between the effects of benevolent motives and the effects of selfish motives. The social order can proceed "from love, from gratitude, from friendship, and esteem." It can also be derived from self-interest:

But though the necessary assistance should not be afforded from such generous and disinterested motives, though among the different members of the society there should be no mutual love and affection, the society, though less happy and agreeable, will not necessarily be dissolved. Society may subsist among different men, as among different merchants, from a sense of its utility, without any mutual love or affection; and though no man in it should owe any obligation, or be bound in gratitude to any other, it may still be upheld by a mercenary exchange of good offices according to an agreed valuation.[140]

In Smith's Stoic perspective, there are certainly many cases in which the pursuit of self-interest goes against the interest of all. In order to show how the private good and the public good converge, Smith proposes a comparison between life and sport:

In the race for wealth, and honors, and preferments, he may run as hard as he can, and strain every nerve and every muscle, in order to outstrip all his competitors. But if he should jostle, or throw down any of them, the indulgence of the spectators is entirely at an end. It is a violation of fair play, which they cannot admit of. This man is to them, in every respect, as good as he: they do not enter into that self-love by which he prefers himself so much to this other, and cannot go along with

---

[138] Ibid., p. 341.   [139] Smith, *The Wealth of Nations*, IV.ii.9.
[140] Smith, *The Theory of Moral Sentiments*, II.ii.3.1.

the motive from which he hurt him. They readily, therefore, sympathize with the natural resentment of the injured, and the offender becomes the object of their hatred and indignation. He is sensible that he becomes so, and feels that those sentiments are ready to burst out from all sides against him.[141]

In sport, all competitors do everything they can to seek their own advantage (winning the competition). Yet they agree to certain rules, including a complete prohibition against hurting others. For Smith, the sport metaphor (which belongs to the Stoic tradition) is remarkably appropriate because it captures two aspects that are often seen as contradictory. On the one hand, as Cicero puts it in *De Officiis*, "we are not required to sacrifice our own interests and surrender to others what we need for ourselves." On the other hand, "each one should consider his own interests, as far as he may without injury to his neighbor's."[142] The Stoic metaphor of life as sport helps us to understand how the relentless pursuit of self-interest can be compatible with the public good:

When a man enters the foot-race, says Chrysippus with his usual aptness, "it is his duty to put forth all his strength and strive with all his might to win; but he ought never with his foot to trip, or with his hand to foul a competitor." Thus in the stadium of life, it is not unfair for anyone to seek to obtain what is needful for his own advantage, but he has no right to wrest it from his neighbor.[143]

Smith's choice of a Stoic scheme rather than an Epicurean/Augustinian scheme sheds light on a fundamental aspect of what we now call liberal ideology. As Carl Schmitt, a fierce critic of liberalism, puts it, "liberalism in one of its typical dilemmas of intellect and economics has attempted to transform the enemy from the viewpoint of economics into a competitor."[144] The Stoic metaphor of life as sport, appropriated by liberals, suggests that other human beings are competitors, not enemies. On the contrary, the choice of an Epicurean/Augustinian scheme would have implied that other human beings are enemies rather than competitors. In the Augustinian scheme, the path to social order includes the notion that self-love makes us enemies of one another: "Self-love which is the cause of this war, will easily tell the way how to make them live in peace."[145]

More generally, the Stoic account of Providence, preferred by Adam Smith, emphasizes the harmony of the universe and the harmony of systems of government, which are the object of philosophical contemplation.

---

[141] Ibid., II.2.1.
[142] Cicero, *De Officiis*, translated by Walter Miller, Cambridge, MA: Harvard University Press, 1913, III.x.42.
[143] Ibid.
[144] Carl Schmitt, *The Concept of the Political*, Chicago: University of Chicago Press, 1996, p. 28.
[145] Nicole, *Moral Essays*, p. 80.

The highest form of philosophical speculation consists in perceiving the harmony between the parts and the whole, in nature as well as in society. Augustinians, on the other hand, insist on the paradoxical, even miraculous, character of the divine providence that turns evils things (e.g. the sin of pride) to good use (e.g. the prosperity of the Roman Empire). Augustinian accounts describe a social order that is, in a sense, safe and sound because it is based on concupiscence. As Pascal remarks, there is no surer foundation because nothing is more certain or predictable than human concupiscence. Yet this order is always on the verge of chaos, because the road from self-interest to social order requires cooperation. The Stoic model, on the contrary, takes the harmony between individual interest and the general interest as a given. Augustine's admiration for the beneficent effects of self-love was quite limited. In *The City of God*, Augustine's final judgment on the effects of pride on the character of Romans is simply: *minus turpes sunt* (they are less depraved).[146] As to pride itself, it is an indirect manifestation of self-love's tyrannical tendencies: an apparently selfless behavior aimed at winning respect and consideration from others. But Augustine reminds his reader that the love of glory was never universal at Rome. Self-love often manifested itself as an immediate lust for power.[147] Borrowing from Sallust, he explains that Rome was for many years on the verge of civil war, and only external threats, like the Second Punic War, "checked their restless spirits, and distracted them from these disorders, by a more urgent anxiety, and recalled them to domestic concord."[148] In the Augustinian conception of Providence, it is a matter of faith that God conducts the events of human history with an unequivocally good purpose. However, from a human perspective, the message contained in the workings of self-love is necessarily an ambiguous one. Self-love, when it manifests itself as love of glory, can have beneficial consequences as far as the social order is concerned. But self-love is and remains an evil. It can just as well manifest itself as an immediate, tyrannical impulse, and cause chaos and civil strife. Augustine sometimes marvels, like the Stoics, at the harmony of the universe. Most often, however, it is the ambiguous meaning of human history that is the focus of his meditation. Self-love can have admirable or catastrophic consequences. The catastrophic consequences of self-love are a proof and manifestation of the original sin. The beneficial consequences of self-love are an indication of God's providential ability to turn evil into good. For Augustine, this puzzle is a sign of the inscrutable ways in which God works through human history to redeem the human race from original sin.

[146] Augustine, *The City of God*, v, 13.   [147] Ibid., v, 19.   [148] Ibid., v, 12.

Irrespective of the theological context, the Augustinian meditation on the ambiguous effects of self-love is based on the observation that cooperation based on self-interest is necessarily precarious. Elaborating on the classic Prisoner's Dilemma (a situation in which cooperation would yield an optimal outcome, but self-interest dictates a refusal to cooperate), Jon Elster observes that "self-interest might seem an unlikely motivation" for cooperation, "since the collective action problem is defined in part by the clause that it is not selfishly rational to cooperate."[149] In a one-shot problem, Elster adds, "this is indeed true." However, when people have to deal with each other many times, "it may be in their self-interest to cooperate, out of hope of reciprocation, fear of retaliation or both."[150] This is Nicole's argument: "Self-love which is the cause of this war, will easily tell the way how to make them live in peace." As we have seen above, the argument has a flipside. As Elster puts it, "the conditions under which people will cooperate out of self-interest are quite stringent." These conditions include some foresight, concern about the future, confidence that others are behaving rationally, etc. This leads Elster to conclude that "most cooperation is due to nonselfish motivations of one kind or another."[151] Elster's conclusion would make him a Stoic rather than an Augustinian. At any rate, his analysis helps to explain the Augustinian point of view: cooperation induced by self-interest is fragile because the primary dictate of self-interest remains a refusal to cooperate.

Another way of contrasting the Augustinian and Stoic concepts of Providence is to look at the physical theories associated with them. In his *Moral Essays*, Nicole compares the social order to Descartes' whirlwinds. The self-love of each individual seeks to expand and occupy as much space as possible. It is constrained by a similar tendency in the self-love of others. These opposite forces produce whirlwinds:

Behold already the picture of constraint, whereto the self-love of each particular is reduced by that of others, which does not permit it to set itself out at large so much as it would. We are going to see all the motions in the sequel of this comparison. For these little confined bodies coming to muster up their forces, and their motions do form great heaps of matter, which philosophers call whirlwinds, which are states and kingdoms. And these whirlwinds are themselves pressed and imprisoned by other whirlwinds, as it were by neighboring kingdoms ... Lastly, as these little bodies drawn by the whirlwinds do yet turn as much as they can upon their own center, so likewise the little ones who follow the fortune of the grandees

---

[149] Jon Elster, *Nuts and Bolts for the Social Sciences*, Cambridge: Cambridge University Press, 1989, p. 132.
[150] Ibid.   [151] Ibid.

and that of the state, do not forbear with all their endeavors, and all their services, which they render them, to look upon themselves, and to have always their own proper interest in prospect.[152]

The image of states and kingdoms as whirlwinds is a clear indication of the limited confidence Augustinians have in the beneficent effects of self-love. Whirlwinds are powerful, yet unstable, because equilibrium is the product of opposite forces. While Nicole proposes a centrifugal model based on Cartesian physics, Adam Smith favors a centripetal scheme, reminiscent of Newton's physics, which he lauded abundantly in his *History of Astronomy*.[153] Sympathy, like universal gravitation, is a univocal principle of order. Self-love, like Descartes' whirlwinds, is a principle of chaos and order at the same time.

VIRTUE, SELF-LOVE, AND THE ENLIGHTENMENT

In his classic work, *The Role of Providence in the Social Order*, Jacob Viner relates Smith's "invisible hand" to a form of "optimistic providentialism" that became dominant in the eighteenth century. He argues that this optimistic providentialism "was not shared by those in the Augustinian tradition whether Protestant or Catholic," because the belief in the original sin and the curse of Adam "were insurmountable barriers to acceptance of optimistic pictures of the destiny of man while on this earth." Viner adds that he knows "of no evidence that any of the strict Augustinians in English or Scottish or Dutch or Genevese Calvinism, or any of the Jansenists, participated in the search for evidences of a benevolent providence in the physical nature of the earth." This may be true regarding the physical nature of the earth, but, as we have seen, Augustinians in the seventeenth and eighteenth centuries (Jansenists like Pascal or Nicole, a Calvinist like Bayle, or an author brought up in the Calvinist tradition like Mandeville) had a strong and coherent picture of Providence, albeit a "pessimistic" one. The terms "optimistic" and "pessimistic" may in fact be misleading. Adam

---

[152] Nicole, *Moral Essays*, p. 83. "C'est l'image de la contrainte où l'amour-propre de chaque particulier est réduit par celui des autres, qui ne lui permet pas de se mettre au large autant qu'il voudrait. Car, comme ces petits corps emprisonnés venant à unir leurs forces et leurs mouvements forment de grands amas de matière que l'on appelle tourbillons, qui sont comme les états et les royaumes; et que ces tourbillons étant eux-mêmes pressés et emprisonnés par d'autres tourbillons, comme par des royaumes voisins ... comme tous ces petits corps entraînés par les tourbillons tournent encore autant qu'ils peuvent autour de leur centre, de même les petits qui suivent la fortune des Grands et celle de l'État ne laissent pas, dans tous les devoirs et les services qu'ils rendent aux autres, de se regarder eux-mêmes, et d'avoir toujours en vue leur propre intérêt." *Essais de morale*, p. 385.

[153] I thank Allan Silver for suggesting this connection between moral philosophy and physics.

Smith's neo-Stoicism is "optimistic" only in a very technical sense: Providence works to optimize the outcome of the social exchange. The dividing line is between two conceptions of Providence: one that adheres to the original-sin doctrine, and one that does not. The question of the original sin determines all other doctrinal choices, including the understanding of self-love and its consequences. If one believes in the original sin, self-love is an evil that can (sometimes) be put to good use by providential action. If one rejects the original-sin doctrine, self-love is a benign sentiment at the service of nature's ends. It is important to notice that, at the beginning of the eighteenth century, with the enormous success of Nicole's *Moral Essays*, and the *succès de scandale* of *The Fable of the Bees*, it is the Epicurean/Augustinian doctrine of self-love and the Augustinian doctrine of Providence that dominated the debate. In that sense, Viner's notion that the original-sin doctrine prevented the Augustinians from accepting the optimistic pictures of the destiny of man ought to be reversed. It is because they rejected the original-sin doctrine, or accepted it in a much-subdued form, that thinkers like Shaftesbury, Butler, and Smith chose to adopt a neo-Stoic rather than Augustinian concept of Providence.

The original sin is the unspoken issue that lies behind the reception of the interest doctrine by most Enlightenment thinkers. Because the interest doctrine is tied to the notion of original sin, it provokes violently polemical responses from Voltaire and the *encyclopédistes*. In his *Dictionnaire philosophique*, Voltaire dedicates an article to blasting the author of the treatise on the *Falsity of Human Virtues*:

> After the Duke of La Rochefoucauld wrote his thoughts on self-love and uncovered this motive of human action, a certain Monsieur Esprit, of the Oratory, wrote a specious book entitled *On the Falsity of Human Virtues*. This Esprit says there is no such thing as virtue, but he does us the favor of ending each chapter by mentioning Christian charity. Thus according to Monsieur Esprit, neither Cato, nor Aristides, nor Marcus Aurelius, nor Epictetus, were good people; such people can only be found among Christians. Among Christians, only Catholics have virtue; among Catholics, Jesuits (enemies of the Oratorians) must be excluded; so much so that virtue can only be found among the Jesuits' enemies . . . Such arrogance is revolting. I will not say more, because it would make me lose my temper.[154]

---

[154] "Quand le duc de La Rochefoucauld eut écrit ses pensées sur l'amour-propre, et qu'il eut mis à découvert ce ressort de l'homme, un monsieur Esprit, de l'Oratoire, écrivit un livre captieux, intitulé: *De la Fausseté des vertus humaines*. Cet Esprit dit qu'il n'y a point de vertu; mais par grâce il termine chaque chapitre en renvoyant à la charité chrétienne. Ainsi, selon le sieur Esprit, ni Caton, ni Aristide, ni Marc-Aurèle, ni Épictète n'étaient des gens de bien; mais on n'en peut trouver que chez les chrétiens. Parmi les chrétiens, il n'y a de vertu que chez les catholiques; parmi les catholiques, il fallait encore en excepter les jésuites, ennemis des oratoriens; partant, la vertu ne

It is remarkable that Voltaire does not wage a frontal attack on La Rochefoucauld. Augustinianism and the doctrine of the original sin lie in the background of the *Maxims*, but they are never explicitly mentioned. As a consequence, it is possible to assume that self-love is a morally neutral sentiment, and perform a "secular" reading of La Rochefoucauld. That is not the case with Esprit, who states the theological assumptions of the *Maxims* very clearly. When Esprit says that only Christians can be truly virtuous, he simply states a point of the Augustinian doctrine: only God's grace can save humans from the deleterious effects of self-love. That is exactly what causes Voltaire's anger. Against the Augustinian critique of virtues, he affirms the possibility of virtue by human efforts alone. It is no coincidence that Voltaire's list of virtuous pagans should include two Stoic philosophers, Epictetus and Marcus Aurelius.

Similarly, the "Intérêt" article in the *Encyclopédie* criticizes Nicole, La Rochefoucauld and Pascal for describing self-love as a malign principle:

Friendship will always be a virtue, even though it is based on the need a soul has for another soul.

Love of order, justice, will always be the prime virtue and the true heroism, even though it has its source in the love of oneself.

These truths should be commonplace and never questioned, but a certain group of people in the last century meant to turn self-love into an ever-malign principle. This was the basis on which Nicole made twenty volumes of morals, which are but a collection of methodically arranged and gracelessly written sophisms.

Pascal himself, the great Pascal, meant to view as an imperfection this love of ourselves that God gave us... M. de la Rochefoucauld, who expressed himself with precision and grace, wrote nearly in the same spirit as Pascal and Nicole... La Rochefoucauld's book, and Pascal's, which were in everybody's hands, have gradually accustomed the French public to take the word *self-love* always in a bad sense. It is only recently that a small number of men have begun to dissociate it from the ideas of vice, pride, etc.[155]

---

se trouvait guère que chez les ennemis des jésuites... Une telle insolence révolte. Je n'en dirai pas davantage, car je me mettrais en colère." Voltaire, *Dictionnaire philosophique*, edited by J. Benda and R. Naves. Paris: Garnier, 1954 [Paris, 1764], art. "Fausseté des vertus humaines."

[155] "L'amitié sera toujours une vertu, quoiqu'elle ne soit fondée que sur le besoin qu'une âme a d'une autre âme.

"La passion de l'ordre, de la justice, sera la première vertu, le véritable héroïsme, quoiqu'elle ait sa source dans l'amour de nous-mêmes.

"Voilà des vérités qui ne devraient être que triviales et jamais contestées; mais une classe d'hommes du dernier siècle a voulu faire de l'amour-propre un principe toujours vicieux; c'est en partant d'après cette idée que Nicole a fait vingt volumes de morale, qui ne sont qu'un assemblage de sophismes méthodiquement arrangés et lourdement écrits.

"Pascal même, le grand Pascal, a voulu regarder en nous comme une imperfection ce sentiment de l'amour de nous-mêmes que Dieu nous a donné... M. de la Rochefoucauld qui s'exprimait avec

The author of the article[156] vilifies Nicole and treats Pascal and La Rochefoucauld (both of them greatly admired literary figures) with more caution. Nevertheless, all three authors are subjected to the same critique: they view self-love as a vice. What makes this article particularly interesting is that it testifies to the popularity of the interest doctrine (La Rochefoucauld's book and Pascal's "were in everybody's hands"); in addition, it shows that this doctrine was still closely associated with Augustinianism (Nicole, La Rochefoucauld and Pascal are all Augustinians). The article also gives evidence of the fact that the *encyclopédistes* viewed the reappraisal of virtues as a new and counterintuitive stance taken by an enlightened elite ("a small number of men").

Adam Smith, who published an enthusiastic review of the first volumes of the *Encyclopédie*,[157] shared these principles entirely. In his examination of the various systems of moral philosophy in Part VII of *The Theory of Moral Sentiments*, the tone is less strident than in the *Encyclopédie*. Nevertheless, Mandeville and La Rochefoucauld appear under the heading of "Licentious Systems."[158] From Smith's Stoic perspective, saying, like the Epicureans and the Augustinians, that self-love is the cause of all human behavior, is an encouragement to vice. Smith sees the Augustinian critique of virtues as a dangerous threat to virtue. He enjoins parents not to chastise self-love in their children, but rather to redirect their vanity toward "the real love of true glory; a passion which, if not the very best passion of human nature, is certainly one of the best."[159] Like Rousseau, Smith constructs his moral philosophy on a refutation of the Epicurean/Augustinian concept of self-love. Regarding Smith's concept of providence, one could agree with Viner that "optimistic providentialism has its roots in the Enlightenment, and

---

précision et avec grâce, a écrit presque dans le même esprit que Pascal et Nicole; . . . Ce livre de M. de la Rochefoucauld, celui de Pascal, qui étaient entre les mains de tout le monde, ont insensiblement accoutumé le public français à prendre toujours le mot d'amour-propre en mauvaise part; et il n'y a pas longtemps qu'un petit nombre d'hommes commence à n'y plus attacher nécessairement les idées de vice, d'orgueil, etc." *Encyclopédie ou dictionnaire raisonné des sciences, des arts et des métiers*, Paris, 1751–1772 (17 vols.), art. "Intérêt."

[156] Tradition attributes this article to Diderot, but its author is Saint-Lambert. See Lafond, *La Rochefoucauld*, p. 267, correcting error of p. 157.

[157] Adam Smith, "Letter to the *Edinburgh Review*," in *Essays on Philosophical Subjects, The Glasgow Edition of the Works and Correspondence of Adam Smith*, vol. 3, Oxford: Oxford University Press, 1980, pp. 242–256.

[158] La Rochefoucauld's name was deleted from the 1790 edition, in compliance with a promise made by Smith to his descendant, Louis Alexandre de La Rochefoucauld (1743–1792), who objected to the association between La Rochefoucauld and Mandeville. See Letter 199 from Le Duc de La Rochefoucauld in *Correspondence of Adam Smith*, pp. 238–239. Smith inadvertently left the title of the chapter "On Licentious Systems" in the plural.

[159] Smith, *The Theory of Moral Sentiments*, VI.iii.45.

in the 'secularization' of even religious thought, more than in traditional Christian orthodoxy when it is understood in the Augustinian sense."[160] More precisely, we must say that Smith's optimistic providentialism asserts itself polemically against the Augustinian concept of Providence.

[160] Jacob Viner, *The Role of Providence in the Social Order. An Essay in Intellectual History*, Princeton: Princeton University Press, 1972, p. 26.

3

Self-interest and reason

Man is an indifferent egoist: even the cleverest regards his habits as more important than his advantage.

Nietzsche, *Fragments of 1887–1888*

THE RATIONAL PURSUIT OF SELF-INTEREST

According to Amartya Sen, standard economic theory defines rational behavior in two different ways: "One is to see rationality as internal *consistency* of choice, and the other is to identify rationality with *maximization of self-interest*."[1] Sen adds that, "in terms of historical lineage, the self-interest interpretation of rationality goes back a long way, and it has been one of the central features of mainline economic theorizing for several centuries."[2] Having discussed the status of self-interest as a first principle, we still need to explain what economists mean by "the rational pursuit of self-interest." In order to do this, we must understand the genealogy of the association between reason and self-interest.

The leading advocate of the "economic approach" claims that a comprehensive account of human behavior can be grounded in a set of related assumptions: (a) maximizing behavior; (b) market equilibrium; (c) stable preferences. In Becker's view, these assumptions, "used relentlessly and unflinchingly, form the heart of the economic approach."[3] The assumption of "maximizing behavior" means that we do not behave inconsistently. As Elster puts it, once a set of beliefs is assumed, our behavior is considered "maximizing behavior" when it is "the best action with respect to the full set of weighed desires."[4] In other words, we choose the behavior that, in

---

[1] Amartya Sen, *On Ethics and Economics*, Oxford: Blackwell, 1987, p. 12.   [2] Ibid., p. 15.

[3] Gary Becker, "The Economic Approach to Human Behavior," in *Rational Choice*, edited by Jon Elster, New York: New York University Press, 1986, p. 110.

[4] Jon Elster, "The Nature and Scope of Rational-Choice Explanations," in *Actions and Events: Perspectives on the Philosophy of Donald Davidson*, edited by Ernest LePore and Brian P. McLaughlin, Oxford: Blackwell, 1985, p. 65.

our estimation, will result in what we consider to be the best outcome. This is what Elster and others call "rational choice." In this expression, the term "rational" should not be understood in a strongly normative way. What is meant by "rational" is simply the idea that we act in accordance with both our beliefs and our desires.

The second assumption is "market equilibrium." This is the modern form of the "invisible hand" argument. It means that the aggregation of individual choices will necessarily result in the best possible outcome for all. For the purpose of this discussion, we shall ignore the assumption of optimality, because it is not a discriminating factor.

Finally, Becker assumes that we have "stable preferences." This is a controversial aspect of his doctrine when compared with that of other rational choice theorists. It is also a very important one as far as our subject matter is concerned. By taking the radical step of assuming that we have stable preferences, Becker formalizes an assumption that remains implicit in the work of many economists. When Becker says that we have "stable preferences," he does not refer to our choices regarding market goods and services, but rather to something that underlies our actual choices:

The preferences that are assumed to be stable do not refer to market goods and services, like oranges, automobiles, or medical care, but to underlying objects of choice that are produced by each household using market goods and services, their own time, and other inputs. These underlying preferences are defined over fundamental aspects of life, such as health, prestige, sensual pleasure, benevolence or envy, that do not always bear a stable relation to market goods and services.[5]

In order to understand what Becker means by "underlying preferences," it will be useful to compare Becker's doctrine with that of the eighteenth-century authors he claims as his predecessors. In addition to Adam Smith, Becker mentions Jeremy Bentham, who was "explicit about his belief that the pleasure–pain calculus is applicable to human behavior."[6] Indeed Bentham wrote that

Nature has placed mankind under the governance of two sovereign masters, *pain* and *pleasure*. It is for them alone to point out what we ought to do, as well as to determine what we shall do. On the one hand the standard of right and wrong, on the other the chain of causes and effects, are fastened to their throne. They govern us in all we do, in all we say, in all we think: every effort we can make to throw off our subjection, will serve but to demonstrate and confirm it.[7]

---

[5] Becker, "The Economic Approach to Human Behavior," p. 110.   [6] Ibid.
[7] Jeremy Bentham, *An Introduction to the Principles of Morals and Legislation*, edited by J.H. Burns and H.L.A. Hart, Oxford: Clarendon Press, 1996 [London, 1789], i.i, p. 11.

A criticism often addressed to earlier formulations of the economic approach was that economic theory was grounded in questionable hedonistic assumptions. Becker, for his part, does not endorse the neo-Epicurean notion that pleasure and pain are the only motives of human action. However, the reference to Bentham indicates that Becker's theory remains indebted to eighteenth-century neo-Epicureanism.

What Becker shares with philosophers like Bentham or Helvétius is the desire to identify some stable principle of behavior behind the bewildering variety of human choices and preferences. For Helvétius, who presents the most radical formulation of the interest doctrine, this stable principle is "personal interest":

In effect, what man, if he sacrifices the pride of styling himself more virtuous than others, to the pride of being more sincere; and if, with a scrupulous attention, he searches all the recesses of his soul; will not perceive that his virtues and vices are wholly owing to the different modifications of personal interest; that all equally tend to their happiness; that it is the diversity of the passions and tastes, of which some are agreeable, and others contrary to the public interest, which terms our actions either vices or virtues?[8]

One may object to the parallel between Becker's theory and the interest doctrine by pointing out that Becker does not claim that self-interest is the only motive. Becker's view (which, on this point, is the mainstream view of economists) is that self-interest is the dominant motive. "Some benevolence"[9] coexists with self-interest. However, Helvétius himself does not claim that benevolence does not exist. Some human beings are disposed in such a way that they sincerely choose the interests of others over their own:

There are men whom a happy disposition, a strong desire of glory and esteem, inspire with the same love of justice and virtue, which men in general have for riches and honors.

The actions personally advantageous to these virtuous men are so truly just, that they tend to promote the general welfare, or, at least not to lessen it.[10]

---

[8] Claude-Adrien Helvétius, *Essays on the Mind*, London: Albion Press, 1810, p. 41. "Quel homme, en effet, s'il sacrifie l'orgueil de se dire plus vertueux que les autres à l'orgueil d'être plus vrai, et s'il sonde, avec une attention scrupuleuse, tous les replis de son âme, ne s'apercevra pas que c'est uniquement à la manière différente dont l'intérêt personnel se modifie, que l'on doit les vices et les vertus? que tous les hommes sont mus par la même force? que tous tendent également à leur bonheur? que c'est la diversité des passions et des goûts, dont les uns sont conformes et les autres contraires à l'intérêt public, qui décide de nos vertus et de nos vices?" *De l'Esprit*, Paris: Durand, 1758, vol. I, II, I, p. 69.

[9] Gary Becker, "Altruism, Egoism, and Genetic Fitness: Economics and Sociobiology," in *The Economic Approach to Human Behavior*, Chicago: University of Chicago Press, 1976, p. 282.

[10] Helvétius, *Essays on the Mind*, p. 40. "Il est des hommes auxquels un heureux naturel, un désir vif de la gloire et de l'estime, inspirent pour la justice et la vertu le même amour que les hommes ont

Helvétius makes therefore two claims, which must be distinguished. The first claim is that self-interest is the dominant, but not the exclusive, motive of human actions. The second claim is that all human actions, including benevolence, must be analyzed in terms of personal advantage, or utility. A benevolent person is someone who finds it either useful or pleasurable to help others. Let us note here that, in the neo-Epicurean tradition, "pleasure," "utility," and "interest" are often used interchangeably. For instance, Helvétius explains that he uses "interest" as a synonym for "pleasure":

The word interest is generally confined to the love of money; but the intelligent reader will perceive that I use it in a more extensive sense, and that I apply it in general to whatever may procure us pleasure, or exempt us from pain.[11]

Similarly, for Bentham, our interest is our pleasure:

A thing is said to promote the interest, or to be *for* the interest, of an individual, when it tends to add to the sum total of his pleasures: or, what comes to the same thing, to diminish the sum total of his pains.[12]

Neo-Epicureans therefore do not deny the existence of virtuous or benevolent behavior. They simply posit pleasure as the motive for all behavior, moral or immoral:

The humane man is he to whom the sight of another's misfortunes is insupportable, and who, to remove this afflicting spectacle, is, as it were, forced to relieve the wretched. The cruel man, on the contrary, is he to whom the sight of another's misfortunes gives a secret pleasure, and it is to prolong that pleasure, that he refuses all relief to the wretched. Now these two persons, so very opposite, both equally tend to their pleasures, and are actuated by the same spring.[13]

Becker, for his part, does not explain altruistic behavior by invoking the search for pleasure. All preferences, however, whether egoistic or altruistic,

communément pour les grandeurs et les richesses. Les actions personnellement utiles à ces hommes vertueux sont les actions justes, conformes à l'intérêt général, ou du moins qui ne lui sont pas contraires." *De l'Esprit*, vol. 1, 11, 1, p. 69.

[11] Ibid., p. 37. "Le vulgaire restreint communément la signification de ce mot *intérêt* au seul amour de l'argent; le lecteur éclairé sentira que je prends ce mot dans un sens plus étendu, et que je l'applique généralement à tout ce qui peut nous procurer des plaisirs, ou nous soustraire à des peines." *De l'Esprit*, vol. 1, 11, 1, p. 64.

[12] Bentham, *An Introduction to the Principles of Morals and Legislation*, 1.5, p. 12.

[13] Helvétius, *Essays on the Mind*, p. 41, footnote. "L'homme humain est celui pour qui la vue du malheur d'autrui est une vue insupportable, et qui, pour s'arracher à ce spectacle, est, pour ainsi dire, forcé de secourir le malheureux. L'homme inhumain au contraire est celui pour qui le spectacle de la misère d'autrui est un spectacle agréable; c'est pour prolonger ses plaisirs qu'il refuse tout secours aux malheureux. Or, ces deux hommes si différents tendent cependant tous deux à leur plaisir, et sont mus par le même ressort." *De l'Esprit*, vol. 1, 11, 11, p. 72, footnote (h).

are expressed in the form of utility functions.[14] Fundamentally, what Becker's approach has in common with the neo-Epicurean theories of Bentham and Helvétius is the idea that a satisfactory explanation of human behavior must postulate objects of choice or principles of choice that are more abstract or more general than the objects of choice that can be observed empirically. In his "New Theory of Consumer Behavior," Becker criticizes the traditional notion that the objects of choice are empirically defined market goods. Instead, he proposes to view "as the primary objects of consumer choice various entities, called commodities, from which utility is directly obtained."[15] While presenting his theory as "a fundamental break with the standard approach to the theory of choice,"[16] Becker refers to Bentham's list of fifteen "simple pleasures" which was meant to constitute "the inventory of our sensations."[17] Becker sees Bentham's system as an anticipation of his own because it postulated objects of choices that were abstract entities, removed from empirical observation. With this list of fifteen pleasures, Becker adds, Bentham was able to account for every aspect of human behavior:

These pleasures, which were supposed to exhaust the list of basic arguments in one's pleasure (i.e. utility) function are of senses, riches, address, friendship, good reputation, power, piety, benevolence, malevolence, knowledge, memory, imagination, hope, association and relief of pain. Presumably these pleasures are "produced" partly by the goods purchased in the market sector.[18]

This passage shows clearly that, in Becker's mind, the modern notion of utility (fundamental in economic theory) is directly issued from the neo-Epicurean concept of pleasure. The word pleasure should of course not be understood in a strictly physical sense. However, Bentham's fifteen pleasures do account for all the examples Becker gives when he explains the objects of our "stable preferences": "health, prestige, sensual pleasure, benevolence or envy." According to Becker, these goods "do not always bear a stable relation to market goods and services," but the theorist can safely assume that we all want health, prestige, sensual pleasure, benevolence or envy in the same degree because of the pleasure these goods bring us. In that sense, "tastes neither change capriciously nor differ importantly between people."[19] Consequently, differences in behavior result not from varying

---

[14] Becker, "Altruism, Egoism, and Genetic Fitness," p. 285.
[15] Gary Becker, "On the New Theory of Consumer Behavior," in *The Economic Approach to Human Behavior*, Chicago: University of Chicago Press, 1976, p. 134.
[16] Ibid.   [17] Ibid., p. 137.   [18] Ibid.
[19] Gary Becker and George Stigler, "De Gustibus Non Est Disputandum," *American Economic Review* 67:2 (1977), p. 76.

preferences "over fundamental aspects of life," but simply from differences in the individual's opportunity set: "All changes in behavior are explained by changes in prices and incomes, precisely the variables that organize and give power to economic analysis."[20]

In many ways, Becker's assumption regarding the stability of preferences is an abstract formulation of the Epicurean/Augustinian principle we discussed in chapter 2: pleasure is the motive of all human conduct. Beyond Bentham, Becker could very well claim Mandeville and La Rochefoucauld as advocates of the notion of stable preferences. In the first volume of *The Fable of the Bees*, Mandeville asserts that "men are never, or at least very seldom, reclaimed from their darling passions, either by reason or precept, and...if anything draws them from what they naturally propose to do, it must be a change in their circumstances or their fortunes."[21] In the second volume, he claims: "The same motives may produce very different actions, as men differ in temper and circumstances. Persons of an easy fortune may appear virtuous, from the same turn of mind that would show their frailty if they were poor."[22] Mandeville postulates a strict determinism of the passions: we can only do what our passions prompt us to do. If our behavior changes, it is not because our passions have changed, but simply because the opportunities available to us have changed. The same line of thinking can be found in La Rochefoucauld. At first sight, La Rochefoucauld says, some people are greedier than others. For instance, philosophers express contempt for material wealth. This contempt, however, is the expression of a preference that philosophers share with those who possess wealth: the desire to be esteemed and admired:

Scorn for wealth, among philosophers, was a concealed desire to avenge themselves against fate, by despising the very thing of which she deprived them; it was a secret way of guarding against the humiliations of poverty; it was a roundabout way of gaining the esteem they could not gain through wealth.[23]

"Pride," La Rochefoucauld writes, "exists equally in all men: the only difference lies in what ways they manifest it."[24] Under the apparent variety in

[20] Ibid., p. 89.
[21] Bernard Mandeville *The Fable of the Bees*, edited by F.B. Kaye, Oxford: Clarendon Press, 1924 [sixth edition, London: J. Tonson, 1732], vol. 1, p. 182.
[22] Ibid., vol. 2, p. 110.
[23] François de la Rochefoucauld, *The Maxims*, translated by Louis Kronenberger, New York: Stackpole, 1936, maxim 54. "Le mépris des richesses était dans les philosophes un désir caché de venger leur mérite de l'injustice de la fortune par le mépris des mêmes biens dont elle les privait; c'était un secret pour se garantir de l'avilissement de la pauvreté; c'était un chemin détourné pour aller à la considération qu'ils ne pouvaient avoir par les richesses." *Maximes*, edited by Jean Lafond, Paris: Gallimard, 1976 [Paris: Barbin, 1678], maxim 54.
[24] Ibid., maxim 35. "L'orgueil est égal dans tous les hommes, et il n'y a de différence qu'aux moyens et à la manière de le mettre à jour."

human tastes and preferences, the passion of pride lies as a stable, unchanging, and universal preference. More generally, La Rochefoucauld makes a distinction between our "tastes" (which are ever-changing) and our "inclinations" (which are stable): "It is as common for tastes to change as it is uncommon for inclinations."[25]

Although it may appear odd to claim that Becker's theory has anything to do with the idea of original sin, it is important to recall that the "economic approach," with its assumption of stable preferences, can be traced back to Augustinians like La Rochefoucauld and Mandeville, who claim that the universal bent for pleasure is characteristic of the fallen state of humanity. The assumption of stable preferences implies that human nature is the same everywhere. As Becker puts it, the economic approach is applicable to "rich or poor persons, men or women, adults or children, brilliant or stupid persons, patients or therapists, businessmen or politicians, teachers or students." Becker's words seem to echo *The Fable of the Bees*, where Mandeville claims that human nature has always and everywhere been the same since the Fall of Adam:

If we consult history both ancient and modern, and take a view of what has past the world, we shall find that human nature since the Fall of Adam has always been the same, and that the strength and frailties of it have been conspicuous in one part of the globe or other, without any regard to ages, climates, or religion.[26]

If we try to re-inject some of the psychological content that its terminology tends to obfuscate, we shall say that the economic approach postulates that we behave rationally (maximizing behavior), that our behavior is driven by pleasure, or interest (stable preferences) and that the outcome of the rational pursuit of pleasure is the best for everyone (optimality).

PREFERENCES AND UTILITY

By most accounts, rational choice theory consists in the application of the assumptions and methodology of economics to all social sciences. However, there is an important difference between Becker's radical formulation of the "economic approach" and rational choice according to theorists like Elster. Like Becker, Elster assumes that, in order to qualify for a rational-choice explanation, behavior must exhibit characteristics of "rationality"[27] and "optimality."[28] Unlike Becker, Elster chooses not to assume anything about the nature of preferences:

---

[25] Ibid., maxim 252 (translation modified). "Il est aussi ordinaire de voir changer les goûts qu'il est extraordinaire de voir changer les inclinations."

[26] Mandeville, *The Fable of the Bees*, vol. 1, p. 229.

[27] Becker, "The Nature and Scope of Rational-Choice Explanations," p. 62.   [28] Ibid., p. 65.

We can then say that the person acts so as to maximize utility, as long as we keep in mind that this is nothing but a convenient way of saying that he does what he most prefers. There is no implication of hedonism. In fact, his preferred option might be one that gives pleasure to others and none to himself.[29]

According to Elster, the calculus implied by rational choice is not necessarily a pleasure–pain calculus. Preferences can be geared toward many things other than the search for pleasure and the avoidance of pain. In his rejection of the hedonist assumption, Elster seems to agree with Sen, who sought to refine the concept of preference by remarking that we sometimes act on the basis of preferences about preferences, or "meta-preferences." One example of meta-preference is commitment. When I commit to something, I choose to act in ways that will sometimes go against my own welfare. As Sen puts it, the most important characteristic of commitment is "the fact that it drives a wedge between personal choice and personal welfare," while "much of traditional economic theory relies on the identity of the two."[30] Sen insists on the ambiguity of the term "preference." In one sense, what we prefer is what we like best, and what we like best is what gives us pleasure. In another sense, to prefer means simply to choose.

In chapter 1, we have seen the affinities between Sen's critique of the behavioral foundations of economic theory and Smith's critique of Epicureanism in *The Theory of Moral Sentiments*. It is worth noticing that for Smith, "to prefer" also means "to choose":

> We never are generous except when in some respect we prefer some other person to ourselves, and sacrifice some great and important interest of our own to an equal interest of a friend or of a superior. The man who gives up his pretensions to an office that was the great object of his ambition, because he imagines that the services of another are better entitled to it; the man who exposes his life to defend that of his friend, which he judges to be of more importance; neither of them act from humanity, or because they feel more exquisitely what concerns that other person than what concerns themselves. They both consider those opposite interests, not in the light in which they naturally appear to themselves, but in that in which they appear to others.[31]

When Smith defines generosity by saying that "we prefer some other person to ourselves," he doesn't mean that generosity consists in liking some other

[29] Jon Elster, *Nuts and Bolts for the Social Sciences*, Cambridge: Cambridge University Press, 1989, p. 23.
[30] Amartya Sen, "Rational Fools: A Critique of the Behavioral Foundations of Economic Theory," *Philosophy and Public Affairs* 6 (1977), p. 329.
[31] Adam Smith, *The Theory of Moral Sentiments* (sixth edition), *The Glasgow Edition of the Works and Correspondence of Adam Smith*, vol. 1, edited by D.D. Raphael and A.L. Macfie, Oxford: Oxford University Press, 1976, IV.2.10 [London and Edinburgh, 1790; first edition, 1759].

person better than ourselves. No matter what our behavioral choices are, it is true that "every individual, in his own breast, naturally prefers himself to all mankind."[32] Generosity simply means that we choose someone else's interest over ours.

As Hirschman points out, "there is a close link between preference change and the concept of meta-preferences."[33] Changes in someone's choice behavior can be an indication that a newly formed meta-preference is at work, or that preferences have won over a meta-preference. If our preferences and meta-preferences are always in agreement, our behavior will always be the same. In the same way, if our preferences always win over our meta-preferences, our behavior will be similarly unchanging. But if the struggle within the self between preferences and meta-preferences results in alternating victories and defeats for our meta-preferences, behavioral change will take place.

Here we must add, with Hirschman, that there are two kinds of preference changes. The preference changes of the first kind are "impulsive, uncomplicated, haphazard, publicity-induced, and generally minor (apple vs. pears) changes in tastes."[34] According to Hirschman, only this kind of preference change has traditionally attracted the attention of economists. However, a change in preferences can also be caused by the formation of a meta-preference, and reflect a change in values rather than a simple change in tastes. The difference between preferences as tastes and preferences as values is that one does not argue about tastes. On the contrary, values are, by definition, a matter of debate. Hirschman's response to the title of the article by Becker and Stigler on stable preferences ("De Gustibus Non Est Disputandum") is: *de valoribus est disputandum.*

This point goes to the heart of the debate. When Becker asserts that preferences do not change, he is of course not referring to the first kind of preferences (apples vs. pears). He is referring to the second kind (changes in values). This appears clearly in the manner in which he defends his approach. According to Becker, when an economic agent appears to behave in a way that goes against self-interest, the analyst should not take refuge in "assertions about irrationality" or "convenient shifts in values (that is, preferences)."[35] The assumption of stable preferences means either that our values do not change, or that shifts in values, if they take place, do not

---

[32] Ibid., II.ii.2.2.
[33] Albert O. Hirschman, "Against Parsimony: Three Easy Ways of Complicating Some Categories of Economic Discourse," in *Rival Views of Market Society*, Cambridge, MA: Harvard University Press, 1992 [1986], p. 144.
[34] Ibid., p. 145.   [35] Becker, "The Economic Approach to Human Behavior," p. 112.

cause behavioral change. The whole question is whether our principles and values guide our behavior. Here again, Becker's view is consistent with Mandeville's description of human behavior. In a passage rich in allusions, Mandeville explains that values have no influence whatsoever on behavior:

These are his words: *Some impose on the world, and would be thought to believe what they really don't; but much the greater number impose upon themselves, not considering nor thoroughly apprehending what it is to believe.* But this is making all mankind either fools or impostors, which to avoid, there is nothing left us, but to say what Mr. Bayle has endeavored to prove at large in his *Reflexions on Comets*: that man is so unaccountable a creature as to act most commonly against his principle.[36]

Mandeville begins by quoting Montaigne, who derides those who choose a belief, or a system of beliefs, without understanding "what it is to believe." In other words, without understanding that one must draw the practical consequences of one's belief. According to Mandeville, Montaigne implies that, if this is true, we are either irrational or hypocritical. Instead of blaming the human race, Mandeville proposes to adopt Bayle's formula, which consists simply in saying that we generally act against our principles. The formula comes from Bayle's *Pensées diverses*:

Man does not act according to his principles.

However rational a creature man may be, he hardly ever acts in accordance with his principles... Although he hardly ever adopts false principles, and almost always retains in his conscience the principles of natural equity, he, nevertheless, almost always decides to the advantage of his unchecked desires. Why is it that, in spite of the tremendous diversity in opinions regarding the ways of serving God and living properly, we see that some passions exert a continuous rule in all countries and all centuries?... What is the cause of this, if not the fact that the true principle of human actions is nothing but our temper, our natural inclination for pleasure, the taste we acquire for certain objects, the desire to please someone, some habit contracted in dealing with friends, or some other disposition resulting from our nature, no matter where we are born, and whatever knowledge has been poured into our minds?[37]

---

[36] Mandeville, *The Fable of the Bees*, vol. 1, p. 166.
[37] *"Que l'homme n'agit pas selon ses principes.*

"Que l'homme soit une créature raisonnable, tant qu'il vous plaira, il n'en est pas moins vrai, qu'il n'agit presque jamais conséquemment à ses principes... Ne donnant presque jamais dans des faux principes, retenant presque toujours dans la conscience les idées de l'équité naturelle, il conclut néanmoins presque toujours à l'avantage de ses désirs déréglés. D'où vient, je vous prie, qu'encore qu'il y ait parmi les hommes une prodigieuse diversité d'opinions touchant la manière de servir Dieu et de vivre selon les lois de la bienséance, on voit néanmoins certaines passions régner constamment dans tous les pays et dans tous les siècles?... D'où vient tout cela, sinon de ce que le véritable principe des actions de l'homme, (j'excepte ceux en qui la grâce du St. Esprit se déploie avec toute

It goes without saying that Bayle's purpose in presenting these views had nothing to do with economic theory. Bayle meant to show that, in spite of their beliefs, Christians were not better people than pagans or atheists (a statement that could be interpreted either as an exhortation to Christians to start living according to their principles, or an apology of atheism). On the other hand, the assumptions of Becker's economic approach are surprisingly close to Bayle's Epicurean/Augustinian anthropology. Like Bayle and Mandeville, Becker assumes that values play no role in behavioral changes. Values and opinions of course vary from one country to the next, or from one person to the next, or even from one person to that same person, but this apparent diversity masks a universal and unchanging bent for pleasure.

Any attempts to translate the language of economic science and rational choice theory into the language of early modern moral philosophy (and vice versa) should be carried out with caution. This book is based on the premise that such translations are not only possible, but also enlightening, because they help reveal the axiomatic choices of both languages. The exercise is authorized by the practice of economists themselves, who never fail to invoke the authority and the language of an eighteenth-century moral philosopher, Adam Smith, when they discuss the first principles of their discipline. In his preface to a 1976 edition of *The Wealth of Nations*, George Stigler equated the "drive of self-interest" with "utility-maximizing behavior."[38] This will do as a rough-and-ready approximation, but our discussion has shown that self-interest and utility-maximizing behavior are two different things. Saying that behavior maximizes utility is another way of saying that behavior is consistent or rational. Conversely, if we attempt to translate the traditional notion that behavior is driven by "pleasure" or "interest" into the language of rational choice theory, we shall say that choice behavior reveals stable preferences.

The reason why Stigler equates self-interest with utility-maximizing behavior is because his understanding of the concept of utility is grounded in the utilitarian tradition. Going back to the definitions proposed by Bentham, we find that utility is

son efficace) n'est autre chose que le tempérament, l'inclination naturelle pour le plaisir, le goût que l'on contracte pour certains objets, le désir de plaire à quelqu'un, une habitude gagnée dans le commerce de ses amis, ou quelque autre disposition qui résulte du fond de notre nature en quelque pays que l'on naisse, et de quelques connaissances que l'on nous remplisse l'esprit?" Pierre Bayle, *Pensées diverses écrites à un docteur de Sorbonne à l'occasion de la comète qui parut au mois de décembre 1680*, in *Œuvres diverses*, vol. 3, The Hague: P. Husson, F. Boucquet et al., 1727 [Rotterdam: Reinier Lees, 1682], § 136.

[38] George J. Stigler, "Preface," in *The Wealth of Nations*, Chicago: University of Chicago Press, 1976, p. xi.

That property in any object, whereby it tends to produce benefit, advantage, pleasure, good, or happiness (all this in the present case comes to the same thing) or (what comes again to the same thing) to prevent the happening of mischief, pain, evil, or unhappiness to the party whose interest is considered: if that party be the community in general, then the happiness of the community: if a particular individual, then the happiness of that individual.[39]

As we have seen above, for Bentham, our interest is our pleasure, or happiness. All those terms are synonymous. It is clear, however, from this definition, that interest and utility are not synonymous. The utility of an object is its ability to provide pleasure. A judgment about utility is therefore a judgment on the adequacy between means and ends: is this the best way of providing pleasure? This is why the "principle of utility" is always associated with rational calculation:

By the principle of utility is meant that principle which approves or disapproves of every action whatsoever, according to the tendency which it appears to have to augment or diminish the happiness of the party whose interest is in question.[40]

To the extent that utility is understood as the adequacy between means and ends, Bentham's definition of utility is consistent with that of rational choice theorists like Elster, who postulate that the ends can be anything the agent chooses. Bentham, on the other hand, postulated that the end was pleasure. Consequently, he saw a close link between utility and pleasure, so much so that he decided to modify his vocabulary to make the link more apparent. Because "the word *utility* does not so clearly point to the ideas of *pleasure* and *pain* as the words *happiness* and *felicity* do,"[41] Bentham decided to use the terms "greatest happiness principle," or "greatest felicity principle" instead of "principle of utility." From a utilitarian point of view, the connection between interest and utility is therefore so strong, that economists have tended to equate the two notions.

On the issue of preferences, the dividing line is the same as in chapter 1 regarding the status of self-interest as a first principle. The assumption of stable preferences implies that "pleasure" or "interest" is the sole engine of human behavior. Values and principles do not matter because we never act according to our principles. Pleasure is the only motive and the stable preference behind our capricious changes in tastes and opinions. In this sense, Becker's "economic approach" is consistent with the Epicurean/Augustinian tradition exemplified by Mandeville, Bayle, and La Rochefoucauld. On the other hand, the assumption of changing preferences

---

[39] Bentham, *An Introduction to the Principles of Morals and Legislation*, 1.3, p. 12.
[40] Ibid., 1.2, p. 12.   [41] Ibid., footnote (a), added in 1822.

implies that we (sometimes) are capable of acting according to our principles. If that is the case, pleasure cannot be the only motive for human action. If one assumes changing preferences, one must also assume that motives other than pleasure are at work. Elster's assumption of changing preferences and the critique of Becker's "economic approach" that we find in Sen and Hirschman are consistent with Adam Smith's neo-Stoic critique of Mandeville in *The Theory of Moral Sentiments*.

In his summary of Mandeville's doctrine, Smith insists on the fact that, for Mandeville, it is impossible to sincerely prefer something other than one's interest:

> Dr Mandeville considers whatever is done from a sense of propriety, from a regard to what is commendable and praise-worthy, as being done from a love of praise and commendation, or as he calls it from vanity. Man, he observes, is naturally much more interested in his own happiness than in that of others, and it is impossible that in his heart he can ever really prefer their prosperity to his own ... All public spirit, therefore, all preference of public to private interest, is, according to him, a mere cheat and imposition upon mankind; and that human virtue which is so much boasted of, and which is the occasion of so much emulation among men, is the mere offspring of flattery begot upon pride.[42]

According to Mandeville, a preference for the public interest cannot be genuine, because we can only prefer our private interest. On the contrary, for Smith, understanding morality means understanding "how and by what means does it come to pass, that the mind prefers one tenor of conduct to another."[43] Like the Stoics, Smith understands human life in terms of choices and preferences. Preferences do matter.

Smith's account of the Stoic doctrine (which is in many ways also an account of his own) reveals the differences and similarities between his approach and Mandeville's. First of all, according to Stoic doctrine,

> The self-love of man embraced, if I may say so, his body and all its different members, his mind and all its different faculties and powers, and desired the preservation and maintenance of them all in their best and most perfect condition.[44]

Self-love, as a natural instinct, guides us and orients our behavior in such a way that the outcome will be the best possible one for us. What we find enunciated here is a principle of optimality, which Smith shares with Bentham as well as Mandeville. However, as we have seen in chapter 2, the Stoic conception of self-love is quite different from the Augustinian one. For the Stoics, self-love as an instinctual force converges with rational

---

[42] Smith, *The Theory of Moral Sentiments*, VII.ii.4.7.   [43] Ibid., VII.i.2.   [44] Ibid., VII.ii.1.16.

choice in carrying out the ends of nature. Therefore, self-love is not the only engine of human behavior. Self-love points the way, but the choices are made rationally.

For the Stoics, as Smith understands them, "virtue and the propriety of conduct" consist "in selecting always from the several objects of choice presented to us, that which was most to be chosen, when we could not obtain them all."[45] The objects of choice are not important in themselves. What matters is the way in which the preference rankings take place:

> By choosing and rejecting with this just and accurate discernment, by thus bestowing upon every object the precise degree of attention it deserved, according to the place which it held in this natural scale of things, we maintained, according to the Stoics, that perfect rectitude of conduct which constituted the essence of virtue. This was what they called to live consistently, to live according to nature, and to obey those laws and directions which nature, or the Author of nature, had prescribed for our conduct.[46]

Here again, it will be helpful to understand Smith's advocacy of Stoicism as a polemical response to the Epicurean/Augustinian tradition exemplified by Mandeville. For the Epicureans, morality and rational choice are not ends in themselves. The *summum bonum* is pleasure. For the Augustinians, the ultimate end is God (the only object capable of giving lasting pleasure). For Smith, advocating Stoicism implies that the ultimate end is neither God nor pleasure. The ultimate end is to live a good life by living "according to nature," i.e. rationally or "consistently." Modern rational choice theory would certainly not endorse the expression "living according to nature," but, like Smith and the Stoics, Elster postulates that, in order to be defined as rational, behavior must be made of internally consistent choices. The agent's beliefs must be internally consistent. The agent's set of desires must be internally consistent as well. Finally, as we have seen above, a set of beliefs being given, the agent's behavior must be "the best action with respect to the full set of weighed desires."[47] Elster even suggests some stronger forms of rationality that may include "rational" beliefs ("The best belief, given the available evidence") and even "rational" desires.

In a "deceptively simple sentence," Elster summarizes rational choice theory by saying that "when faced with several courses of action, people usually do what they believe to have the best overall outcome."[48] This sentence seems to echo the Stoic definition of moral action according to Smith: "Selecting always from among the several objects of choice presented to us,

---

[45] Ibid.   [46] Ibid.   [47] Elster, "The Nature and Scope of Rational-Choice Explanations," p. 64.
[48] Elster, *Nuts and Bolts for the Social Sciences*, p. 22.

that which was most to be chosen, when we could not obtain them all."
At the same time, Elster insists that "rational choice is instrumental: it is
guided by the outcome of the action."[49] The Stoics, on the contrary, insist
that the outcome of an action does not matter. What matters is the fact
that the agent chooses a course of action over another course of action.
We need therefore to complicate our classification by adding one notion:
consequentialism. We do find similar arguments against the interest doctrine in Hirschman, Sen, and Elster. All three agree that motives other
than pleasure or interest must be brought into play in the explanation of
human conduct. Elster, however, insists that rational choice is, by definition, guided by the outcome of the action. This is an instrumentalist, or
consequentialist view. To the extent that it espouses this consequentialist
view, rational choice theory belongs to the utilitarian tradition exemplified
by Bentham and Hume. It is quite possible to be a utilitarian and to reject
the interest doctrine at the same time. In fact, this position, which Elster
advocates, is very close to the position of the founder of utilitarianism,
David Hume. In his *Enquiry Concerning the Principles of Morals*, Hume
makes two main assertions. On the one hand, he states that actions should
be evaluated solely on the basis of their utility:

It may justly appear surprising, that any man, in so late an age, should find it
requisite to prove, by elaborate reasoning, that PERSONAL MERIT consists altogether in the possession of mental qualities, *useful* or *agreeable* to the *person himself*
or to *others*... Whatever is valuable in any kind, so naturally classes itself under
the division of useful or agreeable, the *utile* or the *dulce*, that it is not easy to
imagine, why we should ever seek farther, or consider the question as a matter of
nice research and inquiry.[50]

At the same time, Hume distances himself from the interest doctrine.
Saying that acts should be judged only with regard to their consequences
does not mean that self-interest is or should be the only motive for human
action. Of course, it pleases us to pursue our own interest, but we also find
pleasure in sympathy:

No man is absolutely indifferent to the happiness and misery of others. The first
has a natural tendency to give pleasure; the second, pain. This every one may find
in himself. It is not probable, that these principles can be resolved into principles
more simple and universal.[51]

---

[49] Ibid.
[50] David Hume, *Enquiry Concerning the Principles of Morals*, edited by J.B. Schneewind, Indianapolis: Hackett, 1983 [1777 edition; first edition, 1751], IX, I, p. 72.
[51] Ibid., V, II, p. 43.

The principle of sympathy must be distinguished from the principle of self-interest. Against Mandeville and La Rochefoucauld, Hume argues that self-interest is not a more universal and general principle to which the principle of sympathy could be subordinated. As first principles, self-interest and sympathy must remain separate. As we have seen in chapter 1, Smith followed and developed this line of reasoning in *The Theory of Moral Sentiments*.

Smith follows Hume's argument regarding first principles. However, he departs from Hume's utilitarian assumptions. Like Hume, Smith allowed sympathy as a motive, but he did it on very different philosophical grounds. As we have seen in chapter 2, Smith refutes the interest doctrine from a neo-Stoic point of view. Like the Stoics, Smith does not primarily judge an action on the basis of its outcome, but rather on the adequacy between means and ends. For Smith, the highest form of philosophical activity consists in admiring not the "conveniency or pleasure" of something, but rather "the exact adjustment of the means for attaining any conveniency or pleasure."[52] This applies to what we now call the economy: "the perfection of police, the extension of trade and manufactures." On the one hand, "all constitutions of government...are valued only in proportion as they tend to promote the happiness of those who live under them."[53] This is the utilitarian or consequentialist point of view: the value of an act is determined by its outcome. However, according to Smith, "from a certain love of art and contrivance, we sometimes seem to value the means more than the end, and to be eager to promote the happiness of our fellow-creatures, rather from a view to perfect and improve a certain beautiful and orderly system, than from any immediate sense or feeling of what they suffer or enjoy."[54] This is a non-consequentialist view, grounded in Stoic assumptions. What matters is not the outcome, but the harmonious relationship between the means and the ends. It is this relationship itself, rather than the outcome, that is the end of moral action. For Smith, this view has political consequences. One is unlikely to motivate citizens to serve the public good by showing them "what superior advantages the subjects of a well-governed state enjoy; that they are better lodged, that they are better clothed, that they are better fed."[55] According to Smith, "these considerations will commonly make no great impression."[56] In other words, utilitarian arguments, and the use of incentives (to borrow a term from the vocabulary of economics) will do little to produce public-minded citizens. A much more effective approach

[52] Smith, *The Theory of Moral Sentiments*, IV.1.3.　　[53] Ibid., IV.1.11.
[54] Ibid.　[55] Ibid.　[56] Ibid.

will consist in focusing not on the results, but on the way the results are achieved:

> You will be more likely to persuade, if you describe the great system of public police which procures these advantages, if you explain the connexions and dependencies of its several parts, their mutual subordination to one another, and their general subserviency to the happiness of the society; if you show how this system might be introduced into his own country, what it is that hinders it from taking place there at present, how those obstructions might be removed, and all the several wheels of the machine of government be made to move with more harmony and smoothness, without grating upon one another, or mutually retarding one another's motions. It is scarce possible that a man should listen to a discourse of this kind, and not feel himself animated to some degree of public spirit.[57]

From a Stoic point of view, the value of a system does not result in its output, but rather in its "economy," that is to say in the relationship between the whole and the parts. According to Smith, to admire the relationship between the whole and the parts, to admire the adequacy between means and ends, is the highest form of philosophical activity. It is also the strongest source of inspiration for "public virtue."[58]

It appears that Sen and Hirschman are very close to these views when they question the value of economic incentives in the formulation of public policy. Hirschman takes issue with those who seek to deal with unethical or antisocial behavior by raising the cost of this behavior. This approach, says Hirschman, overlooks the fact that people are capable of changing their values, and that changes in values may result in changes in behavior.[59] In the same spirit, Sen remarks that the economic approach gives good results when applied to market goods and services, but questionable results when applied to "public goods" (roads or public parks, for instance). When people are being asked to state their preferences regarding public goods, they will often give responses that are not dictated by their own interest, but rather by a concern for the public interest:

> What is at issue is not whether people invariably give an honest answer to every question, but whether they always give a gains-maximizing answer, or at any rate, whether they give gains-maximizing answers often enough to make that the appropriate general assumption for economic theory. The presence of non-gains-maximizing answers, including truthful ones, immediately brings in commitment as a part of behavior.[60]

By positing "commitment" as an important motive for human behavior, Sen implies at least two things. On the one hand, he rejects the notion that

---

[57] Ibid.   [58] Ibid.
[59] Hirschman, "Against Parsimony," p. 146.   [60] Sen, "Rational Fools," p. 332.

self-interest alone motivates human conduct. In this, he is in agreement with the type of utilitarianism exemplified by Hume. On the other hand, he rejects the consequentialist view according to which the value of an action is determined by its utility. According to Sen, "commitment sometimes relates to a sense of obligation going beyond the consequences."[61] An act based on commitment should not be judged primarily on its outcome, but rather on its conformity with a rule of conduct. This position contradicts Hume's (and Elster's) utilitarianism. More generally, it contradicts the assumption of utility-maximizing behavior. As Elster puts it, there are two main mechanisms at work in human behavior: "rational choice" and "social norms."[62] Rational choice is instrumental, and maximizes utility. Behavior based on norms does not maximize utility: "Action guided by social norms is not outcome-oriented."[63] A good example of norms-based behavior is the behavior of the Stoic sage in *The Theory of Moral Sentiments*. For Smith, the Stoic wise man concerns himself with the propriety of the choices he makes, but not with the outcome of these choices, because the outcome is not up to us:

The propriety or impropriety of his endeavours might be of great consequence to him. Their success or disappointment could be of none at all; could excite no passionate joy or sorrow, no passionate desire or aversion. If he preferred some events to others, if some situations were the objects of his choice and others of his rejection, it was not because he regarded the one as in themselves in any respect better than the other, or thought that his own happiness would be more complete in what is called the fortunate than in what is regarded as the distressful situation; but because the propriety of action, the rule which the Gods had given him for the direction of his conduct, required him to choose and reject in this manner.[64]

Let us go back to the example of public policy we discussed earlier. Smith postulates that the best way of having public-minded citizens is to show them the beautiful adequacy between means and ends in a particular system of government. This view questions not only the assumption of self-interest (people are not motivated by the idea that a better system of government will make them better off personally). It also questions the assumption of maximizing utility: the public-minded citizen who works to improve the system of government is not interested in the outcome (better housing for all, better food production for all, etc.). Building an efficient system is an end in itself. This is non-instrumental behavior.

It appears that there are at least three ways of understanding the relationship between "preferences" and "utility-maximizing behavior." For Becker,

[61] Ibid., p. 342.   [62] Elster, *Nuts and Bolts for the Social Sciences*, p. 13.
[63] Ibid., p. 113.   [64] Smith, *The Theory of Moral Sentiments*, VII.ii.1.21.

we have stable preferences *and* we maximize utility. Therefore, maximizing utility means pursuing pleasure rationally. This position is consistent with Bentham's utilitarianism. For Elster, on the other hand, maximizing utility has no implication of hedonism. A non-selfish choice may maximize utility just as well as a selfish one. At the same time, Elster's position remains a utilitarian one in the sense that the choice is guided by the outcome of the action. These views are consistent with Hume's form of utilitarianism. Finally, Sen and Hirschman also argue for changing preferences, thus rejecting the notion that self-interest or pleasure alone is the motive of human conduct. But they assume that preference changes are caused by the formation of meta-preferences, which are one step removed from the consequences of an action. In that sense, choices cannot always be guided by the outcome of the action. This position consists in arguing that norms-based behavior must be taken into account when explaining human activity in general, and economic activity in particular. As we have seen above, the assumption of self-interest is not essential to utilitarianism. However, utilitarianism demands utility-maximizing behavior. Because behavior based on commitment does not maximize utility, Sen and Hirschman question not only the assumption of self-interest, but also the utilitarian foundations of economic theory. It is no small irony that Adam Smith's neo-Stoicism is consistent with both the notion of changing preferences (self-interest is not the only first principle) and the rejection of utilitarianism (behavior is not always concerned with outcomes).

BAYLE AND MANDEVILLE ON INCONSISTENCY

According to Hirschman, two elements characterize interest-propelled action: self-centeredness, and rational calculation. Hirschman believes that the second element is the defining one:

> Calculation could be considered the dominant or fundamental element: once action is supposed to be informed only by careful estimation of costs and benefits, with most weight necessarily being given to those that are better known and more quantifiable, it tends to become self-referential by virtue of the simple fact that each person is best informed about his or her own desires, satisfactions, disappointments, and sufferings.[65]

For Hirschman, saying that human action is self-interested can have two meanings. The thesis can be understood to mean that we act according

---

[65] Albert O. Hirschman, "The Concept of Interest: From Euphemism to Tautology," in *Rival Views of Market Society*, p. 36.

to what we think is best for us. This is a near-tautology: our interest is what we think it is. The thesis may also mean that action is preceded by a cost–benefit analysis. Such a proposition is not empty. What gives content to the concept of self-interest is the idea of rational calculation. As we have seen above, the assumption of self-interest is not essential to utilitarianism, nor is it to rational choice theory. However, the assumption of maximizing utility (or, as Hirschman puts it, "rational calculation") is indispensable.

Economic theory is based upon the close association between the notion of self-centeredness and the notion of rational calculation. As we have seen above, economists often see these two notions as so intricately related that they tend to subsume them into one notion: self-interest. Hirschman is quite right to notice that rational calculation is what gives meaning to the notion of self-interest as economists understand it. However, if one looks back to the original debates on the notion of self-interest, it appears that self-centeredness is not necessarily tied to rational calculation. So far, we have considered three combinations: utility maximization and stable preferences (standard economic theory); utility maximization and changing preferences (rational choice according to Elster); and attempts by Sen and Hirschman to revise economic theory by questioning both utility maximization and stable preferences. The remaining combination is: stable preferences (i.e. selfish motives) without maximization of utility (i.e. without rational calculation, or with faulty rational calculation). This remaining combination, generally absent from contemporary theory, coincides with the vast field of Epicurean/Augustinian thinking in the seventeenth and eighteenth centuries.

In *The Fable of the Bees*, Cleomenes seeks to show that it is possible to assume that all human behavior is self-interested, even when empirical observation informs us that we do not do what is best for us:

Cleomenes. Every individual is a little world by itself, and all creatures, as far as their understanding and abilities will let them, endeavor to make that self happy. This in all of them is the continual labor, and seems to be the whole design of life. Hence it follows, that in the choice of things men must be determined by the perception they have of happiness; and no person can commit or set about an action, which at that then present time seems not to be the best for him.

In this passage, Cleomenes begins by posing the Epicurean/Augustinian principle according to which all actions are motivated by pleasure. He then takes the reasoning one step further. If it is true that we seek happiness in everything we do, this must mean that the search for happiness is our actual intent, even when what we do makes us unhappy. In response, Horatius

brings up Ovid's famous line: "I see the better and approve it, but I follow
the worse":

Horatius. What will you say then to, *video meliora proboque, deteriora sequor?*[66]

In Ovid's poem, the character uttering these words is Medea, who realizes
she is falling in love with Jason against her best judgment. The objection
consists in saying that it cannot possibly be Medea's intent to be happy
because she can foresee that loving Jason will make her miserable. This
objection does not deter Cleomenes:

Cleomenes. That only shows the turpitude of our inclinations. But men may say as
they please. Every motion in a free agent which he does not approve of, is either
convulsive, or it is not his; I speak of those that are subject to the will. When two
things are left to a person's choice, it is a demonstration, that he thinks that most
eligible which he chooses, how contradictory, impertinent, or pernicious soever
his reason for choosing it may be. When two things are left to a person's choice,
it is a demonstration, that he thinks that most eligible which he chooses, and it
would be injustice to punish men for their crimes.[67]

Cleomenes distinguishes between involuntary and voluntary actions, in
order to show that the pleasure principle applies to all voluntary actions
("those that are subject to the will"). Whenever we act against our best
interests, even when we know we are acting against our best interests, it
remains true that we are choosing what we think is "most eligible." Our
reasoning may be faulty or inconsistent, but our behavior remains entirely
intentional. As Elster puts it, behavior can be intentional and irrational at
the same time.[68]

   Mandeville's point on *video meliora* is not the trivial remark that passions
point one way and reason points the other way. It is that acts dictated by the
passions are voluntary. They are acts of the will.[69] Mandeville's perspective is
Augustinian. It must be understood in the light of Augustine's conception
of a will structurally divided against itself (see chapter 2). These kinds
of intrinsically contradictory psychological states have attracted Elster's

---

[66] Ovid, *Metamorphoses*, translated by Frank Justus Miller, Cambridge, MA: Harvard University Press,
   1916, vol. I, VII, 20–21.
[67] Mandeville, *The Fable of the Bees*, vol. 2, p. 178.
[68] Elster, "The Nature and Scope of Rational-Choice Explanations," p. 65.
[69] The Augustinian conception of the will may be hard to grasp for the modern reader, who understands
   the will in a Cartesian way as the ability to act against one's strongest inclinations. For Augustine,
   voluntas is the sum total of our desires. For a modern discussion of what it is "to want to want,"
   see Harry G. Frankfurt, "Freedom of the Will and the Concept of Reason," *Journal of Philosophy*
   68:1 (1971), pp. 5–20; also by the same author, *Necessity, Volition and Love*, Cambridge: Cambridge
   University Press, 1999.

attention. The simplest case is a contradiction between two desires. A more subtle case is a contradiction within the desire itself. As Elster points out, there is an internal contradiction in the will to be natural or spontaneous. Similarly, one cannot logically will an absence of will, or will to believe.[70] Yet this type of contradictory willing is common. In the Augustinian tradition, weakness of the will is a sign of the fallen nature of humanity. As we have seen in chapter 2, Augustine meditates on the fact that the human will is never in control of itself. The body obeys the commands of the will. However, the will does not obey its own commands:

Finally, in the very fever of my indecision, I made many motions with my body; like men do when they will to act but cannot, either because they do not have the limbs or because their limbs are bound or weakened by disease, or incapacitated in some other way. Thus if I tore my hair, struck my forehead, or, entwining my fingers, clasped my knee, these I did because I willed it. But I might have willed it and still not have done it, if the nerves had not obeyed my will. Many things then I did, in which the will and power to do were not the same. Yet I did not do that one thing which seemed to me infinitely more desirable, which before long I should have power to will because shortly when I willed, I would will with a single will. For in this, the power of willing is the power of doing; and as yet I could not do it. Thus my body more readily obeyed the slightest wish of the soul in moving its limbs at the order of my mind than my soul obeyed itself to accomplish in the will alone its great resolve.[71]

When the will commands itself to love God and hate sin, the will does not act upon that command. The reason for this, according to Augustine, is that the will does not will entirely, "for if the will were whole and entire, it would not even command it to be, because it would already be."[72] In that sense "it is, therefore, no strange anomaly partly to will and partly to be unwilling. This is actually an infirmity of mind."[73]

As Elster points out, "although rational action is instrumental, some forms of instrumental action are downright irrational. Insomnia, impotence

---

[70] See Jon Elster, *Ulysses and the Sirens: Studies in Rationality and Irrationality*, Cambridge: Cambridge University Press, 1979, 3.9, *Sour Grapes: Studies in the Subversion of Rationality*, Cambridge: Cambridge University Press, 1983, 2.2, and *Nuts and Bolts for the Social Sciences*, chapter 3.

[71] "Denique tam multa faciebam corpore in ipsis cunctationis aestibus, quae aliquando volunt homines, et non valent, si aut ipsa membra non habeant, aut ea vel colligata vinculis, vel resoluta languore, vel quoquo modo impedita sint. Si vulsi capillum, si percussi frontem, si consertis digitis amplexatus sum genu; quia volui, feci. Potui autem velle et non facere, si mobilitas membrorum non obsequeretur. Tam multa ergo feci, ubi non hoc erat velle quod posse: et non faciebam quod et incomparabili affectu amplius mihi placebat, et mox ut vellem, possem; quia mox ut vellem, utique vellem. Ibi enim facultas ea quae voluntas, et ipsum velle jam facere erat; et tamen non fiebat: faciliusque obtemperabat corpus tenuissimae voluntati animae, ut ad nutum mentis membra moverentur, quam ipsa sibi anima ad voluntatem suam magnam in sola voluntate perficiendam." Augustine, *Confessions*, translated by Albert C. Outler, Philadelphia: Westminster Press, 1955, 8.8.20.

[72] "Nam si plena esset [voluntas], nec imperaret ut esset, quia jam esset." Ibid., 8.8.21.

[73] "Non igitur monstrum partim velle, partim nolle; sed aegritudo animi est." Ibid.

and stuttering get worse if one tries to do something about them."[74] Similarly, "we cannot believe at will or forget at will, at least not in the sense in which one can raise one's arm at will."[75] The mention of sexual impotence is particularly interesting from an Augustinian point of view. For Augustine, the workings of sexual desire have a paradigmatic value. They are the clearest symptom of the original sin. According to Augustine, before the Fall, Adam was able to move his sexual organ at will, exactly in the way in which one can raise one's arm at will:

Is there any reason why we should not believe that before the sin of disobedience and its punishment of corruptibility, the members of a man's body could have been the servants of man's will without any lust, for the procreation of children?[76]

The lesson to be learned from the workings of sexual desire is that we cannot will to will. Desire comes and goes no matter what we will. This, according to Augustine, is the consequence and manifestation of the original sin:

It was because man forsook God by pleasing himself that he was handed over to himself, and because he did not obey God he could not obey himself.[77]

For the Augustinians, akratic behavior, or weakness of the will, is not a specific pathology, to be distinguished from commonly healthy behavior. It is a disease that affects human nature itself. The disease manifests itself most clearly in the relationship between desire and time. According to the Augustinian tradition, our bent for pleasure is such that we necessarily seek immediate gratification. As Derek Parfit points out, seeking immediate gratification is not necessarily irrational. I could rationally decide that only my present desires matter, and act consistently upon that belief.[78] Irrationality arises when our discounting of the future is such that we do not hold consistently to past decisions. If I make the rational calculation that a great pleasure next month is more desirable than a small pleasure now, start acting upon that belief, and suddenly decide to have the small pleasure now, for no other reason than its immediate availability, my behavior is irrational.

Saying that such behavior is irrational is another way of saying that it does not maximize utility. Augustinian anthropology is based on the observation that human behavior rarely maximizes utility (this, of course, for reasons

---

[74] Elster, *Nuts and Bolts for the Social Sciences*, p. 24.   [75] Ibid.

[76] "Quid causae est, ut non credamus ante inobedientiae peccatum corruptionisque supplicium, ad propagandam prolem sine ulla libidine servire voluntati humanae humana membra potuisse?" Augustine, *The City of God*, translated by John O'Meara, London: Penguin Books, 1984, XIV, 24.

[77] "Donatus est itaque homo sibi, quia deseruit Deum placendo sibi: et non obediens Deo, non potuit obedire nec sibi." Ibid.

[78] See Derek Parfit, *Reasons and Persons*, Oxford: Clarendon Press, 1984, chapter 6.

entirely different from those proposed by Sen). This human irrationality
and inconsistency is rendered more acute by the assumption that human
behavior, except when inspired by divine grace, is always self-centered. As
Pascal puts it, "each has fancies contrary to his own good, in the very idea
he has of good, and this oddity is disconcerting."[79]

The Augustinian interpretation of suicide, which we have discussed already in chapter 1, offers a clear example of self-centered yet irrational
behavior. Mandeville insists that

whoever kills himself by choice, must do it to avoid something which he dreads
more than that death which he chooses. Therefore, how absurd soever a person's
reasoning may be, there is in all suicide a palpable intention of kindness to one's
self.[80]

Mandeville begins by positing that suicide is a voluntary act. This is
consistent with his assumption that "when two things are left to a person's choice, it is a demonstration, that he thinks that most eligible which
he chooses."[81] Because we can only do what pleases us, those who commit suicide seek their own welfare. Their behavior, however, is irrational,
because concern for their own welfare prompts them consecutively, and inconsistently, to seek to preserve themselves, and then to destroy themselves.
Suicide is an example of self-interested behavior that does not maximize
utility. This, according to Augustine, is true of human behavior in general.
We seek happiness in all we do. Yet, all we do makes us unhappy: "Man
has undoubtedly the will to be happy, even when he pursues happiness by
living in a way which makes it impossible of attainment."[82] For Augustine,
the hedonistic impulse combined with a failure to maximize utility is the
very definition of sin:

For sin only happens by an act of will; and our will is for our own welfare, or for the
avoidance of misfortune. And hence the falsehood: we commit sin to promote our
welfare, and it results instead in our misfortune; or we sin to increase our welfare,
and the result is rather to increase our misfortune.[83]

It is worth noticing that Augustine does not condemn the hedonistic
impulse per se. On the contrary, the desire to be happy is a sign that

<hr/>

[79] Blaise Pascal, *Pensées*, translated by A.J. Krailsheimer, London: Penguin Books, 1966, fragment 805.
"Chacun a des fantaisies contraires à son propre bien dans l'idée même qu'il a du bien. Et c'est une
bizarrerie qui met hors de gamme." *Pensées*, edited by Louis Lafuma, Paris: Seuil, 1963, fragment 805
(Sellier 653).
[80] Mandeville, *The Fable of the Bees*, vol. 2, p. 136.   [81] Ibid., p. 178.
[82] "Beatus quippe vult esse, etiam non sic vivendo ut possit esse." Augustine, *The City of God*, XIV, 4.
[83] "Non enim fit peccatum, nisi ea voluntate, qua volumus ut bene sit nobis, vel nolumus ut male sit
nobis. Ergo mendacium est, quod cum fiat ut bene sit nobis, hinc potius male est nobis; vel cum
fiat ut melius sit nobis, hinc potius pejus est nobis." Ibid.

humans aspire to the full happiness they enjoyed before the Fall. The focus of Augustinian moral reflection is on the failure to maximize utility. For instance Pascal notices that, while "all men seek happiness," no one has ever found a way of reaching it:

Yet for very many years no one without faith has ever reached the goal at which everyone is continually aiming. All men complain: princes, subjects, nobles, commoners, old, young, strong, weak, learned, ignorant, healthy, sick, in every country, at every time, of all ages, and all conditions.[84]

Experience tells us that the things we do to reach happiness do not bring happiness. Yet we keep doing these things in order to reach happiness. In that sense, human behavior is fundamentally irrational. According to Pascal, we rationalize this irrational behavior by minimizing the value of experience:

A test which has gone on so long, without pause or change, really ought to convince us that we are incapable of attaining the good by our own efforts. But example teaches us very little. No two examples are so exactly alike, that there is not some subtle difference, and that is what makes us expect that our expectations will not be disappointed this time as they were last time.[85]

If we applied the rules of scientific induction to our own lives, we would necessarily draw the conclusion that there is a fundamental inadequacy between means and ends in our search for happiness. However, in the moral realm, we see every event as unique. This prevents us from seeing the moral value of experience.

A similar focus on irrationality is present in Pascal's wager. In the wager argument, Pascal compares human life to a game of dice, or a game of cards, where players bet money.[86] The concrete problem Pascal refers to (a problem for which his gambler friends had requested a mathematical solution) is the following: one player wishes to leave the game before the end. His bets are on the table. How much can he fairly take back in order to let the other players continue the game without him? In Pascal's argument,

---

[84] "Et cependant depuis un si grand nombre d'années jamais personne, sans la foi, n'est arrivé à ce point où tous visent continuellement. Tous se plaignent, princes, sujets, nobles, roturiers, vieux, jeunes, forts, faibles, savants, ignorants, sains, malades, de tous pays, de tous les temps, de tous âges, et de toutes conditions." Pascal, *Pensées*, fragment 148 (Sellier 181).

[85] "Une épreuve si longue, si continuelle et si uniforme devrait bien nous convaincre de notre impuissance d'arriver au bien par nos efforts. Mais l'exemple nous instruit peu. Il n'est jamais si parfaitement semblable qu'il n'y ait quelque délicate différence et c'est de là que nous attendons que notre attente ne sera pas déçue en cette occasion comme en l'autre." Ibid.

[86] I follow the interpretation of Pascal's wager proposed by Laurent Thirouin in *Le Hasard et les règles. Le modèle du jeu dans la Pensée de Pascal*, Paris: Vrin, 1991, pp. 130–189.

human life is such a game. The game is going to be interrupted soon (by death). The question for the player is: should I take my money (my life) back, or should I leave it on the table in the hope that I might get more than I wagered? Pascal then performs a rational calculation of probabilities, and shows that it is infinitely advantageous for the player to stay in the game, provided that there is at least one chance of winning against a finite number of chances of losing. Hirschman argues that Pascal's wager "was nothing but an attempt to demonstrate that belief in God (hence conduct in accordance with His precepts) was strictly in our (long-term) self-interest."[87] This characterization is not inaccurate, but the focus of Pascal's argument lies elsewhere. Pascal is not exactly saying that you should believe in God because it is in your interest to do so. As Abbadie pointed out, such an interpretation of the wager is open to the criticism that it is irrational to believe something because one wishes it to be true:

> It has been objected to Monsieur Pascal, who has worked to illustrate this thought, that persuasion does not always succeed when it is based on something one wishes to be true, or if it does, that one should be suspicious of a belief born of our desires; so much so that we must prove the existence of God, rather than show that it is in our interest to believe. Those who reason in this way, do not understand the real use of this thought, which is not to convince the mind, but rather to pull the heart in the direction of a truth from which it has strayed, and to answer the secret objections of self-love: but what if religion were not true? But what if there were not God?[88]

For Abbadie, saying that one should demonstrate the existence of God rather than saying that it is in our interest to believe misses the point. It is true enough that the wager is not, nor does it mean to be, a proof of the existence of God. The rational calculation is aimed at proving that, in the absence of any knowledge regarding the existence of God, it is prudent to bet that he exists. However, Pascal does not expect his interlocutor to act on this belief. The interlocutor is convinced of the validity of the rational calculation that has been presented to him: "This is conclusive, and if men are capable of any truth, this is it." Yet he says: "I am being held fast and

---

[87] Hirschman, "The Concept of Interest," p. 48.

[88] "On a objecté à Monsieur Pascal, qui s'est attaché à donner du jour à cette pensée, qu'on ne se persuade pas toujours ce qu'on désire, ou que si l'on en vient là, on doit se défier d'une opinion qui naît de nos désirs, et qu'ainsi il faut nous prouver l'existence de Dieu, et non pas nous faire voir qu'il est de notre intérêt de la croire. Ceux qui raisonnent ainsi, ne connaissent pas le véritable usage de cette pensée, qui est non de convaincre l'esprit, mais d'ôter au cœur l'éloignement qu'il a pour cette vérité, et de répondre à ces objections secrètes de l'amour propre: mais si la religion n'était point véritable? Mais s'il n'y avait point de Dieu?" Jacques Abbadie, *Traité de la vérité de la religion chrétienne*, Rotterdam: Reinier Leers, 1684, p. 139.

I am so made that I cannot believe." At this point, Pascal's argument consists in saying: you believe that it is rational to bet that God exists, yet you do not act upon this belief. Your behavior does not maximize utility. It is irrational. The realization that his behavior is irrational must lead the interlocutor to look into himself in order to understand the causes of his irrationality. These causes reside essentially in the fact that the interlocutor does not assess the value of his own life in a consistent way. On one hand, he agrees with Pascal that his life is one life, to be compared to the possibility of eternal life. On the other hand, self-love secretly prompts him to put an inordinately high price on his own life. Pascal's response to his interlocutor is that the fault does not lie with the argument, but rather with the interlocutor himself, who behaves inconsistently: "If you are unable to believe, it is because of your passions."[89] The conclusion of the wager argument is therefore a moral one:

Since reason impels you to believe and yet you cannot do so, concentrate then not on convincing yourself by multiplying proofs of God's existence but by diminishing your passions.[90]

Pascal's wager is characteristic of an Augustinian strategy that consists in positing the rational pursuit of self-interest as a norm, in order to show that human behavior ordinarily deviates from this norm. For Bayle, we do not pursue self-interest rationally, because our pleasure–pain calculus is always skewed in favor of pleasure:

One sees no difficulty in going toward sorrow and pain, provided that we encounter joy first, nor in going through pain and sorrow, provided that we are headed toward pleasure. This is made manifest in the example of so many girls, who get carried away by the weight of immediate pleasure, and allow themselves to act in ways they know will bring a long series of bitter consequences, and also in the example of so many people who know from experience that consuming certain foods or drinking excessively has resulted in horrible pain, and still satisfy their appetite with those things whenever the opportunity arises. I have heard of Corsicans who, after suffering an offense, remained for days in the bushes waiting for their enemy, and were quite happy grazing on roots, as long as they could experience the joy of making a successful ambush.[91]

[89] "Votre impuissance à croire vient de vos passions." Pascal, *Pensées*, fragment 418 (Sellier 680).
[90] "Puisque la raison vous y porte et que néanmoins vous ne le pouvez, travaillez donc non pas à vous convaincre par l'augmentation des preuves de Dieu, mais par la diminution de vos passions." Ibid.
[91] "On ne fait pas difficulté d'aller au chagrin et à la douleur, pourvu qu'on passe par la joie, ni de passer par la douleur et par le chagrin, pourvu qu'on aille au plaisir. Cela paraît par l'exemple de tant de jeunes filles qui emportées par le poids victorieux du plaisir présent, se laissent aller à des actions, qu'elles savent bien qui entraînent après elles une longue suite d'amertumes, et par l'exemple de tant de gens qui ont éprouvé mille fois que l'usage de certaines viandes et le trop boire leur ont causé des

Bayle considers the behavior of those drawn by the weight of immediate pleasure (*le poids du plaisir présent*). They seek immediate gratification while being rationally convinced that they will pay dearly for it later. Under a strict rational choice interpretation, this type of behavior is not irrational. It is driven by a strong preference for the present, but preference for the present, as Elster points out "is just another preference."[92] As such, it is not "subject to rational assessment."[93] Elster adds that we cannot expect addicts and other people with very high time discounting "to reduce their rate of time discounting, because to want to be motivated by long-term concerns ipso facto is to be motivated by long-term concerns."[94] This is true enough: as Augustine puts it, "if the will were whole and entire, it would not even command it to be, because it would already be."[95] Strictly speaking, to want to be motivated by long-term concerns and to be motivated by long-term concerns is the same thing. The point of Augustinian psychology, however, is to show that our desires themselves are inconsistent. The will is divided against itself. We want immediate gratification and long-term gratification at the same time, even though we can only have one or the other.

To illustrate this point, let us take Pascal's analysis of *divertissement* (diversion). Philosophers, say Pascal, have noticed the following paradox: men go through a lot of trouble in order to reach the rest they would have if they did not exercise themselves in the first place. The classic philosophical criticism of human behavior is therefore: why don't you stay home instead of going through all this hustle and bustle? You would enjoy the rest you say you're looking for. To this criticism, those who practice *divertissement* could respond that what they are really after is not the rest, but rather the agitation itself:

When men are reproached for pursuing so eagerly something that could never satisfy them, their proper answer, if they really thought about it, ought to be that they simply want a violent and vigorous occupation to take their minds off themselves, and that is why they choose some attractive object to entice them in ardent pursuit.[96]

---

douleurs épouvantables, qui ne laissent pas de contenter leur appétit là-dessus, quand ils en trouvent l'occasion. Il y a des Corses, qui, après une offense reçue, se sont tenus cachés quinze jours entiers dans les broussailles pour attendre leur ennemi, trop satisfait d'y brouter quelques racines, pourvu qu'ils eussent la joie de voir réussir l'embuscade." Bayle, *Pensées diverses*, § 167.

[92] Jon Elster, *Strong Feelings: Emotion, Addiction and Human Behavior*, Cambridge, MA: MIT Press, 1999, p. 146.

[93] Ibid.   [94] Ibid.

[95] "Nam si plena esset [voluntas], nec imperaret ut esset, quia jam esset." Augustine, *Confessions*, 8.9.21.

[96] "Et ainsi quand on leur reproche que ce qu'ils recherchent avec tant d'ardeur ne saurait les satisfaire, s'ils répondaient comme ils devraient le faire, s'ils y pensaient bien, qu'ils ne recherchent en cela qu'une occupation violente et impétueuse qui les détourne de penser à soi et que c'est pour cela qu'ils se proposent un objet attirant qui les charme et les attire..." Pascal, *Pensées*, fragment 136 (Sellier 168).

Such a response, says Pascal, would be perfectly rational, and "their opponents could find no answer to that."[97] In other words, if we pursued *divertissement* knowingly and consistently, our behavior could not be criticized. However, Pascal adds, "they do not answer like that because they do not know themselves. They do not know that all they want is the hunt and not the capture."[98] According to Pascal, the true paradox of *divertissement* lies not in the inadequacy between means and ends (pursuing rest through agitation). It lies in the fact that our desires themselves are inconsistent. We want rest and agitation at the same time:

They have a secret instinct driving them to seek external diversion and occupation, and this is the result of their constant sense of wretchedness. They have another secret instinct, left over from the greatness of our original nature, telling them that the only true happiness lies in rest and not in excitement. These two contrary instincts rise to a confused plan buried out of sight in the depth of their soul, which leads them to seek rest by ways of activity and always to imagine that the satisfaction they miss will come to them once they overcome certain obvious difficulties and can open the door to welcome rest.

All our life passes in this way: we seek rest by struggling against certain obstacles, and once they are overcome, rest proves intolerable because of the boredom it produces. We must get away from it and crave excitement.[99]

In other words, we generally fail to maximize utility but, paradoxically, this does not come from a failure of rationality: we do everything we reasonably can to obtain the things we want. The problem is that the things we want are incompatible: what we must do to enjoy rest prevents us from enjoying excitement, and vice versa. The most perfect rational calculation could never maximize utility when the desires themselves are inconsistent.

There are important similarities between the Augustinian meditations on self-interest, and the utilitarian doctrine developed by Bentham at the end of the eighteenth century. Augustinians and Epicureans always reason

---

97 "Ils laisseraient leurs adversaires sans répartie." Ibid.
98 "Mais ils ne répondent pas cela parce qu'ils ne se connaissent pas eux-mêmes. Ils ne savent pas que ce n'est que la chasse et non la prise qu'ils recherchent." Ibid.
99 "Ils ont un instinct secret qui les porte à chercher le divertissement et l'occupation au-dehors, qui vient du ressentiment de leurs misères continuelles. Et ils ont un autre instinct secret qui reste de la grandeur de notre première nature, qui leur fait connaître que le bonheur n'est en effet que dans le repos et non pas dans le tumulte. Et de ces deux instincts contraires il se forme en eux un projet confus qui se cache à leur vue dans le fond de leur âme qui les porte à tendre au repos par l'agitation et à se figurer toujours que la satisfaction qu'ils n'ont point leur arrivera si en surmontant quelques difficultés qu'ils envisagent ils peuvent s'ouvrir par là la porte au repos. Ainsi s'écoule toute la vie, on cherche le repos en combattant quelques obstacles. Et si on les a surmontés, le repos devient insupportable par l'ennui qu'il engendre. Il en faut sortir et mendier le tumulte. " Ibid.

on the basis of a pleasure–pain calculus. They all assume that pleasure is the
only motivating factor in human behavior. The difference lies in the views
regarding rationality, or maximizing utility. The focus of the combined
Epicurean/Augustinian tradition (up to and including Mandeville) is on
the failure to maximize utility: we seek pleasure, but we do it inconsistently.
A critique of human behavior is always implied. This critique may state
its religious assumptions (Pascal), present itself simply as moral reflections
(La Rochefoucauld), or it may manifest itself as satire (Bayle, Mandeville).
By the middle of the eighteenth century, the idea that our desires are
internally inconsistent because of the original sin disappears almost entirely.
As Vauvenargues puts it, "there are no contradictions in nature."[100] This
goes against the traditional Augustinian idea that there is a contradiction
within human nature itself. Without naming them, Vauvenargues criticizes
the seventeenth-century moralists who presented human nature as a puzzle:

> False philosophers try to attract the attention of men by mentioning contrarieties
> and difficulties in our minds that are of their own making. They are like those who
> amuse children with card tricks and fool their judgment, even though the cards
> are natural, and without magic. Those who make up difficulties in order to resolve
> them are the charlatans of morals.[101]

Because there is no inconsistency in our desires, Vauvenargues submits
that we should trust our heart to determine our preferences, and our reason
to maximize utility: "Our heart should list our interests in the proper order,
and our reason should pursue them."[102] This maxim is a direct echo, and
an implicit critique, of La Rochefoucauld's maxim 66, which presents a
more complicated picture of the human heart:

> Clever men should list their interests in the proper order, and pursue each in turn.
> In our eagerness we often attempt too many things at once, and by wishing too
> much for the small ones we lose the big.[103]

[100] "Il n'y a point de contradictions dans la nature." Luc de Clapiers, marquis de Vauvenargues,
Réflexions et maximes, in *Introduction à la connaissance de l'esprit humain*, Paris: Briasson, 1747,
maxim 289.
[101] "Les faux philosophes s'efforcent d'attirer l'attention des hommes, en faisant remarquer dans notre
esprit des contrariétés et des difficultés qu'ils forment eux-mêmes, comme d'autres amusent les
enfants par des tours de cartes qui confondent leur jugement, quoique naturels et sans magie. Ceux
qui nouent ainsi les choses pour avoir le mérite de les dénouer sont les charlatans de la morale."
Ibid., maxim 288.
[102] "C'est à notre cœur à régler le rang de nos intérêts, et à notre raison de les conduire." Ibid., maxim
306.
[103] La Rochefoucauld, *The Maxims*, maxim 66 (translation modified). "Un habile homme doit régler le
rang de ses intérêts et les conduire chacun dans son ordre. Notre avidité le trouble souvent en nous
faisant courir à tant de choses à la fois que, pour désirer trop les moins importantes, on manque les
plus considérables."

Table 3.1.

	Bentham, Becker	Smith, Sen	Hume, Elster	Bayle, Mandeville
Utility maximizing	yes	no	yes	no
Stable preferences	yes	no	no	yes

According to La Rochefoucauld, we do not pursue self-interest rationally because the way we rank our interests is itself inconsistent. As La Rochefoucauld puts it in another maxim, "the ultimate acumen consists in knowing well the price of things."[104] But precisely: we do not price things consistently. The same desirable things appear to us as "small" sometimes, and sometimes "big."

In the neo-Epicurean tradition exemplified by Helvétius and Bentham, one finds the same hedonic assumption as in La Rochefoucauld and Mandeville, but the focus is on the ways in which utility can be maximized. For Helvétius, we are capable of maximizing utility because, most of the time, our preferences are internally consistent. Bentham continues and develops this utilitarian tradition, which has informed standard economic doctrine.

It may be useful to summarize in a table the distinctions we have made regarding the relationship between reason and self-interest. Table 3.1 distinguishes four traditions. Bentham and Hume assume that human behavior maximizes utility. Smith (in *The Theory of Moral Sentiments*) notices that truly virtuous behavior does not maximize utility. Mandeville argues that self-love skews our practice of rational calculation. Therefore, we rarely maximize utility. Bentham and Mandeville agree on the hedonist assumption (stable preferences, in Becker's vocabulary). Hume and Smith reject the hedonist assumption. These four doctrines have a complex genealogy, overlapping assumptions, and mutually exclusive principles.

SELF-LOVE AND RATIONAL CALCULATION

In chapter 1, we have seen how Rousseau and Smith build their systems on a refutation of the interest doctrine, and how they incorporate the "selfish hypothesis" into their own thought. Rousseau and Smith have a complex

[104] Ibid., maxim 244 (translation modified). "La souveraine habileté consiste à bien connaître le prix des choses."

position on this issue. On the one hand, they reject the notion that human nature is motivated by self-interest alone. On the other hand, they agree that in modern commercial society, human behavior is driven by self-interest. Therefore, we still need to examine the relationship between reason and self-interest in the descriptions of civil society provided by Rousseau and Smith.

As we have seen before, in the first half of the eighteenth century, it is the Epicurean/Augustinian scheme that sets the terms of the debate on self-interest. Rousseau takes a decisive step when, against Mandeville and La Rochefoucauld, he asserts that self-love (*amour-propre*), far from being a basic, instinctual impulse, is a product of reason and reflection: "Reason engenders amour-propre, and reflection fortifies it."[105] For Rousseau, the basic impulse is love of oneself (*amour de soi*). In the state of nature, human reason is undeveloped. Man is driven only by natural and necessary desires, which are easy to satisfy. In that sense, without any efforts, primitive man realizes the ideal of tranquility contemplated by Epicureans and Stoics alike:

The savage breathes nothing but liberty and repose; he desires only to live and be at leisure; and the *ataraxia* of the Stoic does not approach his indifference for every other object.[106]

According to Rousseau, human reason has developed because of the need to satisfy human desires:

We seek to know only because we desire to have pleasure; and it is impossible to conceive why one who had neither desires nor fears would go to the trouble of reasoning.[107]

---

[105] Jean-Jacques Rousseau, *Discourse on the Origin of Inequality*, in *The Collected Writings of Rousseau*, vol. 3, edited by Roger D. Masters and Christopher Kelly, translated by Judith R. Bush, Roger D. Masters, Christopher Kelly, and Terence Marshall, Hanover, NH: University Press of New England, 1992, p. 37. "C'est la raison qui engendre l'amour-propre, et c'est la réflexion qui le fortifie," *Discours sur l'origine et les fondements de l'inégalité*, in *Œuvres complètes*, edited by Bernard Gagnebin and Marcel Raymond, Paris: Gallimard, Bibliothèque de la Pléiade, vol. 3, 1964, p. 156.

[106] Rousseau, *Discourse on the Origin of Inequality*, translated by Adam Smith in "Letter to the *Edinburgh Review*," No. 2 (1756), in *Essays on Philosophical Subjects, The Glasgow Edition of the Works and Correspondence of Adam Smith*, vol. 3, Oxford: Oxford University Press, 1976, p. 253. "Le [sauvage] ne respire que le repos et la liberté, il ne veut que vivre et rester oisif, et l'ataraxie même du stoïcien n'approche pas de sa profonde indifférence pour tout autre objet." *Discours sur l'origine et les fondements de l'inégalité*, p. 192. Ataraxia is originally an Epicurean concept, appropriated later by the Stoics. Rousseau restricts the reference to Stoicism only because of the bad reputation attached to Epicurean ideas.

[107] Rousseau, *Discourse on the Origin of Inequality*, p. 27. "Nous ne cherchons à connaître que parce que nous désirons de jouir, et il n'est pas possible de concevoir pourquoi celui qui n'aurait ni désirs ni craintes se donnerait la peine de raisonner." *Discours sur l'origine de l'inégalité*, p. 143.

Conversely, the use of reason has generated new and artificial desires:

The Passions in turn derive their origin from our needs and their progress from our knowledge. For one can desire or fear things only through the ideas one can have of them or by the simple impulsion of Nature; and savage man, deprived of every kind of enlightenment, feels only the passions of this last kind.[108]

In Rousseau's narrative, savage man has natural desires and very little reason. Reason develops gradually as a consequence of the need to satisfy these natural desires. The newfound ability to make comparisons between himself and others leads man to desire things he did not desire before. As it develops, reason produces countless new passions and desires. For Rousseau, these artificial passions and desires are summarized in the concept of self-love (*amour-propre*). The important point here is that Rousseau identifies self-love with rational calculation.[109] At the end of the process (modern commercial society), human life has little to do with natural and necessary desires, and almost everything to do with unnatural and unnecessary needs. In other words, nearly all (modern) passions are caused by the exercise of reason. Here is, in Adam Smith's translation, Rousseau's satirical description of human behavior in civil society:

The citizen, on the contrary, toils, bestirs and torments himself without end, to obtain employments which are still more laborious; he labours on till his death, he even hastens it, in order to put himself in a condition to live, or renounces life to acquire immortality. He makes his court to the great whom he hates, and to the rich whom he despises; he spares nothing to obtain the honour of serving them; he vainly boasts of his own meanness and their protection, and, proud of his slavery, speaks with disdain of those who do not have the honour to share it. What a spectacle to a *Carib* would be the painful and envied labours of a European minister of state? How many cruel deaths would not that indolent savage prefer to the horror of such a life, which is often not even sweetened by the pleasure of doing well? But to see the end of so many cares, it is necessary that the words, *power* and *reputation* should have an intelligible meaning in his understanding; that he should be made to comprehend that there is a species of men who count for something the looks of the rest of the universe; who can be happy and contented with themselves upon the testimony of another, rather than upon their own. For such in reality

---

[108] "Les passions, à leur tour, tirent leur origine de nos besoins, et leur progrès de nos connais-sances; car on ne peut désirer ou craindre les choses que sur les idées qu'on en peut avoir, ou par la simple impulsion de la nature; et l'homme sauvage, privé de toute sorte de lumières, n'éprouve que les passions de cette dernière espèce; ses désirs ne passent pas ses besoins physiques." Ibid.

[109] "Reason" is to be understood in a narrow sense as the ability to compute, compare, and reflect. In the context of these analyses, the "rational" for Rousseau is what involves comparison and computation. It should not be taken in its Kantian sense as a synonym for the universal. Otherwise, Rousseau's thesis that self-love is a product of reason would make little sense.

is the true cause of all those differences: the savage lives in himself; the man of society, always out of himself; cannot live but in the opinions of others, and it is, if I may say so, from their judgment alone that he derives the sentiment of his own existence.[110]

For Rousseau, the "citizen," instead of enjoying the goods and services produced by commercial society, is engaged in an endless process of post-poned gratification. He never ceases to perform interest calculations, with the idea that forfeiting a pleasure at hand will buy a greater pleasure later. Unfortunately, gratification never comes, because the object of desire is no longer the satisfaction of physical needs, but rather the satisfaction of one's vanity. We want to be admired and esteemed by others. Since the source of happiness is now outside of ourselves, we are engaged in a quest without end.

Adam Smith appropriated the arguments and even the tone of Rousseau's satire in *The Theory of Moral Sentiments*. In a chapter entitled "Of the Origin of Ambition, and of the Distinction of Ranks" (a clear indication that he is addressing the issue discussed in the *Discourse of the Origin of Inequality*), he remarks that, in modern commercial society, human behavior is not aimed at the satisfaction of natural needs:

For to what purpose is all the toil and bustle of this world? What is the end of avarice and ambition, of the pursuit of wealth, of power, and preheminence? Is it to supply the necessities of nature? The wages of the meanest labourer can supply them. We see that they afford him food and clothing, the comfort of a house, and of a family. If we examined his œconomy with rigour, we should find that he spends a great part of them upon conveniencies, which may be regarded as superfluities, and that, upon extraordinary occasions, he can give something even to vanity and distinction.[111]

---

[110] Rousseau, *Discourse on the Origin of Inequality*, translated by Adam Smith, p. 253. "Au contraire, le citoyen toujours actif sue, s'agite, se tourmente sans cesse pour chercher des occupations encore plus laborieuses: il travaille jusqu'à la mort, il y court même pour se mettre en état de vivre, ou renonce à la vie pour acquérir l'immortalité. Il fait sa cour aux grands qu'il hait et aux riches qu'il méprise; il n'épargne rien pour obtenir l'honneur de les servir; il se vante orgueilleusement de sa bassesse et de leur protection et, fier de son esclavage, il parle avec dédain de ceux qui n'ont pas l'honneur de le partager. Quel spectacle pour un Caraïbe que les travaux pénibles et enviés d'un ministre européen! Combien de morts cruelles ne préférerait pas cet indolent sauvage à l'horreur d'une pareille vie qui souvent n'est pas même adoucie par le plaisir de bien faire? Mais pour voir le but de tant de soins, il faudrait que ces mots, *puissance* et *réputation*, eussent un sens dans son esprit, qu'il apprît qu'il y a une sorte d'hommes qui comptent pour quelque chose les regards du reste de l'univers, qui savent être heureux et contents d'eux-mêmes sur le témoignage d'autrui plutôt que sur le leur propre. Telle est, en effet, la véritable cause de toutes ces différences: le sauvage vit en lui-même; l'homme sociable toujours hors de lui ne sait vivre que dans l'opinion des autres, et c'est, pour ainsi dire, de leur seul jugement qu'il tire le sentiment de sa propre existence." *Discours sur l'origine de l'inégalité*, p. 192.

[111] Smith, *The Theory of Moral Sentiments*, I.iii.2.1.

In other words, the "minimum wage" is sufficient to satisfy all basic needs, and then some. The reason why we work so hard is because our vanity prompts us to seek the esteem and admiration of others:

From whence, then, arises that emulation which runs through all the different ranks of men, and what are the advantages which we propose by that great purpose of human life which we call bettering our condition? To be observed, to be attended to, to be taken notice of with sympathy, complacency, and approbation, are all the advantages which we can propose to derive from it. It is the vanity, not the ease, or the pleasure, which interests us. But vanity is always founded upon the belief of our being the object of attention and approbation.[112]

This point is so fundamental for Smith, that he stresses it again in Part VI of *The Theory of Moral Sentiments*. Our behavior in modern commercial society has little do to with the satisfaction of physical needs, and almost everything to do with the satisfaction of our vanity. The possession of material goods is apparently aimed at satisfying physical needs. Upon closer inspection however, it appears that materials goods are only a means to an end. This end is the acquisition of "respect," "credit," and "rank":

Though it is in order to supply the necessities and conveniencies of the body, that the advantages of external fortune are originally recommended to us, yet we cannot live long in the world without perceiving that the respect of our equals, our credit and rank in the society we live in, depend very much upon the degree in which we possess, or are supposed to possess, those advantages. The desire of becoming the proper objects of this respect, of deserving and obtaining this credit and rank among our equals, is, perhaps, the strongest of all our desires, and our anxiety to obtain the advantages of fortune is accordingly much more excited and irritated by this desire, than by that of supplying all the necessities and conveniencies of the body, which are always very easily supplied.[113]

At first sight, it seems difficult to reconcile this satire of commercial society with Smith's description of the rational pursuit of self-interest in *The Wealth of Nations*. Comparison between the two works is rendered difficult by the fact that they follow opposite methods. In *The Theory of Moral Sentiments*, Smith operates *more geometrico*. He starts from first principles, and gradually develops the consequences of these first principles. In *The Wealth of Nations*, the order is analytical. Smith starts from a problem (what are the causes of the wealth of nations?), and he gradually analyzes the problem, by identifying explanatory principles that are more and more general. However, he does not seem overly concerned with the need to ascend to first principles (perhaps because the first principles have already

---

[112] Ibid.   [113] Ibid., vi.i.3.

been addressed in *The Theory of Moral Sentiments*). It can be argued, however, that Smith's description of the search for honor, credit and rank in *The
Theory of Moral Sentiments* is consistent with his emphasis on "the desire
to better our condition" in *The Wealth of Nations*. Furthermore, Smith's
philosophical innovation, following Rousseau's lead, consists in describing
the desire to better our condition as a consequence of the exercise of reason.

That the rational pursuit of self-interest is the first principle of human behavior in *The Wealth of Nations* has been an article of faith among
economists for two centuries. This faith has been questioned by revision-
ist historians like Donald Winch, who cautions us against the temptation
to confuse "the creature called rational economic man" (which is an invention of nineteenth-century social science) with the desire to better our
condition and the propensity to truck and barter as described by Smith.[114]
Furthermore, Winch argues, since Smith described the desire to better our
condition and the propensity to barter as *instincts*, it makes little sense
to identify these principles with the *rational* pursuit of self-interest.[115] Is
the conventional interpretation of *The Wealth of Nations* a simple case of
anachronistic projection of modern categories? We need to look at both
sides of this issue.

Near the beginning of *The Wealth of Nations*, Smith poses the question
of the origins of commerce and the division of labor. The response lies in
"the propensity to truck, barter, and exchange one thing for another."[116]
However, almost as an afterthought, Smith adds that this propensity to
barter and trade can probably be accounted for by a more fundamental
principle:

Whether this propensity be one of the original principles in human nature, of
which no further account can be given; or whether, as seems probable, it be the
necessary consequence of the faculties of reason and speech, it belongs not to our
present subject to inquire.[117]

"The faculties of reason and speech" are probably a more fundamental
principle than the propensity to barter and trade. It therefore seems difficult
to argue that the propensity to barter and trade, based as it is on "reason and
speech," is "sub-rational." Even Viner, who coined the term "sub-rational"

[114] Donald Winch, *Riches and Poverty. An Intellectual History of Political Economy in Britain, 1750–1834*, Cambridge: Cambridge University Press, 1996, p. 105.
[115] Ibid., p. 106. Winch makes the same point in "Adam Smith: Scottish Moral Philosopher as Political Economist," *Historical Journal* 35:1 (1992), p. 106.
[116] Adam Smith, *An Inquiry into the Nature and Causes of the Wealth of Nations*, The Glasgow Edition of the Works and Correspondence of Adam Smith, vol. 2, Oxford: Oxford University Press, 1976 [London: Strahan and Cadell, 1776], I.ii.1.
[117] Ibid.

to describe the realm of sentiments that "begins where animal instincts shared by man end" and "ends where human reason begins,"[118] is far from categorical in labeling the propensity to trade as "sub-rational." Following Smith's inconclusive discussion, he only states that "in this sub-rational area Smith *perhaps* even includes the psychological drives which lead man to engage in trade."[119]

Does Smith have any doubts as to the origin of commerce? Probably not. If he declines to make a final call on the issue of first principles, it is not because he is in doubt as to whether the faculties of reason and speech precede the propensity to trade, but because an analytical work such as the *Inquiry into the Nature and Causes of the Wealth of Nations* does not need to concern itself with first principles. There may also be additional reasons for the inconclusiveness of the discussion. As Thomas Lewis has shown, the notion that the faculties of reason and speech were the cause of the propensity to trade was controversial.[120] In his September 25, 1776 letter to Adam Smith, Pownall commented at length on the only passage in *The Wealth of Nations* that discusses (or rather avoids discussing) first principles. He agreed with Smith that the propensity to barter was *not* the first principle of the division of labor, but he felt that Smith's discussion was unsatisfactory because it did not state explicitly what the first principles of the analysis were: "I think you have stopped short in your analysis before you have arrived at the first natural cause and principle of the division of labour."[121] In addition, he disagreed with Smith's suggestion that the first principle of the division of labor might be the faculties of reason and speech. For Pownall, the first principle of the division of labor was necessarily the same as the first principle of government. If one ascribed the origins of government to the faculties of reason and speech, one had to believe that government was "an artificial succedaneum to an imagined theoretic state of nature."[122] In other words, positing the division of labor as

---

[118] Jacob Viner, *The Role of Providence in the Social Order. An Essay in Intellectual History*, Princeton: Princeton University Press, 1972, p. 79.

[119] Ibid.

[120] Thomas J. Lewis, "Persuasion, Domination and Exchange: Adam Smith on the Political Consequences of Markets," *Canadian Journal of Political Science* 33:2 (2000), pp. 273–289. Lewis claims in a footnote (without developing his thought): "Smith's insistence that the propensity to persuade is the response to the fundamental human need for recognition and approval is very close to Rousseau's concept of social dependence in the *Discourse on the Origin and Foundations of Inequality among Men*. Smith also shares with Rousseau the view that human characters and attributes (the philosopher and the street porter) and the resulting inequalities are decisively shaped by society" (p. 281, note 23).

[121] Letter from Governor Pownall to Adam Smith, in *Correspondence of Adam Smith*, The Glasgow Edition of the Works and Correspondence of Adam Smith, vol. 6, Oxford: Oxford University Press, 1985, p. 338.

[122] Ibid., p. 339.

a consequence of reason and speech implied an acceptance of the subversive theories of Mandeville and Rousseau. Even though it was made *en passant* and tentatively, the remark was dangerous:

And as I think that great danger may arise ... in deriving the source of community and government from passions or caprice, creating by will an artificial succedaneum to nature, I could not but in the same manner, *en passant*, make this cursory remark.[123]

Pownall's warning did not lead Smith to make any changes to the incriminated passage, but it is sufficient indication of the fact that ascribing a first principle to the division of labor was a contentious issue, and it can certainly explain why Smith was cautious in the first place, and make the remark *en passant*.

There was at least one potentially subversive implication of the remark that Smith dared to make explicitly. Against the views of people like Pownall, who believed that social inequalities were the result of natural differences in talents and abilities, Smith insisted that the various positions one occupied on the social ladder were entirely a consequence of the division of labor. The prevailing view at the time was Pownall's, and it could be summarized in this maxim by Vauvenargues: "The inequality of conditions proceeds from the inequality in talent and courage."[124] Smith, on the contrary, asserted in his *Lectures on Jurisprudence* that "the disposition to barter is by no means founded upon different genius and talents," and that "genius is more the effect of the division of labor than the latter is of it."[125] He made the same point, in a slightly more subdued way, in *The Wealth of Nations*:

The difference of natural talents in different men is, in reality, much less than we are aware of; and the very different genius which appears to distinguish men of different professions, when grown up to maturity, is not upon many occasions so much the cause as the effect of the division of labour. The difference between the most dissimilar characters, between a philosopher and a common street porter, for example, seems to arise not so much from nature as from habit, custom, and education.[126]

In saying that the differences between a street porter and a philosopher came "not so much from nature as from habit, custom, and education," Smith agreed with Rousseau, who made a fundamental distinction between

[123] Ibid.
[124] "L'inégalité des conditions est née de celle des génies et des courages." Vauvenargues, *Réflexions et maximes*, maxim 226.
[125] Adam Smith, *Lectures on Jurisprudence, The Glasgow Edition of the Works and Correspondence of Adam Smith*, vol. 5, Oxford: Oxford University Press, 1978, p. 492.
[126] Smith, *The Wealth of Nations*, I.ii.4.

"two sorts of inequality in the human Species: one, which I call natural or Physical... the other, which may be called moral or Political inequality, because it depends upon a sort of convention and is established, or at least authorized, by the consent of Men."[127]

The point that reason and speech are the cause of commerce is therefore much more than a casual remark. It goes to the core of Smith's axiomatic choices. Furthermore, we shall now see that, if we put it in the context of Smith's appropriation of Rousseau's anthropology, it brings with it a crucial distinction regarding the nature of self-love.

As the editors of *The Wealth of Nations* point out, Smith argued in his *Lectures on Jurisprudence* that the real foundation of the division of labor is "that principle to persuade which so much prevails in human nature."[128] Indeed, Smith describes the division of labor as founded on explicit transactions, where one party seeks to persuade the other party that the exchange is in his interest. As Smith puts it in the *Lectures on Jurisprudence*, "the offering of a shilling, which to us appears to have so plain and simple a meaning, is in reality offering an argument to persuade one to do so and so as it is for his interest."[129] One may then ask: according to Smith, what is the foundation of the propensity to barter and trade: is it "reason and speech" or the "principle to persuade"? An answer to this question can be found in *The Theory of Moral Sentiments*. The faculty of speech is a consequence of our desire to persuade others:

The desire of being believed, the desire of persuading, of leading and directing other people, seems to be one of the strongest of all our natural desires. It is, perhaps, the instinct upon which is founded the faculty of speech, the characteristical faculty of human nature. No other animal possesses this faculty, and we cannot discover in any other animal any desire to lead and direct the judgment and conduct of its fellows.[130]

As to the foundation of the desire to persuade others, it is of course the principle of sympathy, because "nothing pleases us more than to observe in other men a fellow-feeling with all the emotions of our own breast."[131] Smith observes in the *Lectures on Jurisprudence* that "you are uneasy whenever anyone differs from you, and you endeavour to persuade [?him] to be of your mind."[132] In Smith's psychology, nothing gives greater pleasure

[127] Rousseau, *Discourse on the Origin of Inequality*, p. 18. "Je conçois dans l'espèce humaine deux sortes d'inégalité; l'une, que j'appelle naturelle ou physique... l'autre, qu'on peut appeler inégalité morale ou politique, parce qu'elle dépend d'une sorte de convention, et qu'elle est établie, ou du moins autorisée par le consentement des hommes." *Discours sur l'origine de l'inégalité*, p. 131.
[128] Smith, *Lectures on Jurisprudence*, p. 493.   [129] Ibid., p. 352.
[130] Smith, *The Theory of Moral Sentiments*, VII.iv.25.   [131] Ibid., 1.i.2.1.
[132] Smith, *Lectures on Jurisprudence*, p. 352.

than mutual sympathy, and nothing is more unpleasant than disagreement. As a consequence, "if one advances anything concerning China or the *more distant moon* which contradicts what you imagine to be true, you immediately try to persuade [your interlocutor] to alter his opinion."[133] Persuasion is the privileged way of avoiding the uneasiness of disagreement and obtaining the pleasure of mutual sympathy.

The same logic of persuasion is at work in the famous passage on the baker and the butcher in *The Wealth of Nations*:

But man has almost constant occasion for the help of his brethren, and it is in vain from him to expect it from their benevolence only. He will be more likely to prevail if he can interest their self-love in his favor, and show them that it is for their own advantage to do for him what he requires of them. Whoever offers to another a bargain of any kind, proposes to do this. Give me that which I want, and you shall have this which you want, is the meaning of every such offer; and it is in this manner that we obtain from one another the far greater part of those good offices which we stand in need of. It is not from the benevolence of the butcher, the brewer, or the baker, that we expect our dinner, but from their regard to their own interest. We address ourselves, not to their humanity but to their self-love, and never talk to them of our own necessities but of their advantages.[134]

The conventional reading of this passage stresses the role of self-interest as an explanatory principle for economic behavior. Yet this passage can also be read as the description of various strategies of persuasion. Self-interest is important only insofar as it is a component in a successful strategy of persuasion. In that sense, self-interest is far removed from the status of a first principle. Smith's point is not that those who engage in commercial transactions are self-interested (that would be a tautology). It is that commercial transactions are a form of persuasion where self-interest is used as an argument.

This passage is entirely consistent with Rousseau's anthropology, at least for two reasons. First, from Smith's point of view, obtaining a good or a service from someone in a commercial transaction is not an end in itself. The ultimate end is the pleasure we derive from obtaining someone's agreement and approbation. Similarly, in Rousseau, *amour-propre* is not ultimately geared towards the acquisition of material goods: it is aimed at securing respect, approbation, and admiration from others. However, as we have seen above, one of Rousseau's main points in the *Second Discourse* is that in modern commercial society, there is a contamination between material needs (the desire to be fed, clothed, etc.) and symbolic needs (the desire

[133] Ibid.   [134] Smith, *The Wealth of Nations*, i.ii.2.

to be approved of). Because of the division of labor, in order to satisfy our material needs, we must seek the assistance of others. Conversely, in order to obtain the respect and admiration of others, we must accumulate material goods. Like Rousseau, Smith argues that, in modern commercial society, the only way of obtaining the assistance of others is to appeal to their self-interest. In other words, *the satisfaction of needs in commercial society must go through a rational calculation of interests.* This calculation is an explicit one, subject to debate and persuasion. Hence the fundamental role of "reason and speech." Smith's remark that we "never talk to them of our own necessities but of their advantages" echoes Rousseau's contention that man in civil society must use his powers of persuasion in order to avail himself of the assistance of others. The only valid argument in such situations is the appeal to self-interest:

He must therefore incessantly seek to interest them in his fate, and to make them find their own profit, in fact or in appearance, in working for his.[135]

The only difference between Smith's description and Rousseau's is that, according to Rousseau, the appeal to self-interest may be fraudulent (the profit may exist "in fact or in appearance"). However, in an earlier draft of the passage, which can be found in the *Lectures on Jurisprudence*, Smith does mention the possibility of a deceitful appeal to self-interest:

Man continually standing in need of the assistance of others, must fall upon some means to procure their help. This he does not merely by coaxing and courting; he does not expect it unless he can turn it to your advantage or make it appear to be so.[136]

The same link between man's state of mutual dependency and the appeal to self-interest as an argument in commercial transactions can be found in the *Second Discourse*, which we shall now quote in Smith's translation:

Thus man, from being free and independent, became by a multitude of new necessities subjected in a manner, to all nature, and above all to his fellow creatures... He is obliged therefore to interest them in his situation, and to make them find, either in reality or in appearance, their advantage in laboring for his.[137]

Even Smith's comparison between man and animals (which precedes the passage in question) makes sense in the light of the parallel between the

---

[135] Rousseau, *Discourse on the Origin of Inequality*, p. 52. "Il faut donc qu'il cherche sans cesse à les intéresser à son sort, et à leur faire trouver en effet ou en apparence leur profit à travailler pour le sien." *Discours sur l'origine de l'inégalité*, p. 175.
[136] Smith, *Lectures on Jurisprudence*, p. 347.
[137] Rousseau, *Discourse of the Origin of Inequality*, translated by Adam Smith, p. 252.

Second Discourse and *The Wealth of Nations*. Smith contrasts the human state of mutual dependency with the independence of animals. Rousseau contrasts it with the independence of primitive man.

When, at the beginning of *The Wealth of Nations*, in the oft-quoted passage on the baker and the butcher, Smith mentions self-love as a motive for human action, he is not making a vague reference to what we have called the "interest doctrine" (the suspicion that self-interest may be the only motive of human actions). He is making some very specific claims, consistent with Rousseau's analyses in the *Second Discourse*: (a) that in modern commercial society, the satisfaction of natural needs *must* occur through commerce and the division of labor; (b) that commerce (and henceforth the division of labor) is founded on persuasion; (c) that the only way of persuading someone to trade is to appeal to his self-love. Self-love is mentioned only as a tool for persuasion: you should trade with me because it is in your interest to do so.

Against the points that have just been made, one could argue that Smith saw the desire to better our condition as an instinct: "a desire which, though generally calm and dispassionate, comes with us from the womb, and never leaves us till we go into the grave."[138] However, in *The Theory of Moral Sentiments*, Smith equates "that great purpose of human life which we call bettering our condition" with "vanity,"[139] a concept that is very close to Rousseau's *amour-propre* (see chapter 1). Vanity is the desire "to be taken notice of with sympathy, complacency, and approbation."[140] Vanity is not an instinct, because it involves constant comparisons between ourselves and others, and constant computations of the ways in which we could improve our position in the eyes of others. As we have seen before, in Smith's system, vanity is based on "the pleasure of mutual sympathy," and sympathy is, with self-love, the principal axiom of Smith's psychology. What is worth noticing here is that even in his descriptions of the most basic forms of sympathy, Smith mentions "reason and judgment" as being an integral part of sympathy:

The compassion of the spectator must arise altogether from the consideration of what he himself would feel if he was reduced to the same unhappy situation, and, what perhaps is impossible, was at the same time able to regard it with his present reason and judgment.[141]

As we have seen in chapter 1, Smith's concept of *sympathy* is very close to Rousseau's concept of *identification*. Whether one calls it sympathy or

---

[138] Smith, *The Wealth of Nations*, II.iii.28. See Winch, *Riches and Poverty*, p. 106.
[139] Smith, *The Theory of Moral Sentiments*, I.iii.2.1.   [140] Ibid.   [141] Ibid., I.i.1.11.

identification, "changing places in fancy"[142] with a fellow human being is an operation that involves reason and reflection. For Rousseau, reason (the ability to compare and reflect) is the cause of our ability to identify with others, and the ability to identify is itself the cause of *amour-propre* (we compare ourselves with others, and we want them to see us the way we see ourselves). In so far as it is based on sympathy, a first principle in Smith's psychology, the desire to better our condition can certainly be described as something that is always with us (from the womb to the grave). This does not mean, however, that it is an instinct. Even in its most basic forms, it involves the use of reason.

When Rousseau made the claim that *amour-propre* was founded on reason and reflection, the claim was perceived as a paradox. Voltaire responded with the following comment: "What a strange idea! Do we need reasoning to want our well-being?"[143] Voltaire's reaction reveals the fact that he shared the idea of self-love prevailing at the time: self-love as a basic, instinctual impulse. The philosophical innovation, in Rousseau and Smith, consists in establishing a fundamental link between self-love and rational calculation. This is not to say that self-love had not been associated with reason before. Butler had made a distinction between self-love (the rational pursuit of one's interests) and the passions (which sometimes cause us to act against our interests). What is new and different in Rousseau's concept of *amour-propre* (and Smith's concept of vanity) is that new needs and desires are created by the exercise of our rational faculties (we shall examine this in greater detail in the following chapter). For Voltaire and most of his contemporaries, we do not need to think in order to know what we want. Our desires are a given. Rousseau's paradoxical point (appropriated by Smith) is that in modern commercial society, the exercise of reason and speech engenders commerce, and the rise in commerce creates new needs and new desires. The better we become at performing rational calculations, the stronger our desire is to "better our condition."

It appears that "the rational pursuit of self-interest" can be understood at least in two different ways. In the Benthamite tradition, the emphasis is on pleasure. It is rational to pursue self-interest, because self-interest is pleasure, and pleasure is the universal goal of human actions, from both a descriptive and a normative point of view. To the extent that it is grounded in Bentham's utilitarianism, Gary Becker's economic approach shares this

---

[142] Ibid., 1.i.1.3.
[143] "Quelle idée! Faut-il donc des raisonnements pour vouloir son bien-être?" See George Remington Havens, *Voltaire's Marginalia on the Pages of Rousseau. A Comparative Study of Ideas*, Columbus: Ohio State University Press, 1933, p. 10.

conception of self-interest. On the contrary, Rousseau and Smith insist that, in modern commercial society, human behavior has paradoxically very little to do with a search for pleasure. The logic of self-interest is one of saving, not consumption. The "desire to better our condition" implies that gratification must be postponed indefinitely to maximize utility. In that sense, rational calculation is what gives all its content to the concept of self-interest. When economists talk about the rational pursuit of self-interest, they refer to a notion that is grounded in two different, and in many ways incompatible, traditions.

4

Passions, interests, and society

> *The power and sagacity as well as labor and care of the politician in civilizing the society has been nowhere more conspicuous than in the happy contrivance of playing our passions against one another.*
>
> Mandeville, *The Fable of the Bees* (1732)

A peculiar feature of Adam Smith's thought is the absence of the political argument in support of capitalism that Montesquieu in France and Sir James Steuart in England had expressed most forcefully: the idea that the development of commerce was the most effective safeguard against arbitrary and despotic government. The "Montesquieu–Steuart doctrine," as Hisrchman calls it, consisted essentially in saying that motives of self-interest would restrain the behavior of rulers who would otherwise succumb to their passions (lust for power, vanity, greed, etc.) and seek to govern tyrannically. Adam Smith, instead of arguing that interests can usefully be pitted against passions, seems to erase the distinction between passions and interests.[1] Understanding the reasons why Smith chose not to adopt the Montesquieu–Steuart doctrine is an essential aspect of understanding the genealogy of economic science.

INTERESTS AND PASSIONS IN REASON OF STATE THEORY

The Montesquieu–Steuart doctrine combines two intellectual traditions: reason of State theory and the Augustinian principle of countervailing passions. Reason of State theory provides the notion that self-interest is a reliable rule of conduct. The countervailing passions principle states that passions can be checked by other passions or even check themselves. For instance, a ruler driven by the passion of greed will refrain from confiscating his subjects' property because maximization of his own wealth is dependent upon the economic well-being of his subjects.

---

[1] See Albert O. Hirschman, *The Passions and the Interests. Political Arguments for Capitalism before its Triumph*, Princeton: Princeton University Press, 1997 [1977], p. 111.

Reason of State theory has its roots in the work of Machiavelli, but the first explicit mention of an opposition between the interests of a ruler and his passions is found in a little book published by Henri de Rohan in 1638 and dedicated to Cardinal Richelieu, *On the Interest of Princes and the States of Christendom*.[2] Rohan's book begins with the assertion that self-interest dictates the behavior of rulers:

Princes rule over peoples and interest rules over princes. Knowledge of this interest takes as much pre-eminence over the actions of princes as do the princes over the peoples. The prince may err, his advisors may be corrupt, but interest alone can never fail.[3]

What is most remarkable about this pronouncement is its normative nature. The rule of interest consists in commands issued from a higher authority (reason of State) comparable to the orders the prince gives to the people. The prince's duty is to behave rationally by obeying the commands of the abstract higher authority called reason of State.

In Hirschman's narrative, the notion of self-interest, having originated in reason of State theory and being originally restricted to the behavior of rulers, was subsequently used to explain the behavior of groups and individuals and human behavior in general. An important early example of this application of self-interest to the psychology of individuals is La Rochefoucauld's *Maxims*. As we shall see, it is highly problematic.

La Rochefoucauld describes the workings of *amour-propre* with a vocabulary drawn from the reason of State doctrine. "Self-love is cleverer than the cleverest man in the world,"[4] says maxim 4. The concept of "cleverness" refers to political skill. In other words, self-love is cleverer than the cleverest Machiavellian prince. In this perspective, the epitome of political skill consists in feigning not to have any political skill:

Very clever men pretend all their lives to condemn trickery so that, at a big moment and for a big interest, they may profit from it.[5]

---

[2] Henri de Rohan, *De l'intérêt des princes et des États de la chrétienté*, edited by Christian Lazzeri, Paris: PUF, 1995 [Paris, 1638].

[3] "Les princes commandent aux peuples, et l'intérêt commande aux princes. La connaissance de cet intérêt est d'autant plus relevée par-dessus celle des actions des princes qu'eux-mêmes le sont par-dessus les peuples. Le prince se peut tromper, son conseil peut être corrompu, mais l'intérêt ne peut jamais manquer." Ibid., p. 161.

[4] François de la Rochefoucauld, *The Maxims*, translated by Louis Kronenberger, New York: Stackpole, 1936. "L'amour-propre est plus habile que le plus habile homme du monde." *Maximes*, edited by Jean Lafond, Paris: Gallimard, 1976 [fifth edition, Paris: Barbin, 1678] maxim 4.

[5] Ibid., maxim 124 (translation modified). "Les plus habiles affectent toute leur vie de blâmer les finesses pour s'en servir en quelque grande occasion et pour quelque grand intérêt."

The logic of self-interest extends to all human behavior. In many ways, La Rochefoucauld describes the individual motivated by self-love as a Machiavellian prince who bases every decision on a calculation of his interests. Since it is not possible to have everything, rational calculation prompts us to give up smaller interests in order to focus on bigger ones. An example of such calculation characterizes the virtue of generosity:

> What looks like generosity is often but ambition in disguise, scorning small interests to pursue larger ones.[6]

Similarly, friendship must be understood in the context of the court society as a political alliance based on the trading of favors:

> What men call friendship is just an alliance, a pooling of mutual interests, and an exchange of favors; in short, a commerce where self-love always sets out to obtain something.[7]

Of self-love, La Rochefoucauld says: "It only seeks *to be*, and as long as it *is*, it will gladly become its own enemy."[8] The only goal of self-love is the continuation of its existence. Similarly, Rohan describes the goal of the statesman as "the growth, or at least the preservation"[9] of the State. There is no transcendent *telos*. As a Machiavellian prince strives to stay in power, self-love only seeks its own preservation. The art of self-preservation implies an ability to adapt, transform and reinvent oneself constantly. La Rochefoucauld notices that when self-love appears to have renounced its pleasure, "it has only suspended, or changed it, and even when it has lost the battle, and one seems to have defeated it, one finds it again triumphant in its own defeat."[10] An example of this extraordinary capacity for survival is the virtue of humility, where self-love hides under its very negation:

> Humility is often just a feigned submissiveness employed to subdue others. It is a stratagem of pride, which lowers itself in order to raise itself, and though it wears

---

[6] Ibid., maxim 246 (translation modified). "Ce qui paraît générosité n'est souvent qu'une ambition déguisée qui méprise de petits intérêts, pour aller à de plus grands."

[7] Ibid., maxim 83 (translation modified). "Ce que les hommes ont nommé amitié n'est qu'une société, qu'un ménagement réciproque d'intérêts, et qu'un échange de bons offices; ce n'est enfin qu'un commerce où l'amour-propre se propose toujours quelque chose à gagner."

[8] Ibid., deleted maxim 1. "Enfin, il ne se soucie que d'être, et pourvu qu'il soit, il veut bien être son ennemi."

[9] "L'accroissement ou, pour le moins, la conservation." Rohan, *De l'intérêt des princes et des États de la chrétienté*, p. 161.

[10] La Rochefoucauld, *The Maxims*, deleted maxim 1. "Il ne fait que le suspendre, ou le changer, et lors même qu'il est vaincu ou qu'on croit en être défait, on le retrouve qui triomphe dans sa propre défaite."

a thousand masks, is never better disguised or more deceptive than when it wears the mask of humility itself.[11]

This capacity for continuous self-transformation is a characteristic of the statesman according to Rohan. Because circumstances change, the definition of the prince's interest changes as well. Because the goal (self-preservation) is unchanging, it is necessary for the prince's understanding of his interest to "change with time."[12] For instance, when King Henri III of France died, Henri de Navarre, who was chief of the rebellious Protestant party, became heir to the French crown. His interest was no longer that of the Protestant party. It had become the interest of France:

> This prince, seeing himself elevated to such a high dignity, was prompted by his changed condition to change his interest. He abandoned the interest he had held until then, and embraced the interest of France.[13]

Since his interest had changed, Henri de Navarre had to transform himself: he gave up the Protestant faith and converted to Catholicism, so that "adapting to changing times, and preferring his interest over any other consideration, he seized the opportunities so aptly that he encountered great success."[14]

Henri de Navarre thus provides a remarkable example of political skill. This type of self-interested behavior is paradoxically difficult to emulate, because, as La Rochefoucauld points out, the rational calculation of our interests is often disturbed by our passions:

> Clever men should list their interests in the proper order, and pursue each in turn. In our eagerness we often attempt too many things at once, and by wishing too much for the small ones we lose the big.[15]

Such is the predicament of the prince according to Rohan. Although it is true that interest "can never fail," the whole question is whether self-interest

---

[11] Ibid., maxim 254 (translation modified). "L'humilité n'est souvent qu'une feinte soumission dont on se sert pour soumettre les autres; c'est un artifice de l'orgueil qui s'abaisse pour s'élever; et bien qu'il se transforme en mille manières, il n'est jamais mieux déguisé et plus capable de tromper que lorsque qu'il se cache sous la figure de l'humilité."

[12] "Qu'il se change selon le temps." Rohan, *De l'intérêt des princes et des États de la chrétienté*, p. 161.

[13] "Ce prince, se voyant élevé en une si haute dignité fut invité par le changement de sa condition à changer d'intérêt et quittant celui qu'il avait tenu jusqu'alors, il embrassa celui de France." Ibid., p. 190.

[14] "Si bien que ce prince s'accommodant au temps, et préférant à toute autre considération son intérêt sut prendre ses avantages si à propos que ses affaires lui succédèrent heureusement." Ibid., p. 195.

[15] La Rochefoucauld, *The Maxims*, maxim 66 (translation modified). "Un habile homme doit savoir régler le rang de ses intérêts et les conduire chacun dans son ordre. Notre avidité le trouble souvent en nous faisant courir à tant de choses à la fois que, pour désirer trop les moins importantes, on manque les plus considérables."

is properly understood. According to reason of State doctrine, the prince will succeed only if he manages to keep his passions at bay and to base his decisions on purely rational considerations:

> In matters of State, one should not yield to those unruly desires that often prompt us to undertake things beyond our strength; nor to those violent passions that move us according to the power they have over us; nor to those superstitious opinions that give us ill-conceived scruples; but to our own interest, guided by reason alone, which must be the rule of our actions.[16]

In reason of State theory, interest calculations are rational in the strongest sense of the term. Any rational observer should be able to calculate the interests of a prince in his stead. That is exactly what Rohan does when, in the most detached fashion, he describes the interests of every European power and then shows "how one strayed from this true interest, either because the prince failed to understand it properly, or because his corrupt ministers concealed it from him."[17] For instance, Rohan believes that Henri de Navarre, after he became King Henri IV, strayed from the true interest of France when he made peace with Spain too soon: he was tired of making war because he had a natural inclination for pleasure. The decision to make peace with Spain, however reasonable it may have seemed, was not rational. La Rochefoucauld follows the same logic (and also complicates the picture) when he writes: "Passions are so unjust and self-interested, that even when they seem most reasonable, to follow them is a danger, to mistrust them a necessity."[18]

According to Rohan's doctrine, success in decision-making depends upon the ability to control one's passions in order to follow the dictates of interest. However, reason of State theory offers no suggestions as to how the ruler can control his passions. La Rochefoucauld exploits this shortcoming of reason of State theory. He shows how human behavior follows the logic of self-interest and how, at the same time, it fails to live up to this logic. In addition, La Rochefoucauld injects ambiguity into the concept of self-interest by noticing that our passions themselves have an interest of their

---

[16] "En matière d'État on ne doit se laisser conduire aux désirs déréglés qui nous emportent souvent à entreprendre des choses au-delà de nos forces, ni aux passions violentes qui nous agitent diversement selon qu'elles nous possèdent, ni aux opinions superstitieuses qui nous donnent des scrupules mal conçus, mais à notre propre intérêt, guidé par la seule raison, qui doit être la règle de nos actions." Rohan, *De l'intérêt des princes et des États de la chrétienté*, p. 187.

[17] "Combien on s'est éloigné de ce vrai intérêt, ou pour n'avoir pas été bien entendu par le prince, ou pour lui avoir été déguisé par la corruption des ministres." Ibid., p. 162.

[18] La Rochefoucauld, *The Maxims*, maxim 9 (translation modified). "Les passions ont une injustice et un propre intérêt qui fait qu'il est dangereux de les suivre, et qu'on doit s'en défier lors même qu'elles paraissent les plus raisonnables."

own. He also suggests that actions that appear to be dictated by self-interest could have been rationalized *ex post facto*. What appears as the product of rational calculation could have been caused by irrational motives:

> It is politic to explain those great and shining actions which dazzle the eyes as deriving from great designs, but in general they derive from whim and passions. Thus the war between Augustus and Antony, which we ascribe to their ambition to become masters of the world, was perhaps only the result of jealousy.[19]

For Rohan, passions and interests are strictly antithetical. La Rochefoucauld also opposes passions and interests when he asserts: "Clever men should list their interests in the proper order." However, when La Rochefoucauld transports the categories of reason of State theory into individual psychology, the opposition between passions and interests becomes much more complex and ambiguous. For La Rochefoucauld, the psychological reality is such that our passions do more than disturb the calculation of our interests. In many ways, our passions *define* our interests.

A similar ambiguity can already be found in Montaigne's *Essays*. In the chapter entitled "Of the Useful and the Honorable," two definitions of interest coexist. On the one hand, there is "the common interest,"[20] "the public welfare."[21] When a conflict arises between the honorable and the useful, and the prince, mindful of the public good, chooses what is useful for the State against what is honorable for the State, "he has abandoned his own reason to a more universal and powerful reason."[22] In a limited endorsement of reason of State theory, Montaigne takes the Stoic view that an act is comparatively better when it serves larger interests. The prince, against his personal sense of what might be honorable, chooses what is useful for the State. The welfare of the State ("a more universal reason") outweighs the prince's personal preferences ("his own reason"), because reason dictates that the public interest must take precedence over a private interest. According to this definition, interest and reason are nearly synonymous.

On the other hand, Montaigne also uses the term *interest* to designate the violent and irrational impulses that cause civil wars:

---

[19] Ibid., maxim 7 (translation modified). "Ces grandes et éclatantes actions qui éblouissent les yeux sont représentées par les politiques comme les effets des grands desseins, au lieu que ce sont d'ordinaire les effets de l'humeur et des passions. Ainsi la guerre d'Auguste et d'Antoine, qu'on rapporte à l'ambition qu'ils avaient de se rendre maîtres du monde, n'était peut-être qu'un effet de jalousie."

[20] Michel Eyquem de Montaigne, *Essays*, translated by Donald Frame, Stanford: Stanford University Press, 1965, III, 1, p. 609. "L'intérêt commun." *Les Essais*, edited by Pierre Villey and V.-L. Saulnier, Paris: PUF, 1992 [Paris: 1598], III, 1, p. 802.

[21] "Le bien public." Ibid., p. 600/791.

[22] "Il a quitté sa raison à une plus universelle et puissante raison." Ibid., p. 607/799.

But we must not call "duty" as we do every day, an inner bitterness and asperity that is born of private interest and passion; nor "courage" a treacherous and malicious conduct. Their propensity to malignity and violence they call zeal. It is not the cause that inflames them, it is their self-interest. They kindle war not because it is just, but because it is war.[23]

For Montaigne, the cause of civil war is the unbridled pursuit of individual self-interest. By self-interest, Montaigne means not a rational purpose but the "sickly qualities: ambition, jealousy, envy, vengeance, superstition, despair," with which "our being is cemented."[24] Under the banner of a great religious or political cause, individual passions manifest themselves in all their injustice and destructiveness. From this point of view, interest is not synonymous with reason. Rather, it is another name for the passions.

Hirschman's narrative focuses on the passions and the interests of the ruler. However, in seventeenth-century moral philosophy, there is also considerable attention paid to the relationship between passions and interests in the subjects or the citizens. Following Montaigne, Hobbes and Locke mention private interest as a destructive force because the content of private interest is defined by private passions. As Quentin Skinner points out, Hobbes speaks of interest to refer to the public good, but also "to describe what individuals take to be in line with their profit or advantage."[25] For Hobbes, individual interest is what prevents us from having a clear sense of justice:

Ignorance of the causes, and original constitution of right, equity, law, and justice, disposeth a man to make custom and example the rule of his actions; in such manner as to think that unjust which it hath been the custom to punish; and that just, of the impunity and approbation whereof they can produce an example or (as the lawyers which only use this false measure of justice barbarously call it) a precedent; like little children that have no other rule of good and evil manners but the correction they receive from their parents and masters; save that children are constant to their rule, whereas men are not so; because grown strong and stubborn, they appeal from custom to reason, and from reason to custom, as it serves their turn, receding from custom when their interest requires it, and setting themselves against reason as oft as reason is against them.[26]

---

23 "Mais il ne faut pas appeler devoir (comme nous faisons tous les jours) une aigreur et âpreté intestine qui naît de l'intérêt et passion privée; ni courage, une conduite traîtresse et malicieuse. Ils nomment zèle leur propension vers la malignité et violence: ce n'est pas la cause qui les échauffe, c'est leur intérêt; ils attisent la guerre non parce qu'elle est juste, mais parce que c'est la guerre." Ibid., p. 602/793.

24 "Notre être est cimenté de qualités maladives: l'ambition, la jalousie, l'envie, la vengeance, la superstition, le désespoir." Ibid., p. 599/790.

25 Quentin Skinner, *Reason and Rhetoric in the Philosophy of Hobbes*, Cambridge: Cambridge University Press, 1996, p. 349.

26 Thomas Hobbes, *Leviathan*, edited by Edwin Curley, with selected variants from the Latin edition of 1668, Indianapolis: Hackett, 1994 [London: Andrew Crooke, 1651], I, XI, p. 61.

On the other hand, not having an agreement on what is just leads men to focus on their self-interest, which leads necessarily to civil war:

For being distracted in opinions concerning the best use and application of their strength, they do not help, but hinder one another, and reduce their strength by mutual opposition to nothing: whereby they are easily, not only subdued by a very few that agree together, but also, when there is no common enemy, they make war upon each other for their particular interests.[27]

For Hobbes, private interest equals private passions. This is the fundamental reason why monarchy is a better system of government. Speaking of the monarch, Hobbes remarks:

And though he be careful in his politic person to procure the common interest, yet he is more, or no less, careful to procure the private good of himself, his family, kindred and friends; and for the most part, if the public interest chance to cross the private, he prefers the private: for the passions of men are commonly more potent than their reason. From whence it follows that where the public and private interest are most closely united, there is the public most advanced. Now in monarchy the private interest is the same with the public.[28]

The monarch has a duty to defend the common interest, but the propensity to indulge in one's private interest is irresistible because private interest is defined by the passions, and the passions almost always have their way. This, however, does not constitute a predicament in a monarchy because there is by definition no difference between the king's private interest and the public interest. The monarch pursues the public interest even when he is driven by his passions.

Locke understands the relationship between interest and passions in a similar way. He affirms that, because the law of nature exists only in the minds of men, it is necessary to write it down in the form of "promulgated standing laws," for fear that men "through passion or interest, shall mis-cite or misapply it."[29] In a different context, he again lumps the two notions together when he states what leads us to give our assent to a proposition in the absence of a definite proof:

Whatsoever credit or authority we give to any proposition more than it receives from the principles and proofs it supports itself upon, is owing to our inclinations

---

[27] Ibid., II, XVII, p. 107.

[28] Ibid., II, XIX, p. 120. Hirschman mentions the Hobbesian conception of monarchy in his discussion of the physiocrats. Interestingly, he overlooks the aspect of the doctrine mentioned here: the coincidence between the king's passions and the interest of the State (*The Passions and the Interests*, p. 97).

[29] John Locke, *Second Treatise of Government*, edited by C.B. Macpherson, Indianapolis: Hackett, 1980 [London, 1690], § 136, p. 71.

that way, and is so far a derogation from the love of truth as such: which, as it can receive no evidence from our passions or interests, so it should receive no tincture from them.[30]

From Montaigne to Locke, there is a consensus on the idea that private interest is dictated by the passions. This instills some ambiguity into the relationship between private and public interest. In Montaigne, this ambiguity is limited by the fact that there is a clear separation between the private and the public spheres. The public interest is defined by reason. The private interests are defined by the passions. Montaigne insists that private passions and interests should not taint the feelings and obligations one has with respect to the common interest:

Moreover, I am not pressed by any passion either of hate or love toward the great, not is my will bound by any personal injury or obligation. I look upon our kings simply with a loyal and civic affection, which is neither moved nor removed by private interest.[31]

In La Rochefoucauld, the ambiguity goes further. As we have seen above, La Rochefoucauld uses a political-military vocabulary to analyze individual psychology. He talks about large and small interests, victories, defeats, enemies and allies, etc. On the other hand, he looks at political and military history through the prism of individual psychology: great men like Caesar and Alexander make history; these men are moved into action by passions like ambition, or perhaps even envy or jealousy. This double movement has two contradictory consequences. On the one hand, self-love can be compared to a Machiavellian prince, who behaves according to a rational calculation of his interests. That is the meaning of the maxim: "Self-love is cleverer than the cleverest man in the world."[32] On the other hand, self-love is at its calculating best when it is moved by the most violent passions:

In its greatest interests, in its most important dealings, when the violence of its desires leads it to pay full attention, it sees, it feels, it hears, it imagines, it suspects, it understands, it guesses everything.[33]

[30] John Locke, *An Essay Concerning Human Understanding*, edited by Peter Harold Nidditch, Oxford: Clarendon Press, 1975 [London, 1689], XIX, I.

[31] Montaigne, *Essays*, III, I, p. 601. "Au demeurant, je ne suis pressé de passion ou haineuse ou amoureuse envers les grands; ni n'ai ma volonté garrottée d'offense ou d'obligation particulière. Je regarde nos rois d'une affection simplement légitime et civile: ni émue ni démue par intérêt privé." *Essais*, III, I, p. 792.

[32] La Rochefoucauld, *The Maxims*, maxim 4. "L'amour-propre est plus habile que le plus habile homme du monde."

[33] Ibid., deleted maxim I (my translation). "Dans ses plus grands intérêts, et dans ses plus importantes affaires, où la violence de ses souhaits appelle toute son attention, il voit, il sent, il entend, il imagine, il soupçonne, il pénètre, il devine tout."

Having insisted on the opposition between interests and passions in seventeenth-century moral philosophy, Hirschman presents Adam Smith's reference to "the private interests and passions of individuals" as a philosophical innovation. But we have just seen that reason of State theory has a flipside. From Montaigne to Locke, private interests and passions are constantly associated. In reason of State theory, there is a clear opposition between passions and interests. In La Rochefoucauld's psychology, the picture is more complex: in one sense, there is still an opposition between interests and passions; in another sense, passions and interests are synonymous. While La Rochefoucauld relies heavily on the concepts of reason of State theory in his analysis of self-love, the migration from the political sphere to the individual sphere undermines the consistency of the theory – which is probably La Rochefoucauld's intent. To be sure, there is a fundamental difference between the way Smith associates passions and interests, and the equivalency between passions and interests we find from Montaigne to Locke. For Montaigne, La Rochefoucauld, and Locke, private passions and interests are inherently destructive. For Smith, they are the foundation of the wealth of nations. This observation does not contradict the point made by Hirschman: that Smith's view of the relationship between passions and interests is a puzzling one. It makes it even more puzzling.

THE MONTESQUIEU–STEUART DOCTRINE

According to Hirschman, early modern political philosophy proposes three ways of managing the passions. First, the political system could be built in order to *repress* the passions. Secondly, the system could be aimed at *harnessing* the passions, instead of simply repressing them. Thirdly, a system could be designed around the belief that the best way of checking a passion is to oppose another passion to it. Such doctrine is based upon the *countervailing passions* principle.

An example of the first category, in Hirschman's analysis, is Calvin's political doctrine, inspired by Augustine's view of the passions. The classic "invisible hand" argument is presented under the second category (harnessing the passions). In that sense, Pascal is a precursor of Adam Smith because he marveled at the role of concupiscence in the foundation of the social order.[34] Hirschman adds, in a rather skeptical tone, that the invisible hand argument never says exactly *how* individual passions and interests

---

[34] Blaise Pascal, *Pensées*, translated by A.J. Krailsheimer, London: Penguin Books, 1966, fragments 106 and 118 (Sellier 138 and 150).

(Smith) or concupiscence (Pascal) are transformed into a stable political and economic order: "We are left in the dark about the conditions under which that marvelous metamorphosis of destructive 'passions' into 'virtue' actually takes place."[35] Mandeville also falls into this category, because he advocated the skillful management of the passions by politicians in order to turn private vices into public benefits. According to Hirschman, Mandeville restricted his demonstration to the manner in which greed (passion for material goods) can be harnessed for the common interest. Building upon Mandeville's demonstration, "Smith was able to take a further giant step in the direction of making the proposition palatable and persuasive: he blunted the edge of Mandeville's shocking paradox by substituting for 'passion' and 'vice' such bland terms as 'advantage' or 'interest'."[36] Consequently, "in this limiting and domesticated form the harnessing idea was able to survive and to prosper both as a major tenet of nineteenth-century liberalism and as a central construct of economic theory."[37] In the third category (countervailing passions), one finds Bacon, Spinoza, Hume, d'Holbach and the authors of the American constitution, whose preoccupation with checks and balances was based upon the belief that the only effective counterweights of the passions are the passions themselves. The next step in the countervailing passions scheme is the idea that interests can be pitted against passions. One set of passions, previously known as avarice, greed, etc., is euphemistically redefined as *interest*, and pitted against all the other passions: ambition, lust for power, sexual desire, etc. "At this point," says Hirschman, "a junction is effected between the previously developed train of thought on countervailing passions and the doctrine of interest."[38] This association of reason of State theory with the countervailing passions principle is the Montesquieu–Steuart doctrine.

As we have seen in chapter 2, the various thinkers involved in this story belong to two different traditions. On the one hand, an Epicurean/Augustinian tradition, exemplified by Pascal, La Rochefoucauld, Bayle, and Mandeville, which sees pleasure as the only motive for human action, and focuses on the ambiguous function of self-interest: a destructive force that provides a (precarious) foundation for the social order. On the other hand, a Stoic tradition, exemplified by Shaftesbury, Hutcheson, Rousseau (to some extent), and Smith, which postulates a harmony between individual self-interest and the interest of all (the invisible hand argument). In many ways, Hirschman's concept of harnessing the passions

---

[35] Hirschman, *The Passions and the Interests*, p. 17.   [36] Ibid., p. 19.
[37] Ibid.   [38] Ibid., p. 41.

is consistent with the Stoic tradition described in chapter 2 (the invisible hand is a neo-Stoic notion). As to the principle of countervailing passions, Hirschman himself notices that it is originally Augustinian.[39] In that sense, it is consistent with the Epicurean/Augustinian tradition described in chapter 2.

If that is correct, we must question Hirschman's suggestion that Pascal's political doctrine foreshadows the invisible hand argument. Pascal is an Augustinian thinker, who does not believe in the harmony between individual self-interest and the interest of all. On the contrary, Pascal's reasoning is based on the countervailing passions principle. When Pascal marvels at the role of concupiscence in establishing the social order, he means that the populace, because of the force of "imagination,"[40] is easily impressed by displays of power. This checks their tendency to question authority and rebel against it ("They throw off the yoke as soon as they recognize it"[41]). One vice (gullibility) checks another vice (rebelliousness). As Pascal puts it elsewhere, "we do not keep ourselves virtuous by our own power, but by the counterbalance of two opposing vices, just as we stay upright between two contrary winds."[42] As an Augustinian, Pascal does marvel at the providential effects of countervailing passions. Yet at the same time he is aware that divine Providence always sends out mixed messages. Because gullibility checks rebelliousness, nothing is easier than starting a civil war. The only thing needed is to make the populace a bit less gullible by showing them that the foundations of the political order are arbitrary: "The art of subversion, of revolution, is to dislodge established customs by probing down to their origins in order to show that they lack authority and justice."[43]

The same can be shown with other authors belonging to the Epicurean/Augustinian tradition. Nicole follows the countervailing passions principle when he writes that "fear of death is ... the first tie of civil society, and the first check of self-love."[44] The passion of fear neutralizes the lust for power. La Rochefoucauld develops various aspects of the same

[39] "For the latter argument of this essay, it is of considerable interest that St. Augustine conceives here of the possibility that one vice may check another." Ibid., p. 10.

[40] Pascal, *Pensées*, fragment 44 (Sellier 78).

[41] "Ils secouent le joug dès qu'ils le reconnaissent." Ibid., fragment 60 (Sellier 94).

[42] "Nous ne nous soutenons pas dans la vertu par notre propre force, mais par le contrepoids de deux vices opposés, comme nous demeurons debout entre deux vents contraires." Ibid., fragment 674 (Sellier 553).

[43] "L'art de fronder, bouleverser les états est d'ébranler les coutumes établies en sondant jusque dans leur source pour marquer leur défaut d'autorité et de justice." Ibid., fragment 60 (Sellier 94).

[44] Pierre Nicole, *Moral Essays*, London: Manship, 1696, p. 81. "La crainte de la mort est donc le premier lien de la société civile, et le premier frein de l'amour-propre." *Essais de morale*, edited by Laurent Thirouin, Paris: PUF, 1999 [Paris: Desprez, 1675], p. 384.

principle in his *Maxims*. First of all, he states that within the human heart, passions are in an adversarial relationship:

In the human heart there is an endless generation of passions, so that the downfall of one almost always means the establishment of another.[45]

An example of one passion taming other passions is the power of laziness:

We deceive ourselves thinking that only violent passions, like ambition and love, can overpower our other passions. Laziness, thoroughly languid though it be, very seldom fails to be master; it interferes with all our plans and actions; it very gradually wears down and consumes our passions and our virtues.[46]

The countervailing passions principle appears in its most subtle form when resistance to a passion comes not from another passion, but from the passion itself:

The passions often beget their opposites: avarice sometimes gives rise to extravagance, extravagance to avarice; one is often firm through weakness and bold through timidity.[47]

Regarding *The Fable of the Bees*, Hirschman rightly points out the importance of greed in Mandeville's scheme. However, Mandeville's demonstration regarding the beneficial effects of vice is not restricted to greed. Pride plays an even larger role in the system. One can understand why Hirschman would see Mandeville as someone who subscribes to the idea that passions can be harnessed into producing beneficial consequences. Mandeville insists on the manipulation of popular passions by politicians. However, this manipulation takes place in accordance with the countervailing passions principle. For instance, in *The Fable of the Bees*, Cleomenes and Horatius discuss the function of pride in the education of children. Cleomenes argues that it is useful to cultivate both shame and pride in children. Horatius objects that inflating pride must have deleterious consequences. Cleomenes agrees, but he argues that it is possible to neutralize pride by playing it against itself:

[45] La Rochefoucauld, *The Maxims*, maxim 10 (translation modified). "Il y a dans le cœur humain une génération perpétuelle de passions, en sorte que la ruine de l'une est presque toujours l'établissement d'une autre."

[46] Ibid., maxim 266 (translation modified). "C'est se moquer que de croire qu'il n'y ait que les violentes passions comme l'ambition et l'amour, qui puissent triompher des autres. La paresse, toute languissante qu'elle est, ne laisse pas d'en être souvent la maîtresse; elle usurpe sur tous les desseins et sur toutes les actions de la vie; elle y détruit et y consume insensiblement les passions et les vertus."

[47] Ibid., maxim 11. "Les passions en engendrent souvent qui leur sont contraires. L'avarice produit quelquefois la prodigalité, et la prodigalité l'avarice; on est souvent ferme par faiblesse, et audacieux par timidité."

Horatius. I should have thought that this increase of pride would render children more stubborn and less docile.

Cleomenes. You judge right, it would so; and must have been a great hindrance to good manners, till experience taught men, that, though pride was not to be destroyed by force, it might be governed by stratagem, and that the best way to manage it, is by playing the passion against itself. Hence it is that in an artful education we are allowed to place as much pride as we please in our dexterity of concealing it.[48]

Elsewhere, Cleomenes elaborates on this idea. The natural manifestations of pride are offensive to others. However, in civilized society, pride expresses itself in ways that are not offensive to others, because people are taught to put their highest pride in their ability to dissimulate their pride:

Where pride is so much indulged, and yet to be so carefully kept from all human view, as it is in persons of honor of both sexes, it would be impossible for mortal strength to endure the restraint, if men could not be taught to play the passion against itself, and were not allowed to change the natural home-bred symptoms of it for artificial foreign ones.[49]

The "artificial" symptoms of pride are "fine clothes and other orna-ments," "costly equipages," "titles of honor," etc., which are "less offensive, and more beneficial to others" than the natural ones. For the purpose of our analysis, the important point is that conquering pride is "impossible for mortal strength." The only thing capable of conquering pride is pride itself.

The countervailing passions principle is also at the root of Bayle's phi-losophy. Bayle states that the human soul "is subject to so many passions that they are sufficient to hold back one another."[50] Like all authors in the Augustinian tradition, Bayle believes that a "repressing principle" is necessary to hold society together. Unlike Calvin, who saw religion as the repressing principle, Bayle agrees with Nicole that fear of death is sufficient to hold society together:

Whoever cares to reflect on the most unchanging passions in our nature will find (without injecting religion into it *velut Deum ex machina*) this repressing principle they say is needed to preserve the human race. Man naturally loves the preservation of his own life. This necessarily leads him to get away from a condition where he

[48] Bernard Mandeville *The Fable of the Bees*, edited by F.B. Kaye, Oxford: Clarendon Press, 1924 [sixth edition, London: J. Tonson, 1732], vol. 2, p. 78.
[49] Ibid., p. 125.
[50] Pierre Bayle, *Continuation des pensées diverses*, in *Œuvres diverses*, vol. 3, The Hague: P. Husson, F. Boucquet et al., 1727 [Rotterdam: Reinier Leers, 1704], § 121, p. 357.

would have to be continuously at war with everyone. Hence the suspension of all acts of hostility between families that seek to remain independent, or the confederations of entire peoples under one chief.[51]

According to Bayle, the principle of countervailing passions is also at work in the exercise of political power. Ambition is by nature a destructive force, but its detrimental effects are limited because ambition often checks itself:

Of all human passions, there is none more contrary to the tranquility of societies than the ambition of those who enslave their homeland or set themselves up as conquerors; but this very ambition is one of the most effective ways of preserving society as a whole and preventing anarchy; because the tyrants by usurpation, the tyrants by administration, and the conquerors have no stronger motive than increasing their power. Therefore, nothing would be more contrary to their interests than anarchy or the breakdown of society and of all form of government.[52]

This passage is remarkable because, like La Rochefoucauld, Bayle combines the vocabulary of reason of State theory (he mentions the "interests" of the rulers) with the Augustinian analysis of countervailing passions. The "interests" of the ruler have a psychological content: a ruler's interest is the satisfaction of his ambition. At the same time, ambition must control itself in order to be satisfied. Bayle gives the example of the Roman dictators, Marius and Sylla, who stopped slaughtering their opponents not because they suddenly became aware of moral considerations, but simply because their ambition demanded it:

Marius, Sylla, and the triumvirs did not push the fury of their massacres any further, not because they were afraid of offending the gods, but because, having satisfied their anger, they realized that it was in their own interest to stop there. They wanted to have some people left over whom they could rule.[53]

---

[51] Ibid., § 121, p. 358. "Quiconque prendra la peine de réfléchir sur les passions les plus inaliénables de notre nature y trouvera sans y mêler la religion *velut Deum ex machina* ce principe réprimant que l'on dit être nécessaire à conserver le genre humain. L'homme aime naturellement la conservation de sa vie. Cela le porte de toute nécessité à se tirer d'une condition où il faudrait être continuellement sous les armes contre tout le monde. De là émanent ou les suspensions de tous actes d'hostilité entre des familles dont chacune se veut maintenir dans l'indépendance, ou les confédérations de tout un peuple sous un seul chef."

[52] Ibid., "De toutes les passions de l'homme il n'y en a point de plus opposée au repos des sociétés que l'ambition, ou de ceux qui subjuguent leur patrie, ou de ceux qui s'érigent en conquérants; mais cette ambition même est l'un des moyens les plus efficaces de conserver la société généralement et de prévenir l'anarchie; car les tyrans d'usurpation, les tyrans d'administration, les conquérants n'ont point de plus fort motif que d'augmenter leur puissance. Rien donc ne serait aussi opposé à leurs intérêts que l'anarchie ou que la rupture de la société et de toute forme de gouvernement."

[53] Ibid., "Si Marius et Sylla et les triumvirs ne poussèrent pas plus loin la fureur de leurs massacres, ce ne fut point par la crainte d'irriter les dieux, mais parce que leur colère étant assouvie, ils connurent que leurs propres intérêts les engageaient à s'arrêter là. Ils voulurent qu'il restât des gens à qui l'on pût commander."

In reason of State theory, interests are pitted against passions, but the definition of a ruler's interests is a rationalistic one. Rohan does not explain how the ruler can prevent his passions from interfering with the calculation of his interests. In the Augustinian interpretation of reason of State theory, interests are successfully pitted against the passions because the interests are an expression of the passions themselves. Ambition as an unruly passion is tamed by ambition as interest. It is worth mentioning that this psychological analysis is part of a providential interpretation of history. Bayle ends his analysis of the "repressing principle" with the contention that "God's Providence" can find as many ways of "repressing human wickedness"[54] in atheistic societies as in pagan societies.

The Augustinian interpretation provides a response to a question that remained unanswered in reason of State theory: how can the ruler control his passions? According to the Augustinians, passions have a providential way of checking themselves. However, this self-regulating mechanism is not entirely reliable. The passions of the rulers sometimes manifest themselves directly as what they are: a destructive force. In such instances, interest calculations are irrelevant:

Monarchs do not always orient their passions by the wind of their interest. They are being accused of this fault: they are supposed to abandon friendship or hatred very easily, as soon as their ambition requires that they should hate or love. This may be true in general. But they have, just like private persons, some secret passions, or some dislikes, which on some occasions force them to govern themselves according to those instincts, and to give up their glory, their prudence, and their most fundamental interests.[55]

Two points emerge from this overview. First, it is the case that well before Montesquieu, reason of State theory had been combined with the countervailing passions principle. Secondly, in keeping with the Augustinian tradition, there was also some skepticism regarding the self-regulating power of passions. As we shall now see, Montesquieu's analysis of the passions and the interests is consistent with both of these aspects of the Epicurean/Augustinian tradition.

---

[54] Ibid.

[55] Pierre Bayle, *Dictionnaire historique et critique*, Amsterdam: P. Brunel, 1740 [Rotterdam: Reinier Leers, 1697], article "Louis XI." "Cela montre que les monarques ne tournent pas toujours leurs passions selon le vent de leur intérêt. On les accuse de ce défaut, on suppose qu'ils se défont et de l'amitié et de la haine, avec la dernière facilité, dès que leur grandeur demande ou qu'ils haïssent ou qu'ils aiment: cela peut être vrai ordinairement parlant; ils ont tout comme les particuliers certaines passions secrètes, ou certaines antipathies, qui en quelques rencontres, ne leur permettent pas de se gouverner autrement que selon l'instinct de cette disposition: ils lui sacrifient leur gloire, leur prudence, leurs intérêts les plus capitaux."

In book XXI of *The Spirit of the Laws*, Montesquieu studies the origins of commerce in Europe. The story begins with a dramatic description of the persecutions suffered by Jews at the hands of greedy kings who robbed them of their wealth and forced them into exile. In response, Jewish merchants invented the bill of exchange, which made wealth intangible and immune to confiscation. As a consequence, kings had to respect the Jewish merchants upon whom they depended, and commerce prospered:

Nevertheless, one saw commerce leave this seat of harassment and despair. The Jews, proscribed by each country in turn, found the means for saving their effects. In that way, they managed to fix their refuges forever; a prince who wanted very much to be rid of them would not, for all that, be in a humor to rid himself of their silver.

They invented the bill of exchange, and in this way commerce was able to avoid violence and maintain itself everywhere, for the richest trader had only invisible goods, which could be sent everywhere and leave no trace anywhere.[56]

Montesquieu concludes his narrative with the following generalization, which Hirschman takes as the motto of the Montesquieu–Steuart doctrine:

And, happily, men are in a situation such that, though their passions inspire in them the thought of being wicked, they nevertheless have an interest in not being so.[57]

Kings, motivated by greed, would like to rob the Jews of their possessions. They cannot do so because those possessions have become intangible. Commerce, now unhampered by the greed of kings, prospers. As a consequence, the nations are now prosperous, and the kings begin to understand that it is in their interest not to interfere with the development of commerce. As Hirschman remarks, Sir James Steuart, a disciple of Montesquieu, made a similar point when he stated that modern economies are such complex mechanisms that any interference from the prince would have disastrous

---

[56] Charles-Louis de Montesquieu, *The Spirit of the Laws*, translated and edited by Anne M. Cohler, Basia Carolyn Miller, and Harold Samuel Stone, Cambridge: Cambridge University Press, 1989, XXI, 20, p. 389. "Cependant on vit le commerce sortir du sein de la vexation et du désespoir. Les Juifs, proscrits tour de chaque pays, trouvèrent le moyen de sauver leurs effets. Par là ils rendirent pour jamais leurs retraites fixes; car tel prince qui voudrait bien se défaire d'eux, ne serait pas pour cela d'humeur à se défaire de leur argent.

"Ils inventèrent les lettres de change; et par ce moyen, le commerce put éluder la violence, et se maintenir partout; le négociant le plus riche n'ayant que des biens invisibles, qui pouvaient être envoyés partout, et ne laissaient de trace nulle part." *De L'Esprit des lois*, in *Œuvres complètes*, Paris: Seuil, 1964 [Geneva, 1748], XXI, 20, p. 672.

[57] "Et il est heureux pour les hommes d'être dans une situation où, pendant que leurs passions leur inspirent la pensée d'être méchants, ils ont pourtant intérêt de ne pas l'être." Ibid., p. 389/673.

effects. As a consequence, it can be said that the advancement of commerce is the best check against despotism.[58]

In the conclusion of his narrative, Montesquieu opposes interest to passions (consistent with reason of State theory) but the way in which interest triumphs over passions is entirely consistent with the countervailing passions principle. The ruler's "interest" is his greed. It can be said in that sense that greed checks itself. But Montesquieu appears to make an even stronger claim. Jewish merchants invented the bill of exchange in order to protect their wealth from the exactions of kings. Thus they continued trading in spite of the kings' efforts to dispossess them. Or perhaps, it is *because* of the kings' efforts to dispossess them that Jewish merchants invented ways of making commerce immune to political interference. In that sense, the greed of kings is the indirect and providential cause of the extraordinary development of commerce in Europe. In spite of any explicit references to divine Providence, Montesquieu's analysis must be understood within the Epicurean/Augustinian tradition because of its combination of moral pessimism and upbeat assessment of the beneficial consequences of vice. It must be noticed here that, in Montesquieu's view, greed motivates the behavior of merchants as well as rulers: "The Jews, who were made wealthy by their exactions, were pillaged with the same tyranny by the princes."[59] This narrative bears some superficial resemblance to the invisible hand argument (the pursuit of self-interest by individuals contributes to the interest of all), but its logic is in many ways foreign to it. As we have seen in chapter 2, the invisible hand argument is based on the premise that there exists a natural harmony between individual interest and the interest of all. Here, Montesquieu explains how a vice (greed) begins by having catastrophic consequences and ends up producing beneficial consequences. As Montesquieu puts it, we owe to the avarice of princes "the establishment of a device" (the bill of exchange) that puts commerce "out of their power."[60] In other words, the development of commerce is a consequence of the avarice of princes. Another beneficial consequence is the fact that commerce, which had traditionally been associated with bad faith, both in theology and in popular opinion, "returned, so to speak, to the bosom of integrity."[61] It is

---

[58] Hirschman, *The Passions and the Interests*, pp. 81–84. See Sir James Steuart, *An Inquiry into the Principles of Political Economy*, Edinburgh: Oliver & Boyd, 1966 [London: A. Millar and T. Cadell, 1767], II, XXII, pp. 276–283.

[59] Montesquieu, *The Spirit of the Laws*, XXI, 20, p. 388. "Les Juifs, enrichis par leurs exactions, étaient pillés par les princes avec la même tyrannie." *De L'Esprit des lois*, XXI, 20, p. 672.

[60] "Ainsi nous devons . . . à l'avarice des princes, l'établissement d'une chose qui le met [le commerce] en quelque façon hors de leur pouvoir." Ibid., p. 389/672.

[61] "Rentra, pour ainsi dire, dans le sein de la probité." Ibid.

important to notice that the "good faith" which makes commerce possible is itself based on greed, as La Rochefoucauld points out:

Gratitude is like the good faith of merchants: it keeps trade brisk, and we pay up, not because it is the proper thing to do, but because it makes it easier to borrow again.[62]

Commercial honesty and integrity are therefore examples of virtues proceeding from vice. To quote La Rochefoucauld again, "vices go into the making of virtues, as poisons into that of medicines."[63] This type of reasoning, and the image of poisons used as beneficial drugs, can be traced back to Augustine's conception of Providence. In Book XI of *The City of God*, Augustine criticizes those who see fire, cold and wild beasts as evidence against a providential interpretation of the world:

They fail to see how much those same things contribute to our benefit, if we make wise and appropriate use of them. Even poisons, which are disastrous when improperly used, are turned into wholesome medicines by their proper application.[64]

This quote from *The City of God* exemplifies the logic of the Epicurean/Augustinian doctrine. The social order is based upon forces that are potentially disastrous, and yet produce beneficial consequences. Montesquieu's analysis of the development of commerce in Europe is entirely consistent with this logic, which we also find at work in Pascal, La Rochefoucauld, Bayle, and Mandeville.

It must be added that, like Bayle, Montesquieu is skeptical regarding the effectiveness of interest calculations in checking the passions of rulers. In the *Persian Letters*, Usbek satirizes the exercise of public law in the Western world (public law is what regulates the relations between governments, as opposed to civil law, which regulates the relations between citizens). He notices that public law has been corrupted by "the passions of princes." As it is today, public law "is a science that teaches princes just how far they can violate justice without jeopardizing their own interests."[65] In other words,

---

[62] La Rochefoucauld, *The Maxims*, maxim 223 (translation modified). "Il est de la reconnaissance comme de la bonne foi des marchands: elle entretient le commerce; et nous ne payons pas parce qu'il est juste de nous acquitter, mais pour trouver plus facilement des gens qui nous prêtent."

[63] Ibid., maxim 182 (translation modified). "Les vices entrent dans la composition des vertus comme les poisons entrent dans la composition des remèdes."

[64] Augustine, *The City of God*, translated by John O'Meara, London: Penguin Books, 1984, XI, 22. "Nobis ipsis si eis congruenter atque scienter utamur, commoditatis adtribuant, ita ut venena ipsa, quae per inconvenientiam perniciosa sunt, convenienter adhibita in salubria medicamenta vertantur."

[65] Charles-Louis de Montesquieu, *Persian Letters*, translated by J. Robert Loy, New York: Meridian Books, 1961, letter XCIV, p. 179. "Ce droit, tel qu'il est aujourd'hui, est une science qui apprend aux princes jusqu'à quel point ils peuvent violer la justice sans choquer leurs intérêts." *Lettres persanes*, in *Œuvres complètes*, Paris: Seuil, 1964 [Paris, 1721], Letter 94.

interest calculations do check the behavior of princes to some extent, but the passions of princes have corrupted public law in such a way that justice is violated whenever princes pursue their interests.

In Rousseau's narrative of the origin of commerce, self-love (*amour-propre*) is a paradoxical passion, born of reason and reflection (see chapters 1 and 3). According to Rousseau, the most significant aspect of modern commercial society is that interest calculations drive human behavior in its entirety. As a consequence, true passion has become extinct. Rousseau makes this point in a very revealing passage of *Rousseau Judge of Jean-Jacques*. Observing himself, Rousseau notices that he is "lax and soft," as long as reason alone pushes him. On the contrary, "he becomes completely enflamed the moment he is animated by some passion."[66] The interlocutor may object that this is standard human behavior. Rousseau insists that these psychological features are highly unusual:

> You will say all men are like that. I think the very opposite, and you yourself would think this way if I had put the word *interest* in place of the word *reason*, which basically means the same thing here.[67]

Because, from Rousseau's point of view, interest and reason are nearly synonymous, the psychological observation means that Rousseau is "lax and soft" when his interest is at stake. On the contrary, he is strongly motivated to act when he is moved by his passions. In order to stress the point, Rousseau compares himself to the rest of humankind, who behave in the opposite way. They are prompted to act by their interests, not their passions:

> For what is practical reason if not sacrificing a present and temporary good to the means for procuring greater and more solid ones someday, and what is interest if not the augmentation and continuous extension of these same means? The interested

---

[66] Jean-Jacques Rousseau, *Rousseau Judge of Jean-Jacques*, in *The Collected Writings of Rousseau*, vol. 1, edited by Roger D. Masters and Christopher Kelly, translated by Judith R. Bush, Christopher Kelly, and Roger D. Masters, Hanover, NH: University Press of New England, 1990, p. 122. "Il est lâche et mou tant que la seule raison l'excite, il devient tout de feu sitôt qu'il est animé par quelque passion." *Rousseau juge de Jean-Jacques*, in *Œuvres complètes*, vol. 1, edited by Bernard Gagnebin and Marcel Raymond, Paris: Gallimard, Bibliothèque de la Pléiade, 1959, p. 818.

[67] "Vous me direz que c'est comme cela que sont tous les hommes. Je pense tout le contraire, et vous ne penseriez pas ainsi vous-même si j'avais mis le mot intérêt à la place du mot raison qui dans le fond signifie ici la même chose." Ibid.

man thinks less of enjoying than of multiplying for himself the instrument of enjoyments. He has no passions as such, just as the miser doesn't.[68]

Here, Rousseau touches upon the paradox he developed in the *Second Discourse*. Modern commercial society is based on postponed gratification because the citizen is engaged in endless calculations of interest. As we have just seen, when his interlocutor suggests that Rousseau's psychological profile is common, Rousseau strongly disagrees. He does it for two reasons. First of all, it is a bold assertion of psychological singularity. Secondly, and more importantly, it comes from a realization that Rousseau's ideas on the relationship between self-love and self-interest are counterintuitive. Rousseau seems to be saying: you believe that humans are moderately moved by reason and strongly by the passions; you are right, as far as human nature and common sense are concerned. But the only living human being for whom this is true is Jean-Jacques Rousseau. All other human beings are (unnaturally) moved by reason (self-interest) alone, and not at all by their passions. As a consequence, passions have almost entirely disappeared:

True passions, which are rarer than one might think among men, become even more so day by day. Interest erodes them, diminishes them, swallows them all up, and vanity, which is only a folly of *amour-propre*, helps to stifle them more. The motto of Baron de Feneste can be read in big letters in all the actions of the men of today: *It is for appearances*. These habitual dispositions are hardly suited to allowing the true movement of the heart to act.[69]

Rousseau draws a fundamental distinction between strong, natural passions and the passions induced by the exercise of reason and reflection. Self-interested persons manage to hide their passions easily because the passions generated by *amour-propre* are weak. Natural passions, on the contrary, are hard to dissimulate:

But since *amour-propre* and the impulses derived from it are only secondary passions produced by reflection, they do not act so sensibly on the machine [the body]. This

---

[68] "Qu'est-ce que la raison pratique, si ce n'est le sacrifice d'un bien présent et passager aux moyens de s'en procurer un jour de plus grands ou de plus solides, et qu'est-ce que l'intérêt si ce n'est l'augmentation et l'extension continuelle de ces mêmes moyens? L'homme intéressé songe moins à jouir qu'à multiplier pour lui l'instrument des jouissances. Il n'a point proprement de passions non plus que l'avare." Ibid.

[69] "Les véritables passions, plus rares qu'on ne pense parmi les hommes, le deviennent de jour en jour davantage, l'intérêt les élime, les atténue, les engloutit toutes, et la vanité, qui n'est qu'une bêtise de l'amour-propre, aide encore à les étouffer. La devise du baron de Feneste se lit en gros caractères sur toutes les actions des hommes de nos jours: c'est pour paraître. Ces dispositions habituelles ne sont guère propres à laisser agir les vrais mouvements du cœur." Ibid.

is why those governed by that sort of passion have more mastery over appearances than those who surrender to the direct impulses of nature.[70]

Similarly, in his *Considerations on the Government of Poland*, Rousseau insists that "greed" is "the littlest and weakest of all passions to those who know the human heart well," and that it reigns supreme in human hearts only because "the other passions have been unnerved and smothered when they should have been excited and developed."[71]

Against the behavior of his fellow human beings, Rousseau affirms that wisdom consists in escaping "the narrow prison of personal interest and petty earthly passions," in order to "rise on the wings of imagination above the vapors of our atmosphere," in order to reach the "ethereal regions" where the sage can sustain himself with "sublime contemplations" and "brave from there the blows of fate and the senseless judgments of men."[72] In spite of the stylistic differences, Rousseau's portrait of the sage is remarkably close to the portrait we find in *The Theory of Moral Sentiments*. Rousseau's text was first published in England in 1780.[73] It is quite possible that Smith had it in mind when he composed his portrait of the sage for the last edition of *The Theory of Moral Sentiments*, which was published in 1790. At any rate, the passages quoted above show some remarkable points of convergence between Rousseau and Smith regarding the relationship between passions and interests and the definition of wisdom.

Like Rousseau, Smith paints the portrait of a neo-Stoic sage, who rises above his own narrow point of view in order to embrace the interests of the universe:

In the greatest public as well as private disasters, a wise man ought to consider that he himself, his friends and countrymen, have only been ordered upon the forlorn station of the universe; that had it not been necessary for the good of the whole, they would not have been so ordered; and that it is their duty, not only

---

[70] "L'amour-propre et les mouvements qui en dérivent n'étant que des passions secondaires produites par la réflexion n'agissent pas si sensiblement sur la machine. Voilà pourquoi ceux que ces sortes de passions gouvernent sont plus maîtres des apparences que ceux qui se livrent aux impulsions directes de la nature." Ibid., p. 156/861.

[71] "L'intérêt pécuniaire est . . . le moindre et le plus faible aux yeux de qui connaît bien le cœur humain," ". . . c'est qu'on a énervé, étouffé toutes les autres qu'il fallait exciter et développer." Jean-Jacques Rousseau, *Considérations sur le gouvernement de Pologne*, in *Œuvres complètes*, vol. 3, p. 1005.

[72] Rousseau, *Rousseau Judge of Jean-Jacques*, p. 120. "Mais celui qui, franchissant l'étroite prison de l'intérêt personnel et des petites passions terrestres, s'élève sur les ailes de l'imagination au dessus des vapeurs de notre atmosphère, celui qui . . . sait s'élancer dans les régions éthérées, y planer et s'y soutenir par de sublimes contemplations, peut de là braver les coups du sort et les insensés jugements des hommes." *Rousseau juge de Jean-Jacques*, p. 815.

[73] *Rousseau juge de Jean-Jacques. Dialogues. D'après le manuscrit de M. Rousseau, laissé entre les mains de M. Brooke Boothby*, Lichfield: J. Jackson, 1780.

with humble resignation to submit to this allotment, but to endeavour to embrace it with alacrity and joy.[74]

Smith adds that "the man whom we believe to be principally occupied in this sublime contemplation, seldom fails to be the object of our highest veneration,"[75] and he mentions "Marcus Antoninus" (Marcus Aurelius) as the most illustrious example of this type of activity.

The narrow point of view of the individual is defined by his "individual interest and petty terrestrial passions." Here again, passions and interests appear not as antonyms, but as near-synonyms. Earlier in this chapter, we have seen that, while Hirschman presents Smith's reference to "the private interests and passions of individuals" in *The Wealth of Nations* as a philosophical innovation, there is an entire philosophical tradition from Montaigne to Locke where interest and passions appear as synonyms. At the same time, the equivalency between passions and interests has a different meaning in Montaigne and Locke than it does in Smith. For Montaigne, La Rochefoucauld, and Locke, individual passions and interests are inherently destructive. For Smith (and also for Rousseau, as we have just seen) individual passions and interests are simply a narrow point of view. The sage must rise above his individual passions and interests in order to contemplate the order of the universe, but individual interest is not inherently destructive. It is simply a small element in the larger order of the universe. In this Stoic scheme, passions and interests are of course denigrated from the point of view of greater wisdom. At the same time (and this is crucial for the emergence of economic science): (1) there is no opposition between passions and interests; (2) passions and interests are no longer seen as destructive forces; (3) passions and interests, now assimilated, contribute to the harmony of the whole.

ADAM SMITH ON "SPLENETIC PHILOSOPHY"

In his classic work, *The Machiavellian Moment*, Pocock presents Rousseau as the embodiment of the contradictions of civic humanism according to which "by its nature society humanized man and by the same process distracted and alienated him again."[76] The contradictions of civic

---

[74] Adam Smith, *The Theory of Moral Sentiments* (sixth edition), *The Glasgow Edition of the Works and Correspondence of Adam Smith*, vol. 1, edited by D.D. Raphael and A.L. Macfie, Oxford: Oxford University Press, 1976 [London and Edinburgh, 1790; first edition, 1759], VI.ii.3.4.

[75] Ibid., VI.ii.3.5.

[76] J.G.A. Pocock, *The Machiavellian Moment. Florentine Political Thought and the Atlantic Republican Tradition*, Princeton: Princeton University Press, 1975, p. 504.

humanism can be observed in Smith as well. Alluding to the proverbial expression *le doux commerce*, Hirschman observes that "the *douceur* that was celebrated by Montesquieu and others meant corruption and decadence not only to Rousseau but to some extent also to Smith."[77] Smith laments the fact that interest calculations drive most human behavior in modern commercial society. He paints a vivid portrait of "the poor man's son, whom heaven in its anger has visited with ambition."[78] This young man "admires the condition of the rich." Rich people appear to him as belonging to "some superior rank of beings, and in order to arrive at it, he devotes himself forever to the pursuit of wealth and greatness." Such behavior is futile, Smith insists, because "to obtain the conveniencies which these afford, he submits in the first year, nay in the first month of his application, to more fatigue of body and more uneasiness of mind than he could have suffered through the whole of his life from the want of them."[79] In other words, the poor man's son believes that his life would be more comfortable with servants, horse carriages, etc. but in order to obtain the means towards greater comfort, he submits himself to so much discomfort that the whole enterprise seems self-defeating. Rousseau had made much the same point in the *Second Discourse*, only in a different style, which Adam Smith characterized as "sublime and pathetic".[80] While "the savage breathes nothing but liberty and repose," "the citizen, on the contrary, toils, bestirs and torments himself without end, to obtain employments which are still more laborious: he labours on till his death, he even hastens it, in order to put himself in a condition to live, or renounces life to acquire immortality."[81]

Smith insists that, in addition to being futile, the pursuit of wealth and fame is corrupting because it forces the young man to constantly seek favors and services from others, and to debase himself in the process:

He studies to distinguish himself in some laborious profession. With the most unrelenting industry he labours night and day to acquire talents superior to all his competitors. He endeavours next to bring those talents into public view, and with equal assiduity solicits every opportunity of employment. For this purpose he makes his court to all mankind; he serves those whom he hates, and is obsequious to those whom he despises.[82]

---

[77] Hirschman, *The Passions and the Interests*, p. 107.
[78] Smith, *The Theory of Moral Sentiments*, IV.1.8.   [79] Ibid.
[80] Adam Smith, "Letter to the *Edinburgh Review*," No. 2 (1756), *The Glasgow Edition of the Works and Correspondence of Adam Smith*, vol. 3, Oxford: Oxford University Press, 1976, p. 251.
[81] Rousseau, *Discourse on the Origin of Inequality*, translated by Adam Smith, ibid., p. 253.
[82] Smith, *The Theory of Moral Sentiments*, IV.1.8.

This passage echoes the *Second Discourse* word for word. Of the "citizen" Rousseau writes (in Adam Smith's translation): "He makes his court to the great whom he hates, and to the rich whom he despises."[83]

This parallel between Smith and Rousseau highlights the principal themes of civic humanism: critique of the corrupting influence of luxury and wealth, praise of poverty and virtue. In the conclusion of his review of the *Second Discourse*, Smith characterized Rousseau's book as manifesting "the true spirit of a republican carried a little too far."[84] In other words, Smith saw Rousseau as someone who shared his republican values, but expressed them in an extremist fashion.

Indeed, Smith tried to strike a balance between Rousseau's republican critique of civil society and a more positive view of the function of wealth in the modern economy. Immediately after describing the toils and sufferings of the poor man's son who tries to emulate the rich, Smith proposes a counter-argument to Rousseau's satire:

But though this splenetic philosophy, which in time of sickness or low spirits is familiar to every man, thus entirely depreciates those great objects of human desire, when in better health and in better humour, we never fail to regard them under a more agreeable aspect.[85]

According to this view, Rousseau's *Second Discourse* would be an example of "splenetic philosophy," which consists in denigrating the value of all human endeavors in civil society. Whenever we are in a better mood than melancholic Rousseau is, we can appreciate the value and utility of wealth in the great scheme of things:

Our imagination, which in pain and sorrow seems to be confined and cooped up within our own persons, in times of ease and prosperity expands itself to every thing around us. We are then charmed with the beauty of that accommodation which reigns in the palaces and œconomy of the great; and admire how every thing is adapted to promote their ease, to prevent their wants, to gratify their wishes, and to amuse and entertain their most frivolous desires.[86]

It is true that luxury goods and services are not in themselves worth the trouble one has to incur in order to obtain them. There is, however, another consideration. The modern economy is a beautiful system of marvelous complexity. As such, it is worthy of admiration. This in itself justifies the desire to become rich:

---

[83] Rousseau, *Discourse on the Origin of Inequality*, translated by Adam Smith, "Letter to the *Edinburgh Review*," p. 253.
[84] Ibid., p. 251.   [85] Smith, *The Theory of Moral Sentiments*, IV.1.9.   [86] Ibid.

If we consider the real satisfaction which all these things are capable of affording, by itself and separated from the beauty of that arrangement which is fitted to promote it, it will always appear in the highest degree contemptible and trifling. But we rarely view it in this abstract and philosophical light. We naturally confound it in our imagination with the order, the regular and harmonious movement of the system, the machine or œconomy by means of which it is produced. The pleasures of wealth and greatness, when considered in this complex view, strike the imagination as something grand and beautiful and noble, of which the attainment is well worth all the toil and anxiety which we are so apt to bestow upon it.[87]

   This apology of capitalism is very different from the Montesquieu–Steuart doctrine (the interests of the ruler checking his despotic tendencies). Smith praises modern commercial society from a neo-Stoic point of view. Striving to become rich is the proper thing to do, because the modern economy is a well-ordered and harmonious system. From this point of view, differences in wealth and rank (what Rousseau calls inequality) are necessary for prosperity and good order: "Upon this disposition of mankind, to go along with the passions of the rich and the powerful, is founded the distinction of ranks, and the order of society."[88] As to the passions themselves, they are no longer thought of as an evil. The passions of the rich and the powerful are nothing but their interests, and as such they constitute the engine of wealth creation. In the Montesquieu–Steuart doctrine, social order is the result of opposite forces. As Pascal puts it, moral and political equilibrium comes from "the counterbalance of two opposite vices, just as we stay upright between two contrary winds." This equilibrium is always precarious however: "Take one of these vices away and we fall into the other."[89] Smith's own idea of the social order is entirely foreign to this Epicurean/Augustinian way of thinking. Moral and political equilibrium is not the result of opposite forces. Rather, it is a consequence of the natural harmony between individual passions and the welfare of society as a whole.
   As we have just seen, what Smith derides under the term "splenetic philosophy" is Rousseau's account of the origin of inequality. Elsewhere, Smith calls "splenetic philosophers" those who, "in judging human nature, have done as peevish individuals are apt to do in judging of the conduct of one another, and have imputed to the love of praise, or to what they call vanity, every action which ought to be ascribed to that of praise-worthiness."[90]

---

[87] Ibid.   [88] Ibid., I.iii.2.3.

[89] "Nous ne nous soutenons pas dans la vertu par notre propre force, mais par le contrepoids de deux vices opposés, comme nous demeurons debout entre deux vents contraires. Otez un de ces vices, nous tombons dans l'autre." Pascal, *Pensées*, fragment 674 (Sellier 553).

[90] Smith, *The Theory of Moral Sentiments*, III.ii.27.

Those who see vanity behind every human action are of course La Rochefoucauld and Mandeville. It is, however, no coincidence that Smith would use the same term to refer to Rousseau on the one hand and to La Rochefoucauld and Mandeville on the other. As we have seen in chapter 1, Smith reads the *Second Discourse* as an appropriation by Rousseau of *The Fable of the Bees*. In addition, although Rousseau rejects Mandeville's axiomatic choices regarding the relationship between pity and self-interest, he entirely subscribes to Mandeville's analysis regarding the role of self-interest in modern commercial society. In that sense, from Smith's point of view, a "splenetic philosopher" is one who sees human behavior as entirely driven by calculations of interest.

There is a strange and paradoxical relationship between the interest doctrine, exemplified by La Rochefoucauld and Mandeville, and Smith's understanding of the relationship between passions and interest. As Hirschman points out, Smith reduces passions to interests in *The Wealth of Nations* because, in *The Theory of Moral Sentiments*, he has already described the "great purpose of human life" as "bettering our condition."[91] In *The Wealth of Nations*, Smith claims that "an augmentation of fortune is the means by which the greater part of men propose and wish to better their condition."[92] In other words, according to Smith, the desire to become rich is the overriding passion in modern commercial society.[93] All other passions are subsumed into the desire to increase one's wealth. Why Smith would operate such a reduction becomes less puzzling if one bears in mind the great similarities between Smith's doctrine and Rousseau's anthropology. As we have seen in chapter 3, Rousseau takes a step of decisive importance when he argues against La Rochefoucauld and Mandeville that self-love (*amour-propre*) is a product of reason and reflection. Self-love is a weak and artificial passion, which paradoxically reigns supreme in commercial society. It is both the cause and the consequence of social interaction, and of the constant comparisons we make between ourselves and others. Furthermore, for Rousseau, because self-love is intrinsically tied to interest calculations, there is no difference between self-love and self-interest: in modern commercial society, self-love is the engine of a behavior that consists in constantly evaluating one's position on the social ladder and calculating ways of improving it. All the transactions we perform have only one purpose: improving our standing in the eyes of others.

Rousseau refutes and reinterprets Mandeville at the same time. On the one hand, he agrees with Mandeville that self-love is the only engine

[91] Ibid., I.iii.2.1. [92] Ibid., II.iii.28. [93] Hirschman, *The Passions and the Interests*, p. 108.

of human behavior in modern commercial society. On the other hand, Rousseau's definition of self-love is different from Mandeville's. As an Augustinian, Mandeville (like La Rochefoucauld) sees self-love as the foundation of all kinds of strong, unpredictable, and dangerous passions. Rousseau, however, redefines self-love as a weak, derivative passion, induced by interest calculations. *Adam Smith, having appropriated Rousseau's definition of self-love, is therefore in a position to subsume all passions into the pursuit of self-interest.* In that sense, the conventional wisdom is correct: Smith does assume that human behavior in modern commercial society is generally driven by the pursuit of self-interest. What is more unexpected is that in making this assumption, Smith agrees with a "splenetic philosopher" like Rousseau, who was the first thinker to establish the conceptual connection between self-love, rational calculation, and commercial society.

The difference between the two thinkers lies in the fact that Smith argues on both sides of the issue. While Rousseau's analysis presents itself as part of a univocal critique of commercial society, Smith develops Rousseau's arguments, and then criticizes them as "splenetic philosophy." And yet, with the passage of time, Smith seems to have moved even closer to Rousseau's position. After comparing the 1759 and 1790 editions of *The Theory of Moral Sentiments*, Laurence Dickey concludes that "Smith was becoming increasingly alarmed by what Hirsch has called the 'depleting moral legacy' of commercial society."[94] Indeed, the 1790 edition includes a new chapter entitled: "Of the corruption of our moral sentiments, which is occasioned by this disposition to admire the rich and the great, and to despise or neglect persons of poor and mean condition."[95] According to Smith, "the candidates for fortune frequently abandon the paths of virtue: for unhappily, the road which leads to the one, and that which leads to the other, lie sometimes in very opposite directions."[96] The goal remains the same in all cases: receiving the approbation and esteem of others. However, two very different paths lead to this goal:

To deserve, to acquire, and to enjoy the respect and admiration of mankind, are the great objects of ambition and emulation. Two different roads are presented to us, equally leading to the attainment of this so much desired object; the one, by the study of wisdom and the practice of virtue; the other, by the acquisition of wealth and greatness.[97]

Smith draws a sharp distinction between the acquisition of wealth, which he now describes as corrupting, and the path of virtue, taken by "the

---

[94] Laurence Dickey, "Historicizing the 'Adam Smith Problem': Conceptual, Historiographical, and Textual Issues," *Journal of Modern History* 58 (1986), p. 608.
[95] Smith, *The Theory of Moral Sentiments*, I.iii.3.   [96] Ibid., I.iii.3.8.   [97] Ibid., I.iii.3.2.

wise and the virtuous," who are "but a small party."[98] As to "the great mob of mankind," they are the "admirers and worshippers of wealth and greatness."[99] Hirschman notices that in his *Lectures on Jurisprudence*, Smith had already expressed ambivalence regarding the progress of commerce. The "commercial spirit" has an adverse effect on military virtue. A classic example of this is the contrast between Rome and Carthage:

The Carthaginians were often victorious abroad, but when the war was carried into their own country they had no share with the Romans. These are the disadvantages of a commercial spirit. The minds of men are contracted and rendered incapable of elevation, education is despised or at least neglected, and heroic spirit is almost utterly extinguished. To remedy those defects would be an object worthy of serious attention.[100]

Smith was certainly not alone in this opinion. As Pocock points out, the opposition between commerce and virtue was a *topos* of civic humanism: "Commerce is the source of all social values save one...but that one, the *vertu politique*, is that which makes man a *zoon politikon* and consequently human...Commerce, which makes men cultured, entails luxury, which makes them corrupt."[101]

But here again, Smith's position can be best understood in relation to Rousseau's critique of commerce. Acquisition of wealth and greatness is corrupting because, as Rousseau had shown in his *Second Discourse*, it makes it a compelling matter of self-interest to deceive others:

Thus are all our natural qualities exerted, the rank and condition of every man established, not only upon the greatness of his fortune and his power to serve or to hurt, but upon his genius, his beauty, his strength, or his address, upon his merit or his talents; and those qualities being alone capable of attracting consideration, he must either have them or affect them: he must for his advantage show himself to be one thing, while in reality he is another.[102]

In commercial society, according to Rousseau's expression, "we cannot live but in the opinion of others."[103] Consequently, we must use every means necessary to shape the opinion of others, including dissimulation and deception. Smith gives an example of an extreme and self-defeating use of deception. Since wealth is the surest means towards obtaining the

---

[98] Ibid.   [99] Ibid.
[100] Adam Smith, *Lectures on Jurisprudence, The Glasgow Edition of the Works and Correspondence of Adam Smith*, vol. 5, Oxford: Oxford University Press, 1978, p. 541.
[101] Pocock, *The Machiavellian Moment*, p. 492.
[102] Rousseau, *Discourse on the Origin of Inequality*, translated by Adam Smith, "Letter to the *Edinburgh Review*," p. 252.
[103] Ibid., p. 253.

esteem of others, some have calculated that it is in their interest to *simulate* wealth:

There are hypocrites of wealth and greatness, as well as of religion and virtue; and a vain man is as apt to pretend to be what he is not, in the one way, as a cunning man is in the other. He assumes the equipage and splendid way of living of his superiors, without considering that whatever may be praise-worthy in any of these, derives its whole merit and propriety from its suitableness to that situation and fortune which both require and can easily support the expence. Many a poor man places his glory in being thought rich, without considering that the duties (if one may call such follies by so very venerable a name) which that reputation imposes upon him, must soon reduce him to beggary, and render his situation still more unlike that of those whom he admires and imitates, than it had been originally.[104]

From Rousseau's point of view, the systematic use of deception does not only constitute a danger for individual morality. It is a threat to the social fabric itself:

To conclude, an insatiable ambition, an ardor to raise his relative fortune, not so much from any real necessity, as to set himself above others, inspires all men with a direful propensity to hurt one another; with a secret jealousy, so much more dangerous, as to strike its blow more surely, it often assumes the mask of good will; in short, with concurrence and rivalship on one side; on the other, with opposition of interest; and always with the concealed desire of making profit at the expense of some other person. All these evils are the first effects of property, and the inseparable attendants of beginning inequality.[105]

This passage offers a stunning refutation of the *doux commerce* thesis. Far from taming the passions, the pursuit of self-interest incessantly generates new and dangerous passions. As Rousseau puts it in *Émile*, "*amour-propre*, which makes comparisons, is never content, and never could be... hateful and irascible passions are born of *amour-propre*."[106] Inequality triggers envy and jealousy. Furthermore, as citizens become more aware of their interests, they begin to see the pursuit of interest as a zero-sum game, where my gain is your loss. The passion of envy, generated by the growth of commerce and the concurrent growth in inequality, is the greatest threat to civil society. This, according to Rousseau, is due to the fact that while we sympathize

---

[104] Smith, *The Theory of Moral Sentiments*, I.iii.3.7.

[105] Rousseau, *Discourse on the Origin of Inequality*, translated by Adam Smith, "Letter to the *Edinburgh Review*," p. 253.

[106] Jean-Jacques Rousseau, *Émile*, translated by Allan Bloom, New York: Basic Books, 1979, p. 213. "Mais l'amour-propre, qui se compare, n'est jamais content et ne saurait l'être... les passions haineuses et irascibles naissent de l'amour-propre." *Émile ou de L'Education*, in *Œuvres Complètes*, vol. 4, Paris, Gallimard, 1969 [Amsterdam: Marc-Michel Rey, 1762], p. 493.

with the sorrow of others, the sight of happiness and prosperity hurts our self-love:

> If our common needs unite us by interest, our common miseries unite us by affection. The sight of a happy man inspires in others less love than envy. They would gladly accuse him of usurping a right he does not have in giving himself an exclusive happiness; and *amour-propre* suffers, too, in making us feel that this man has no need of us.[107]

Rousseau's position is a complex one. On the one hand, self-interest is an agent of social cohesion because it prompts us to serve our common needs. On the other hand, the pursuit of self-interest, being both a cause and a consequence of the growth in inequality, is accompanied by a growth in envy, a destructive passion.

Smith must have been aware of these implications of Rousseau's doctrine, because he goes out of his way to assert, rather counterintuitively, that we sympathize with joy more readily than we do with sorrow:

> We often feel a sympathy with sorrow rid of it; and we often miss that with joy when we would be glad to have it. The obvious observation, therefore, which it naturally falls in our way to make, is, that our propensity to sympathize with sorrow must be very strong, and our inclination to sympathize with joy very weak.
>
> Notwithstanding this prejudice, however, I will venture to affirm, that, when there is no envy in the case, our propensity to sympathize with joy is much stronger than our propensity to sympathize with sorrow; and that our fellow-feeling for the agreeable emotion approaches much more nearly to the vivacity of what is naturally felt by the persons principally concerned, than that which we conceive for the painful one.[108]

In what Jean-Pierre Dupuy characterizes as a *coup de force*,[109] Smith reverses the conventional wisdom. The implications of this move are far-reaching. It allows Smith to contend against Rousseau that we naturally sympathize with the feelings of "the rich and the great." Yet at the same time Smith seems to remain aware of the dangers of envy. He concedes to the reader that the idea of a natural sympathy with the feelings of the wealthy is hard to believe:

[107] "Si nos besoins communs nous unissent par intérêt, nos misères communes nous unissent par affection. L'aspect d'un homme heureux inspire aux autres moins d'amour que d'envie; on l'accuserait volontiers d'usurper un droit qu'il n'a pas en se faisant un bonheur exclusif, et l'amour-propre souffre encore, en nous faisant sentir que cet homme n'a nul besoin de nous." Ibid., p. 221/504.
[108] Smith, *The Theory of Moral Sentiments*, 1.iii.1.4.
[109] Jean-Pierre Dupuy, "De l'émancipation de l'économie: retour sur 'le problème d'Adam Smith'," *L'Année sociologique* 37 (1987), p. 333.

The great mob of mankind are the admirers and worshippers, and, *what may seem more extraordinary* [my emphasis], most frequently the disinterested admirers and worshippers, of wealth and greatness.[110]

In addition, every time Smith advances the idea that we sympathize with the feelings of the wealthy and the great, he qualifies his statement by saying that, for this to be true, we must take "the odious and detestable passion of envy"[111] out of the picture. For instance, in the passage quoted above, Smith writes: "I will venture to affirm, that, *when there is no envy in the case* [my emphasis], our propensity to sympathize with joy is much stronger than our propensity to sympathize with sorrow."[112] In another chapter, entitled "Of the Selfish Passions," he expresses the same idea in a slightly different way: "Joy is a pleasant emotion, and we gladly abandon ourselves to it upon the slightest occasion. We readily, therefore, sympathize with it in others, *whenever we are not prejudiced by envy* [my emphasis]."[113] An example of behavior generating envy is the behavior of the *nouveau riche*: "An upstart, though of the greatest merit, is generally disagreeable, and a sentiment of envy commonly prevents us from heartily sympathizing with his joy."[114] Among many passages, one could still quote this one, where the rule according to which we sympathize with joy is qualified by the reference to envy: "It is agreeable to sympathize with joy; and *wherever envy does not oppose it* [my emphasis], our heart abandons itself with satisfaction to the highest transports of that delightful sentiment."[115]

In fact, Smith sees envy as the single most potent threat to the social order:

The great source of both the misery and disorders of human life, seems to arise from over-rating the difference between one permanent situation and another. Avarice over-rates the difference between poverty and riches: ambition, that between a private and a public station: vain-glory, that between obscurity and extensive reputation. The person under the influence of any of those extravagant passions, is not only miserable in his actual situation, but is often disposed to disturb the peace of society, in order to arrive at that which he so foolishly admires.[116]

In this passage, what avarice, ambition, and vain-glory have in common is the fact that the individual "foolishly admires" something he does not have. In other words, the natural tendency to sympathize with the feelings of the rich and the great can easily turn into an irrepressible and socially disruptive desire to obtain what the rich and the great possess. In sum, sympathy can easily become envy. Indeed, Smith uses the word *envy* to

---

[110] Smith, *The Theory of Moral Sentiments*, I.iii.3.2.   [111] Ibid., VI.iii.15.   [112] Ibid., I.iii.1.4.
[113] Ibid., I.ii.5.1.   [114] Ibid.   [115] Ibid, I.iii.1.9.   [116] Ibid., III.3.31.

describe the feelings one has vis-à-vis the rich and the great. According to Smith, it is the fact that "the man of rank and distinction . . . is observed by all the world" that "renders greatness the object of envy."[117] In the chapter added in 1790, he also characterizes wealth as an "envied situation."[118] In those instances, the line between sympathy and envy seems to be blurred. Finally in *The Wealth of Nations*, Smith observes that the main purpose of establishing civil government is to protect the rich from the envy of the poor: "The affluence of the rich excites the indignation of the poor, who are often both driven by want, and prompted by envy, to invade his possessions."[119] This point is reminiscent of Rousseau's *Second Discourse*, where the establishment of civil government is described as an initiative of the rich who manage to persuade the poor that it is in everyone's interest to have laws to protect property. It is worth noticing here that, of course, Smith does not question the legitimacy of civil government, but neither does Rousseau. The conclusion of the *Second Discourse* is that inequality "finally becomes stable and legitimate by the establishment of property and Laws."[120]

It thus appears that Smith's position on the relationship between passions and interests is at least as complex as Rousseau's. Hont and Ignatieff are right to point out that "Rousseau is an important if unavowed interlocutor in the passages in *The Theory of Moral Sentiments* which Smith devoted to the pursuit of wealth in modern society."[121] However, they express only one side of the issue when they claim that "Smith broke decisively with the modern Stoic and Rousseauian critique of modern deception."[122] Two contradictory arguments can be made on the basis of Rousseau's analyses. On the one hand, it is the case that human behavior in commercial society is entirely driven by interest calculations. These calculations are both the cause and consequence of artificial, derivative, and weak passions. From this point of view, there is no difference between passions and interests. Smith

---

[117] Ibid., I.iii.2.1.   [118] Ibid., I.iii.3.8.

[119] Adam Smith, *An Inquiry into the Nature and Causes of the Wealth of Nations*, The Glasgow Edition of the Works and Correspondence of Adam Smith, vol. 2, Oxford: Oxford University Press, 1976 [London: Strahan and Cadell, 1776], v.i.b.2.

[120] Jean-Jacques Rousseau, *Discourse on the Origin of Inequality*, in *The Collected Writings of Rousseau*, vol. 3, edited by Roger D. Masters and Christopher Kelly, translated by Judith R. Bush, Roger D. Masters, Christopher Kelly, and Terence Marshall, Hanover, NH: University Press of New England, 1992, p. 67. ". . . devient enfin stable et légitime par l'établissement de la propriété et des lois." *Discours sur l'origine de l'inégalité*, in *Œuvres complètes*, edited by Bernard Gagnebin and Marcel Raymond, Paris: Gallimard, Bibliothèque de la Pléiade, 1959–1969, vol. 3, p. 193.

[121] Istvan Hont and Michael Ignatieff, "Needs and Justice in the 'Wealth of Nations,'" in *Wealth and Virtue. The Shaping of Political Economy in the Scottish Enlightenment*, edited by Istvan Hont and Michael Ignatieff, Cambridge: Cambridge University Press, 1983, p. 10.

[122] Ibid.

appropriates this aspect of Rousseau's thought in order to reduce passions to interest, and to develop a harmonic scheme whereby the passions of individuals contribute to the common good. On the other hand, Smith remains aware of the other side of Rousseau's argument. The pursuit of self-interest and the growth of inequality result in the growth of dangerous and destructive passions like envy. Smith limits the implications of this idea by making the paradoxical assertion that we sympathize naturally with the feelings of the wealthy, but, as we have seen above, there seems to be a very short distance from sympathy to envy. Pocock draws a distinction between Rousseau and the Scottish school of moral philosophy by pointing out that

Rousseau was the Machiavelli of the eighteenth century, in the sense that he dramatically and scandalously pointed out a contradiction that others were trying to live with. If the Scottish school believed that the contradiction between virtue and culture might be managed by men in society with good hopes of reasonable success, it was his role to insist that the contradiction was intolerable.[123]

The distinction may not be quite as sharp as Pocock claims. It is indeed illuminating to read Smith's work as an attempt to resolve the contradiction between virtue and culture, or, in the case of the present discussion, between passions and interests. Whether the attempt was successful is an open question. It is certain, at any rate, that Rousseau's work reminded Smith of the acuteness of the contradiction.

---

[123] Pocock, *The Machiavellian Moment*, p. 504.

5

Interested and disinterested commerce

Here then is the mutual commerce of good offices in a manner lost among mankind, and every one reduced to his own skill and industry for his well-being and subsistence.

Hume, *A Treatise of Human nature* (1739)

THE ETHICS/ECONOMICS DICHOTOMY

In his volume entitled *On Ethics and Economics*, Amartya Sen criticizes the "anti-ethicalism"[1] that characterizes modern economic theory. Sen does not mean that economists have a bias against moral judgments per se (even though he suggests that some of them actually do). The claim is that, to its detriment, economic theory has historically asserted itself by excluding any form of moral consideration from its reasoning. This turn of events is rather paradoxical, if one recalls that economics was originally a branch of ethics. Aristotle discussed money and exchange in Book V of the *Nicomachean Ethics*. Adam Smith's position at the University of Glasgow was professor of moral philosophy. According to Sen, the methodological distinction between ethics and economics was expressed most sharply by F.Y. Edgeworth in his *Mathematical Psychics*. In this work, Edgeworth distinguishes between the "Economical Calculus," which "investigates the equilibrium of a system of hedonic forces each tending to maximum individual utility," and the "Utilitarian Calculus," which studies "the equilibrium of a system in which each and all tend to maximum universal utility."[2] In economical calculus, the motives of the agent are characterized as "Egoistic Hedonism" (a reference to Sidgwick's *Methods of Ethics*[3]). In utilitarian calculus, the motives of

---

[1] Amartya Sen, *On Ethics and Economics*, Oxford: Blackwell, 1987, p. 31.
[2] Francis Y. Edgeworth, *Mathematical Psychics. An Essay on the Application of Mathematics to the Moral Sciences*, London: C. Kegan Paul, 1881, p. 15.
[3] Henry Sidgwick, *The Methods of Ethics* (seventh edition), London: Macmillan, 1907 [London, 1874], pp. 119–121.

the agents pertain to "Universalistic Hedonism."[4] In Edgeworth's system, utilitarian calculus is the first principle of ethics, while egoistic calculus is the first principle of economics.[5] The egoistic hedonist works exclusively toward individual happiness. The universalistic hedonist only cares about the happiness of others.

In this presentation, ethics and economics seem to constitute two entirely separate fields, especially since they are grounded in first principles that are incompatible. Edgeworth praises Sidgwick for having "forever dispelled" the notion "that the interest of all is the interest of each, an illusion to which the ambiguous language of Mill, and perhaps Bentham, may have led some countenance."[6] Sidgwick's "masterly analysis" acknowledges "two supreme principles – Egoism and Utilitarianism, of independent authority, conflicting dictates, irreconcilable, unless indeed by religion."[7] Because the interest of each is incompatible with the interest of all, economics and ethics are incompatible. Sen, who believes this dichotomy has informed modern economic discourse, proposes to overcome it by bringing up ethical issues in the field of economics, and raising economic issues in the field of ethics.

One may wonder, however, if the ethics/economics dichotomy is as clear as Sen suggests. Edgeworth is indeed the direct predecessor of those twentieth-century economists who took their discipline on a path of ever-increasing formalization, and sought an approach free of normative or ethical considerations. At the same time, it is clear that Edgeworth saw his own effort as belonging to the field of morals in the broad sense. The full title of his book is: *Mathematical Psychics. An Essay on the Application of Mathematics to the Moral Sciences.* Edgeworth's explicit reference to Sidgwick's *Methods of Ethics* gives further indication of this. For Sidgwick, universalistic hedonism and egoistic hedonism are two "methods of ethics," having in common the fact that they "take happiness as an ultimate end."[8] Sidgwick refers universalistic hedonism to "Bentham and his successors," and informs the reader that he uses the term "Utilitarianism" as a synonym for "Universalistic Hedonism."[9] As to egoistic hedonism, he often simply calls it "Egoism." In addition, says Sidgwick, "it may sometimes be convenient to call it Epicureanism."[10] We thus have two ethical systems, each being referred (albeit loosely) to a historically defined moral doctrine: Utilitarianism for universalistic hedonism, Epicureanism for egoistic hedonism. In that sense, it cannot be said that "economical calculus," according to Edgeworth, is free of moral considerations. Economics is a particular

---

[4] Ibid., pp. 411–413.   [5] Edgeworth, *Mathematical Psychics*, p. 1.   [6] Ibid., p. 52.
[7] Ibid.   [8] Sidgwick, *The Methods of Ethics*, p. 11.   [9] Ibid.   [10] Ibid.

system of ethics, grounded in the neo-Epicurean principle of egoistic hedonism.

On the other hand, as we have already seen, Edgeworth views the distinction between "economical calculus" and "utilitarian calculus" as the foundation of the distinction between economics and ethics. In this perspective, economics is not a particular system of ethics. It is to be distinguished from ethics as a whole. In fact, Edgeworth is arguing on the basis of two different conceptions of ethics. On the one hand, a broad historical and conceptual view, which encompasses all possible moral systems including "selfish" systems such as Epicureanism. On the other hand, a more restricted view, which regards behavior as moral to the extent that it is free of selfish motives. In other words, the ethics/economics dichotomy implies a conception of ethics that equates moral behavior with unselfish behavior.

It thus appears that the discriminating notion is the notion of self-interest. Edgeworth sees two separate spheres: one in which self-interest is the only motive (he calls it economics), and one in which self-interest is not allowed at all (he calls it ethics). Like his predecessors Mill and Bentham, Edgeworth is a utilitarian (in the broad sense of the term, as opposed to the restricted sense in which Sidgwick uses it).[11] In order to inquire about the origin of the aforementioned dichotomy, we must begin with the works of the founder of utilitarianism, David Hume. In the *Treatise of Human Nature*, Hume draws a distinction between "interested commerce" and "disinterested commerce." The distinction appears in a chapter on promises, which analyzes the relationship between self-interest and the keeping of promises. Hume's purpose is to prove that, while helping the poor or taking care of one's children are virtues grounded in natural inclinations, keeping one's word is not a natural virtue. Hume starts with the assumption that men are "naturally selfish, or endowed only with a confined generosity."[12] Consequently, "they are not easily induced to perform any action for the interest of strangers, except with a view to some reciprocal advantage, which they have no hope of obtaining but by such a performance."[13] Self-interest would in principle dictate that we should engage in mutually profitable exchange. However, in concrete situations,

[11] The terminology may appear confusing here. Edgeworth and Sidgwick call "utilitarian" a moral system that maximizes the interest of all. At the same time, their distinction between "utilitarian hedonism" and "egoistic hedonism" is itself utilitarian in the broad sense.

[12] David Hume, *A Treatise of Human nature, being an attempt to introduce the experimental method of reasoning into moral subjects*, Oxford: Clarendon Press, 1975 [London: John Noon, 1739], III.II.V, p. 519.

[13] Ibid.

the exchange can rarely be instantaneous. Someone has to give first, and then wait for the recipient to give back. For this to happen, one may count on the feeling of gratitude, but "so much corruption is there among men, that, generally speaking, this becomes but a slender security."[14] In fact, since the exchange was started with a motive of self-interest, the recipient, being now in possession of what he needs, would have every reason not to give anything back. The solution to the problem does not consist in trying to make human nature less selfish. It consists it establishing a convention that makes it a matter of self-interest to pay something back. The obligation of promises is that convention. It signals explicitly that the exchange is a matter of self-interest. When I promise to pay back, it is in my interest to comply with my promise, because I would immediately lose all credit if I did not:

After these signs are instituted, whoever uses them is immediately bound by his interest to execute his engagements, and must never expect to be trusted any more, if he refuse to perform what he promised.[15]

For Hume, this is a modern form of commerce, to be distinguished from an older form of commerce, which relies on feelings of gratitude in order to make the exchange possible. However, "self-interested" commerce, based on explicit transactions and made possible by the institution of promises, has not entirely eclipsed the commerce based on gratitude:

But though this self-interested commerce of man begins to take place, and to predominate in society, it does not entirely abolish the more generous and noble intercourse of friendship and good offices. I may still do services to such persons as I love, and am more particularly acquainted with without any prospect of advantage; and they may make me a return in the same manner, without any view but that of recompensing my past services.[16]

Hume adds that promises have been instituted precisely "to distinguish those two different sorts of commerce, the interested and the disinterested."[17] In the older form of commerce, someone makes a gift to someone else. The gift creates an obligation and a feeling of gratitude in the recipient. Moved by his feeling of gratitude, the recipient subsequently makes a counter-gift, in order to acquit himself of his obligation. This commerce is "disinterested" in the sense that reciprocity is never explicitly required or mentioned. In fact, as Pierre Bourdieu points out in a discussion of traditional forms of exchange in North Africa, any explicit

---

[14] Ibid.   [15] Ibid., p. 522.   [16] Ibid., p. 521.   [17] Ibid.

mention of the fact that reciprocity is required or expected would make the exchange impossible.[18] The initial gift must appear one-sided, without any expectation of return ("without any prospect of advantage", says Hume). The counter-gift, even though it is a response to the initial gift, must not present itself that way; rather, it must appear spontaneous as well. This is the reason why there must be a time interval between the initial gift and the counter-gift. If the counter-gift came immediately after the initial gift, its reciprocal nature would be too obvious. After some time has elapsed, the counter-gift can be given, and appear spontaneous:

The lapse of time interposed is what enables the gift or counter-gift to be seen and experienced as an inaugural act of generosity, without any past or future, i.e. without calculation.[19]

To the modern mind, the expression "disinterested commerce" may seem like a contradiction in terms. If there is commerce, there is an exchange of goods or services; an exchange cannot take place unless it is mutually beneficial; therefore, it must be "interested" in some way. However, in commerce, the manner is just as relevant as the matter. Even though the outside observer (and the participants themselves in some way) can see the reciprocal nature of the gifts and counter-gifts, the circulation of goods and services would stop if it did not appear to the participants as one-sided, gratuitous, or "disinterested":

The theoretical construction which retrospectively projects the counter-gift into the project of the gift has the effect of transforming into mechanical sequences of obligatory acts the at once risky and necessary improvisation of the everyday strategies which owe their infinite complexity to the fact that the giver's undeclared calculation must reckon with the receiver's undeclared calculation, and hence satisfy his expectations without appearing to know what they are.[20]

It thus appears that the true discriminating factor between "interested commerce" and "disinterested commerce" is not the nature of the motives or feelings underlying the transaction. These motives and feelings are hard to guess anyway. Hume's distinction between "two different sorts of commerce" is a *formal* one:

When a man says *he promises any thing*, he in effect expresses a *resolution* of performing it; and along with that, by making use of this *form of words*, subjects himself to the penalty of never being trusted again in case of failure.[21]

---

[18] Pierre Bourdieu, *Outline of a Theory of Practice*, translated by Richard Nice, Cambridge: Cambridge University Press, 1977, p. 171.
[19] Ibid.   [20] Ibid.   [21] Hume, *A Treatise of Human nature*, III.II.V, p. 522.

In other words, the only thing that distinguishes interested commerce from disinterested commerce is the presence or absence of a *promise*. If there is a promise, the transaction is explicit. If there is no promise, the transaction remains implicit.

Unlike the Epicureans and the Augustinians, Hume believes that human nature is capable of limited generosity. He criticizes the proponents of the "selfish hypothesis," who ascribe all human conduct to self-love. At the same time Hume acknowledges that we do act, in general, out of selfish motives. However, Hume does not spend much time sorting out the motives. Rather than scrutinizing all aspects of human conduct to inquire whether the motives are selfish or generous, he focuses on the *form* of human relations. Because we are mostly selfish, "moralists" and "politicians," instead of trying to amend our nature, have instituted a convention (the obligation of promises) whereby "I learn to do a service to another, without bearing him any real kindness; because I foresee, that he will return my service, in expectation of another of the same kind."[22] The remedy to human selfishness is therefore to establish a *conventional space* where human relations are explicitly a matter of self-interest. This new space does not make human beings any more or less selfish than they were before. By assuming (conventionally) self-interest as the only motive, it clears up any ambiguities regarding the nature of the transactions taking place. No guessing is necessary regarding the motives and intentions of others. In the traditional form of commerce, gratitude was the engine of all transactions. Because selfishness is "the true mother of ingratitude,"[23] self-interest was the biggest obstacle to commerce. Modern commerce, on the contrary, is established on artificial rules that cleverly make it a matter of self-interest to return any service rendered. Self-interest is, *by convention*, the engine of modern commerce.

The space of disinterested commerce is perhaps harder to characterize. Hume seems to describe it as a holdover from ancient aristocratic culture. He refers to it in nostalgic and morally favorable terms as "the more generous and noble intercourse of friendship and good offices,"[24] which has not been entirely abolished by interested commerce. At the same time, as Allan Silver suggests,[25] Hume's "disinterested commerce" can be seen as an emerging private space where human relations can take place without any

[22] Ibid., p. 521.   [23] Ibid., p. 519.   [24] Ibid., p. 521.
[25] Allan Silver, " 'Two Different Sorts of Commerce' – Friendship and Strangership in Civil Society," in *Public and Private in Thought and Practice*, edited by Jeff Weintraub and Krishan Kumar, Chicago: University of Chicago Press, 1998, pp. 43–74.

consideration of interest. Indeed, for Hume, what characterizes friendship is the fact that calculations of interest are banished from it:

It is remarkable, that nothing touches a man of humanity more than any instance of extraordinary delicacy in love or friendship, where a person is attentive to the smallest concerns of his friend, and is willing to sacrifice to them the most considerable interest of his own. Such delicacies have little influence on society; because they make us regard the greatest trifles. But they are the more engaging, the more minute the concern is, and are a proof of the highest merit in any one, who is capable of them.[26]

Because a friend is capable of overlooking "the most considerable interest of his own," the logic of self-interest does not apply to friendship. One could even say that the value of friendship is a function of how far it departs from the logic of self-interest. The most important point is perhaps that "such delicacies have little influence on society." In other words, friendship operates in a different sphere, independent of the regular conduct of business. As Silver puts it, "Hume argues that distinguishing friendship from instrumental concerns creates a distinctive moral domain for personal relations."[27]

THE EPICUREAN/AUGUSTINIAN CRITIQUE
OF DISINTERESTEDNESS

Hume's distinction between interested and disinterested commerce comes in response to the interest doctrine (the "selfish hypothesis,"[28] according to which all behavior is driven by self-interest) and the Epicurean/Augustinian critique of virtues. In his *Maxims*, La Rochefoucauld suggests that there is no such thing as disinterested behavior. Self-interest, personified as a hypocrite, "speaks all sorts of languages and plays all sorts of roles, even that of the disinterested person."[29] Interest calculations enter into friendship:

---

[26] Hume, *A Treatise of Human nature*, III.III.III, p. 604.

[27] Silver, " 'Two Different Sorts of Commerce,' " p. 50.

[28] David Hume, *Enquiry Concerning the Principles of Morals*, edited by J.B. Schneewind, Indianapolis: Hackett, 1983 [1777 edition; first edition, 1751], Appendix II, p. 89 .

[29] "L'intérêt parle toutes sortes de langues, et joue toutes sortes de personnages, même celui de désintéressé." François de la Rochefoucauld, *The Maxims*, Paris: Barbin, 1665 [first edition] maxim 43. The first edition of the *Maxims* is used here, as opposed to the more widely quoted fifth edition (1678) because it makes a more extensive use of the words "intérêt" and "désintéressé." There is no change in views between the first edition and the fifth, but the latter edition reflects a desire to use a vocabulary that seems less technical. Consequently, in the fifth edition, La Rochefoucauld's indebtedness to reason of State theory is less visible.

"The most disinterested friendship is but a trade, where self-love always seeks its gain."[30] About kindness, La Rochefoucauld writes:

Self-love seems to yield naively to kindness. However, this is the most useful of all the means self-love uses to reach its goals. It is a hidden path, upon which self-love comes back to itself with greater and more abundant returns; it is a form of disinterestedness that carries a usurious rate of interest; finally it is a subtle device self-love uses to gather, turn, and incline all men favorably toward itself.[31]

Finally, La Rochefoucauld sees ulterior motives in generosity itself:

Generosity makes clever use of disinterestedness in order to cut a shorter path toward greater interests.[32]

La Rochefoucauld's description of the workings of self-interest must be understood in the context of the court of Louis XIV. As Norbert Elias points out, "it was not only in the sphere of bourgeois-capitalist competition that the idea of egoism as a motive for human action was formed, but first of all in the competition at court, and from the latter came the first unveiled descriptions of the human affects in modern times. La Rochefoucauld's *Maxims* are one example."[33] The world of the *Maxims* is the court society, where every agent is motivated by self-interest. In the context of the court, a person's interest is this person's position within a scale of hierarchy and prestige. Everyone competes to attain and keep the highest possible rank on this scale. It is mostly the king who decides (within certain limits) what a person's rank is. At the same time, maximizing one's symbolic capital requires complex negotiations with others, and the continuous exchange of favors and services. Elias notices that "this whole bustle of activity had a certain resemblance to a stock exchange. In it, too, a society actually present formed changing assessments of value."[34] The difference is that "at a stock exchange, what is at stake is the value of commercial houses in the opinion of investors; at court, it was the value of the people present in each other's opinion."[35] This system may appear artificial or even "unreal" to the

---

[30] "L'amitié la plus désintéressée n'est qu'un trafic où notre amour-propre se propose toujours quelque chose à gagner." Ibid., maxim 94.

[31] "Il semble que l'amour-propre soit la dupe de la bonté. Cependant c'est le plus utile de tous les moyens dont l'amour-propre se sert pour arriver à ses fins; c'est un chemin dérobé, par où il revient à lui-même, plus riche et plus abondant; c'est un désintéressement qu'il met à une furieuse usure; c'est enfin un ressort délicat avec lequel il réunit, il dispose et tourne tous les hommes en sa faveur." Ibid., maxim 250.

[32] "La générosité est un industrieux emploi du désintéressement pour aller plus tôt à un plus grand intérêt." Ibid., maxim 268.

[33] Norbert Elias, *The Court Society*, New York: Pantheon Books, 1983, p. 105.

[34] Ibid., p. 91.   [35] Ibid.

modern eye, but it was very real to the courtiers. Loss of prestige meant ruin in the eyes of the court and in the eyes of the courtier himself. In that sense, Elias rightly insists that the behavior of courtiers was "rational," even if the courtiers' rationality was different from the modern bourgeois rationality, which consists in maximizing one's financial position. As Elias puts it, "in the bourgeois type of 'rational' behavior-control, the calculation of financial gains and losses plays a primary role, while in the court aristocratic type the calculation is of gains and losses of prestige, finance and prestige respectively being the means to power in these societies."[36]

We might say that, when Elias describes the court society, he does it with an abundance of economic metaphors. The process of ranking individuals is compared to a stock exchange. The quest for prestige is compared to the quest for financial gain, etc. Describing the court etiquette after it became detached from its real significance in terms of power and influence in the eighteenth century, Elias writes that "the mechanism perpetuated its own ghostly existence like an economy uncoupled from its purpose of providing the means of life."[37] This use of "economic" vocabulary is certainly consistent with La Rochefoucauld's own description of his world. It suffices to mention a few of the maxims we have seen before. Kindness "is a form of disinterestedness that carries a usurious rate of interest."[38] Friendship is a "trade,"[39] or a "commerce where self-love always sets out to obtain something."[40] La Rochefoucauld also compares gratitude to "business credit" because "it keeps trade brisk, and we pay up, not because it is the proper thing to do, but because it makes it easier to borrow again."[41]

Without question, La Rochefoucauld describes the exchange of favors and services and the quest for prestige with a vocabulary borrowed from the field of commerce and finance. We may wonder, however, if we are speaking properly when we say that La Rochefoucauld uses "economic metaphors." First of all, he also makes abundant use of words coming from the field of war and politics. As Hirschman pointed out, the concept of interest was originally used in reason of State theory. Secondly, it may be that we are projecting our notion of what "the economy" is (complete with a price system and financial markets) onto a reality that has little to do with

---

[36] Ibid., p. 92.   [37] Ibid., p. 86.   [38] La Rochefoucauld, *The Maxims*, maxim 250.
[39] Ibid., maxim 94.
[40] François de la Rochefoucauld, *The Maxims* (1678 edition), translated by Louis Kronenberger, New York: Stackpole, 1936, maxim 83 (translation modified). "Un commerce où l'amour-propre se propose toujours quelque chose à gagner."
[41] Ibid., maxim 223. "Il est de la reconnaissance comme de la bonne foi des marchands: elle entretient le commerce; et nous ne payons pas parce qu'il est juste de nous acquitter, mais pour trouver plus facilement des gens qui nous prêtent."

the modern market system. As Bourdieu remarks, "those who apply the categories and methods of economics to archaic economies without taking into account the ontological transmutation they impose on their object are ... treating this type of economy 'as the fathers of the Church treated the religions which preceded Christianity' (Marx)."[42] This "ethnocentrism" Bourdieu adds, has its roots in "the unconscious acceptance of a *restricted definition of economic interest*, which in its explicit form, is the product of capitalism."[43] This may be true in general, but the aristocratic society of the seventeenth and eighteenth centuries is a special case. Elias is right to stress the fact that the idea of self-interest as a motive for individual action was initially formed in the context of the court society, long before it became the first principle of economics. In fact, the behavior of courtiers as described by La Rochefoucauld is consistent with the two principal axioms of mainstream economic theory. Firstly, the courtier acts exclusively upon self-seeking motives (he wants power and prestige). Secondly, the courtier's behavior maximizes his utility: every move the courtier makes can be interpreted as an attempt to get the most power and prestige at the lowest cost for himself in terms of services rendered and favors done to others. The interest doctrine was born in the context of seventeenth-century politics and extended by La Rochefoucauld to the behavior of the entire aristocracy – that is to say, for La Rochefoucauld, all human behavior. Because Hume and Smith appropriated and modified the interest doctrine in order to construct what would later be called "political economy" the vocabulary of the interest doctrine has been transported into economic science. It is therefore not surprising that the vocabulary and the notions of economic science should come to mind so naturally when one describes the court society. It can be argued, however, that when we refer to the court society in economic terms, we have our metaphors backwards. Historically, it is the court society that has served as a model for understanding what we now call "the economy" and not the reverse.

In order to distinguish the court society from today's market society, Elias refers to the conventional distinction between "bourgeois" behavior, which consists in maximizing one's financial position, and "aristocratic" behavior, which seeks to maximize symbolic gains (glory, prestige, etc.). The bourgeois is opposed to the aristocrat in the same way as content is opposed to form. The bourgeois cares about what is "real" and tangible (wealth). The aristocrat concerns himself with external and superficial forms of respect

---

[42] Bourdieu, *Outline of a Theory of Practice*, p. 177.   [43] Ibid.

and consideration. This distinction, which seems clear and obvious to us, was far from self-evident in the eighteenth century. As Elias himself points out, "what we often refer to by the inexact term 'Enlightenment' is not solely to be understood in relation to bourgeois capitalist rationalism, since it has strong links to court rationality."[44] According to Elias, this link between "rationalism" and court rationality could be easily demonstrated in the case of Leibniz or Voltaire. In many ways, this applies to Adam Smith as well. As we have seen in chapters 1 and 4, one of the points Smith stresses most strongly in *The Theory of Moral Sentiments* (following Rousseau on this) is the fact that the "great purpose of human life which we call bettering our condition"[45] is ultimately geared toward symbolic gains rather than material ones:

To be observed, to be attended to, to be taken notice of with sympathy, complacency, and approbation, are all the advantages which we can propose to derive from it. It is the vanity, not the ease, or the pleasure, which interests us.[46]

In other words, we never pursue wealth for its own sake, but because wealth buys us a higher position on the social ladder, a position that will draw greater marks of consideration and esteem from others. It must be noted that, unlike some modern economists who take vanity and peer-pressure (keeping up with the Joneses) as one factor among others in explaining consumer behavior, Smith insists that vanity is the *only* motive. Smith's description of the desire to better our condition must be understood in the context of a hierarchical society, where the only thing that matters is "rank": "Upon this disposition of mankind, to go along with all the passions of the rich and the powerful, is founded the distinction of ranks, and the order of society."[47]

It is quite symptomatic that the passage in *The Theory of Moral Sentiments* where the expression "invisible hand" appears is an analysis of what Smith calls "the œconomy of greatness."[48] The conspicuous consumption of the rich and the great, their addiction to useless "baubles and trinkets"[49] has the providential effect of giving work to thousands of craftsmen who would not otherwise find a means of subsistence. But this conspicuous consumption is itself based on a desire that plays itself out entirely on a symbolic level. The

[44] Elias, *The Court Society*, p. 113.
[45] Adam Smith, *The Theory of Moral Sentiments* (sixth edition), *The Glasgow Edition of the Works and Correspondence of Adam Smith*, vol. 1, edited by D.D. Raphael and A.L. Macfie, Oxford: Oxford University Press, 1976 [London and Edinburgh, 1790; first edition, 1759], I.iii.2.1.
[46] Ibid.   [47] Ibid., I.iii.2.3.   [48] Ibid., IV.1.10.   [49] Ibid.

rich and the great consume great quantities of goods and services not for reasons of pleasure and enjoyment, but simply because they wish to keep their rank within the social hierarchy. In the same chapter, Smith describes the destiny of the "poor man's son, whom heaven in its anger has visited with ambition."[50] To be sure, this description implies a social mobility that the court society excluded in principle (although it was in fact possible over time to buy one's way into the nobility). Yet it is remarkable that Smith does not seem to make a distinction between what we now call economic concerns (the desire to increase one's wealth) and the symbolic goal of securing esteem and consideration from others. In fact, the two purposes are inextricably linked. In Smith's description, the young man who wishes to become rich and great "makes his court to all mankind; he serves those whom he hates, and is obsequious to those whom he despises."[51] We have seen in chapter 4 that this passage echoes the words of the *Second Discourse*, where Rousseau describes the toils of the "citizen": "He makes his court to the great whom he hates, and to the rich whom he despises."[52] Rousseau is more explicit than Smith in saying that ambition consists in trying to break into aristocratic circles (the rich and the great). Smith's perspective is more general: the ambitious young man "makes his court to all mankind." Both authors, however, describe the means towards the goal of "bettering our condition" in similar ways, and with a uniformly negative moral tone: servility, obsequiousness, trading of favors and services, influence peddling, etc. The expression itself ("He *makes his court* to all mankind") says it all. It is as if the customs of the court society were now applicable to the society at large.

La Rochefoucauld's critique of disinterestedness, and his analysis of the court society, are therefore present in the incipient political economy. At the same time, the interest doctrine undergoes profound transformations. A comparison between La Rochefoucauld's views and Hume's distinction between interested and disinterested commerce is illuminating in that respect, because it shows how Hume managed to accommodate, rather than simply reject, the "selfish hypothesis." Long before La Rochefoucauld's connection with Augustinianism was established,[53] Paul Bénichou described the *Maxims* as an enterprise of "demolition of the hero."[54] La Rochefoucauld

[50] Ibid., IV.i.8.   [51] Ibid.

[52] Jean-Jacques Rousseau, *Discourse on the Origin of Inequality*, translated by Adam Smith in "Letter to the *Edinburgh Review*," No. 2 (1756), *The Glasgow Edition of the Works and Correspondence of Adam Smith*, vol. 3, Oxford: Oxford University Press, 1976, p. 253.

[53] See Jean Lafond, *La Rochefoucauld. Augustinisme et littérature*, Paris: Klincksieck, 1977.

[54] Paul Bénichou, *Morales du grand siècle*, Paris: Gallimard, 1948.

examines all aspects of the traditional aristocratic values and codes of conduct, and takes them apart. For instance, La Rochefoucauld compares gratitude to "business credit" and explains that we return favors not because it is the right thing to do but because it will allow us to keep seeking favors from others. In so doing, he goes squarely against the logic of traditional aristocratic behavior. According to the traditional aristocratic code of conduct, gratitude has no ulterior motives: I return a favor because I am sincerely grateful. As we have seen before, there is no *quid pro quo*. The returned favor presents itself as spontaneous and one-sided. Looking now at the process from the perspective of the initial giver, the aristocratic code of conduct prescribes generosity. True generosity consists in giving without any expectation of return. La Rochefoucauld demolishes aristocratic generosity by saying, as we have seen above, that "what looks like generosity may be ambition in disguise, scorning small interests to pursue larger ones."[55]

It would be a misunderstanding to say that the traditional aristocratic code of conduct prescribes that generosity and gratitude should be "unselfish." On the one hand, it is true that gifts and counter-gifts must appear as spontaneous and one-sided. On the other hand, as we have seen above, the agents *know* that an exchange is taking place. The initial giver knows that the gift will probably be reciprocated at some point; it is rational for him to give, because giving creates obligations in others. In a traditional structure of exchange, the power goes to whoever has the greatest number of people in his debt. In that sense, the giver is acting in his own interest when he gives. La Rochefoucauld's critique consists in *revealing* the fact that an exchange is taking place. Once that fact is revealed, generosity and gratitude appear as hypocritical postures. Fundamentally, La Rochefoucauld is applying the logic and calculations of reason of State theory to a whole range of behavior and customs that was foreign to it. In reason of State theory, everyone's interests are clear, unambiguous, and explicitly stated. Everyone knows that each prince is pursuing the interests of his country in a methodical, rational, and open fashion. In traditional aristocratic behavior, agents do have "interests" too, but they must pursue them with the appearance of disinterestedness. La Rochefoucauld's critique puts the aristocracy in a state of moral crisis: once it has been revealed that aristocratic disinterestedness is the customary way of pursuing aristocratic interests, the aristocrat is in a bind because the only acceptable means of pursuing

[55] La Rochefoucauld, *The Maxims* (1678 edition), maxim 246.

his interests (generosity and gratitude) have been morally discredited. In traditional aristocratic behavior, there is no contradiction between the pursuit of one's interests (power, glory, honor, etc.) and the practice of virtues that the modern mind would deem "unselfish" (generosity, clemency, gratitude, etc.). In fact, these virtues are the recommended path towards power and glory. But once the logic of the interest doctrine is applied to it, the aristocratic code of conduct becomes untenable.

La Rochefoucauld does not offer any solutions to the problem. In the court society as Elias describes it, aristocrats seem to have been pursuing their interests in accordance with the logic of the interest doctrine, but with due reverence to the appearance of disinterestedness required by the traditional code. Hence the prevailing sense (certainly shared by Rousseau and Smith) that courtly behavior was corrupt and "hypocritical," because of a growing distance between conduct and motives, appearances and reality. Hume does offer a solution to La Rochefoucauld's critique of disinterestedness. He says essentially this: La Rochefoucauld asserts that all human behavior is dictated by self-interest. This is mostly true, although human beings are also capable of limited generosity. However, instead of trying to scrutinize motives (which would lead to infinite regress) let's assume that the regular exchange of services is done out of self-interest. The presence of a promise is the conventional sign that an exchange is taking place, and that self-interest is the motive. This is not a psychological judgment about the agent's state of mind and inner motives. This is simply a way for the agent to state his intentions clearly. In this perspective, self-interest is a convenient assumption, which will free us from the need (always prevalent in the courtly context) to guess what the interlocutor's true motives and intentions are. Now that everyone's intentions are clear, the exchange of services can take place in a safe and predictable way. This type of human relations is called "interested commerce."

For La Rochefoucauld, all human relations are contaminated by self-interest. Hume segregates interest-driven behavior, which becomes *explicitly* self-interested, from disinterested behavior. Now that the sphere of "interested commerce" has been defined, everything else falls under the category of "disinterested commerce." As we have seen above, Hume tends to have an idealized view of "the more generous and noble intercourse of friendship and good offices."[56] This view stems logically from the definition of "interested commerce." *Because motives of self-interest have been conventionally confined to the sphere of interested commerce, the disinterestedness of older forms*

---

[56] Hume, *A Treatise of Human nature*, III.II.V, p. 521.

of exchange is now taken at face value. We are thus left with a dichotomy. There are two sorts of commerce: a modern one, based on self-interest, and an archaic one (which may well thrive in the private sphere) excluding motives of self-interest.

DISINTERESTEDNESS AS A MORAL AND THEOLOGICAL CATEGORY

A paradoxical consequence of the interest doctrine and of the critique of the interest doctrine is the emergence of disinterestedness as a moral value. A quick philological survey of the term *désintéressé* is in order here (the English use of this term follows the French). In the first half of the seventeenth century, the word *désintéressé* is used rather sparingly (only twelve occurrences in the University of Chicago ARTFL database). It has two related meanings. To be *désintéressé* means that one does not take sides in a conflict or a dispute (one is not an *interested party*). The expression *désintéresser quelqu'un* means to compensate a person who has a claim to something, in order to cause this person to drop his or her claim. In the second half of the seventeenth century, there is a remarkable surge in the use of the term (287 occurrences in ARTFL). During this time period (when the interest doctrine becomes a common reference) one finds the first occurrences of the modern sense of *désintéressé*, notably in La Rochefoucauld's *Maxims* (first published in 1665). In the *Maxims*, to be disinterested means *to have motives other than self-interest*. The notion of self-interest, brought forward by reason of State theory and its application to individual psychology, produces a new moral category, *désintéressé*, which is the opposite of *intéressé*. This category is subsequently used by religious writers such as Arnauld d'Andilly in his *Mémoires* (1667), Nicole in his *Essais de morale* (first volume published in 1671), Fléchier in his funeral oration for Turenne (1676), Jacques Esprit in his *Fausseté des vertus humaines* (1678) and Jacques Abbadie in his *Traité de la vérité de la religion chrétienne* (1684). In all these religious works, disinterestedness is used as a synonym for unselfish, charitable behavior.

The term *désintéressé* appears most often in a religious context. This pre-occupation with disinterestedness culminates in a late-seventeenth-century theological dispute: the controversy on Quietism, which centered on the figure of Madame Guyon, a mystic who developed the doctrine of *pure love* stipulating that one should love God in an entirely disinterested fashion. Madame Guyon's position is perhaps best exemplified with an anecdote reported by Bossuet, a bishop who was initially acquainted with Madame

Guyon and later became her most resolute critic. Madame Guyon had written that one should never pray to God in order to obtain anything for oneself, because "every demand for oneself is self-interested, contrary to the doctrine of pure love, and to the obligation to conform oneself to God's will."[57] Bossuet reports that, having asked her if that really was her opinion, Madame Guyon responded in the affirmative. He then asked her if she would ask God to forgive her for her sins. She replied that she could not. From this conversation, Bossuet concluded that Madame Guyon's doctrine was heretical. It must be noted that the controversy was closely watched from England: most of the pieces related to the controversy were translated into English just a few months after they appeared in French.

Madame Guyon had an ally and defender, Fénelon, the archbishop of Cambrai. In a book entitled *The Maxims of the Saints Explained*, Fénelon attempted to distinguish, in the doctrine of pure love, between what was heretical and what was not. He also sought to exonerate Madame Guyon from the criticisms directed at her personal piety. According to Fénelon, there are five degrees of perfection in the way we love God. The most imperfect way consists in loving God "not for the sake of himself, but for some other good things depending on his Almighty power, which we hope to obtain from him."[58] Fénelon associates this love with "the Carnal Jews, who observed the Law in hopes of being recompensed with the dew of Heaven and the fertility of the Earth."[59] Such love has little value, Fénelon believes, because it is "neither chaste nor filial, but merely servile."[60] He who loves God in this way does not really love God, but "his own dear self."[61] The second step on the ladder of Christian perfection consists in having faith "and not one degree of charity with it."[62] We love God because we know that God is the only object that can make us happy. Because the ultimate end is our own happiness, "this would rather be a self-love than a love of God."[63] Even though we see God as the only reward, this love would "prove wholly mercenary and of mere concupiscence."[64] In the third

---

[57] Jacques Bénigne Bossuet, *Relation sur le quiétisme*, in *Œuvres*, Versailles: Lebel, 1817 [Lyon: J. Anisson, 1698], vol. 29, p. 543.

[58] François de Salignac de la Mothe Fénelon, *The Maxims of the Saints Explained, Concerning the Interiour Life, by the Lord Archbishop of Cambrai*, London: H. Rhodes, 1698, p. 1. "On peut aimer Dieu, non pour lui, mais pour les biens distingués de lui, qui dépendent de sa puissance, et qu'on espère en obtenir, en sorte qu'on ne l'aimerait point sans ce motif." *Explication des maximes des saints*, Paris: Blond, 1911 [Paris: B. Aubouin, 1697], p. 118.

[59] "... les juifs qui étaient charnels, et qui observaient la loi, pour être récompensés par la rosée du ciel, et par la fertilité de la terre." Ibid.

[60] "Cet amour n'est ni chaste, ni filial, mais purement servile." Ibid.   [61] Ibid.

[62] "Aucun degré de charité." Ibid.

[63] "Cet amour serait plutôt un amour de soi qu'un amour de Dieu." Ibid., p. 2/119.

[64] "... il serait purement mercenaire, et de pure concupiscence." Ibid.

degree, we love God "with a love of hope, which love is not entirely selfish, for it is mixed with a beginning of love to God for himself, only our own interest is the chief and dominant motive."[65] The fourth degree "is a love of charity, which is yet alloyed with some mixture of self-interest, but is the true justifying love."[66] The fifth and supreme degree of perfection consists in loving God "with a love of pure charity, and without any mixture of the motive of self-interest."[67] The soul, now entirely disinterested, would love God even if there were no rewards in doing so, and even if loving God made the soul unhappy:

God is no more beloved either in regard of the merit or perfection, or for the happiness which is found in loving him. We would love him as much, though by an impossible supposition he should know nothing of his being beloved, or would render eternally unhappy those who had loved him.[68]

In Fénelon's presentation, the gradual ascension toward spiritual perfection consists in purifying the soul from motives of self-interest. From step one to step two, the soul elevates itself from a material to a spiritual definition of self-interest. From step two to step five, self-interest diminishes gradually as a motive till it becomes entirely eliminated in step five.

One may wonder what this theological exposé has to do with the issues of moral philosophy we discussed at the beginning of this chapter. The response to this question can be found in Fénelon's own work. For Fénelon, moral and theological issues are closely related. In a pamphlet aimed at the spiritual instruction of the aristocracy,[69] Fénelon attempts to define pure love by drawing on the experience of his readers, and especially their experience of friendship in the context of the court. Although La Rochefoucauld is not explicitly mentioned, Fénelon's many references to the relationship between self-love and friendship indicate that La Rochefoucauld's critique of friendship is the starting point of moral reflection. Fénelon begins by agreeing with the author of the *Maxims* that true friendship, if it exists, ought to exclude the trading of favors that goes with it in courtly practice.

[65] "On peut aimer Dieu d'un amour qu'on nomme d'espérance et qui peut précéder la justification du pécheur, alors l'homme qui a cet amour ne rapporte point Dieu comme moyen à soi, comme fin, de même que dans l'amour de pure concupiscence." Ibid., p. 2/120.

[66] "Il y a un état d'amour véritablement justifiant où l'âme ne fait pas encore fréquemment des actes de charité." Ibid., p. 3/121.

[67] "On peut aimer Dieu d'un amour que les saints ont appelé pur." Ibid., p. 5/124.

[68] "Par intérêt et par motif intéressé, il est naturel d'entendre un amour de soi qui est autre que cet amour de nous si pur et si parfait, suivant lequel on ne s'aime plus que comme le reste des créatures, dans l'ordre de Dieu et du même amour dont on aime sa beauté souveraine. Alors on aimerait autant Dieu quand même par supposition impossible, il devrait ignorer qu'on l'aime ou qu'il voudrait faire souffrir des peines éternelles à ceux qui l'auraient aimé." Ibid., p. 5/127.

[69] François de Salignac de la Mothe Fénelon, *Instructions et avis sur divers points de la morale et de la perfection chrétienne*, in *Œuvres*, Versailles: Lebel, 1822–1824, vol. 18.

However, Fénelon takes La Rochefoucauld's suspicion about motives one step further. Even in the case of a perfectly disinterested friendship, self-love remains as the central, sinful motive. Even though we do not seek to obtain favors or services from our friends, we want them to love us for the fact that we are showing such perfect disinterestedness:

We therefore seek, in these friendships that seem so disinterested to others and to us, the pleasure of loving without any interest, of rising above all those weak hearts which cling to base interests. Beyond this statement directed at ourselves in order to flatter our pride, we still seek, in the world, the glory attached to disinterestedness and generosity. We seek to be loved by our friends even though we do not seek favors from them. We hope they will by charmed by all the things we do for them without any selfish motive; and this is precisely where the selfish motive appears again, even though we had seemed to abandon it. Is there anything sweeter and more flattering for someone's self-love than being praised to the point that it no longer appears as self-love?[70]

In this passage, Fénelon seeks to outdo La Rochefoucauld in the game of suspicion. He displays an astonishing virtuosity tracking down selfish motives in the apparently most unselfish conduct. Elsewhere, Fénelon makes an explicit connection between disinterested friendship and the pure love of God. He starts with the observation that "everyone, in his relations with his friends, wants to be loved without any motive of interest, and exclusively for himself."[71] He adds that, when the requirement of friendship is disinterestedness, we are extraordinarily clever at detecting potentially selfish motives in the behavior of our friends:

Our capacity for discernment goes to infinity when it comes to identifying the subtlest motives of interest, politeness, pleasure, or honor that attach our friends to us. We are deeply sorry when they love us only out of gratitude, and even more so when the motives are more offensive. We only want love of pure inclination, of esteem, of admiration. Friendship is so jealous and delicate that an obstacle as small as an atom hurts it.[72]

[70] "On cherche donc, dans ces amitiés qui paraissent et aux autres et à nous-mêmes si désintéressées, le plaisir d'aimer sans intérêt et de s'élever, par ce sentiment noble, au-dessus de tous les cœurs faibles et attachés à des intérêts sordides. Outre ce témoignage qu'on veut se rendre à soi-même pour flatter son orgueil on cherche encore, dans le monde, la gloire du désintéressement et de la générosité; on cherche à être aimé de ses amis, quoiqu'on ne cherche pas à être servi par eux; on espère qu'ils seront charmés de tout ce que l'on a fait pour eux sans retour sur soi; et, par là, on retrouve le retour sur soi qu'on semble abandonner; car, qu'y a-t-il de plus doux et de plus flatteur pour un amour-propre sensé et d'un goût délicat que de se voir applaudir jusqu'à ne passer plus pour un amour-propre?" Ibid., p. 402.
[71] "Chacun veut, dans la société de ses amis, être aimé sans motif d'intérêt, et uniquement pour lui-même." Ibid., p. 318.
[72] "On est pénétrant jusqu'à l'infini pour démêler jusqu'aux plus subtils motifs d'intérêt, de bienséance, de plaisir ou d'honneur qui attachent nos amis à nous; on est au désespoir de n'être aimé d'eux que

Fénelon is well aware of the infinite regress that characterizes this game of suspicion. If we look for motives of self-interest, any small detail will become a matter of investigation, and the "selfish hypothesis" will never fail to provide explanatory schemes. It is precisely the aporetic nature of the game that requires a jump from ethics to theology. The problem is insoluble on a moral level. It has a clear solution, however, from a theological point of view. According to Fénelon, we are infinitely clever in discerning motives of self-interest in our friends because our self-love is infinitely sensitive to manifestations of self-love in others. As Fénelon puts it, "this jealousy is but a tyranny of self-love."[73] Anyone with a modicum of self-knowledge is aware of this, Fénelon adds. The desire to be loved in a disinterested way is an insufferable tyranny among human beings. But in God, whom the Bible describes as "jealous," this desire is entirely legitimate: "What is the most ridiculous and contemptible injustice in us, is the supreme justice in God."[74] This conclusion supports the notion of pure love, and the idea that Christian perfection consists in loving God in a disinterested way. For the purposes of our discussion, the remarkable point is that the idea of equating spiritual perfection with disinterestedness originates in a zealous application of the "selfish hypothesis."

Fénelon's views on disinterested love were extremely controversial within the Catholic Church. The archbishop of Cambrai waged a battle on two fronts. On the one hand, he sided with the orthodoxy in attacking the Jansenists, and likening their views to the heretical doctrine of Calvin. On the other hand, he had to defend himself from attacks by the bishop of Meaux, Bossuet, who represented the Catholic orthodoxy. In a book addressed to his flock in the diocese of Cambrai, Fénelon waged a violent attack against Jansenism. He drew a parallel between Calvinist and Jansenist views on grace.[75] The book was a series of letters, meant to evoke Pascal's hugely successful *Provincial Letters*, which had defended the Jansenist doctrine on grace fifty years before. One of Fénelon's main targets was the Augustinian doctrine of "opposite delights." Of course, Augustine being a Father of the Church, Fénelon claimed the doctrine was not genuinely Augustinian. According to this doctrine, the soul will move in the direction

---

par reconnaissance, à plus forte raison par d'autres motifs plus choquants; on veut l'être par pure inclination, par estime, par admiration. L'amitié est si jalouse et si délicate, qu'un atome qui s'y mêle la blesse." Ibid.

[73] "Cette jalousie n'est qu'une tyrannie de l'amour-propre." Ibid., p. 319.

[74] "Ce qui est en nous l'injustice la plus ridicule et la plus odieuse, est la souveraine justice en Dieu." Ibid.

[75] François de Salignac de la Mothe Fénelon, *Instruction pastorale en forme de dialogues* [Cambrai: Douilliez, 1714], in *Œuvres*, Versailles: Lebel, 1822–1824, vol. 16.

of what gives it the greatest pleasure. God's grace moves the soul by providing an attraction that is infinitely superior to the attraction of sin. Fénelon
found this view particularly repugnant, because it was in direct contradiction with his idea of disinterested love. One of the letters proposes "a
comparison between the system of Jansenius and that of Epicurus."[76] Given
the near-universal reprobation attached to Epicureanism, this was an extraordinarily violent attack. The polemical tone notwithstanding, Fénelon
points out the fact (discussed in chapter 2 of this book) that Augustinians
and Epicureans make the same hedonist assumptions about the motives of
human behavior:

Epicurus believed that every man must follow his greatest pleasure, because pleasure
is the end of human life and happiness. Don't your theologians say that *pleasure is
the only spring moving the hearts* of all men?[77]

Fénelon goes on to say that the primacy of pleasure is what orients the
whole Jansenist doctrine on the matter of grace:

If *pleasure is the only spring moving the human heart*, then it is the heart's unique
motive and end. God himself cannot move the heart directly. He can only do it
by using the spring of pleasure. Finally, this spring being the only thing animating
the heart, it is absolutely clear that, between two opposite pleasures, the greater
pleasure is the spring that animates the human heart. Our will must prefer what
provides the greatest pleasure. *Quod amplius nos delectat, secundum id operemur
necesse est* ... Therefore, your party agrees entirely with the Epicureans on this
fundamental principle.[78]

The Latin sentence (*Quod amplius nos delectat ...*) is a quote from Augustine's commentary on the *Letter to the Galatians*: "We can only do what
pleases us the most."[79] As we have seen in chapter 2, Pascal uses it in
his exposition of the Augustinian doctrine on grace.[80] As Fénelon makes

---

[76] Ibid., letter 23.

[77] "Epicure croyait que tout homme doit suivre son plus grand plaisir, qui est la fin du bonheur et de
la vie humaine. Vos théologiens ne disent-ils pas que *le plaisir est le seul ressort qui remue le cœur* de
tous les hommes?" Ibid.

[78] "Si *le plaisir est le seul ressort qui remue le cœur de l'homme*, il est son seul motif et son unique fin.
Dieu lui-même ne peut point immédiatement remuer le cœur. Il ne peut le remuer qu'en recourant
au ressort du plaisir. Enfin ce ressort étant le seul qui remue le cœur, il est clair comme le jour,
qu'entre deux plaisirs opposés, le plus grand est le ressort qui a le plus de force pour remuer le cœur
de l'homme. Il est nécessaire que notre volonté préfère ce qui nous donne le plus de plaisir *Quod
amplius nos delectat secundum id operemur necesse est* ... Voilà donc votre parti qui est entièrement
d'accord avec les Epicuriens sur ce principe fondamental." Ibid.

[79] Augustine, *Expositio in Epistolam ad Galatas*, § 49.

[80] Blaise Pascal, *Écrits sur la grâce*, in *Œuvres complètes*, edited by Jean Mesnard, vol. 3, Paris: Desclée
de Brouwer, 1991, p. 704.

clear, this issue is of fundamental importance, because it regards first principles. Jansenists and Epicureans posit that pleasure is the sole motive of human behavior, including religious behavior. For the Jansenists, as well as for Epicureans like Gassendi, the soul seeks its own pleasure in the act of loving God. Fénelon dismisses such thinking as heretical: in order to love God perfectly, the soul must not seek its own pleasure.

Against Fénelon's doctrine of *pure love*, Bossuet reaffirmed the orthodox doctrine according to which one should have an interest in one's salvation. Bossuet, as one would expect, bases his argument primarily on references to Augustine. According to Bossuet, Fénelon has taken the obligation of disinterestedness to an indefensible extreme:

> It is always true, according to Saint Augustine's principle, that disinterestedness cannot go so far as losing, in any act whatsoever, the will to be happy, which prompts our desire for all things.[81]

Bossuet always comes back to the first principle of Augustine's psychology: the desire to be happy. This desire, according to Augustine, is the sole motive of human actions, including the purest forms of religious worship. Bossuet insists that the existence of this desire is a universal truth, grounded in nature as well as in divine revelation:

> Here is Augustine's unshakeable principle (*De Trinit. Lib.* XIII, chap. VIII, n. II), which has never been questioned by anyone. It is the truest, the best understood, the clearest, the most unchanging thing in the world: *tam illa perspecta, tam examinata, tam eliquata, tam certa sententia*: not only do we want to be happy, but also we seek nothing but this, and we seek all other things for this purpose: *quod omnes homines beati esse volunt, idque unum ardentissimo amore appetunt, et propter hoc caetera quaecumque appetunt*. This is the cry of truth, he says, this is the call of nature: *hoc veritas clamat, hoc natura compellit*.[82]

In support of the idea that perfect virtue implies disinterestedness, Fénelon had invoked some classic examples from antiquity: Socrates dying for the cause of virtue, heroic pagans dying for their homeland, heroic or

---

[81] "Il demeure toujours véritable, selon le principe de saint Augustin, qu'on ne peut se désintéresser jusqu'au point de perdre dans un seul acte, quel qu'il soit, la volonté d'être heureux, pour laquelle on veut toutes choses." Jacques-Bénigne Bossuet, *Réponse à quatre lettres de Monseigneur l'archevêque duc de Cambrai*, in *Œuvres*, vol. 29, Versailles: Lebel, 1817 [Paris: J. Anisson, 1698], p. 31.

[82] "Voici le principe inébranlable de saint Augustin (*De trinit. Lib.* XIII, cap. VIII, n. II.) que personne ne révoqua jamais en doute: la chose du monde la plus véritable, la mieux entendue, la plus éclaircie, la plus constante: *tam illa perspecta, tam examinata, tam eliquata, tam certa sententia*: c'est non seulement qu'on veut être heureux, mais encore qu'on ne veut que cela, et qu'on veut tout pour cela: *quod omnes homines beati esse volunt, idque unum ardentissimo amore appetunt, et propter hoc caetera quaecumque appetunt*. C'est, dit-il, ce que crie la vérité, c'est à quoi nous force la nature; *hoc veritas clamat, hoc natura compellit*." Ibid., p. 30.

virtuous suicides, etc. Bossuet counters this with the traditional Augustinian interpretation of suicide (also discussed by Pascal and Mandeville – see chapter 2). However absurd their reasoning may be, those who kill themselves are still seeking happiness:

When a man kills himself, this Father says, "in order to avoid insufferable pain, he mistakenly believes that he will cease to be, but he also has in his mind a natural desire for repose: *in opinione habet errorem omnimodae defectionis, in sensu autem naturale desiderium quietis*" (*De Lib. Arbitr.* II, chap. VII, n. 23). Thus there is always a secret desire for eternal living, either in the memory of men (which is called the life of glory) or in the body of the republic, as a member striving for survival in the whole. In any case, we never aim at pure nonbeing, and we never fail to see it with concrete circumstances that make us associate it with a form of happiness.[83]

During the same period, another polemic took place on a related issue: the metaphysical and moral value of pleasure. The starting point of the polemic was Malebranche's interpretation of the Augustinian theory of pleasure. Against the Stoics, who sought to demonstrate that one can be happy while experiencing violent pain, Malebranche contends, in *The Search after Truth*, that "one must tell it the way it is: pleasure is always a good, and pain is always an evil."[84] In Malebranche's metaphysics, external objects are not capable of producing pleasure. Only God's "invisible hand," which "covers us with riches,"[85] is capable of doing so: "Only God is powerful enough to act within us, and to make us feel pleasure and pain."[86] Malebranche agrees with the Epicureans' belief that pleasure is always a good thing. The Epicureans' only error, he says, is to see the source of pleasure in external objects, when "only God can satiate us with all the pleasures of which we are capable."[87] As an Augustinian, Malebranche believes that a desire for happiness, and an attraction to the good, are inscribed in human

---

[83] "Quand un homme se tue lui-même, dit ce Père, 'pour éviter des douleurs insupportables, il a dans l'opinion l'erreur d'une totale cessation d'être, mais cependant il a dans le sens le désir naturel du repos: *in opinione habet errorem omnimodae defectionis, in sensu autem naturale desiderium quietis*' (*De lib. Arbitr.* II, cap. VIII, 23). Ainsi on a toujours pour objet secret une subsistance éternelle, ou dans la mémoire des hommes, ce qui s'appelle la vie de la gloire, ou une autre espèce de vie dans le corps de la république, dont on est membre qui veut se sauver dans son tout: quoi qu'il en soit, on n'a jamais en vue le pur néant; et on ne cesse de la revêtir, malgré qu'on en ait, de circonstances réelles qui nous y font établir un certain bonheur." Ibid.

[84] "Il faut dire les choses comme elles sont: le plaisir est toujours un bien, et la douleur toujours un mal." Nicolas Malebranche, *De la Recherche de la vérité*, in *Œuvres complètes de Malebranche*, Paris: Vrin, 1962 [Paris: Pralard, 1674], vol. 2, IV, x, § I, p. 77.

[85] "Cette main invisible qui nous comble de biens." Ibid., IV, x, § 2, p. 83.

[86] "Il n'y a que Dieu qui soit assez puissant pour agir en nous, et pour nous faire sentir le plaisir et la douleur." Ibid., IV, x, § I, p. 77.

[87] "Il n'y a que lui qui puisse nous combler de tous les plaisirs dont nous sommes capables." Ibid., vol. I, I, XVII, § 3, p. 173.

nature. We all want to be happy, but we seek happiness in external things. This is the malady of human nature:

We must speak to men the way Jesus Christ spoke to them, not the way the Stoics did. These philosophers knew neither the nature nor the malady of the human mind ... We must show them that they are compelled to do the opposite of what they desire, so that they may perceive their inaptitude for the good. Men unfailingly want to be happy, and one cannot be happy if one cannot do what one wants.[88]

True to the Augustinian tradition, Malebranche associates the hedonist assumption with the notion of the will divided against itself (see chapter 3). The hedonist assumption is of fundamental importance, and appears frequently in Malebranche's works: "Man only seeks pleasure";[89] "Man unfailingly wants to be happy";[90] "Men at all times want to be happy, and they never want to be unhappy";[91] etc. Malebranche even insists that physical pleasure makes us actually happy, albeit momentarily: "Present pleasure makes us presently happy, and present pain makes us presently unhappy."[92] These views drew criticism from another Augustinian: Antoine Arnauld argued that God wants to be loved in a disinterested fashion, and that loving him "in view of the kind of happiness we think we receive from him when we experience physical pleasure"[93] is not loving him at all:

It means loving [God] like Epicureans loved virtue, which they professed just as much as the philosophers did, because they saw it as necessary to establish a firm ground for the enjoyment of physical pleasure.[94]

Bayle, yet another Augustinian, sided with Malebranche in the polemic. In the "Epicurus" entry of his *Dictionary*, he affirmed the validity of the Epicurean doctrine on the relationship between happiness and pleasure:

As to the doctrine regarding the chief good, or happiness, it was likely to be misinterpreted, and it had adverse consequences that gave the [Epicurean] sect a

[88] Ibid.
[89] "L'homme ne cherche que le plaisir." Nicolas Malebranche, *Traité de morale*, in *Œuvres complètes de Malebranche*, vol. 11, Paris: Vrin, 1966, 1, 1, § xviii, p. 24.
[90] "L'homme veut invinciblement être heureux." Ibid., 1, iii, § xii, p. 44.
[91] "Les hommes en tous temps veulent être heureux, ils ne veulent jamais être malheureux." Ibid., 1, x, § viii, p. 119.
[92] "Le plaisir actuel rend actuellement heureux, et la douleur malheureux." Ibid.
[93] "Aimer Dieu dans la vue de ce bonheur que l'on croit recevoir de lui par la jouissance et le plaisir des sens." Antoine Arnauld, *Réflexions philosophiques et théologiques sur le nouveau système de la nature et de la grâce*, in *Œuvres de Messire Antoine Arnauld*, vol. 39, Paris: Sigismond d'Arnay, 1781 [Cologne: N. Schouten 1685], 1, xxiv, p. 396.
[94] "C'est l'aimer comme les Epicuriens aimaient la vertu, qu'ils faisaient profession d'embrasser autant que les philosophes, parce qu'ils la jugeaient nécessaire pour avoir un contentement solide dans la jouissance de la volupté." Ibid.

bad reputation. But it was in fact very reasonable, and no one could deny that if we understand the word happiness as he did, the felicity of man consists in pleasure. Mr. Arnauld criticized this doctrine in vain.[95]

The dividing line in these debates is consistent with the categories we have seen in chapter 2. On one side, Epicureans and Augustinians agree that pleasure is the only motivating factor in human actions, and that salvation is a matter of self-interest (however elevated and spiritual the definition of this interest may be). The opposite, neo-Stoic point of view says that spiritual and moral perfection consists in a holy indifference: we should contemplate the beautiful order of God's creation, assent to it, and refrain from preferring an outcome over another, because the outcome of our actions is a consequence of God's will. What is remarkable in these debates about disinterestedness is the way in which the antagonistic positions are related. As we have seen above, Fénelon, in his defense of the Quietist doctrine, goes even further than La Rochefoucauld in casting suspicion upon the motives of human action. La Rochefoucauld restricts the selfish hypothesis to human interaction within the court society. Fénelon extends the suspicion to man's relationship with God. Once this move has been made, there is a theological and metaphysical foundation for the (now commonplace) idea that the moral worth of an act is a function of the purity of its motives. Disinterestedness is now the foundation of morality.

The conceptual connections between the polemic on Quietism and eighteenth-century moral philosophy may not be obvious. They do exist, however. In the 1726 preface to his *Sermons*, Joseph Butler puts the main argument of his book in the context of the longstanding dispute between Epicureans and their critics. He identifies his adversaries as "the Epicureans of old, Hobbes, the author of *Réflexions, Sentences et Maximes Morales* [La Rochefoucauld], and this whole set of writers."[96] In other words, Butler's polemical target is the interest doctrine as expressed in the Epicurean/Augustinian tradition. Against this doctrine, Butler invokes an opinion "maintained by the several ancient schools of philosophy" that "virtue is to be pursued as an end, eligible in and for itself."[97] He then

---

[95] "Quant à la doctrine touchant le souverain bien ou le bonheur, elle était fort propre à être mal interprétée, et il en résulta de mauvais effets qui décrièrent la secte. Mais au fond elle était très raisonnable, et l'on ne saurait nier qu'en prenant le mot de bonheur comme il le prenait, la félicité de l'homme ne consiste dans le plaisir. C'est en vain que M. Arnauld a critiqué cette doctrine." Pierre Bayle, *Dictionnaire historique et critique*, Amsterdam: P. Brunel, 1740 [Rotterdam: Reinier Leers, 1697], article "Épicure."

[96] Joseph Butler, "Fifteen Sermons," in *British Moralists, 1650–1800*, edited by D.D. Raphael, Oxford: Clarendon Press, 1969, preface, p. 332.

[97] Ibid., p. 336.

makes an explicit connection between this dispute in moral philosophy and a dispute that had taken place recently within the field of theology:

> The question which was a few years ago disputed in France concerning *the love of God*, which was there called enthusiasm, as it will everywhere by the generality of the world, the question I say, answers in *religion* to that old one in *morals* now mentioned. And both of them are, I think, fully determined by the same observation, namely that the very nature of affection, the idea itself necessarily implies resting in its object as an end.[98]

For Butler, the controversy on Quietism is the theological version of the questions of moral philosophy he discusses in his *Fifteen Sermons*. Butler vehemently rejects the interest doctrine because this doctrine implies that all human actions are subordinated to the pursuit of pleasure or happiness. Consequently, according to the Epicurean/Augustinian tradition, virtue is not to be sought for its own sake, but rather as a means towards happiness. The theological translation of the same question is: should we love God because loving God makes us happy (as Bossuet argued), or should our love of God be entirely disinterested (as Fénelon believed)? In Sermon XIII, "Upon the Love of God," Butler makes it clear that he sides with Fénelon on this issue: "Resignation to the will of God is the whole of piety. It includes in it all that is good, and is a source of the most settled quiet and composure of mind."[99] Butler acknowledges that the Quietist doctrine has been embraced by fanatics but, he adds, this should not obscure the fact that this doctrine is true:

> Everybody knows, you therefore need only just to be put in mind, that there is such a thing as having so great a horror of the extreme as to run insensibly and of course into the contrary; and that a doctrine having been a shelter for enthusiasm, or made to serve the purposes of superstition, is no proof of the falsity of it.[100]

Like Joseph Butler, Adam Smith was quite aware of the theological implications of his analysis of virtue. In Part VII of *The Theory of Moral Sentiments*, Smith classifies moral systems according to the three possible ways in which virtue can be defined: prudence, propriety, and benevolence. Having laid out these three categories, he shows that they can account for all existing moral systems. Examining "that system which places virtue in obedience to the will of the Deity," Smith argues that it "may be counted

---

[98] Joseph Butler, *Fifteen Sermons preached at the Rolls Chapel*, sixth edition, London: Rivington, 1792 [London: Knapton, 1726], preface.
[99] Sermon XIII, "Upon the Love of God," ibid., p. 281. This sermon is not included in D.D. Raphael's edition.
[100] Ibid., p. 261.

either among those which make [virtue] consist in prudence, or among those which make it consist in propriety."[101] According to Smith, the question: "Why should we obey God's will?" has only two possible answers:

It must either be said that we ought to obey the will of the Deity because he is a Being of infinite power, who will reward us eternally if we do so, and punish us eternally if we do otherwise: or it must be said, that independent of any regard to our own happiness, or to rewards and punishments of any kind, there is a congruity and fitness that a creature should obey its creator, that a limited and imperfect being should submit to one of infinite and incomprehensible perfections. Besides one or other of these two, it is impossible to conceive that any other answer can be given to this question.[102]

If we obey God because of the rewards and punishments attached to the obligation of obedience, "virtue consists in prudence, or in the proper pursuit of our own final interest and happiness." If we obey God regardless of rewards and punishments, "virtue must consist in propriety, since the ground of our obligation to obedience is the suitableness or congruity of the sentiments of humility and submission to the superiority of the object which excites them."[103] In Smith's analysis, those who equate virtue with prudence are the Epicureans. Those who equate virtue with propriety are the Platonists, the Aristotelians, and principally the Stoics. In Smith's own system, virtue is defined as propriety. Since the mainstream Christian view is that one should take an interest in one's salvation, it could be argued that Smith rejects it by equating it with Epicureanism, and by espousing a neo-Stoic point of view on matters of religious piety.

SELF-INTEREST AND BENEVOLENCE

Fénelon's grounds for equating virtue with disinterestedness are theological. With Shaftesbury and Hutcheson, the debate leaves the field of theology, and takes place mostly within the realm of ethics.

As we have seen in chapter 2, Shaftesbury takes a polemical stance against the interest doctrine. Against those who see self-interest as the single motive of human action, Shaftesbury argues that a variety of motives are at work:

You have heard it (my friend!) as a common saying, that *interest governs the world*. But, I believe, whoever looks narrowly into the affairs of it, will find that *passion, humor, caprice, zeal, faction*, and a thousand other springs which are counter to self-interest, have as considerable a part in the movements of this machine. There are more wheels are counterpoises in this engine than are easily imagined ... It is

---

[101] Smith, *The Theory of Moral Sentiments*, VII.ii.3.20.   [102] Ibid.   [103] Ibid.

hard, that in the plan or description of this clockwork, no wheel or balance should be allowed on the side of the better and more enlarged affections.[104]

In the same pages, Shaftesbury singles out Epicurus as the "primitive father and founder"[105] of the philosophy of self-interest. His most negative judgment goes against La Rochefoucauld, whom he presents as a pale and narrow-minded imitator of Epicurus:

Other authors there have been of yet an inferior kind [than the Epicureans]: a sort of distributors and petty retailers of this wit, who have run changes, and divisions, without end, upon this article of *self-love*. You have the same thought spun out a hundred ways, and drawn into mottos and devises to set forth this riddle: that "act as disinterestedly or generously as you please, *self* still is at the bottom, and nothing else."[106]

Along with this scathing critique of the "selfish hypothesis," one finds a critique of the attempts that have been made to show that the practice of virtue is a matter of self-interest. According to Shaftesbury, such attempts have had the consequence of degrading the idea of virtue:

Men have not been contented to show the natural advantages of honesty and virtue. They have rather lessened these, the better, as they thought, to advance another foundation. They have made *virtue* so mercenary a thing, and have talked so much of its *rewards*, that one can hardly tell what there is in it, after all that can be worth rewarding. For to be bribed only or terrified into an honest practice bespeaks little of real honesty or worth.[107]

For Shaftesbury, too many rewards attached to virtue diminish the price of virtue. If virtue is not desirable for its own sake, then it is probably not worth pursuing. This has far-reaching consequences regarding the relationship between ethics and religion. According to Shaftesbury, the practice of virtue in the Christian religion is tied to the rewards and punishments in the afterlife. On the other hand, what characterizes the truly heroic virtues is a complete disregard for the long-term or short-term consequences of an action. This is why, according to Shaftesbury, the Christian religion has not emphasized the heroic virtues:

I could be almost tempted to think that the true reason why some of the most heroic virtues have so little notice taken of them in our holy religion, is, because there would have been no room left for disinterestedness, had they been entitled

---

[104] Anthony Ashley Cooper, Third Earl of Shaftesbury, *Sensus Communis, viz. An Essay on the Freedom of Wit and Humor*, in *Characteristics of Men, Manners, Opinions, Times*, London: 1711, vol. 1 [London: Egbert Sanger, 1709], p. 115.
[105] Ibid., p. 116.   [106] Ibid., p. 120.   [107] Ibid., p. 97.

to a share of that infinite reward which Providence has by revelation assigned to other duties.[108]

There is something slightly sophistical in this argument, which Shaftesbury presents with precaution and tentativeness. At the same time, it reveals a great deal about Shaftesbury's position. As we have seen above, Fénelon invoked the heroic virtues of the pagans as a proof that true disinterestedness was possible, and he extended that psychological observation to disinterestedness in the love of God. For his part, Shaftesbury seems to take the hedonistic (or at least eudemonistic) principles of the Christian religion for granted: the purpose of religion is the pursuit of eternal happiness; therefore religion is ultimately a matter of self-interest. As a consequence, he examines the idea of disinterestedness outside the sphere of the Christian religion. Shaftesbury professes his reverence for the revealed belief that Christian virtues will be rewarded in the afterlife. In addition, he seems to imply, ironically perhaps, that God's Providence has decided not to reward the heroic virtues because these virtues had to remain disinterested in order to be genuinely heroic.

Because, according to Shaftesbury, the good order of society requires that we should have at least some concern for others, an excessive focus on matters of personal salvation could have adverse consequences for society. Strict religious observance is a matter of self-love and self-interest. Consequently, religious zealots cannot be good citizens:

In this religious sort of discipline, the principle of *self-love*, which is naturally so prevailing in us, being no way moderated or restrained, but rather improved and made stronger every day by the exercise of the passions in a subject of more extended self-interest, there may be reason to apprehend lest the temper of this kind should extend itself in general through all the parts of life. For if the habit be such as to occasion, in very particular, a stricter attention to self-good and private interest, it must insensibly diminish the affections towards public good, or the interest of society, and introduce a certain narrowness of spirit, which (as some pretend) is peculiarly observable in the devout persons and zealots of almost every religious persuasion.[109]

This is not Voltaire's classic argument against religious fanaticism. With the required caution ("as some pretend"), Shaftesbury criticizes religious zealots not because they are likely to cause riots and civil wars, but simply because they selfishly prefer the salvation of their souls to the disinterested

---

[108] Ibid., p. 98.
[109] Anthony Ashley Cooper, Third Earl of Shaftesbury, *An Inquiry Concerning Virtue*, in *Characteristics of Men, Manners, Opinions, Times*, London: 1711, vol. 2 [London: A. Bell, E. Castle, and S. Buckley, 1699], p. 58.

pursuit of the public good. He concludes his analysis with a remark that puts him very close to Fénelon's point of view. The value of true religious piety itself resides in its disinterestedness:

This, too, must be confessed: that if it be true piety, to love GOD *for his own sake*, the over-solicitous regard to private good expected from him, must of necessity prove a diminution of piety. For whilst God is beloved only as the cause of private good, he is no otherwise beloved than as any other instrument or means of pleasure by any vicious creature.[110]

This theological remark further indicates that there is a remarkable conceptual affinity between Fénelon's theory of *pure love* and Shaftesbury's idea that virtue must be disinterested. Fénelon had tried to promote the obligation of disinterestedness in the theological domain, and was rebuked by the defenders of the orthodoxy, who claimed that one should be interested in one's salvation. Shaftesbury agreed that true religious piety should be disinterested, but instead of challenging the commonly accepted notion of piety, he focused on disinterestedness in the moral sphere, where the rewards and punishments of the afterlife are not relevant. This explains his interest in the virtues of pagans, who could practice virtue for its own sake because they did not believe in rewards in the afterlife. This also explains why, in a footnote, Shaftesbury approvingly quotes the author of a contemporary treatise on friendship, who drew all his examples of perfect friendships from non-Christian cultures or pre-Christian times:

Friendships are pure loves, regarding to do good more than to receive it. He that is a friend after death, hopes not for a recompense from his friend, and makes no bargain either for fame or love, but is rewarded with the conscience and satisfaction of doing bravely.[111]

For Shaftesbury, "private friendship, and zeal for the public, and our country, are virtues purely voluntary in a Christian."[112] This implies that non-Christians have practiced these virtues more assiduously than Christians. As Hume would do a few years later, Shaftesbury seems to present disinterested friendship as a thing of the past. However, one may precisely wonder if such an attention paid to the "perfect friendships" of antiquity is not the symptom of the emergence of a private sphere where "the moral quality of friendship is enhanced precisely because it is not implicated in

---

[110] Ibid.
[111] Shaftesbury, *Sensus Communis*, vol. 1, p. 100, footnote (quote from *Treatise of Friendship*, by Bishop Taylor).
[112] Ibid., p. 99.

'self-interested commerce.' "[113] In that sense, disinterested friendship would very much be a thing of the present, not the past.

Hutcheson uses the concept of disinterestedness in a related but slightly different argument. In order to prove the existence of something he calls "moral sense," Hutcheson begins by acknowledging that the practice of virtue may not always be disinterested. Anybody can be bribed into acting morally, if the right incentive is applied:

> A covetous *man* shall dislike any branch of trade, how useful soever it may be to the public, if there is no gain for himself in it; here is an aversion from *interest*. Propose a sufficient premium, and he shall be the first who sets about it, with full satisfaction in his own conduct.[114]

Conversely, anyone could be bribed into acting immorally, but in either case, according to Hutcheson, our sense of the moral value of an act (whether performed by ourselves or by others) remains independent of the advantage we expect to derive from it:

> I may easily be capable of wishing that another would do an action I abhor as *morally evil*, if it were very advantageous to me. Interest in that case may overbalance my desire of *virtue* in another. But no *interest* will make me approve an action as good, which, without that interest to myself, would have appeared *morally evil*. The sense of the moral good, or evil, cannot be overbalanced by *interest*.[115]

In other words, motives of self-interest may always take part in our decision to engage, or not to engage in a certain conduct. However, our judgment regarding the moral worth of a particular act is itself entirely disinterested. We should think of it as the perception of the "beauty"[116] of an act. In addition, for Hutcheson, our moral sense tells us that a perfectly virtuous action must proceed from disinterested motives: "*Virtue* is not pursued from the *interest* or *self-love* of the *pursuer*, or any motives of his own advantage."[117] The fundamental motives of virtuous actions are two kinds of love, love of esteem, and love of benevolence. Both kinds, according to Hutcheson, are disinterested by definition. This is especially true of the love of benevolence:

> If there be any *benevolence* at all, it must be *disinterested*; for the most useful action imaginable loses all appearance of *benevolence* as soon as we discern that it only flowed from *self-love* or *interest*.[118]

---

[113] Silver, " 'Two Different Sorts of Commerce'," p. 50.

[114] Francis Hutcheson, *An Inquiry into the original of our Ideas of Beauty and Virtue, in two treatises, in which the principles of the late Earl of Shaftesbury are explained and defended, against the author of The Fable of the Bees*, in *Collected Works*, vol. 1, Hildesheim: Georg Olms, 1990 [London: J. Darby, 1725], p. 116.

[115] Ibid., p. 119.   [116] Ibid., p. 116.   [117] Ibid., p. 127.   [118] Ibid., p. 129.

To be sure, Hutcheson adds, self-love is also a frequent and powerful motive of human action. Self-love and benevolence "are to be considered as two forces impelling the same body to motion: sometimes they conspire, sometimes are indifferent to each other, and sometimes are in some degree opposite."[119] For Hutcheson, the moral worth of an action can be computed precisely by looking at the quantity of self-interest and benevolence that goes into it, and by assessing whether there is a conflict between the selfish motive and the benevolent motive. On the basis of these assumptions, virtue can be expressed in the form of an equation where B represents the benevolence (= moral worth) of an action, M is the "moment," (the quantity) of good, I is the agent's interest, and A represents the agent's abilities:

When the moment in one action partly intended for the good of the agent is but equal to the moment in the action of another agent influenced only by benevolence, the former is less virtuous, and in this case the interest must be deducted to find the true effect of the benevolence, or virtue. And in the same manner, when interest is opposite to benevolence, and yet surmounted by it, this interest must be added to the moment, to increase the virtue of the action, or the strength of the benevolence. Or thus, in *advantageous virtue* $B = (M - I)/A$. And in *laborious, painful, dangerous or expensive virtue* $B = (M + I)/A$.[120]

If self-interest and benevolence converge, the moral worth of the action is diminished by the quantity of self-interest that goes into it. On the contrary, if there is a conflict between self-interest and benevolence, the moral worth of the action is augmented by the quantity of self-interest that was forfeited in order to carry out the action.

Like Shaftesbury, Hutcheson considers the objection that "in those actions of our own which we call good, there is constant advantage superior to others, which is the ground of our approbation, and the motive to them from self-love, viz. that we suppose the deity will reward them."[121] In other words, the most disinterested action may not be truly disinterested, if it is done in view of a reward in the afterlife. In response, Hutcheson, like Shaftesbury, invokes the virtues of non-Christians. In addition, he argues that the objection would be valid if the logic of self-interest could be applied to God himself. If we could prove that "it is for the advantage of the deity"[122] to reward virtue, we would have to admit that virtue is a matter of self-interest. However, when applied to God, the logic of self-interest appears immediately as absurd:

---

[119] Ibid., p. 130.   [120] Ibid., p. 170.   [121] Ibid., p. 118.   [122] Ibid., p. 138.

Without acknowledging some other principle of action in rational agents than self-love, I see no foundation to expect beneficence or rewards from God, or man, further than it is the interest of the benefactor; and all expectations of benefits from a being whose interests are independent on us, must be perfectly ridiculous.[123]

Such an emphasis on disinterestedness led Adam Smith to put Hutcheson's system in the category of "those systems which make virtue consist in benevolence."[124] However, Hutcheson's "amiable system"[125] does not take into account the fact that "regard to our private happiness and interest, too, appear upon many occasions very laudable principles of action."[126] The moral qualities that stem from self-interested motives are "the habits of œconomy, industry, discretion, attention, and application of thought."[127] In that sense, for Smith, the distinction between interested and disinterested motives does *not* constitute the foundation of morality. On this point, Smith agrees with Butler, who took pains to demonstrate that self-love did not necessarily impede or exclude the love of others, and that benevolence did not necessarily exclude self-love. Therefore, according to Butler, "to those who are shocked to hear virtue spoken of as disinterested, it may be allowed that it is indeed absurd to speak thus of it."[128] For Butler, equating virtue with disinterestedness is an absurd statement, because self-interest is not a discriminating factor. Self-interest may be equally involved in benevolent and in "selfish" behavior: "Benevolence and the pursuit of public good has at least as great respect to self-love and the pursuit of private good, as any other particular passions, and their respective interests."[129]

THE ORIGINS OF EGOISM AS AN ECONOMIC CONCEPT

Let us now go back to the beginning of our discussion. The current, widely accepted separation between ethics and economics was formally enunciated for the first time by Edgeworth in the 1880s. If we look further into the genealogy of the ethics/economics dichotomy, we shall find Edgeworth's own statement that the distinction between ethics and economics is based on Sidgwick's distinction between "Egoistic Hedonism" and "Universalistic Hedonism." According to Sidgwick, the philosophical tradition behind "Egoistic Hedonism" includes "the audacious enunciation of Egoism by Hobbes"[130] and "Epicureanism."[131] As Shaftesbury, Butler, and most eighteenth-century moral philosophers did before him, Sidgwick puts

---

[123] Ibid., p. 139.   [124] Smith, *The Theory of Moral Sentiments*, VII.iii.
[125] Ibid., VII.ii.3.14.   [126] Ibid., VII.ii.3.16.   [127] Ibid.
[128] Butler, Sermon XI, in *British Moralists*, p. 369.   [129] Ibid., p. 371.
[130] Sidgwick, *The Methods of Ethics*, p. 86.   [131] Ibid., p. 10.

Hobbes and the Epicureans together as the standard-bearers of what we have called the interest doctrine, or, as he puts it, of "a system which prescribes actions as means to the end of the individual's happiness or pleasure."[132] Sidgwick also defines "the Rational Egoist" as "a man who had learned from Hobbes that Self-preservation is the first law of Nature and Self-Interest the only rational basis of social morality."[133] In this genealogical perspective, the "method of ethics" that provides its foundation to economic discourse can ultimately be traced back to Hobbes and the Epicurean tradition. In that sense, economic science is a neo-Epicurean doctrine.

At first sight, this genealogy of economic science is not especially controversial, but it will seem more puzzling if we recall that Smith, along with Shaftesbury, Butler, Hutcheson and Rousseau, took a polemical stance against the Augustinian/Epicurean tradition, and used neo-Stoic arguments to refute the notion that self-interest was or should be the sole motive of human actions. As we have seen in chapter 1, that is the meaning of the opening lines of *The Theory of Moral Sentiments*: "How selfish soever man may be supposed, there are evidently some principles in his nature, which interest him in the fortune of others, and render their happiness necessary to him."[134] In that sense, when Edgeworth states that "the first principle of Economics is that every agent is actuated only by self-interest,"[135] he is making a claim that is inconsistent with Adam Smith's view of human nature. Edgeworth's claim, on the other hand, is consistent with the first principles of Hobbes's philosophy. For Edgeworth, the workings of self-interest "may be viewed under two aspects, according as the agent acts without or with the consent of others affected by his actions."[136] If action takes place without the consent of others, it is called "war." If it takes place with the consent of others, it is called "contract."[137] The logic described here (the workings of self-interest result in a war of all against all unless there is cooperation) is reminiscent of Hobbes and the Epicurean/Augustinian tradition in general. The paradox is this: when, at the end of the nineteenth century, economists set out to enunciate the first principles of their discipline, they adopted Hobbes's (and Mandeville's) "selfish hypothesis," a principle that Smith (along with Hume and many others) had adamantly rejected.

As we have seen in chapter 4, in *The Wealth of Nations*, self-love is a motive of human behavior only to the extent that it is used as an argument to persuade others to engage in commercial exchange. The drive behind commerce and the division of labor is the propensity to barter and trade,

[132] Ibid., p. 89.   [133] Ibid., p. xix.   [134] Smith, *The Theory of Moral Sentiments*, I.i.1.1.
[135] Edgeworth, *Mathematical Psychics*, p. 16.   [136] Ibid.   [137] Ibid.

and this propensity is itself based on the faculties of reason and speech and the urge to persuade others. The "desire to better our condition," which Smith invokes as a quasi-universal motive of action in commercial society, is ultimately grounded in neo-Stoic assumptions regarding sympathy and the desire for sympathy, not in Epicurean principles of pleasure or happiness. In that sense, the conventional reading of *The Wealth of Nations* as a paradigm of the interest doctrine is an Epicurean interpretation of a work that is fundamentally anti-Epicurean.

Furthermore, for Smith, invoking first principles other than self-interest did not mean that morality should be equated with disinterestedness. It seems difficult therefore to trace the ethics/economics dichotomy to Adam Smith. Sidgwick himself, whom Edgeworth invokes to provide the conceptual distinction between ethics and economics, makes no such claims: for him, "Egoistic Hedonism" is a "method of ethics" like any other. On the other hand, the distinction between an "egoistic" and a "universalistic" method of ethics lends itself easily to an interpretation that would overlook the fact that egoism is a method of ethics. One may suspect that Edgeworth's methodological distinction between ethics and economics was intuitively appealing because it was consistent with the popular notion that egoism was immoral, and morality implied disinterestedness.

In the *Genealogy of Morals*, Nietzsche praises "these English psychologists, whom one has also to thank for the only attempts hitherto to arrive at a history of the origin of morality."[138] What Nietzsche particularly appreciates in Hume and other "English psychologists" is their willingness to drag "the *partie honteuse* of our inner world into the foreground"[139] in their search for what has been decisive in the evolution of morality. In other words, Hume should be praised for putting the various aspects of human selfishness (hitherto hidden like genital parts) at the center of his history of morality. However, Nietzsche criticizes the English psychologists for making utility the original criterion of what was "good" and "bad":

> Originally – so they decree – one approved unegoistic actions and called them good from the point of view of those to whom they were done, that is to say, those to whom they were useful; later one forgot how this approval originated and, simply because unegoistic actions were always habitually praised as good, one also felt them to be good – as if they were something good in themselves.[140]

Indeed, Hume asserts that "self-interest is the original motive to the establishment of justice," and that "the sense of moral good and evil follows

---

[138] Friedrich Nietzsche, *On the Genealogy of Morals*, translated by Walter Kaufmann, New York: Vintage Books, 1989 [*Zur Genealogie der Moral*, 1887], First Essay, Section 1, p. 24.
[139] Ibid.   [140] Ibid., Section 2, p. 25.

upon justice and injustice."[141] In Hume's genealogy of morals, justice (based on self-interest and utility) comes first. Afterwards comes the sense of moral good and evil, based on "sympathy with public interest."[142] Although he approves the English psychologists' willingness to delve into the least noble parts of human nature, Nietzsche strongly objects to their utilitarian assumptions (their notion that the distinction between moral good and evil comes from a consideration of the public interest). According to Nietzsche, these utilitarian assumptions have crept into popular consciousness in such a way that everyone now spontaneously equates morality with unselfishness:

> It was only when aristocratic value judgments declined that the whole antithesis "egoistic" "unegoistic" obtruded itself more and more on the human conscience... And even then it was a long time before that instinct attained such dominion that moral evaluation was actually stuck and halted at this antithesis (as, for example, is the case in contemporary Europe: the prejudice that takes "moral," "unegoistic," "*désintéressé*" as concepts of equivalent value already rules today with the force of a "fixed idea" and brain-sicknes).[143]

For an example of what Nietzsche sees as a "prejudice" affecting "contemporary Europe," it suffices to go back to Edegworth's *Mathematical Psychics*, written, like the *Genealogy of Morals*, in the 1880s. Like Hume, Edgeworth focuses on the "controlless core of human selfishness,"[144] but more importantly, he takes Hume's utilitarian assumptions to their logical conclusion by equating morality with an exclusive concern for the interest of others. Following Nietzsche's interpretation, one could argue that the English psychologists' common purpose was to respond to what Hume called the "selfish hypothesis." Rather than rejecting it altogether, they sought to restrict its application, either by establishing a field where it would apply as a matter of convention (Hume's distinction between interested and disinterested commerce) or by trying to distinguish between selfish and unselfish motives of action (as Shaftesbury and Hutcheson did). There are two sides to this philosophical enterprise: one side is a sober assessment of the fundamental role of self-interest in human behavior; the other side is a utilitarian view that equates moral goodness with a concern for the public interest. Edgeworth's distinction between ethics and economics must be understood in this context. On the one hand, we find what looks like an unqualified endorsement of the "selfish hypothesis": "a system of hedonic forces each tending to maximum individual utility."[145] But precisely this endorsement of a Hobbesian view of human nature is restricted to the field of economics.

---

[141] Hume, *A Treatise of Human nature*, III.II.II, p. 499.   [142] Ibid.
[143] Nietzsche, *On the Genealogy of Morals*, First Essay, Section 2, p. 26.
[144] Edgeworth, *Mathematical Psychics*, p. 52.   [145] Ibid., p. 15.

The field of ethics is a utilitarian universe where "each and all tend to maximum universal utility."[146] For a complete picture of human nature, one must look at both fields together, and recall that in Edgeworth's view, "it is possible that the moral constitution of the concrete agent would be neither pure Utilitarian nor pure Egoistic, but μικτη τις [some combination of both]."[147] The obvious difficulty with this approach is that in order to have a complete picture of human nature, one must operate simultaneously in two fields that are ruled by mutually exclusive principles. In this perspective, the divorce between ethics and economics is not an unfortunate turn of events that could be remedied if economists paid more attention to ethical concerns, or if moral philosophers studied economics. It is a logical and necessary consequence of the commonly accepted definitions of ethics and economics. The assumption of self-interest carries with it the notion of a separate sphere where this assumption does not hold. In other words, the idea that economic behavior is self-interested *implies* that moral behavior must be disinterested.

[146] Ibid.   [147] Ibid.

6

Self-interest and the public good

How can maxims so clear, so agreeable to plain common sense, and to facts
attested by all who have made commerce their study, have yet been rejected
in practice by all the ruling powers of Europe?... To speak the truth, it
is because the first principles of political economy are as yet but little
known; because ingenious systems and reasonings have been built upon
hollow foundations and taken advantage of, on the one hand, by interested
rulers, who employ prohibition as a weapon of offense, or an instrument
of revenue; and, on the other, by the personal avarice of merchants and
manufacturers, who have a private interest in exclusive measures.

Jean-Baptiste Say, *A Treatise on Political Economy* (1803)

For economists today, the relationship between economics and politics is
a problematic one. Some see the origin of this uneasy relationship in *The*
Wealth of Nations. According to Smith, the "folly of human laws" stands
as an obstacle to the rational pursuit of self-interest, and yet "the natural effort of every individual to better his condition, when suffered to
exert itself with freedom and security, is so powerful a principle" that it is
capable of "surmounting a hundred impertinent obstructions"[1] caused by
ill-conceived laws. Hence the paradox formulated by George J. Stigler: "If
self-interest dominates the majority of men in all commercial undertakings,
why not also in all their political undertakings? Why should legislators erect
"a hundred impertinent obstructions" to the economic behavior which
creates the wealth of nations?"[2] Stigler's paradox challenges a common
assumption that Hirschman characterizes as "widespread today among
economists": that "politics is the province of the 'folly of men' while
economic progress, like Candide's garden, can be cultivated with success provided such folly does not exceed some fairly ample and flexible

---

[1] Adam Smith, *An Inquiry Into the Nature and Causes of the Wealth of Nations, The Glasgow Edition of*
the Works and Correspondence of Adam Smith, vol. 2, Oxford: Oxford University Press, 1976 [London:
Strahan and Cadell, 1776], IV.v.b.43.
[2] George J. Stigler, "Smith's Travels on the Ship of State," *History of Political Economy* 3 (1971), p. 265.

limits."[3] In other words, most economists assume that the rational pursuit of individual self-interest will yield the best possible outcome for society at large through the operation of the invisible hand. At the same time, the direct pursuit of the public good through legislation is almost inevitably tainted with prejudice and misconceptions, and therefore yields results that are less than optimal. Economics and politics are separate domains, with separate principles: economics is driven by the rational pursuit of self-interest; politics is driven by the apparently rational, but most often misguided pursuit of the public good. Hirschman traces the origin of this economics/politics dichotomy to Adam Smith himself. According to Hirschman, the idea that "economics can go it alone"[4] was a novelty: in Adam Smith's time the most authoritative opinion (the "Montesquieu–Steuart doctrine") was that economic progress resulted necessarily in better government.

Even though it may be implied by his doctrine, the separation between economics and politics was not explicitly stated in Adam Smith's work. Against Hirschman's interpretation, Winch argues that Smith "did not feel the need to take upon himself... the whole burden of explaining something quite peculiar, something that was in urgent need of justification, namely how the economic realm had emerged."[5] The official divorce of economics from politics was pronounced in 1803 by Jean-Baptiste Say, who argued that "wealth (...) is essentially independent of political organization. Under every form of government, a state whose affairs are well administered may prosper."[6] According to Say, the first economist to have reasoned along those lines was Adam Smith himself:

In confounding in the same researches the essential elements of good government with the principles on which the growth of wealth, either public or private, depends, it is by no means surprising that authors should have involved these subjects in obscurity, instead of elucidating them. Stewart, who has entitled his first chapter "Of the Government of Mankind," is liable to this reproach; the sect of "Economists" of the last century, throughout all their writings, and J.J. Rousseau, in the article "Political Economy" in the *Encyclopédie*, lie under the same imputation.

---

[3] Albert O. Hirschman, *The Passions and the Interests. Political Arguments for Capitalism before its Triumph*, Princeton: Princeton University Press, 1997 [1977], p. 104.

[4] Ibid., p. 103.

[5] Donald Winch, *Riches and Poverty. An Intellectual History of Political Economy in Britain, 1750–1834*, Cambridge: Cambridge University Press, 1996, p. 106.

[6] Jean-Baptiste Say, *A Treatise on Political Economy*, Philadelphia: Grigg & Elliot, 1832, p. 15. "Les richesses ... sont essentiellement indépendantes de l'organisation politique. Sous toutes les formes de gouvernement, un état peut prospérer, s'il est bien administré." *Traité d'économie politique*, Paris: Guillaumin, 1841 [Paris: Deterville, 1803], p. 1.

Since the time of Adam Smith, it appears to me, these two very distinct inquiries have been uniformly separated; the term *political economy* being now confined to the science which treats of wealth, and that of *politics*, to designate the relations existing between a government and its people, and the relations of different states to each other.[7]

In Say's perspective, Smith was an innovator because unlike Steuart, Rousseau, and the physiocrats, who used the term *political economy* to designate the general science of government, Smith restricted the use of the term to the study of wealth. Is it legitimate then to trace the economics/politics dichotomy to Adam Smith? In order to answer this question, we must first study its context: the eighteenth-century debate on the relationship between private interest and public interest.

HUME ON PRIVATE AND PUBLIC INTEREST

In a little-known fragment, Rousseau proposes to examine luxury, commerce, and the arts, not in relation to morality (as he had done in the *First Discourse*) but "from a new point of view, and in relation to the prosperity of the State."[8] In doing so, he feels the need to refute the novel theories of "two men trying to make themselves famous by peculiar opinions."[9] These two men, according to Rousseau, "have taken it into their heads to upset all the economic maxims of the ancient political thinkers, and of substituting for them an entirely new system of government, so brilliant that it was very

---

[7] "En confondant dans les mêmes recherches les principes qui constituent un bon gouvernement, et ceux sur lesquels se fonde l'accroissement des richesses, soit publiques, soit privées, il n'est pas étonnant qu'on ait embrouillé bien des idées au lieu de les éclaircir. C'est le reproche qu'on peut faire à Steuart, qui a intitulé son premier chapitre: *du gouvernement du genre humain*; c'est le reproche qu'on peut faire aux *économistes* du dix-huitième siècle, dans presque tous leurs écrits, et à J.J. Rousseau dans l'*Encyclopédie* (art. *économie politique*). Il me semble que depuis Adam Smith on a constamment distingué ces deux corps de doctrine, réservant le nom d'*économie politique* à la science qui traite des richesses, et celui de *politique* seul, pour désigner les rapports qui existent entre le gouvernement et le peuple, et ceux des gouvernements entre eux." Ibid. The credit given to Adam Smith for the autonomy of economic science is even more explicit in the original 1803 edition of *Treatise on Political Economy*. The second paragraph of the work (p. i) starts with the following sentence: "Jusqu'au moment où Smith a écrit, on a confondu la *Politique* proprement dite, la science du gouvernement, avec l'*Economie politique*, qui montre comment se forment, se distribuent et se consomment les richesses."

[8] Jean-Jacques Rousseau, *Political Fragments*, in *The Collected Writings of Rousseau*, vol. 4, translated by Judith R. Bush, Roger D. Masters, and Christopher Kelly, Hanover, NH: University Press of New England, 1994, p. 45. "Mais sous un nouveau point de vue et par rapport à la prospérité de l'état." Rousseau, *Fragments politiques*, in *Œuvres complètes*, edited by Bernard Gagnebin and Marcel Raymond, Paris: Gallimard, Bibliothèque de la Pléiade, 1959–1969, vol. 3, p. 517.

[9] "Deux h[ommes] cherchant à se rendre célèbres par des opinions singulières." Ibid., p. 45/518.

difficult not to be seduced by it."[10] Most critics agree that the proponents
of these dangerous maxims are Jean-François Melon, who published his
Essai politique sur le commerce (Political Essay on Commerce) in 1734, and
David Hume, who discussed commerce in his *Political Discourses*,[11] which
were published in 1752 and translated into French the following year. (Let
us note in passing that in the twentieth century, these same essays were
often published as Hume's *Writings on Economics*.)[12]

In his essay "Of Commerce," Hume proposes the new and paradoxical
view that the wealth and power of the sovereign is a function of the wealth
of the subjects. Hume begins by examining the traditional theory according
to which "the ambition of the sovereign must entrench on the luxury of
individuals, so the luxury of individuals must diminish the force, and check
the ambition of the sovereign."[13] Hume acknowledges that this reasoning
is not "merely chimerical, but is founded on history and experience."[14] The
best example of the validity of this idea is the ancient city of Sparta, which
was at one point the most powerful state in the world, "and this was owing
entirely to the want of commerce and luxury."[15] Yet according to Hume,
things have changed:

But though the want of trade and manufactures, among a free and very martial
people, may sometimes have no other effect than to render the public more powerful, it is certain, that, in the common course of human affairs, it will have a quite
contrary tendency. Sovereigns must take mankind as they find them, and cannot
pretend to introduce any violent change in their principles and ways of thinking. A
long course of time, with a variety of accidents and circumstances, are requisite to
produce those great revolutions, which so much diversify the face of human affairs.
And the less natural any set of principles are, which support a particular society,
the more difficulty will a legislator meet with in raising and cultivating them. It
is his best policy to comply with the common bent of mankind, and give it all
the improvements of which it is susceptible. Now, according to the most natural
course of things, industry and arts and trade increase the power of the sovereign as
well as the happiness of the subjects; and that policy is violent, which aggrandizes
the public by the poverty of individuals.[16]

[10] "[Ils] se sont avisés de nos jours de renverser toutes les maximes économiques des anciens politiques,
et de leur substituer un système de gouvernement tout nouveau et si brillant qu'il était très difficile
de ne pas s'en laisser séduire." Ibid., p. 46/518.
[11] David Hume, *Political Discourses*, Edinburgh: A. Kincaid and A. Donaldson, 1752.
[12] See for instance David Hume, *Writings on Economics*, edited by Eugene Rotwein, Madison: University of Wisconsin Press, 1970. The more recent edition by Knud Haakonssen restores the *political*
nature of Hume's essays in its title (see note 13).
[13] David Hume, "Of Commerce," in *Political Essays*, edited by Knud Haakonssen, Cambridge:
Cambridge University Press, 1994 [*Political Discourses*, Edinburgh: A. Kincaid and A. Donaldson,
1752], p. 96.
[14] Ibid.   [15] Ibid.   [16] Ibid., p. 98.

Hume does not propose any theoretical reasons to account for this fact: the power of the modern sovereign is dependent upon trade and commerce; ancient sovereigns, on the other hand, were powerful to the extent that they kept their citizens poor. He simply presents it as an empirical truth. Hume compares Sparta to a military camp, where discipline and courage stemmed from the fact that all luxuries and all kinds of comfort were banned. If a nation could be turned into such a military camp, Hume argues, it would be possible to make it powerful by keeping it poor:

Could we convert a city into a kind of fortified camp, and infuse into each breast so martial a genius, and such a passion for public good, as to make every one willing to undergo the greatest hardships for the sake of the public; these affections might now, as in ancient times, prove alone a sufficient spur to industry, and support the community. It would then be advantageous, as in camps, to banish all arts and luxury; and, by restrictions on equipage and tables, make the provisions and forage last longer than if the army were loaded with a number of superfluous retainers.[17]

However, in the modern age, such a scheme is unlikely to work because "these principles are too disinterested and too difficult to support."[18] Public spirit can, in theory, be fostered by disinterestedness and poverty, but according to Hume this path is arduous and impractical. The statesman should take human beings as they are, and find other ways of attending to the public interest: "It is requisite to govern men by other passions, and animate them with a spirit of avarice and industry, art and luxury."[19] Encouraging avarice and greed has one disadvantage: the nation will be loaded with unnecessary goods and luxuries. However, says Hume, the advantages far outweigh the disadvantages:

The harmony of the whole is still supported; and the natural bent of the mind being more complied with, individuals, as well as the public, find their account in the observance of those maxims.[20]

In sum, the statesman is faced with a choice: encouraging or discouraging the pursuit of self-interest. If he discourages it, the citizens will be poor, and the nation will perhaps be strong militarily. If he encourages it, the citizens will be wealthy, and the nation will certainly be strong militarily. Encouraging the pursuit of individual self-interest has the great advantage of serving the public interest as well as private interests.

In his essay "Of Refinements in the Arts," Hume takes the reasoning one step further. He argues that lack of refinement and luxury is contrary to the public interest, because it makes "men sink into indolence," and

[17] Ibid., p. 100.   [18] Ibid.   [19] Ibid.   [20] Ibid.

"lose all enjoyment of life."[21] Hume supports this point by drawing an example from modern European history. When Charles VIII of France invaded Italy in the sixteenth century, he brought 20,000 men with him, and this endeavor exhausted the French public treasury. Louis XIV, who reigned over a country that was much more developed in its arts and trade, was able to keep an army of 400,000 for nearly thirty years.

A few years before, Jean-François Melon had already argued that luxury was not contrary to military virtue. In his *Political Essay on Commerce*, Melon wrote that "the soldier is courageous only because of ambition, and the merchant works only because of greed."[22] Consequently, it cannot be said that luxury makes a nation soft:

In what sense can we say that luxury makes a nation soft? This cannot apply to the military: soldiers and low-ranking officers are entirely deprived of it. As to the magnificent appearance of high-ranking officers, it has never been a cause of defeat. Ambitious emulation sustains them just as much as all others.[23]

According to Melon, luxury has important moral and political benefits. Idleness and sloth are the vices that pose the greatest threat to the social order, because an idle populace is especially prone to rioting and civil war:

The wisest and best-established monarchy would be in danger of collapsing if part of the inhabitants of the capital were fed and entertained during the idleness of civil peace, and had nothing to lose from the troubles of civil war.[24]

Luxury must therefore be encouraged, because it is the most effective check against sloth and idleness:

Luxury is in a way the destructor of sloth and idleness. The man who likes to display his wealth would soon see the end of it, if he did not work to keep or augment it, and he is much more inclined to carry out his duties with respect to society when others look at him with envy.[25]

---

[21] David Hume, "Of Refinement in the Arts," in *Political Essays*, p. 108.

[22] "Le militaire n'est valeureux que par ambition, et le négociant ne travaille que par cupidité." Jean-François Melon, *Essai politique sur le commerce*, Rouen(?), 1734, p. 106.

[23] "Dans quel sens peut-on dire que le luxe amollit une nation? Cela ne peut pas regarder le militaire: les soldats et les officiers subalternes en sont bien éloignés; et ce n'est pas par la magnificence des officiers généraux qu'une armée a été battue. L'émulation ambitieuse ne les soutient pas moins que les autres." Ibid., p. 108.

[24] "La monarchie la plus sage et la mieux établie aurait bien de la peine à se soutenir, si une partie des habitants de la capitale étaient nourris et amusés dans l'oisiveté de la paix, et n'avaient rien à perdre dans les troubles de la guerre civile." Ibid., p. 101.

[25] "Le luxe est en effet en quelque façon ce destructeur de la paresse et de l'oisiveté. L'homme somptueux verrait bientôt la fin de ses richesses, s'il ne travaillait pas pour les conserver, ou pour en acquérir de nouvelles, et il est d'autant plus engagé à remplir les devoirs de la société qu'il est exposé aux regards de l'envie." Ibid., p. 110.

Melon's views on commerce and luxury must therefore be understood as an expression of the countervailing passions doctrine. A destructive passion (sloth) is neutralized by other passions (ambition and greed). Social order and stability are the result of these opposing forces. For Melon, luxury and wealth are not to be pursued for their own sake, but for their contribution to the order of society. Melon argues for the *political* benefits of commerce.

Hume's views on the relationship between commerce and the public good are consistent with the general principles he discusses in his *Treatise of Human Nature*. In the chapter on the origin of justice and property, Hume argues that the natural affections of human beings are not entirely selfish. Yet the movement of nature, leading us to prefer those we know (our relatives and friends) over those we do not know, makes us inevitably partial and biased in our actions. The solution to this problem is not to be found in nature, but in convention. This convention is the establishment of justice, which makes individual interest agree with the public interest. Justice is a set of artificial rules dealing mainly with the possession of external goods. Through justice, the possession of external goods is rendered stable and secure. Hume insists that the establishment of justice is not contrary to human greed and avarice. It simply restrains and channels greed in ways that are consistent with the public interest. In fact, the establishment of justice is what best serves individual self-interest:

Instead of departing from our own interest, or from that of our nearest friends, by abstaining from the possessions of others, we cannot better consult both these interests, than by such a convention; because it is by that means we maintain society, which is so necessary to their well-being and subsistence, as well as to our own.[26]

From Hume's utilitarian perspective, the beneficial effects of commerce are simply a special case of the beneficial effects of self-interest, which is made to agree with the public interest through the establishment of justice. Hume's position is a particularly interesting one with respect to the question raised by Hirschman in *The Passions and the Interests*:[27] Why did Adam Smith neglect the *political* arguments for capitalism that Montesquieu and Steuart had proposed?

On the one hand, Hume's reasoning is consistent with the Epicurean/Augustinian doctrine of countervailing passions (see chapter 4). According

---

[26] David Hume, *A Treatise of Human nature, being an attempt to introduce the experimental method of reasoning into moral subjects*, Oxford: Clarendon Press, 1975 [London: John Noon, 1739], III.II.II, p. 489.

[27] Hirschman, *The Passions and the Interests*. See esp. pp. 100–113.

to Hume, the love of gain is a destructive passion that makes human beings unfit for society. Our better instincts, like benevolence to strangers, are too weak to counterbalance this passion. As to the other passions, "they rather inflame this avidity."[28] Consequently, the only force capable of checking greed is greed itself:

There is no passion, therefore, capable of controlling the interested affection, but the very affection itself, by an alteration of its direction.[29]

Similarly, in his essay "On the Balance of Power," Hume argues that the military ambition of large monarchies is usually self-defeating, because military success forces the nobility to fight wars in areas that are increasingly remote from the court, thus making military posts unattractive. As a consequence, kings are forced to use mercenaries, and their military enterprises falter. "Thus," Hume concludes, "human nature checks itself in its airy elevations."[30]

On the other hand, Hume departs from the Epicurean/Augustinian doctrine on one important point. Pascal, Nicole, Bayle, Mandeville, and Melon had all insisted on one paradox: private vices serve to establish the social order. Hume, for his part, refuses to pass moral judgment on "the wickedness or goodness of human nature."[31] Whether self-interest is a virtue or a vice is irrelevant to the purpose of studying the origins of society. What matters is the outcome:

For whether the passion of self-interest be esteemed vicious or virtuous, it is all a case, since itself alone restrains it, so that if it be virtuous, men become social by their virtue, if vicious, their vice has the same effect.[32]

This statement is remarkable because, while following the logic of the countervailing passions doctrine, it erases all reference to original sin. Up until Hume, all proponents of this doctrine, including Mandeville, had assumed the wickedness of human nature. Hume does not refute or deny this assumption. He simply dismisses it as unnecessary. Alluding to *The Fable of the Bees*, Hume agrees with Mandeville that "two opposite vices in a state may be more advantageous than either of them alone." This does not mean, however, that one should "pronounce vice itself advantageous."[33] In that sense, Mandeville's slogan, *private vices, public benefits*, is "little less than a contradiction in terms."[34] At any rate, Hume argues that deciding

---

[28] Hume, *A Treatise of Human nature*, III.II.II, p. 492.   [29] Ibid.
[30] David Hume, "On the Balance of Power," in *Political Essays*, p. 160.
[31] Hume, *A Treatise of Human nature*, III.II.II, p. 492.   [32] Ibid.
[33] Hume, "Of Refinement in the Arts," p. 114.   [34] Ibid.

whether private vices beget public benefits is "a *philosophical* question, not a *political* one."[35] From a political point of view, whether or not luxury is a vice is irrelevant. Like Melon, Hume believes that the government has a legitimate interest in encouraging luxury because it is "in general preferable to sloth and idleness, which would commonly succeed in its place, and are more hurtful both to private persons and to the public."[36] Cultivating luxury is consistent with the pursuit of the public good: wealthy nations are strong, while poor nations "can afford nothing to those who are employed in the public service."[37]

One could think of Hume's scheme as a secularized version of the countervailing passions doctrine. This doctrine is a complete psychological and political theory, designed to account for the origin of society. There is no separation between economics and politics. By pursuing self-interest, individuals become rich *and* they contribute to the social and political order. This is a very strong *political* argument for capitalism.

At the same time, it is possible to see how Hume's understanding of self-interest could evolve into what Hirschman calls the reduction of passions to interest. The Montesquieu–Steuart doctrine, as Hirschman describes it, consists in saying that one predictable and calm passion (greed) will check other impetuous and unpredictable passions. The rational pursuit of self-interest will thus result in a stable political order. Yet in Hume's description, the impetuous and unpredictable passions are dismissed from the start. The only strong and dangerous passion is greed itself:

All the other passions, beside this of interest, are either easily restrained, or are not of such pernicious consequence when indulged ... This avidity alone, of acquiring goods and possessions for ourselves and our nearest friends, is insatiable, perpetual, universal, and directly destructive of society.[38]

In the Montesquieu–Steuart doctrine, interests are pitted against passions. In Hume's theory, interests and passions are synonymous, because greed is the over-arching passion. Far from opposing interests to passions, Hume talks about "the passion of self-interest." Self-interest is another name for the passion of greed. Hume departs from the doctrine of countervailing passions, because he describes the human mind as having, for all practical purposes, only one passion. Hume's political argument for capitalism is grounded in the assumption that greed and acquisitiveness are the over-arching human passions.

---

[35] Ibid.   [36] Ibid.   [37] Ibid.
[38] Hume, *A Treatise of Human nature*, III.II.II, p. 491.

Hume places his discussion of the political benefits of self-interest within the broad framework of reason of State theory. In his essay "Of the Independency of Parliament," he alludes to what had then become a matter of conventional wisdom. An effective system of government must be designed with the assumption that human beings have no motive other than self-interest:

> Political writers have established it as a maxim, that in contriving any system of government, and fixing the several checks and controls of the constitution, every man ought to be supposed a knave, and to have no other end, in all his actions, but private interest. By this interest we must govern him, and, by means of it, make him cooperate to public good, notwithstanding his insatiable avarice and ambition.[39]

Hume's own account of the origin of government is consistent with this assumption. Hume therefore acknowledges as "a just *political* maxim, *that every man must be supposed a knave.*"[40] He adds, perhaps more surprisingly: "It appears somewhat strange, that a maxim should be true in *politics*, which is false in *fact*."[41] Political theorists and framers of constitutions are correct in assuming self-interest as the only motive of human action. Yet we must acknowledge that this assumption is empirically false. Hume solves the paradox by noticing that, if *individuals* are rarely selfish to the extreme (because "honor is a great check upon mankind"[42]) parties and factions are unambiguously self-interested, because all sense of shame is lifted when human beings act collectively. Consequently, the assumption of self-interest is a valid one. In any event, this analysis sheds some light on Hume's understanding and use of the "selfish hypothesis." As we have seen in chapter 1, many discussions of self-interest as a first principle of economics focus on the psychological validity of the assumption: is it true that the human mind operates with exclusively selfish motives? Yet, as Hume shows, this question is probably misleading. It is not difficult to show that the selfish hypothesis, when expressed as a statement on human psychology, is empirically false. This does not mean that it cannot be a valid assumption for political science (or economic science). When political writers *suppose* man to be a knave, they do not necessarily mean that man is essentially and intrinsically a knave. The assumption of self-interest, as Hume understands it, sidesteps the issue of the wickedness or goodness of human nature. Self-interest is nothing but a convenient assumption, which makes systems of government possible. Hume reasons in a similar way regarding the obligation of

---

[39] David Hume, "Of the Independency of Parliament," in *Political Essays*, p. 24.
[40] Ibid.   [41] Ibid.   [42] Ibid.

promises. As we have seen in chapter 5, instead of scrutinizing motives, Hume focuses on the *form* of human relations. A person who makes a promise is assumed to engage in "interested commerce." This is not a statement about the person's inner motives. It is simply a conventional way of signaling that the person who makes the promise has a compelling reason to keep it (because a failure to keep the promise will damage that person's credit). It is true, according to Hume, that most of human interaction now falls under the category of interested commerce. Yet this is not a statement about the selfishness or unselfishness of human nature. Self-interest, in and of itself, is an obstacle to commerce. It becomes an engine of commerce only after it has been transformed into a conventional and explicitly stated motive of action.

ROUSSEAU'S CRITIQUE OF COMMERCE

Rousseau submits Hume's views to a radical critique. Like Hume, Rousseau begins his analysis with an examination of the "selfish hypothesis." As we have seen in chapter 1, Rousseau rejects the interest doctrine as an account of human nature, but he endorses it as a description of human behavior in contemporary society. As far as the customs of his contemporaries are concerned, Rousseau appropriates La Rochefoucauld's critique of the trading of favors. In the *Confessions*, he refers to the *Maxims* as "a sad and distressing book, especially when one is young and does not like to see man as he is."[43] The *Maxims* are sad and distressing precisely because they present an accurate description of human behavior. Later in the *Confessions*, Rousseau recalls the natural goodness of an innkeeper, who helped him to establish himself in Lausanne. He then wonders why, having found so many good people in his youth, he finds so few of them in his mature age. The answer is that he now moves in the high spheres of society. In the lower ranks of society, goodness abounds because the feelings of nature are still present. However, "in the more elevated stations they are absolutely stifled, and beneath the mask of feeling nothing but interest and vanity speaks there."[44] In *Émile*, Rousseau takes issue with the ways in which educators try to instill generosity in children. One method, advocated by Locke,

---

[43] Jean-Jacques Rousseau, *The Confessions*, in *The Collected Writings of Rousseau*, vol. 5, translated by Christopher Kelly, Hanover, NH: University Press of New England, 1995, p. 93. "Livre triste et désolant, principalement dans la jeunesse où l'on n'aime pas à voir l'homme comme il est." *Les Confessions*, in *Œuvres complètes*, vol. 1, p. 112.

[44] "Dans les états plus élevés ils sont étouffés absolument, et sous le masque du sentiment il n'y a jamais que l'intérêt ou la vanité qui parle." Ibid., p. 124/147.

consists in showing the child that those who give most generously are those who receive the most in return. Rousseau objects to this method on moral grounds:

Arrange it so, says Locke, that they be convinced by experience that the most liberal man always comes off best. That is to make a child in appearance liberal and in fact a miser. Locke adds that children will contract in this way the habit of liberality. Yes, of a usurious liberality which gives an egg to have a cow. When one stops returning, they will soon stop giving.[45]

In this passage, the critique of generosity is supported by a reference to a French proverb (*Qui vole un œuf, vole un bœuf* – literally, "He who steals an egg, steals a cow"). In addition, the expression "usurious liberality" is probably an allusion to La Rochefoucauld's description of kindness as "a form of disinterestedness that carries a usurious rate of interest."[46] Both references support the idea that generosity is a form of theft.

Having appropriated La Rochefoucauld's critique of the commerce of favors in the court society, Rousseau transforms it into a radical critique of commerce in general. In the *Confessions*, he claims that none of the things that can be bought are worth having:

I would like something of good quality; with my money I am sure of having one of bad quality. I buy a fresh egg dearly, it is old; a fine fruit, it is green; a girl, she is tainted. I love good wine; but where is it to be found? At a wine merchant's? Whatever I might do he will poison me.[47]

In *Julie, or the New Heloise*, Saint-Preux describes the "domestic œconomy" of Clarens, the estate of Monsieur and Madame de Wolmar. He discusses, among other things, the best way of training household servants. Masters, he says, are always afraid that servants will leave them as soon as they have been trained. Saint-Preux then makes the following suggestion:

---

[45] Jean-Jacques Rousseau, *Émile*, translated by Allan Bloom, New York: Basic Books, 1979, p. 103. "Faites en sorte, dit Locke, qu'ils soient convaincus par expérience que le plus libérale est toujours le mieux partagé. C'est là rendre un enfant libéral en apparence, et avare en effet. Il ajoute que les enfants contracteront ainsi l'habitude de la libéralité; oui, d'une libéralité usurière, qui donne un œuf pour avoir un bœuf. Mais quand il s'agira de donne tout de bon, adieu l'habitude; lorsqu'on cessera de leur rendre ils cesseront bientôt de donner." *Émile*, in *Œuvres complètes*, vol. 4, p. 338.

[46] "C'est un désintéressement qu'il [l'amour-propre] met à furieuse usure." François de la Rochefoucauld, *Maximes* (first edition), Paris: Barbin, 1665, maxim 250.

[47] Rousseau, *The Confessions*, p. 31. "Je voudrais une chose bonne dans sa qualité; avec mon argent, je suis sûr de l'avoir mauvaise. J'achète cher un œuf frais, il est vieux; un beau fruit, il est vert; une fille, elle est gâtée. J'aime le bon vin; mais où en prendre? Chez un marchand de vin? Comme que je fasse, il m'empoisonnera." *Les Confessions*, p. 37.

Train them as you should, it could be answered, and they will never serve others. If you think only of yourself when you train them, then they are quite right to think only of themselves when they leave you; but attend a bit more to them and they will remain attached to you.[48]

In other words, masters should not think of their own interest when they train their servants. If they do, they will introduce their servants to the logic of self-interest. Having learned their lesson, the servants will leave them to earn better wages elsewhere. Saint-Preux draws a general lesson from this: "Intention alone creates obligations, and a person who takes advantage of something I want only for myself owes me no gratitude."[49] Rousseau draws radical and paradoxical consequences from La Rochefoucauld's critique of commerce. The *Maxims* reveal the fact that, behind every gift, behind every service rendered, there is a motive of self-interest. For La Rochefoucauld, this critique must be understood within the context of a general critique of virtues: kindness, generosity, liberality, etc. are not true virtues. In order to criticize the virtues, La Rochefoucauld does something that is entirely foreign to the aristocratic culture to which he belongs: he looks at inner motives. In traditional aristocratic conduct, a gift must certainly appear as disinterested, but no one will question the motives of the giver if a number of external signs of disinterestedness are present: there is no obvious *quid pro quo*, the gift does not come as an immediate response to a gift received, there is no explicit expectation of return, etc. On the contrary, under La Rochefoucauld's suspicion, the most selfish intentions are automatically assumed. Rousseau appropriates La Rochefoucauld's suspicion, and he concludes from it that genuine disinterestedness must be a matter of the heart. One could say that the giver now has the burden of proof. Anyone who makes a gift is assumed to act out of self-interest. It is the giver's burden to prove that his intentions are pure, and that no reciprocity is expected. It is only under those conditions that the recipient can legitimately be expected to have a feeling of obligation to the giver. Otherwise, the only valid response is ingratitude.

In response to La Rochefoucauld's critique of the commerce of favors, Rousseau draws pretty much the same distinction as Hume did between

---

[48] Jean-Jacques Rousseau, *Julie, or the New Heloise*, in *The Collected Writings of Rousseau*, vol. 6, translated by Philip Stewart and Jean Vaché, Hanover, NH: University Press of New England, 1997, p. 367. "Formez-les comme il faut, pourrait-on vous répondre, et jamais ils ne serviront à d'autres. Si vous ne songez qu'à vous en les formant, en vous quittant ils font fort bien de ne songer qu'à eux; mais occupez-vous d'eux un peu davantage et ils vous demeureront attachés." *La Nouvelle Héloïse*, in *Œuvres complètes*, vol. 2, p. 446.

[49] "Il n'y a que l'intention qui oblige, et celui qui profite d'un bien que je ne veux faire qu'à moi ne me doit aucune reconnaissance." Ibid.

interested commerce and disinterested commerce, with one exception: in Rousseau, interested commerce is the object of a wholesale moral condemnation. As to disinterested commerce, Rousseau, like Hume, takes a morally favorable view of it. As we have seen in chapter 5, Hume takes a nostalgic look at disinterested commerce, and associates it with the old aristocratic culture. Rousseau shows his esteem for disinterested commerce by associating it with popular culture. Each in his own way, Hume and Rousseau project an idealized view of disinterested commerce upon social practices for which the modern distinction between interested and disinterested behavior is mostly irrelevant. In Rousseau's definition of disinterested commerce, the value of the things exchanged is entirely a function of the inner motives of the giver. Since it is always possible to be suspicious of someone's motives, true purity of motives can perhaps only be obtained if the gift does not happen at all. As we shall see later, in this paradoxical form of commerce, the ideal transaction is the transaction that never takes place.

Since disinterestedness has become a moral criterion, it serves to absolve behavior that, according to usual standards, would be considered immoral. The sexual promiscuity of Madame de Warens was not a serious fault, says Rousseau, because Madame de Warens never made a commerce of the sexual favors she dispensed so liberally: "She never made a low transaction of them; she lavished them but she did not sell them."[50]

In the *Reveries of the Solitary Walker*, Rousseau takes the logic of disinterested commerce to its ultimate consequence. Rousseau describes his warm feelings for the disabled veterans he encounters in his walks near the École Militaire. These veterans, explicitly compared to the soldiers of ancient Sparta, have kept "the old military decorum,"[51] and they salute Rousseau as he passes by. These good military manners fill him with an intense feeling of gratitude: "This salute, which my heart returned a hundredfold, gratified me and augmented the pleasure I had in seeing them."[52]

What touches Rousseau in this military salute is the fact that it is addressed to a total stranger, and without any ulterior motives. The soldiers salute simply because they are following a custom they learned in the army.

---

[50] Rousseau, *The Confessions*, p. 167. "Elle n'en fit jamais un vil commerce; elle les prodiguait, mais elle ne les vendait pas." *Les Confessions*, p. 199.

[51] Jean-Jacques Rousseau, *Reveries of the Solitary Walker*, translated by Charles Butterworth, in *The Collected Writings of Rousseau*, vol. 8, Hanover, NH: University Press of New England, 2000, p. 86. "L'ancienne honnêteté militaire." *Les Rêveries du promeneur solitaire*, in *Œuvres complètes*, vol. 1, p. 1095.

[52] "Ce salut que mon cœur leur rendait au centuple me flattait et augmentait le plaisir que j'avais à les voir." Ibid.

This "republican" form of salute is very different from the salutations practiced in polite society, where expressions of civility are an implicit way of promising a favor, or the return of a favor. As we have seen above, "intention alone creates obligations." Since the soldier's intentions are disinterested and pure, the recipient has a feeling of obligation. Interestingly, this feeling never translates into any action. Rousseau writes that his heart returns the salute a hundredfold. We may suppose that Rousseau responds to the soldier with a salutation of his own, but the "hundredfold" return never leaves the bottom of Rousseau's heart. It is as if the feelings of gratitude, in order to remain pure, had to stay unexpressed.

In a somewhat similar anecdote, Rousseau recounts his crossing of the Seine on a boat with another disabled veteran. He is again charmed by his "forthright manner," and his "open and affable tone."[53] At the end of the crossing, he offers to pay for the passage, and the veteran accepts. Rousseau then feels an immense feeling of gratitude for the fact that the veteran has accepted a small favor from him. These feelings are so overwhelming that he weeps with joy. He also feels an intense desire to give the veteran some money to buy tobacco:

I was dying to put a twenty-four copper piece in his hand for some tobacco; I never dared. The same shame which held me back has often prevented me from doing good works which would have filled me with joy and from which I have abstained only in deploring my foolishness.[54]

Having been unable to act upon his desire, Rousseau consoles himself by thinking that he would have acted against his own principles "by mixing with honorable things a prize of money which degrades their nobility and sullies their disinterestedness."[55] In other words, giving money to the veteran would have been a way of explicitly thanking him for being civil. This would have established a *quid pro quo*, and consequently changed the nature of their relationship. Their disinterested commerce would have turned into interested commerce. Rousseau's feeling of gratitude towards the veteran remains pure and authentic to the extent that it does not translate into any action. It is as if a truly pure gift could only be an intent to give, which becomes impure once it is acted upon.

---

[53] "Son air honnête." "Son ton ouvert et affable." Ibid., p. 87/1095.
[54] "Je mourais d'envie de lui mettre une pièce de vingt-quatre sols dans la main pour avoir du tabac; je n'osai jamais. La même honte qui me retint m'a souvent empêché de faire de bonnes actions qui m'auraient comblé de joie et dont je ne me suis abstenu qu'en déplorant mon imbécillité." Ibid., p. 87/1097.
[55] "En mêlant aux choses honnêtes un prix d'argent qui dégrade leur noblesse et souille leur désintéressement." Ibid.

As we have seen above, Rousseau agrees with Hume's distinction between interested and disinterested commerce. The commerce that takes place in the public sphere is interested. The commerce that takes place in the private sphere is disinterested. In a letter to President de Malesherbes, Rousseau draws a sharp contrast between his dislike for public, interested commerce, and his love for private, disinterested commerce:

A word to say, a letter to write, a visit to make, as soon as it is necessary to do, are tortures for me. That is why, although the ordinary company of men is odious to me, intimate friendship is dear to me, because there are no more duties to it. One follows one's heart and everything is done.[56]

Rousseau ascribes his dislike for public commerce to his "laziness," but also more fundamentally to the fact that he has "always been unable to stand benefits," because "every benefit demands gratitude," and he feels "ungrateful from the very fact alone that gratitude is a duty."[57] More generally, Rousseau rejects any commerce based on self-interest and reciprocity, because it is morally corrupting. For Hume, positing self-interest as a motive for human relations is simply a convenient way of making commerce possible. No statement about human nature is implied. For Rousseau, the practice of interested commerce has produced a change in human nature itself. Interested commerce is both the cause and the consequence of self-love (*amour-propre*), an artificial and deleterious passion (see chapters 1 and 3).

With so much corruption in the public sphere, Rousseau tries to take refuge in the private sphere. In another letter to Malesherbes, he describes his friendship with Monsieur and Madame de Luxembourg: "My heart, which does not know how to attach itself by halves, has given itself to them unreservedly."[58] Since the social distance between Rousseau and the Luxembourgs was considerable, the relationship had to be a private, not a public one, in order to be close. In the *Confessions*, Rousseau mentions the pact he had with the Luxembourgs, which made their friendship possible. Their relationship should exclude any commerce of favors or services:

---

[56] Jean-Jacques Rousseau, "Letter 1 to Malesherbes," in *The Collected Writings of Rousseau*, vol. 5, p. 573. "Lettre 1 à Malesherbes," in *Œuvres complètes*, vol. 1, p. 1132.

[57] "Voilà pourquoi encore j'ai toujours redouté les bienfaits. Car tout bienfait exige reconnaissance; et je me sens le cœur ingrat par cela seul que la reconnaissance est un devoir." Ibid.

[58] Jean-Jacques Rousseau, "Letter 4 to Malesherbes," in *The Collected Writings of Rousseau*, vol. 5., p. 582. "Mon cœur qui ne sait point s'attacher à demi s'est donné à eux sans réserve." "Lettre 4 à Malesherbes," in *Œuvres complètes*, vol. 1, p. 1145.

Since both of us were persuaded that I was right to be content with my station and not want to change it, neither he nor Mme de Luxembourg appeared for an instant to want to give their attention to my purse or my fortune; although I could not doubt the tender interest both of them took in me, they never proposed a position to me and never offered me their influence.[59]

Accepting any favor from the Luxembourgs would have turned their relationship into a traditional and unequal relationship between client and patron. In order to remain equal and private, the relationship had to exclude any type of transaction.

According to Rousseau, private friendship does not exclude gifts and favors in principle. In fact, one is always tempted to express one's feelings by making the most generous gifts. However, acting upon generous feelings carries the danger of changing the nature of the relationship. In *Émile*, Rousseau notices that "it would be sweet to be liberal toward the person one loves, if this did not constitute a purchase."[60] He then proposes a utopian way of being generous without turning the relationship into a form of interested commerce:

I know only one way of satisfying this inclination towards one's mistress without poisoning love. It is to give her everything and then to be supported by her. It remains to be known where there is a woman with whom this procedure would not be a folly.[61]

This scheme could be seen as a private version of the *Social Contract*. In Rousseau's mind, the only acceptable alternative to complete disinterestedness is absolute dependency. Anything in between is a form of prostitution.

In *Émile*, Rousseau describes what he considers to be the ideal way of giving and receiving favors. Émile does need the help of his fellow human beings. However, in order to obtain it, he does not resort to begging. He also refuses to invoke self-interest. The action of giving and receiving assumes that all human beings are equal, and giving is done out of respect for humanity:

[59] Rousseau, *The Confessions*, p. 435. "Persuadés l'un et l'autre que j'avais raison d'être content de mon état et de n'en vouloir pas changer, ni lui ni Madame de Luxembourg n'ont paru vouloir s'occuper un instant de ma bourse ou de ma fortune; quoique je ne pusse douter du tendre intérêt qu'ils prenaient à moi tous les deux, jamais ils ne m'ont proposé une place et ne m'ont offert leur crédit." *Les Confessions*, p. 520.

[60] Rousseau, *Émile*, p. 349. "Il serait doux d'être libéral envers ce qu'on aime si cela ne faisait un marché." *Émile*, p. 683.

[61] "Je ne connais qu'un moyen de satisfaire ce penchant avec sa maîtresse sans empoisonner l'amour; c'est de lui tout donner et d'être ensuite nourri par elle. Reste à savoir où est la femme avec qui ce procédé ne fût pas extravagant." Ibid.

On his side, if he needs some assistance, he will ask for it from the first person he meets without distinction. He would ask for it from the king as from his lackey. All men are still equal in his eyes. You see by the way in which he makes a request that he is aware that he is owed nothing. He knows that what he asks is a favor; he also knows that humanity is inclined toward according it. His expressions are simple and laconic. His voice, his look, and his gesture are those of a being accustomed equally to compliance and refusal. This is neither the crawling and servile submission of a slave nor the imperious accent of a master. It is a modest confidence in his fellow man; it is the noble and touching gentleness of a free but sensitive and weak being who implores the assistance of a being who is free but strong and beneficent.[62]

For Rousseau, Emile's naïveté points to an ideal world where favors could be given and received without any sense of reciprocity. The only obligation one would have would be an obligation to humanity in general. Beyond the private sphere, Rousseau's exemplary man engages his fellow human beings in disinterested commerce.

Rousseau's retreat into the sphere of private friendships (and ultimately into a solitary life) did not mean that he lost interest in the public sphere, or that the public sphere was by necessity the province of interested commerce. For Rousseau, there is in fact a conceptual link between private friendship and disinterestedness applied to the public sphere. On this point, Rousseau follows Shaftesbury, who had noticed the conceptual affinity between "private friendship and zeal for the public, and our country."[63] What private friendship and zeal for the public have in common is the virtue of disinterestedness, which is "purely voluntary in a Christian,"[64] and therefore especially admirable from a purely human point of view.

Rousseau's scathing critique of Melon and Hume is based upon the assumption that disinterestedness is required if one is to attend seriously to the public good. For Rousseau, the novel theories of Melon and Hume are particularly dangerous because they posit that the public good is best

[62] "De son côté, s'il a besoin de quelque assistance, il la demandera indifféremment au premier qu'il rencontre, il la demanderait au roi comme à son laquais: tous les hommes sont encore égaux à ses yeux. Vous voyez à l'air dont il prie qu'il sent qu'on ne lui doit rien. Il sait que ce qu'il demande est une grâce, il sait aussi que l'humanité porte à en accorder. Ses expressions sont simples et laconiques. Sa voix, son regard, son geste sont d'un être également accoutumé à la complaisance et au refus. Ce n'est ni la rampante et servile soumission d'un esclave, ni l'impérieux accent d'un maître; c'est une modeste confiance en son semblable, c'est la noble et touchante douceur d'un être libre mais sensible et faible qui implore l'assistance d'un être libre mais sensible et bienfaisant." Ibid., p. 161/421.
[63] Anthony Ashley Cooper, Third Earl of Shaftesbury, *Characteristics of Men, Manners, Opinions, Times*, London: 1711, vol. I, p. 98.
[64] Ibid., p. 99.

served by the pursuit of self-interest. As we have seen above, Rousseau faults Melon and Hume for subverting all the economic maxims of ancient political theorists, in order to replace them with a dangerously seductive system of government. In addition to the lure and brilliance of paradox, this new system was especially difficult to resist, in Rousseau's view, because "it was very advantageous to private interest."[65] This was "another means to succeed in a century when no one any longer cares about the public good, and when this term – ridiculously profaned – no longer serves as anything but an excuse for Tyrants and a pretext for rogues."[66]

In his description of the estate of Monsieur and Madame de Wolmar, Saint-Preux makes comparisons between the domestic economy of Clarens, and political economy. He asserts that the principle of countervailing passions is just as dangerous in the domestic economy as it is in the political economy:

It is a great mistake in domestic as in civil economy to combat one vice with another or create between them a sort of equilibrium, as if what saps the foundations of order could ever serve to establish it! With this bad system one only ends up compounding all the difficulties. The vices tolerated in a house are not the only ones that prosper therein; let one sprout, a thousand others will follow.[67]

At first sight, the fictional world of *Julie* has little to do with any social reality, and one might think that Rousseau is constructing an ideal economy in complete ignorance of the work of those authors we now read as precursors of Adam Smith. As we have just seen, this is not the case at all. Rousseau is quite aware of Hume's theories on the relationship between the private good and the public good. In this passage, he gives a precise and accurate description of the principle of countervailing passions. He opposes this principle not because he misunderstands it, but because he makes entirely opposite assumptions. For Rousseau, the only way of achieving the public good is to aim for it directly. Vice does not check vice. It simply begets more vice.

---

[65] Rousseau, *Political Fragments*, p. 46. "... l'intérêt particulier y trouvant très bien son compte...", *Fragments politiques*, p. 518.

[66] "C'était un autre moyen de succès dans un siècle où personne ne se soucie plus du bien public et où ce mot ridiculement profané ne sert plus que d'excuse aux tyrans et de prétexte aux fripons." Ibid.

[67] Rousseau, *Julie, or the New Heloise*, p. 379. "C'est une grande erreur dans l'économie domestique ainsi que dans la civile de vouloir combattre un vice par un autre ou former entre eux une sorte d'équilibre, comme si ce qui sape les fondements de l'ordre pouvait jamais servir à l'établir! On ne fait par cette mauvaise police que réunir enfin tous les inconvénients. Les vices tolérés dans une maison n'y règnent pas seuls; laissez en germer un, mille viendront à sa suite." *La Nouvelle Héloïse*, p. 461.

In *Émile*, Rousseau refutes the interest doctrine from a slightly different perspective:

It is said that everyone contributes to the public good for his own interest. But what then is the source of the just man's contributing to it to his prejudice? What is going to one's death for one's interest?[68]

Rousseau acknowledges that "no one acts for anything other than for his good."[69] However, "if there is not a moral good which must be taken into account, one will never explain by private interest anything but the action of the wicked."[70] The *Encyclopédie* article on "Economy" formulates the same principle in a more general way. According to Rousseau, "the second essential rule of public *economy*" is "the law of duty."[71] Rousseau argues that "if political thinkers were less blinded by ambition," they would "feel that the greatest wellspring of public authority lies in the hearts of the citizens, and that for the maintenance of the government, nothing can replace good morals."[72] If the citizens are not virtuous and disinterested, if they do not care about the public good, the best government will necessarily be undermined:

Then, since all the private interests combine against the general interest which is no longer that of anyone, public vices have more force to weaken the laws than the laws have to repress vices. And the corruption of the people and leaders finally extends to the government, however wise it may be.[73]

Once public spirit has disappeared, the leaders "are forced to substitute the cry of terror or the lure of an apparent interest by which they deceive their creatures."[74] In Rousseau's conceptual and historical scheme, "the small, despicable tricks they call *maxims of state* and *cabinet secrets*"[75]

[68] Rousseau, *Émile*, p. 289. "Chacun, dit-on, concourt au bien public pour son intérêt; mais d'où vient que le juste y concourt à son préjudice? Qu'est-ce qu'aller à la mort pour son intérêt?" *Émile*, p. 599.
[69] "Nul n'agit que pour son bien." Ibid.
[70] "S'il n'est un bien moral dont il faut tenir compte on n'expliquera jamais par l'intérêt propre que les actions des méchants." Ibid.
[71] Jean-Jacques Rousseau, *Discourse on Political Economy*, in *The Collected Writings of Rousseau*, vol. 3, translated by Judith R. Bush, Roger D. Masters, Christopher Kelly, and Terence Marshall, Hanover, NH: University Press of New England, 1992, p. 149. "Seconde règle essentielle de l'économie publique." "La loi du devoir." *Discours sur l'économie politique*, in *Œuvres complètes*, vol. 3, p. 252.
[72] "Si les politiques étaient moins aveuglés par leur ambition . . . ils sentiraient que le plus grand ressort de l'autorité publique est dans le cœur des citoyens, et que rien ne peut suppléer aux mœurs pour le maintien du gouvernement." Ibid.
[73] "Alors comme tous les intérêts particuliers se réunissent contre l'intérêt général qui n'est plus celui de personne, les vices publics ont plus de force pour énerver les lois, que les lois n'en ont pour réprimer les vices; et la corruption du peuple et des chefs s'étend enfin au gouvernement, quelque sage qu'il puisse être." Ibid.
[74] "Les chefs sont forcés de substituer le cri de la terreur ou le leurre d'un intérêt apparent dont ils trompent leurs créatures." Ibid., p. 150/253.
[75] "C'est alors qu'il faut recourir à toutes les petites et misérables ruses qu'ils appellent *maximes d'état*, et *mystères du cabinet*." Ibid.

(in other words, the precepts of reason of State theory) are an attempt by the leaders to persuade the citizens that it is in their own interest to support the interests of the government.

In Hume's theory, private and public interest are made to converge through the establishment of justice. Wealthier and more prosperous citizens make a stronger and more secure state. In Rousseau's scheme, private and public interest remain stubbornly at odds. If the citizens do not care primarily about the public interest, private interests will rule, and the State will weaken. This will call for the desperate remedy of Machiavellian government. Unfortunately, reason of State theory serves not the public good, but the interests of the government through a manipulation of private interests. While Hume encouraged the pursuit of wealth as the best way of making the State stronger, Rousseau argues that one of the government's main duties should be to prevent the unequal distribution of wealth among the citizens:

It is, therefore, one of the government's most important tasks to prevent extreme inequality of wealth, not by taking treasures away from those who possess them, but by removing the means of accumulating them from everyone.[76]

For Rousseau, the largest impediment to public spirit is economic inequality. The rich are above the law, the poor ignore the law. Only those in the middle obey the law: "It is only on moderate wealth that the full force of the laws is exerted."[77] Rousseau's "republican" stance, presented as a defense of common sense and philosophical tradition, is a vehement refutation of the paradoxes developed by Melon and Hume regarding the relationship between the private good and the public good.

HARMONY OF INTERESTS VS. COUNTERVAILING PASSIONS

Adam Smith's position regarding the relationship between the private and public good is a complex one, because it constitutes an attempt to reconcile the apparently incompatible positions of Hume and Rousseau. In some ways, Smith agrees with Rousseau's critique of commercial society, and he disagrees with Hume's assessment of the political benefits of commerce. Against Hume and Melon, who had proposed the new and paradoxical view that the wealth of the citizens makes the state stronger militarily, Smith follows Rousseau in reasserting the traditional view: luxury makes the

---

[76] "C'est donc une des plus importantes affaires du gouvernement, de prévenir l'extrême inégalité des fortunes, non en enlevant les trésors à leurs possesseurs, mais en ôtant à tous les moyens d'en accumuler." Ibid., p. 154/258.
[77] "C'est sur la médiocrité seule que s'exerce toute la force des lois." Ibid.

citizens unfit for warfare.[78] In *The Wealth of Nations*, Smith explains that the progress in the division of labor has left virtually no spare time for military exercises, so much so that "the great body of the people becomes altogether unwarlike."[79] In the following chapter, he draws a parallel between ancient republics, which emphasized military exercise in the education of youth, and modern European states where "the martial spirit" of the population "goes gradually to decay."[80] Smith's *Lectures on Jurisprudence* also include a parallel between Rome and Carthage explaining "the disadvantages of a commercial spirit," and ascribing the defeat of Carthage to the fact that in commercial nations "the minds of men are contracted and rendered incapable of elevation, education is despised or at least neglected, and heroic spirit is almost utterly extinguished."[81]

For Smith, the issue is broader than the armed defense of the country. There is both a practical and conceptual connection between martial spirit and public spirit. In "barbarous societies," where there is little division of labor, "the varied occupations of every man oblige every man to exert his capacity."[82] As a result, "invention is kept alive, and the mind is not suffered to fall into that drowsy stupidity, which, in a civilized society, seems to benumb the understanding of almost all the inferior ranks of people."[83] According to Smith, people in archaic societies take advantage of their spare time to exercise for war and to mind the business of the State:

In those barbarous societies, as they are called, every man, as it has already been observed, is a warrior. Every man too is in some measure a statesman, and can form a tolerable judgment concerning the interests of the society, and the conduct of those who govern it. How far their chiefs are good judges in peace, or good leaders in war, is obvious to the observation of almost every single man among them.[84]

[78] On Smith's position within the tradition of civic humanism, see Nicholas Phillipson, "Adam Smith as a Civic Moralist," and Donald Winch, "Adam Smith's 'Enduring Particular Result': A Political and Cosmopolitan Perspective," in *Wealth and Virtue. The Shaping of Political Economy in the Scottish Enlightenment*, edited by Istvan Hont and Michael Ignatieff, Cambridge: Cambridge University Press, 1983, pp. 179–202 and 253–269. Also see Donald Winch, *Adam Smith's Politics. An Essay in Historiographic Revision*, Cambridge: Cambridge University Press, 1978 and Edward J. Harpham "Liberalism, Civic Humanism, and the Case of Adam Smith," *American Political Science Review* 78 (1984), pp. 764–774. For a discussion focusing on Hume's position on these issues, see John Robertson, "The Scottish Enlightenment at the Limits of the Civic Tradition," in *Wealth and Virtue*, pp. 137–178.
[79] Smith, *The Wealth of Nations*, v.i.a.15.   [80] Ibid., v.i.f.59.
[81] Adam Smith, *Lectures on Jurisprudence, The Glasgow Edition of the Works and Correspondence of Adam Smith*, vol. 5, Oxford: Oxford University Press, 1978, p. 541.
[82] Smith, *The Wealth of Nations*, v.i.f.51.   [83] Ibid.   [84] Ibid.

In commercial society, on the contrary, the division of labor is such that most people have no time for war or politics. In addition, their specialization in one particular skill has made them ignorant and incompetent in just about everything else. It is worth noticing here that Smith's position is exactly the reverse of the thesis advocated by Melon in his *Political Essay on Commerce*. Melon argued that idleness was the greatest threat to the social order, because an idle populace would be prone to rioting and civil war. It was therefore necessary to encourage commerce and industry, because that would keep people busy, and exercise their minds. Smith, on the contrary, argues that in ancient republics the undeveloped state of commerce left plenty of time available for military training and the exercise of government.

Smith was of course not alone in holding the "republican" view that the division of labor had detrimental consequences. Adam Ferguson had expressed similar fears in his *Essay on the History of Civil Society*.[85] As Jacob Viner puts it, there is an entire tradition of thinkers, from Smith and Ferguson to Marx, who held that the division of labor resulted in the alienation of the laborers. According to Marx, the inventor of the *Entfremdung* issue was not Smith but Ferguson. Apparently, there was a polemic between Ferguson and Smith as to the originality of the views presented in Ferguson's *Essay on the History of Civil Society*. According to Alexander Carlyle, "Smith had been weak enough to accuse [Ferguson] of having borrowed some of his inventions without owning them."[86] Ferguson denied this accusation, "but owned he had derived many notions from a French author, and that Smith had been there before him."[87] Viner proposes to settle the dispute by noticing that Smith had touched upon the alienation theme as early as 1755 in his review of Rousseau's *Second Discourse* in the *Edinburgh Review*. Therefore, "Adam Smith has clear claims to priority as far as British writers are concerned."[88] However, according to Viner, it is likely that both Smith and Ferguson "were started on this line of thought by a 'French author,' or at least an author writing in French, Jean Jacques Rousseau, and none of them made a secret of his indebtedness, although it has since been very nearly universally overlooked, and seemingly universally left unexplored."[89]

In his *Lectures on Jurisprudence*, Smith gives an account of "that science which inquires into the general principles which ought to be the foundation of the laws of all nations."[90] After mentioning his predecessors, Grotius,

---

[85] Adam Ferguson, *An Essay on the History of Civil Society*, edited by Fania Oz-Salzberger, Cambridge: Cambridge University Press, 1995 [Edinburgh: Kincaid & Bell, 1767].
[86] Alexander Carlyle, quoted in Jacob Viner, "Guide to John Rae's *Life of Adam Smith*," in *Life of Adam Smith*, Reprints of Economic Classics series, New York: Augustus M. Kelley, 1965, p. 36.
[87] Ibid. [88] Ibid., p. 35. [89] Ibid. [90] Smith, *Lectures on Jurisprudence*, p. 397.

Hobbes, and Puffendorf, he spells out the "two principles which induce men to enter into a civil society."[91] These two principles are "authority" and "utility." Authority comes from superior strength, age, and, most importantly, wealth. How wealth strengthens authority "is fully explained in *The Theory of Moral Sentiments*,"[92] Smith adds. Indeed in this work, Smith explains how people sympathize with the passions of the rich: "We admire their happy situation, enter into it with pleasure, and endeavour to promote it."[93] As to the other principle, utility, Smith insists that the social order is based on our deliberate adherence to public utility, rather than private utility:

It is the sense of public utility, more than of private, which influences men to obedience. It may sometimes be for my interest to disobey, and to wish government overturned. But I am sensible that other men are of a different opinion from me and would not assist me in the enterprise. I therefore submit to its decision for the good of the whole.[94]

Smith, like Rousseau, believes that citizens must have a clear notion of the public interest in order to obey the law. This is a point on which Smith and Rousseau disagree with Hume, who argues that the concept of public interest is far too abstract for most people, and cannot explain or justify adherence to the law:

Experience sufficiently proves, that men, in the ordinary conduct of life, look not so far as the public interest, when they pay their creditors, perform their promises, and abstain from theft, and robbery, and injustice of every kind. That is a motive too remote and too sublime to affect the generality of mankind, and operate with any force in actions so contrary to private interest as are frequently those of justice and common honesty.[95]

As we have just seen, Smith has strongly "republican" leanings, and subscribes to many aspects of Rousseau's critique of commerce. On the other hand, Smith cannot accept the conclusions Rousseau draws from his critique. Rousseau argues that the only way of fostering public spirit would be to prevent the citizens from accumulating wealth. Here Smith agrees with Hume that such a remedy might make sense in theory. However, "that policy is violent, which aggrandizes the public by the poverty of individuals."[96] There is no point in trying to reverse the evolution that has produced the wealth of nations. Smith also dismisses the traditional critique of luxury, according to which access to material goods had a corrupting influence on the populace:

[91] Ibid.   [92] Ibid.   [93] Ibid.   [94] Ibid.
[95] Hume, *A Treatise of Human Nature*, III.II.I, p. 481.   [96] Hume, "Of Commerce," p. 96.

Servants, labourers, and workmen of different kinds, make up the far greater part of every great political society. But what improves the circumstances of the greater part can never be regarded as an inconveniency to the whole. No society can surely be flourishing and happy, of which the far greater part of the members are poor and miserable. It is but equity, besides, that they who feed, clothe, and lodge the whole body of the people, should have such a share of the produce of their own labour as to be themselves tolerably well fed, clothed, and lodged.[97]

In addition, as we have seen above, because the poor admire the rich, economic inequality is the strongest foundation of "authority." As such, it is an effective and legitimate way of ensuring the preservation of social order.

It seems at first sight that Smith's system, as a political theory, is built upon a contradiction.[98] To the extent that the social order is founded upon "authority," the State has an interest in encouraging the creation of wealth, and the unequal distribution of this wealth. The richer the rich are, the more the poor will admire and respect them. On the contrary, to the extent that the social order is founded upon "utility," the primary interest of the State is in fostering the disinterested pursuit of the public good. In the first case, there is a clear convergence between private interests and the interest of the public. In the second case, private interest stands in opposition to public interest.

Smith's solution to the contradiction does not consist in making a choice between Hume and Rousseau, between the "liberal" notion that greater wealth and the pursuit of self-interest will secure the foundations of the State, and the "republican" idea that the pursuit of self-interest will weaken the authority of the State. The solution consists in putting forward a scheme whereby the public good can be achieved through the pursuit of self-interest *and* the cultivation of public spirit.

Preventing factions was an essential issue in eighteenth-century political philosophy. As Hume puts it, "factions subvert government, render laws impotent, and beget the fiercest animosities among men of the same nation, who ought to give mutual assistance and protection to each other."[99] For Rousseau, factions are the expression of particular wills that go against the general will:

97 Smith, *The Wealth of Nations*, I.viii.36.
98 For a comprehensive discussion of Smith's theory of government, see T.D. Campbell, *Adam Smith's Science of Morals*, London: Allen & Unwin, 1971, pp. 205–220; Winch, *Adam Smith's Politics*; Knud Haakonssen, *The Science of a Legislator. The Natural Jurisprudence of David Hume and Adam Smith*, Cambridge: Cambridge University Press, 1981.
99 David Hume, "Of Parties in General," in *Political Writings*, p. 34.

All political societies are composed of other, smaller societies of different types, each of which has its interests and maxims; but these societies that everyone perceives, because they have an external, authorized form, are not the only ones that really exist in the State. All the private individuals united by a common interest constitute as many others, permanent or temporary, whose strength is no less real for being less apparent, and whose various relationships, well observed, are the genuine knowledge of morals. It is all these tacit or formal associations which modify in so many ways the appearance of the public will by the influence of their own. The will of these particular societies always has two relations: for the members of the association, it is a general will; for the large society, it is a private will, which is very often found to be upright in the first respect and vicious in the latter.[100]

Rousseau's solution to the problem is well known. In the *Social Contract* Rousseau argues that "in order for the general will to be expressed, it is therefore important that there be no partial society in the State, and that each Citizen give only his own opinion."[101] Hume's solution, on the other hand, has affinities with Montesquieu's famous division of powers. Particular interests should be allowed both to express themselves and to check each other:

When there offers, therefore, to our censure and examination, any plan of government, real or imaginary, where the power is distributed among several courts, and several orders of men, we should always consider the separate interest of each court, and each order; and, if we find, that, by the skillful division of power, this interest must necessarily, in its operation, concur with the public, we may pronounce that government to be wise and happy. If, on the contrary, separate interest be not checked, and be not directed to the public, we ought to look for nothing but faction, disorder, and tyranny from such a government.[102]

---

[100] Rousseau, *Discourse on Political Economy*, p. 144. "Toute société politique est composée d'autres sociétés plus petites, de différentes espèces dont chacune a ses intérêts et ses maximes; mais ces sociétés que chacun aperçoit, parce qu'elles ont une forme extérieure et autorisée, ne sont pas les seules qui existent réellement dans l'état; tous les particuliers qu'un intérêt commun réunit, en composent autant d'autres, permanentes ou passagères, dont la force n'est pas moins réelle pour être moins apparente, et dont les divers rapports bien observés font la véritable connaissance des mœurs. Ce sont toutes ces associations tacites ou formelles qui modifient de tant de manières les apparences de la volonté publique par l'influence de la leur. La volonté de ces sociétés particulières a toujours deux relations; pour les membres de l'association, c'est une volonté générale; pour la grande société, c'est une volonté particulière, qui très souvent se trouve droite au premier égard, et vicieuse au second." *Discours sur l'économie politique*, p. 243.

[101] Jean-Jacques Rousseau, *On the Social Contract*, in *The Collected Writings of Rousseau*, vol. 4, edited by Roger D. Masters and Christopher Kelly, translated by Judith R. Bush, Roger D. Masters, and Christopher Kelly, Hanover, NH: University Press of New England, 1994, p. 147. "Il importe donc pour avoir bien l'énoncé de la volonté générale qu'il n'y ait pas de société partielle dans l'Etat et que chaque citoyen n'opine que d'après lui." *Du Contrat social*, in *Œuvres complètes*, vol. 3, p. 372.

[102] Hume "Of the Independency of Parliament," p. 25.

This solution (like Montesquieu's) is consistent with the countervailing passions doctrine, which is itself characteristic of the Epicurean/Augustinian tradition (see chapter 2). Political equilibrium is the result of a constitutional scheme that pits the interests of one group against the interests of another group, thus preventing any group from seizing total control. In other words, the public good is the outcome of a properly managed conflict between particular interests.

Smith deals with similar issues in *The Wealth of Nations*. He studies the many instances in which "the private interests and prejudices of particular orders of men" have expressed themselves without calculating the consequences of their actions "upon the general welfare of society."[103] It is remarkable, however, that in addressing the relationship between private and public interest, he does not follow the countervailing passions scheme (combating one vice with another or creating between them a sort of equilibrium). Smith's method consists in a cold examination of the relationship between the interests of each group and the interests of society as a whole. Sometimes there is harmony between the interests of one group and the general welfare of society. Sometimes there isn't.

In Book I of *The Wealth of Nations*, Smith studies the interests of "the three great, original, and constituent orders of every civilized society"[104]: landowners, laborers, and merchants. According to Smith, the interest of landowners "is strictly and inseparably connected with the general interest of the society."[105] As to "the interest of the second order" (the laborers), it "is as strictly connected with the interest of the society as that of the first."[106] Only the merchants have an interest that is at odds with the general welfare of society because the rate of profit is high in poor countries, and it is low in rich countries: "The interest of the dealers...in any particular branch of trade or manufactures, is always in some respects different from, and even opposite to, that of the public."[107] As we have seen in chapter 2, this way of thinking is characteristic of Smith's neo-Stoic approach. There are two ways of contributing to the greater good: the deliberate way and the unconscious way. The unconscious way is, in a certain sense, safer. Selfish motives drive individuals to contribute unknowingly to the public good:

He intends only his own gain, and he is in this, as in many other cases, led by an invisible hand to promote an end which was no part of his intention. Nor is it always the worse for the society that it was no part of it. By pursuing his own

---

[103] Smith, *The Wealth of Nations*, Introduction, p. 8.   [104] Ibid., I.xi.p.10.   [105] Ibid.
[106] Ibid.   [107] Ibid.

interest he frequently promotes that of the society more effectually than when he really intends to promote it.[108]

Similarly, the pursuit of self-interest by individuals results in an efficient allocation of capital between domestic and foreign investments. In this case, Smith argues, "the private interests and passions of men naturally lead them to divide and distribute the stock of every society among all the different employments carried on in it as nearly as possible in the proportion which is most agreeable to the interest of the whole society."[109]

There is a fundamental difference between the harmony-of-interests scheme that Smith follows in *The Wealth of Nations*, and the countervailing passions scheme that is characteristic of the Epicurean/Augustinian tradition. An invisible hand explanation consists in saying that individuals contribute unknowingly to the public good. They do what they are doing for their own reasons, and their actions happen to be beneficial to the public. In that sense, the desire to better our condition is to the wealth of nations what sexual instinct is to the propagation of the species. Animals mate because they find pleasure in doing so. The act that gives them pleasure happens to be beneficial to the propagation of the species. There is a providential harmony between the sexual act and the propagation of the species. This is the sense in which the invisible hand scheme is an example of the doctrine of "unintended consequences."[110] The social order is comparable to an ecosystem where the instinctual impulses of individuals work for the harmony of the whole. As Thorstein Veblen puts it, "Smith does not fall back on a meddling Providence who is to set human affairs straight when they are in danger of going askew."[111]

The countervailing passions scheme works differently. In the Epicurean/ Augustinian account of the origins of society (which can be found in Nicole, Mandeville, and many others) human beings are driven by a desire for universal domination, and this desire never leaves them entirely. The desire to "lord it over the earth" can be never satisfied because it is opposed by a similar desire in others. In that sense, one can say that the selfish tendencies of individuals are the foundation of the social order, but this becomes possible only because the desire for universal domination is forced to go against its natural course and to express itself in ways that are supportive of the public good. As we have seen in chapter 2, the countervailing passions scheme

---

[108] Ibid., iv.ii.9.   [109] Ibid., iv.vii.c.87.
[110] See Friedrich A. Hayek, "The Results of Human Action but not of Human Design," in *Studies in Philosophy, Politics and Economics*, London: Routledge & Kegan Paul, 1967, pp. 96–105.
[111] Thorstein Veblen, "The Preconceptions of Economic Science (II)," *Quarterly Journal of Economics* 13:4 (1899), p. 396.

postulates a social order that is born of chaos, and always on the verge of returning to chaos, because the equilibrium between opposite forces is necessarily precarious. There is no harmony of interests here. Symptomatically, Mandeville presents the invention of society as something that came "from God, by miracle."[112] Unlike the invisible hand of Smith's Providence, Mandeville's Providence is rather heavy-handed. A miraculous intervention is necessary to alter the direction of selfish desires and to put them at the service of the public good. Whether or not one takes Mandeville's providential interpretation literally, the use of the word "miracle" means an operation that "deviates from the common course of nature."[113]

In the harmony-of-interests scheme, the unconscious way of contributing to the greater good takes the form of a coincidence between *private* interest (the interest of persons taken individually) and the public interest. The deliberate way of contributing to the public good takes the form of a coincidence, or an absence of coincidence, between the interest of a *group* and the public interest. Whether or not there is such coincidence is subject to public debate and persuasion. The debate is driven by "that principle to persuade which so much prevails in human nature."[114] As we have seen in chapter 3, the desire to persuade is the underlying principle of the division of labor and commercial transactions. The exchange takes place when one party has persuaded the other party that the exchange is in his interest. As Smith puts it at the beginning of *The Wealth of Nations*, we "never talk to them of our own necessities but of their advantages."[115] The difference between the type of persuasion that takes place in commercial exchange and the type of persuasion that takes place in political debate is that the argument shifts from private to public interest. In commercial exchange, I persuade you to enter into a transaction with me because I show you that this transaction is in your interest. In political debate, I persuade you to do something that goes against your private interest because I show you that doing it is in the public interest. In Smith's narrative, the merchants are the most skilled practitioners of this kind of rhetoric. They have managed to persuade the landowners to accept laws that restrict competition by telling them that the interests of the merchants coincided with the interest of the public:

---

[112] Bernard Mandeville, *The Fable of the Bees*, edited by F.B. Kaye, Oxford: Clarendon Press 1924 [London: J. Tonson, 1732], vol. 2, p. 205. This goes against Hayek's reading of Mandeville as an early proponent of the doctrine of unintended consequences. Mandeville insists that political equilibrium is the result of "the dexterous management of a skillful politician" (*Letter to Dion*, Liverpool: University Press of Liverpool, 1954 [London: J. Roberts, 1732], p. 36).

[113] Mandeville, *The Fable of the Bees*, vol. 2, p. 206.

[114] Smith, *Lectures on Jurisprudence*, p. 493.   [115] Smith, *The Wealth of Nations*, i.ii.2.

Their superiority over the country gentleman is not so much in their knowledge of the public interest, as in their having a better knowledge of their own interest than he has of his. It is by this superior knowledge of their own interest that they have frequently imposed upon his generosity, and persuaded him to give up both his own interest and that of the public, from a very simple but honest conviction that their interest, and not his, was the interest of the public.[116]

In this passage, the landowners are described as citizens who sincerely (if naïvely) care about the public interest. It is because they care about the public interest that "the clamor and sophistry of merchants and manufacturers easily persuade them that the private interest of a part, and a subordinate part of the society, is the general interest of the whole."[117]

This scenario differs greatly from the Epicurean/Augustinian system of countervailing passions. In Hume's description, the various groups and factions involved in political debate are assumed to know their interests. As we have seen above, for Hume, the maxim that *that every man must be supposed a knave* is true as a political statement (and not as a psychological statement) because, unlike individuals, parties and factions are univocally self-interested. The constitution of the State provides factions with a framework for negotiating compromises between competing interests. In Smith's scenario, citizens taken individually have an adequate knowledge of their interest, but they do not necessarily know their interests collectively. For instance, the landowners do not have an adequate knowledge of their interest as a group:

When the public deliberates concerning any regulation of commerce or police, the proprietors of land never can mislead it, with a view to promote the interest of their own particular order; at least, if they have any tolerable knowledge of that interest. They are, indeed, too often defective in this tolerable knowledge.[118]

What is remarkable in Smith's approach is that the failure of a group to act in accordance with either its own interests or the public interest is presented as a *cognitive* failure. Landowners are "ignorant," and they let themselves be "deceived"[119] by the merchants. In chapter VI of *The Theory of Moral Sentiments* (added in 1790) Smith argues that "the wise and virtuous man is at all times willing that his own private interest should be sacrificed to the public interest of his own particular order or society."[120] In addition, "he is at all times willing, too, that the interest of his order or society should be

[116] Ibid., I.xi.p.10.   [117] Ibid., I.x.c.25.   [118] Ibid., I.xi.p.10.   [119] Ibid.
[120] Adam Smith, *The Theory of Moral Sentiments* (sixth edition), *The Glasgow Edition of the Works and Correspondence of Adam Smith*, vol. 1, Oxford: Oxford University Press, 1976 [London and Edinburgh, 1770; first edition 1759], VI.ii.3.3.

sacrificed to the greater interest of the state or sovereignty, of which it is only a subordinate part."[121] But precisely in order to subordinate one's interest to the interest of society, one needs to have an adequate knowledge of what that interest is. Such knowledge is the privilege of the "wise and virtuous man." All of this is consistent with Smith's neo-Stoic outlook: nature gives us an adequate knowledge of our individual interest. However, an adequate knowledge of the interests of larger entities ("orders of men," states, or "the greater interest of the universe"[122]) requires wisdom and virtue.

Still in chapter VI of *The Theory of Moral Sentiments*, Smith argues that the stability of the constitution of a state depends upon "the ability of each particular order to maintain its own powers, privileges, and immunities, against the encroachments of every other."[123] In addition, the partiality of citizens who defend the interests of particular orders "may sometimes be unjust," but "not upon that account, useless," because "it checks the spirit of innovation."[124] At first sight, this looks like an endorsement of the countervailing passions doctrine. However, the framework of Smith's analysis is clearly a Stoic, harmony-of-interests scheme. The analysis is part of a discussion "Of the order in which Societies are by nature recommended to our Beneficence,"[125] where Smith analyzes the various feelings and notions that enter into the love of our country. Smith argues that "we do not love our country merely as a part of the great society of mankind: we love it for its own sake, and independently of any such consideration."[126] Loving one's country because it is a part of humanity as a whole would of course be a philosophically superior point of view. However, the interest of humanity as a whole is best served when the inhabitants of each country show partiality towards their homeland:

That wisdom which contrived the system of human affections, as well as that of every other part of nature, seems to have judged that the interest of the great society of mankind would be best promoted by directing the principal attention of each individual to that particular portion of it, which was most within the sphere both of his abilities and of his understanding.[127]

The same logic applies to Smith's discussion of factions. Factions are in a sense unjust because they represent partial points of view. These points of view are partial because of the limitations of human abilities and understanding. On the other hand, the wisdom of nature makes use of these partial points of view in order to achieve political stability. Smith's final word on the love of our country is that it involves two principles. The first

---

[121] Ibid. [122] Ibid. [123] Ibid., vi.ii.2.10. [124] Ibid. [125] Ibid., vi.ii.2.
[126] Ibid., vi.ii.2.4. [127] Ibid.

principle is "a certain respect and reverence for that constitution or form of government which is actually established."[128] The second principle is "an earnest desire to render the condition of our fellow citizens as safe, respectable, and happy as we can."[129] This distinction matches the distinction Smith makes in the *Lectures on Jurisprudence* between the "two principles which induce men to enter into a civil society, which we shall call the principles of authority and utility."[130] As we have seen above, the principle of authority involves respect for established powers. It is ultimately based on the principle of sympathy. The principle of utility involves our ability to understand the greater good. According to Smith, "it is the sense of public utility, more than of private, which influences men to obedience," and makes them submit to the government's decisions "for the good of the whole."[131] The love of our country is therefore a good example of how "natural" tendencies (respect for authority) converge with rational understanding (perception of a greater good) in order to produce an optimal outcome.

At least one solution to the cognitive deficiencies discussed above is a typically "republican" one. In Book V of *The Wealth of Nations*, Smith argues that it is the sovereign's duty to educate the citizenry in order to counterbalance the effects of the division of labor, which makes the citizens' outlook on public affairs narrower and narrower. According to Smith, "an instructed and intelligent people...are more disposed to examine, and more capable of seeing through, the interested complaints of faction and sedition."[132] Among these "interested complaints," one may count the efforts of manufacturers who enroll their employees into campaigns to ban imports, so much so that "like an overgrown standing army, they have become formidable to the government, and upon many occasions intimidate the legislature."[133] In that sense, Smith's approach is closer to Rousseau's than it is to Hume's: it is less a compromise between the interests of competing factions than a public debate on what constitutes the public interest.

One could summarize Smith's outlook by saying that the *individual* pursuit of self-interest can generally be trusted to contribute to the public good, while the pursuit of their interest by *groups* gets mixed results. It is important to notice that, in Smith's harmonic scheme, the pursuit of self-interest and the pursuit of the public good can be not only compatible, but also convergent. The "uniform, constant, and uninterrupted effort of every man to better his condition" is in a sense the more reliable way of reaching

---

[128] Ibid., VI.ii.2.II.   [129] Ibid.   [130] Smith, *Lectures on Jurisprudence*, p. 401.
[131] Ibid., p. 402.   [132] Smith, *The Wealth of Nations*, V.i.f.61.   [133] Ibid., IV.ii.43.

"public and national, as well as private opulence,"[134] because it works like a natural instinct. Smith compares it to "the unknown principle of animal life."[135] However, from Smith's point of view, there is a fundamental convergence between nature and reason. Human beings work unconsciously toward the ends of nature, but they are also capable of achieving the ends of nature in a rational and deliberate way. In order to do this, they must rise above their particular and partial point of view to adopt a larger point of view. This is precisely why the pursuit of their interest by groups is often mistaken and misleading. First, groups may not see their interest clearly (because seeing the interest of a group is much more difficult than seeing one's individual interest). Second, when a group (like the merchants) sees its interest clearly, it is likely to mistake it for the interest of society at large. At any rate, Smith presents the pursuit of the public good as a public deliberation: some join it in good faith and with little knowledge, others with more knowledge and less good faith. *The Wealth of Nations* is Smith's own contribution to the debate: that of an impartial spectator who can see what has been obscured by partial and interested points of view.

In some ways, this distinction between two avenues in the pursuit of the public good coincides with the modern distinction between economics and politics: economics studies the unconscious ways of achieving the public welfare; politics deals with the rational and conscious ways of doing it. This does not mean, however, that Smith believed that good government had to be based on the rational and disinterested pursuit of the public good. As Nathan Rosenberg has shown, Smith was very interested in the *institutional* mechanisms that would "harness man's selfish interests to the general welfare"[136] in general, and to the efficient delivery of public services in particular. In that respect, Smith's principle is the following: "Public services are never better performed than when their reward comes only in consequence of their being performed, and is proportioned to the diligence employed in performing them."[137] In Book V of *The Wealth of Nations*, Smith studies the application of this principle to the administration of justice, public works, the education of youth, and the teaching of religion. In all cases, the challenge is to design the institutional mechanism that will provide the proper incentive for the efficient delivery of a public service.

---

[134] Ibid., II.iii.31.
[135] Ibid. "The effort of every man to better his condition" is *compared* to a natural instinct. This does not mean, however, that Smith sees it as an instinct in the proper sense of the term (see chapter 3).
[136] Nathan Rosenberg, "Some Institutional Aspects of the *Wealth of Nations*," *Journal of Political Economy* 68:6 (1960), p. 560.
[137] Smith, *The Wealth of Nations*, v.i.b.20.

In the case of education, Smith argues that "the discipline of colleges and universities is in general contrived, not for the benefit of the students, but for the interest, or more properly speaking, for the ease of the masters."[138] The distinction Smith makes between *ease* and *interest* is essential here. By *ease*, Smith means the fundamental tendency one has for present enjoyment and immediate gratification. Smith's point is that when a guaranteed salary "constitutes the whole of the revenue which he derives from his office,"[139] a teacher will necessarily neglect his duty because "it is the interest of every man to live as much at his ease as he can."[140] On the other hand, when a teacher's income "arises from the honoraries or fees of his pupils,"[141] he has an incentive to perform his duty properly. One could speak in modern terms of an *economic* incentive, but it is important to see what the teachers' *interest* is in this case: it is no longer defined by the desire for present enjoyment; rather, it has to do with "their success and reputation in their particular professions."[142] The engine of behavior is the desire to be recognized, to be approved of: what Smith calls "vanity," opposing it to "ease," in *The Theory of Moral Sentiments*,[143] or what Rousseau calls *amour-propre*, opposing it to *amour de soi*, in the *Second Discourse*. In modern commercial society, one's "success and reputation" is of course measured in money, but one should not overlook the fact that, in a properly designed institutional framework, the fundamental incentive for the teacher should be "the affection, gratitude, and favourable report of those who have attended upon his instructions."[144]

As Rosenberg puts it, Smith's goal in *The Wealth of Nations* is "an institutional scheme which will establish and enforce an identity of interests between the public and private spheres."[145] Yet precisely, "Smith regards politicians and government officials as a class of men peculiarly insulated not only from the ordinary pressures of the market but from any other institutionalized compulsion which engages the pursuit of their selfish interests with the public welfare."[146] On the one hand, Smith studies the ways in which the self-interest of individuals could be harnessed towards the efficient delivery of public services. On the other hand, Smith expresses skepticism regarding the concrete possibilities of enforcing an identity of interests between "that insidious and crafty animal vulgarly called a statesman or politician,"[147] and the society as a whole. In his discussion of the freedom of trade at the end of Book IV of *The Wealth of Nations*, he points

---

[138] Ibid., v.i.f.15.   [139] Ibid., v.i.f.7.   [140] Ibid.   [141] Ibid., v.i.f.6.   [142] Ibid., v.i.f.5.
[143] Smith, *The Theory of Moral Sentiments*, i.iii.2.1.   [144] Smith, *The Wealth of Nations*, v.i.f.6.
[145] Rosenberg, "Some Institutional Aspects of the *Wealth of Nations*," p. 567.
[146] Ibid., p. 565.   [147] Smith, *The Wealth of Nations*, iv.ii.39.

out that the legislators have every incentive to support the protectionist policies advocated by merchants and manufacturers:

The Member of Parliament who supports every proposal for strengthening this monopoly is sure to acquire not only the reputation of understanding trade, but great popularity and influence with an order of men whose numbers and wealth render them of great importance. If he opposes them, on the contrary, and still more if he has authority enough to be able to thwart them, neither the most acknowledged probity, nor the highest rank, nor the greatest public services can protect him from the most infamous abuse and detraction, from personal insults, nor sometimes from real danger, arising from the insolent outrage of furious and disappointed monopolists.[148]

In this case, it is clearly in the politician's interest to favor partial interests at the expense of the public good, and Smith seems to suggest that only great personal wisdom and virtue could give a politician the strength to do something as dangerous as standing up to merchants and manufacturers. Smith does not propose any institutional solutions to correct this improper system of incentives. Rather, he appeals directly to the wisdom and judgment of the legislators:

The legislature, were it possible that its deliberations could be always directed, not by the clamorous importunity of partial interests, but by an extensive view of the general good, ought upon this very account, perhaps, to be particularly careful neither to establish any new monopolies of this kind, nor to extend further those which are already established. Every such regulation introduces some degree of real disorder into the constitution of the state, which it will be difficult afterwards to cure without occasioning another disorder.[149]

Similarly, in his discussion of the consequences of commerce in the *Lectures on Jurisprudence*, Smith notices that "whenever commerce is introduced into any country, probity and punctuality always accompany it."[150] Therefore, the differences in probity and punctuality among nations should not be attributed to national character, but rather "to self-interest, that general principle which regulates the action of every man, and which leads men to act in a certain manner from views of advantage."[151] Smith explains that the frequency of contracts makes it necessary (for reasons of self-interest) to be seen as trustworthy. However, in situations where contracts are less frequent, people often calculate that it is in their best interest to cheat, "because they can gain more by a smart trick than they can lose by the injury which it does to their character."[152] Those who think they

---

[148] Ibid., IV.ii.43.   [149] Ibid., IV.ii.44.   [150] Smith, *Lectures on Jurisprudence*, p. 538.
[151] Ibid.   [152] Ibid., p. 539.

can gain more by cheating are politicians ("not the most remarkable men in the world for probity and punctuality"[153]) and ambassadors ("they are praised for any little advantage they can take"[154]). In other words, because the dealings of politicians and ambassadors do not have the regularity of commercial exchange, they do not obey the logic of commerce, but the logic of reason of State theory: they are driven by self-interest, but self-interest in this case does not necessarily dictate honesty and trustworthiness. In that sense, the entire political realm is outside the reach of commercial honesty.

Rosenberg hypothesizes that Smith's "antigovernment bias was, in substantial measure, a reflection of the currently limited possibilities for engaging the 'interested diligence' of public officials upon the efficient operation of government undertakings."[155] In other words, it was possible in theory to enforce an identity of interests between the public and the private spheres, but difficult in practice, for historical and institutional reasons (size and nature of the British government, etc.). At any rate, Hirschman is quite right to point out that Smith's position on this issue was a peculiar one, because the conventional wisdom at the time was the "Montesquieu–Steuart doctrine": the idea that an identity of interests between the statesman and society as a whole was a natural consequence of the development of commerce.[156] In the Montesquieu–Steuart doctrine (which is a blend of reason of State theory and the countervailing passions doctrine) the statesman is assumed to understand that his interest as a ruler is intrinsically tied to the wealth of the nation he rules. It is clear that Smith does not subscribe to this interpretation. The reasons for this may be empirical and institutional, as Rosenberg suggests. They are also probably philosophical and conceptual. In Smith's neo-Stoic perspective, the idea that a ruler would work for the public good for reasons of self-interest is implausible. With the proper institutional mechanisms, the self-interested actions of *individuals* can be harnessed toward the public good. However, it is very difficult to imagine a similar scheme for kings or legislators because their actions affect the welfare of society at large in a direct and immediate way. It is possible to give judges and teachers selfish reasons to work for the public good, but a legislator's individual interest is necessarily smaller and more partial than the interest of society as a whole. In other words, when the consequences of someone's actions are very "large" and very general, there can be no identity of interests between the person who acts and the persons affected by those actions. This is why the invisible hand scheme assumes

[153] Ibid.   [154] Ibid.
[155] Rosenberg, "Some Institutional Aspects of the *Wealth of Nations*," p. 565.
[156] Hirschman, *The Passions and the Interests*, pp. 69–93.

atomistic competition, and it is also the reason behind Smith's preference for decisions made at the local level. In Book V of *The Wealth of Nations*, Smith explains that roads are maintained more efficiently in Britain than they are in France, because in Britain they are "under the management of a local and provincial administration,"[157] while in France they are "entirely under the management of the intendant; an officer who is appointed and removed by the king's council."[158] Under the French system, the intendant has an incentive to maintain the main roads properly because they are "frequently seen by the nobility, whose applauses not only flatter his vanity, but even contribute to support his interest at court."[159] For the same reasons, the intendant's interest is also to neglect all the other roads. This does not happen in Britain because it is in the interest of local government to keep the local roads in good condition. The smaller the scope of someone's outlook and responsibilities, the easier it will be to achieve a coincidence between individual self-interest and the public interest. This is why "the abuses which sometimes creep into the local and provincial administration of a local and provincial revenue, how enormous soever they may appear, are in reality, however, almost always very trifling, in comparison of those which commonly take place in the administration and expenditure of the revenue of a great empire."[160]

When the issue is "large," and especially in the case of legislation, which deals with large issues by definition, the only way of achieving the public good is through rational debate and deliberate action. As we have seen above, from Smith's neo-Stoic point of view, having an adequate knowledge of the interests of large entities requires wisdom and virtue. Ultimately, only a properly enlightened statesman can have an adequate understanding of the public good.

HISTORICIZING SELF-INTEREST

In adopting a harmony-of-interests scheme, Smith distanced himself from the Montesquieu–Steuart doctrine and from the philosophical apology of luxury, both of which were based on a countervailing passions scheme. In that sense, he disagreed with Hume's assessment of the political benefits of commerce. For Hume, "laws, order, police, discipline; these can never be carried to any degree of perfection, before human reason has refined itself by exercise, and by an application to the more vulgar arts, at least, of commerce

---

[157] Smith, *The Wealth of Nations*, v.i.d.18.   [158] Ibid., v.i.d.16.   [159] Ibid.   [160] Ibid., v.i.d.19.

and manufacture."¹⁶¹ Once human reason has exercised itself by the practice of commerce, it applies itself to the practice of government, and "knowledge in the arts of government naturally begets mildness and moderation."¹⁶² As a consequence, "factions are then less inveterate, revolutions less tragical, authority less severe, and seditions less frequent."¹⁶³ This type of reasoning is frequent in Hume, and remarkably infrequent in Smith. Yet in Book III of *The Wealth of Nations*, in his account of "How the Commerce of the Towns contributed to the Improvement of the Country,"¹⁶⁴ Smith tells a story that appears consistent with the Montesquieu–Steuart doctrine. He explains that commerce made cities very powerful, and that kings decided to use the cities "as a counterbalance... to the authority of the great lords."¹⁶⁵ This is the origin of "the representation of burghs in the states-general of all the great monarchies of Europe."¹⁶⁶ Smith concludes that "order and good government, and along with them the liberty and security of individuals, were, in this manner, established in cities at a time when the occupiers of land in the country were exposed to every sort of violence."¹⁶⁷ This narrative follows the logic of the countervailing passions doctrine: good government was a consequence of the kings' decision to pit the interests of the lords against the interests of the towns: "mutual interest... disposed [the burghers] to support the king, and the king to support them against the lords."¹⁶⁸ The next step in the narrative is the extension of good government from the cities to the country. This extension happens in parallel with the extension of commerce:

> Thirdly, and lastly, commerce and manufactures gradually introduced order and good government, and with them, the liberty and security of individuals, among the inhabitants of the country, who had before lived almost in a continual state of war with their neighbours and of servile dependency upon their superiors. This, though it has been the least observed, is by far the most important of all their effects. Mr. Hume is the only writer who, so far as I know, has hitherto taken notice of it.¹⁶⁹

What makes this development possible is the behavior of the great lords, who gradually give up the power they had from owning the land. Before the rise of commerce, the surplus generated by agriculture was shared by the lords with a large army of retainers, and with tenants who had no formal leases. Tenants and retainers were in a state of personal dependency with respect to the great lords, who had complete control over the administration

---

¹⁶¹ Hume, "Of Refinement in the Arts," p. 109.   ¹⁶² Ibid.   ¹⁶³ Ibid.
¹⁶⁴ Smith, *The Wealth of Nations*, III.iv.   ¹⁶⁵ Ibid., III.iii.11.   ¹⁶⁶ Ibid.
¹⁶⁷ Ibid.   ¹⁶⁸ Ibid., III.iii.8.   ¹⁶⁹ Ibid., III.iv.4.

of justice at the local level. With the development of commerce, the lords were able to spend the surplus of their estates on manufactured goods coming from the towns ("a pair of diamond buckles, perhaps, or something as frivolous and useless"[170]). In order to generate the funds needed for those purchases, they dismissed the retainers, and they signed long leases with their tenants. As a result, their power vanished: "and thus for the gratification of the most childish, the meanest and the most sordid of all vanities, they gradually bartered their whole power and authority."[171] Because "the great proprietors were no longer capable of interrupting the regular execution of justice,"[172] good government was made possible in the country, as it had been in the cities: "a regular government was established in the country as well as in the city, nobody having sufficient power to disturb its operations in the one, any more than in the other."[173]

This story is a significant counterexample to Hirschman's claim that the Montesquieu–Steuart doctrine is absent from *The Wealth of Nations*. Hirschman reconciles it with his overall hypothesis by arguing that it is not a case of self-interest winning over passion but the exact opposite (the lords relinquish their power because they seek immediate gratification). He adds that Smith's story explains how good government was made possible by economic progress at the *local* level; however, there is nothing in *The Wealth of Nations* to explain how the same logic could apply to the *central* government: by pitting the cities against the lords, the kings have increased their power, but this is no guarantee against arbitrary and despotic government on the part of the kings themselves.[174]

The fundamental issue here is Smith's conception of the nature and function of self-interest in a historical perspective. Here again, a comparison with Rousseau will be helpful. As we have seen a chapter 1, in *The Theory of Moral Sentiments*, Smith posits two principles of human nature: self-love and sympathy. Self-love is the natural, legitimate, and limited concern we have for our own preservation and well-being. Sympathy is our ability to identify with the feelings and emotions of others. What Smith calls *self-love* in *The Theory of Moral Sentiments* is very close to Rousseau's concept of *amour de soi* in the *Second Discourse*. What Smith calls *sympathy* overlaps almost entirely with the concept of *identification* in Rousseau. There are obvious connections between Smith's *sympathy* and Rousseau's *pitié*, but Smith argues that sympathy increases with the progress of civilization while Rousseau says that *pitié* diminishes with it. On the other hand, one of

---

[170] Ibid., III.iv.10.   [171] Ibid.   [172] Ibid., III.iv.15.   [173] Ibid., III.iv.15.
[174] Hirschman, *The Passions and the Interests*, p. 102.

Rousseau's main points in the *Second Discourse* is that the ability to *identify* with others increases with the development of reason and reflection. This ability to identify is the foundation of *amour-propre*, a feeling that is both a cause and a consequence of the development of commerce and civilization. As we have seen in chapter 1, Smith subscribes to Rousseau's description of human behavior in civilized society: human beings, driven by the need to be seen favorably by others ("vanity," in Smith's vocabulary, *amour-propre* in Rousseau), work to accumulate wealth instead of seeking immediate gratification: "it is the vanity, not the ease, or the pleasure, which interests us."[175] The paradox here is that the pursuit of wealth is not based on the "selfish" impulse that is natural to all human beings: *amour de soi* in Rousseau, or self-love in Smith. It originates in an apparently "non-selfish" impulse, the ability to identify with the feelings of others: "vanity is always founded upon the belief of our being the object of attention and approbation."[176]

For Rousseau, *amour-propre* is the result of a historical evolution of human nature. As we have seen in chapter 1, there are three stages in this evolution: primitive man is endowed with *amour de soi* and *pitié*. With the development of reason and an increased capacity for identification, primitive man becomes savage man. He develops *pitié identifiante* (pity based on explicit identification with others) and *amour-propre désintéressé* (a form of vanity that seeks marks of esteem from others at any price for the recipient).[177] In the final stage (modern commercial society), man is almost exclusively driven by *amour-propre intéressé* (a form of vanity that seeks its satisfaction through the accumulation of wealth). Only the man in the final stage fits an economist's description of the rational economic man. According to Rousseau, before the rise of modern commercial society, human beings were driven only by "present and perceptible interest" because "foresight meant nothing to them, and far from being concerned about a distant future, they did not even think of the next day."[178] Smith's own stadial theory is at least in part consistent with this analysis of the evolution of human psychology. In the early stages of economic development, human beings are driven by a desire for immediate gratification, or by

---

[175] Smith, *The Theory of Moral Sentiments*, I.iii.2.1.   [176] Ibid.

[177] The expressions *pitié identifiante* and *amour-propre désintéressé* are Victor Goldschmidt's. See his *Anthropologie et politique. Les principes du système de Rousseau*, Paris: Vrin, 1974, pp. 337–341 and 452–457.

[178] Jean-Jacques Rousseau, *Second Discourse*, in *The Collected Writings of Rousseau*, vol. 3, Hanover, NH: University Press of New England, 1992, p. 45. "... l'intérêt présent et sensible; car la prévoyance n'était rien pour eux, et loin de s'occuper d'un avenir éloigné, ils ne songeaient pas même au lendemain." *Discours sur l'origine de l'inégalité*, in *Œuvres complètes*, vol. 3, p. 166.

"irrational" forms of vanity. This applies to the behavior of the great lords, who bartered away their political power for vain tokens of distinction:

> Having sold their birth-right, not like Esau for a mess of pottage in time of hunger and necessity, but in the wantonness of plenty, for trinkets and baubles, fitter to be the play-things of children than the serious pursuit of men, they became as insignificant as any substantial burgher or tradesman in a city.[179]

In *Rousseau Judge of Jean-Jacques*, Rousseau defines the "interested man" as the one who "thinks less of enjoying than of multiplying for himself the instruments of enjoyment."[180] Rousseau's historical scheme includes the notion that "true passions, which are rarer than one might think among men, become even more so day by day."[181] Passions become weaker because "interest erodes them, diminishes them, swallows them all up, and vanity, which is only a folly of *amour-propre*, helps to stifle them more."[182] In this perspective, the generalization of self-interested behavior goes hand in hand with the rise of "calculating" vanity and *amour-propre*. Indeed, as we have seen in chapter 4, according to Rousseau, self-interest and *amour-propre* are inextricably linked, historically and conceptually. Passionate behavior, which tends to instant gratification, is more "natural," but it corresponds to an earlier stage in the development of civilization. Modern commercial society is based on vanity, *amour-propre*, absence of real passion, and postponed gratification.

Rousseau's portrayal of self-interested behavior is satirical throughout. Smith's description is more equivocal: sometimes satirical, and sometimes laudatory. As we have seen in chapter 1, in *The Theory of Moral Sentiments*, Smith follows Rousseau's satire very closely. He insists on the folly of a behavior that consists in postponing gratification indefinitely.[183] On the other hand, in *The Wealth of Nations* he praises the self-interested behavior

---

[179] Smith, *The Wealth of Nations*, III.iv.15.

[180] Jean-Jacques Rousseau, *Rousseau Judge of Jean-Jacques*, in *The Collected Writings of Rousseau*, vol. 1, edited by Roger D. Masters and Christopher Kelly, translated by Judith R. Bush, Christopher Kelly, and Roger D. Masters, Hanover, NH: University Press of New England, 1990, p. 122. "L'homme intéressé songe moins à jouir qu'à multiplier pour lui l'instrument des jouissances." *Rousseau juge de Jean-Jacques*, in *Œuvres complètes*, vol. 1, p. 818.

[181] "Les véritables passions, plus rares qu'on ne pense parmi les hommes, le deviennent de jour en jour davantage." Ibid.

[182] "L'intérêt les élime, les atténue, les engloutit toutes, et la vanité, qui n'est qu'une bêtise de l'amour-propre, aide encore à les étouffer." Ibid.

[183] See Smith, *The Theory of Moral Sentiments*, I.iii.2.1, following a passage from the *Second Discourse* that Smith translated in his "Letter to the *Edinburgh Review*": "The citizen, on the contrary, toils, bestirs and torments himself without end, etc." Adam Smith, *Essays on Philosophical Subjects*, *The Glasgow Edition of the Works and Correspondence of Adam Smith*, vol. 3, Oxford: Oxford University Press, 1976, p. 253.

of merchants, and contrasts it with the unwise behavior of the great lords, who sought immediate gratification: "the merchants and artificers, much less ridiculous, acted merely from a view of their own interest, and in pursuit of their own pedlar principle of turning a penny whenever a penny was to be got."[184] What is remarkable here is that Smith appropriates Rousseau's analysis of the fundamental role of self-interest in modern commercial society, with one difference: blame has been changed into praise.

The same logic applies to the famous passage where Smith analyzes "the desire of bettering our condition." Human behavior can be derived from two explanatory principles. On the one hand, "the principle which prompts to expense is the passion for present enjoyment."[185] On the other hand, "the principle which prompts to save is the desire of bettering our condition."[186] Both principles are present in human nature. The passion for present enjoyment is ultimately grounded in what Smith calls self-love in *The Theory of Moral Sentiments*: our natural impulse to seek our well-being through immediate gratification. As to the principle which prompts to save, it is derived from sympathy: our ability to identify with the feelings of others, which prompts us to seek their esteem and approval.

In Smith's narrative, the desire to better our condition has always been present in human nature. It is, however, much more prevalent in modern commercial societies, because it requires some preconditions to express itself: the development of commerce, the division of labor, and a legal system that makes it possible to accumulate capital. Smith explains that when men "are secure of enjoying the fruits of their industry, they naturally exert it to better their condition."[187] Therefore, the desire to better one's condition has historically expressed itself in cities long before it has manifested itself in the country: "That industry, therefore, which aims at something more than necessary subsistence, was established in cities long before it was commonly practiced by the occupiers of land in the country."[188] For Rousseau, on the other hand, *amour-propre* is not an original feature of human nature. Rousseau presents the development of *amour-propre* as a change that has affected human nature itself. At the same time, there is an essential similarity between the two narratives. For Rousseau, the development of *amour-propre* is both a consequence and a cause of the development of commerce and the division of labor. For Smith, the development of commerce has allowed the desire to better one's condition to express itself, and in turn the desire to better one's condition has prompted the development of commerce and the

---

[184] Smith, *The Wealth of Nations*, III.iv.17.   [185] Ibid., II.iii.28.   [186] Ibid.
[187] Ibid., III.iii.12.   [188] Ibid.

division of labor. Both Smith and Rousseau agree that what we now call the rational pursuit of self-interest is a historically contingent phenomenon.

The same historical perspective is needed to understand the status of the Montesquieu–Steuart doctrine in Smith. Whether or not it matches the particulars of the Montesquieu–Steuart doctrine as Hirschman describes it (the idea that economic development will check the power of the sovereign) the narrative of Book III of *The Wealth of Nations* is consistent with an idea that was shared by many at the time: that the development of commerce had produced better government. This was often expressed in the form of a stadial theory of the development of society.[189] However, as Shovlin puts it, the stadial theory "was altered significantly by civic-minded political economists who argued that progress can go too far, that while commerce may improve mœurs when societies are still in a barbaric state, too much commercial development can precipitate a society into decadence and corruption."[190] This was Ferguson's position. He agreed that the development of commerce had brought stable and orderly government, but he warned that too much commerce breaks the bonds of society:

The manners of rude nations require to be reformed. Their foreign quarrels, and domestic dissentions, are the operations of extreme and sanguinary passions. A state of greater tranquility hath many happy effects. But if nations pursue the plan of enlargement and pacification, till their members can no longer apprehend the common ties of society, nor be engaged by affection in the cause of their country, they must err on the opposite side, and by leaving too little to agitate the spirits of men, bring on ages of languor, if not of decay.[191]

For Ferguson, an excessive development of commerce meant that citizens had "no common affairs to transact, but those of trade."[192] Another civic-minded thinker who sought to limit the scope of the Montesquieu–Steuart doctrine by putting it in a historical perspective was Condorcet. In his *Sketch for a Historical Picture of the Progress of the Human Mind*, Condorcet alludes to the doctrine according to which the sovereign understands that it is his interest not to stand in the way of economic and political progress:

We shall give a detailed exposition of the causes that have produced in Europe a kind of despotism for which there is no precedent in earlier ages or in other parts of the world, a despotism in which all but arbitrary authority, restrained by

[189] See Ronald L. Meek, *Social Science and the Ignoble Savage*, Cambridge: Cambridge University Press, 1976.
[190] John Shovlin, "Luxury, Political Economy, and the Rise of Commercial Society in Eighteenth-Century France," doctoral dissertation, University of Chicago, 1998, p. 135.
[191] Ferguson, *An Essay on the History of Civil Society*, p. 208.   [192] Ibid.

public opinion, controlled by enlightenment, tempered by self-interest, has often contributed to the progress of wealth, industry, and education, and sometimes even to that of liberty.[193]

This is a clear reference to the Montesquieu–Steuart doctrine. The sovereign favors economic and political progress for reasons of self-interest. Reciprocally, greater civilization is a consequence of the development of commerce: "Manners have become less violent through the weakening of the prejudices that had maintained their savagery," and "through the influence of the spirit of industry and commerce which is inimical to unrest and violence as the natural enemies of wealth."[194] However, in Condorcet's teleological perspective, the political progress made possible by the development of commerce is limited and relative. After taking stock of the progress made in the eighteenth century, Condorcet argues that, since the publication of Rousseau's *Social Contract*, the Montesquieu–Steuart doctrine is no longer valid, philosophically or politically:

Man was thus compelled to abandon that astute and false policy, which, forgetful of the truth that all men possess equal rights by nature, would seek to apportion those rights unequally between countries, according to the character or prosperity of a country, the conditions of its industry and commerce, and unequally between men, according to a man's birth, fortune, or profession, and which then calls into being conflicting interests and opposing forces to restore the balance, measures which would have been unnecessary without this policy and which are in any event impotent to control its more dangerous tendencies.[195]

For Condorcet, trying to achieve stable government by pitting competing interests against each other is clever but ultimately self-defeating because

---

[193] Jean-Antoine-Nicolas de Caritat, marquis de Condorcet, *Sketch for a Historical Picture of the Progress of the Human Mind*, London: Weidenfeld and Nicolson, 1955, p. 126. "Nous exposerons en détail les causes qui ont produit en Europe ce genre de despotisme dont, ni les siècles antérieurs, ni les autres parties du monde, n'ont offert d'exemple; où l'autorité presque arbitraire, contenue par l'opinion, réglée par les lumières, adoucie par son propre intérêt, a souvent contribué aux progrès de la richesse, de l'industrie, de l'instruction, et quelquefois même à ceux de la liberté civile." *Esquisse d'un tableau historique de l'esprit humain*, Paris: Boivin, 1933 [Paris: Agasse, 1794], p. 148.

[194] "Les mœurs se sont adoucies par l'affaiblissement des préjugés qui en avaient maintenu la férocité; . . . par l'influence de cet esprit de commerce et d'industrie, ennemi des violences et des troubles qui font fuir la richesse." Ibid., p. 127/148.

[195] "Ainsi, l'on se vit obligé de renoncer à cette politique astucieuse et fausse, qui, oubliant que tous les hommes tiennent des droits égaux de leur nature même, voulait tantôt mesurer l'étendue de ceux qu'il fallait leur laisser, sur la grandeur du territoire, sur la température du climat, sur le caractère national, sur la richesse du peuple, sur le degré de perfection du commerce et de l'industrie; et tantôt partager, avec inégalité, ces mêmes droits entre diverses classes d'hommes, en accorder à la naissance, à la richesse, à la profession, et créer ainsi des intérêts contraires, des pouvoirs opposés, pour établir ensuite entre eux un équilibre que ces institutions seules ont rendu nécessaire, et qui n'en corrige même pas les influences dangereuses." Ibid., p. 129/151.

it divides humanity into two classes, "the one fated to rule, the other to obey, the one to deceive, the other to be deceived."[196] Such a division overlooks the fact "that all men have an equal right to be informed on all that concerns them, and that none of the authorities established by men over themselves has the right to hide from them a single truth."[197]

These two examples (Ferguson and Condorcet) show, from two very different perspectives, that a limited endorsement of the *doux commerce* thesis in general or the Montesquieu–Steuart doctrine in particular was compatible with a republican point of view. In that sense, Hirschman's insight regarding the absence of the Montesquieu–Steuart doctrine in Smith remains valid. In his discussion of the relationship between private interests and the public interest, Smith follows a harmony-of-interests rather than a countervailing passions scheme. The idea that a vice checks another vice, or that a vice checks itself, which is so frequently expressed in Montesquieu or Hume, is rare in Smith's works. The countervailing passions scheme makes a brief appearance to explain the loss of power of the great lords. This, however, applies to an earlier stage in the development of commerce. In addition, Smith expresses some ambivalent feelings about the chain of causes that led to this development. On the one hand, the loss of power of the great lords, and the extension of prosperity and good government from the cities to the country, are presented as "a revolution of the greatest importance to the public happiness."[198] On the other hand, Smith famously characterizes this evolution as "contrary to the natural course of things."[199] For Smith, the natural evolution should have started with the prosperity of the country, followed by the progress of manufacturing, and, finally, by the progress of commerce. In Europe, the historical sequence was precisely the reverse of the natural one. This aspect of Smith's narrative is puzzling if one recalls the generally accepted interpretation of Smith as a believer in the doctrine of "unintended consequences."[200] On the one hand, good government seems to emerge spontaneously, as a result of the actions of "two different orders of people, who had not the least intention to serve the public."[201] On the other hand, the initial reason why the cities became powerful was a political calculation on the part of the kings who decided to favor them in order to counterbalance the power of the great lords. From

---

[196] "L'une est destinée à gouverner, l'autre à obéir; l'une à mentir, l'autre à être trompée." Ibid.
[197] "Que tous ont un droit égal de s'éclairer sur tous leurs intérêts, de connaître toutes les vérités; et qu'aucun des pouvoirs établis par eux sur eux-mêmes, ne peut avoir le droit de leur en cacher aucune." Ibid.
[198] Smith, *The Wealth of Nations*, III.iv.17.   [199] Ibid., III.iv.19.
[200] See Hayek, *Studies in Philosophy, Politics and Economics*, pp. 96–105.
[201] Smith, *The Wealth of Nations*, III.iv.17.

this point of view, there is nothing unintended in the weakening of the great lords' power: the kings knew exactly what they were doing. In accordance with the precepts of reason of State theory, they allied themselves with the cities in order to tame the lords who were the greatest obstacle to the exercise of their power. In that particular case, the interest of the kings was consistent with the public interest. However, the kings' decision to favor the cities set off a historical process that Smith characterizes as "unnatural."[202] Smith seems to rely on the countervailing passions scheme to explain historical events that went against the natural course of things because of human design.

As to the present situation, there is little indication that Smith was willing to rely on the continuing progress of commerce to achieve the "withering away," as Hirschman puts it,[203] of wrongheaded economic policies. Rather, he was intent "on describing these policies as hard realities that had to be changed rather than on discovering grounds for hope that they would dissolve of their own accord."[204] As Hirschman suggests, Smith's rejection of the Montesquieu–Steuart doctrine was tied to his republican leanings. Criticizing reason of State theory and questioning the countervailing passions doctrine were staples of republican discourse. In that sense, Smith agreed with Rousseau, who dismissed the idea that, as a general rule, the prince could work for the public good for reasons of self-interest:

The best Kings want to be able to be wicked if it so pleases them, without ceasing to be the masters. A political sermonizer tells them in vain that since the force of the people is their own, their greatest interest is that the people should be flourishing, numerous, formidable. They know very well this is not true. Their personal interest is first of all that the People should be weak, miserable, and unable to offer resistance to them ... This is what Samuel so strongly pointed out to the Hebrews; and what Machiavelli showed with clarity. While pretending to give lessons to Kings, he gave great ones to the people. Machiavelli's *The Prince* is the book of republicans.[205]

As we have seen above, Smith was a critic of the rationality of reason of State theory. He made a distinction between the self-interest of merchants,

---

[202] Ibid., III.i.9.   [203] Hirschman, *The Passions and the Interests*, p. 96.
[204] Ibid., p. 104.
[205] Rousseau, *On the Social Contract*, p. 177. "Les meilleurs rois veulent pouvoir être méchants s'il leur plaît, sans cesser d'être les maîtres. Un sermonneur politique aura beau leur dire que la force du peuple étant la leur, leur plus grand intérêt est que le peuple soit florissant, nombreux, redoutable. Ils savent très bien que cela n'est pas vrai. Leur intérêt personnel est premièrement que le peuple soit faible, misérable, et qu'il ne puisse jamais leur résister ... C'est ce que Samuel représentait fortement aux Hébreux; c'est ce que Machiavel a fait voir avec évidence. En feignant de donner des leçons aux rois il en a donné de grandes aux peuples. Le *Prince* de Machiavel est le livre des républicains." *Du Contrat social*, p. 409.

which led them to be honest and trustworthy, and the self-interest of states-
men, which led them to cheat and deceive (and therefore to work against
the public good). Of course, Smith's works do not contain the radical
pronouncements of a Condorcet, who argued that the deceitful and mani-
pulative character of the Montesquieu–Steuart doctrine went against the
natural rights of man. For Smith, a certain amount of deception is in fact inevitable and beneficial: with the proper institutional mechanisms, it allows
the power of individual self-interest to be harnessed for the common good.
However, the type of deception that takes place in a harmony-of-interests
scheme is impersonal and anonymous: the legislator has established a system that harnesses the self-interest of individuals, but he is not manipu-
lating anybody in particular. On the contrary, in a countervailing passions
scheme, the sovereign manipulates the interests of specific groups in order
to obtain political stability. Finally, for Smith, deception cannot be the only
tool. With the help of a proper system of education, the citizens should
be able to discern the common good through public deliberation. This is
especially true "in free countries, where the safety of government depends
very much upon the favourable judgment which people may form of its
conduct."[206]

REPUBLICANISM AND THE AUTONOMY OF ECONOMIC SCIENCE

A comparison between Adam Smith and Jean-Baptiste Say will be useful
here. The traditional image of Say as a classic "liberal" has been recently
challenged by Richard Whatmore, who argues convincingly that Say was
a staunch republican and an admirer of Rousseau.[207] In that respect, Say's
early work is particularly interesting because it features a republican critique
of commerce that invokes Rousseau *and* Smith as its main authorities. In
a work describing the imaginary land of Olbie, published in 1799, Say
brings up all the republican themes regarding the corrupting influence
of commerce.[208] He explains that the love of wealth makes nations weak
militarily, and (like Smith in the *Lectures on Jurisprudence*) he mentions
the example of Carthage, a city that was defeated because it dedicated
itself exclusively to commerce.[209] He warns the Americans that they must
choose between wealth on the one hand and virtue and freedom on the

---

[206] Smith, *The Wealth of Nations*, v.i.f.61.
[207] Richard Whatmore, *Republicanism and the French Revolution. An Intellectual History of Jean Baptiste Say's Political Economy*, Oxford: Oxford University Press, 2000.
[208] Jean-Baptiste Say, *Olbie, ou Essai pour reformer les mœurs d'une nation*, Paris: Deterville, 1799.
[209] Ibid., p. 29.

other hand.[210] Glossing this warning in an endnote, Say explains that "when the influence of money becomes immense in a nation... the policy of this nation becomes narrow, exclusive, even barbarous and perfidious."[211] He backs up this assertion with a reference to *The Wealth of Nations*, where Smith highlights the nefarious influence of merchants on foreign policy: "The capricious ambition of kings and ministers has not, during the present and the preceding century, been more fatal to the repose of Europe than the impertinent jealousy of merchants and manufacturers."[212] In another endnote criticizing Rousseau's *First Discourse*, Say declares that his criticism of Rousseau's views on letters does not diminish the "great veneration" he has for him nor the belief that Rousseau's writings "will be counted among those that will contribute the most to the future improvement of the human race."[213] Like Smith, Say professes a republican belief in the power of education: its main function, according to Say, is to enlighten the people about their "true interests."[214] In a direct echo of *The Wealth of Nations*, Say declares that "in free states, it is especially important that the people be enlightened."[215]

The first edition of Say's *Treatise on Political Economy*, which contains the very first claim of autonomy for economic science, was published in 1803, only four years after this republican pamphlet. It is unlikely that Say had altered his fundamental views in such a short period of time. Say's distinction between political economy and politics is usually interpreted as a tactical move, drawn by his desire to dissociate Smith's doctrine from its subversive, republican interpretation. This may well be the case. Another interpretation (not necessarily incompatible with the first) is possible: it consists in grounding the distinction in Say's own republican principles. In the introduction to his treatise, Say criticizes all of Adam Smith's predecessors for having confused political economy with politics, but he is especially critical of "the maxim that a state is enriched by luxury,"[216] which became popular during the regency of Philippe d'Orléans (1715–1723): "all the talents and wit of the day were exerted in gravely maintaining such a paradox in prose, or in embellishing it with the more attractive charms of

---

[210] Ibid., p. 30.   [211] Ibid., p. 106.
[212] Smith, *The Wealth of Nations*, IV.iii.c.9, quoted in Say, *Olbie*, note (K), p. 106.
[213] "La grande vénération que j'ai pour Rousseau, la persuasion où je suis que ses écrits seront au nombre de ceux qui contribueront le plus au perfectionnement futur de l'espèce humaine, n'a jamais fermé mes yeux à ce que j'ai cru être chez lui des erreurs." Say, *Olbie*, note (M), p. 109.
[214] Ibid., p. 4.   [215] Ibid., p. 6.
[216] Say, *Treatise on Political Economy*, p. 32. "Cette maxime que le luxe enrichit les états." *Traité d'économie politique*, p. 23.

poetry."[217] What Say has in mind is the philosophical apology of luxury, initially proposed by Mandeville, and subsequently illustrated by Voltaire,[218] Melon, and Hume. The *Treatise on Political Economy* offers an extensive refutation of the philosophical apology of luxury, essentially based on the notion that the consumption of luxury goods destroys wealth.[219] Say also takes Montesquieu to task for considering the influence of laws on national wealth: "the nature and origin of wealth he should first have ascertained; of which, however, he did not form any opinion."[220] In other words, because Montesquieu did not know that wealth comes from the desire of individuals to better their condition, he mistakenly associated the creation of wealth with particular systems of government. From Say's point of view, affirming the autonomy of economics was essential because the notion of a reciprocal influence between economics and politics was closely associated with all the ideas that republicans rejected: the *doux commerce* thesis and the philosophical apology of luxury. Say's rejection of the philosophical apology of luxury was based on Smith's argument that long-term economic growth was the result of a surplus in the balance between annual consumption and production. In addition, Say agreed wholeheartedly with the many passages in *The Wealth of Nations* where Smith praises frugality and parsimony. Smith's own take on the issue of luxury was more ambiguous than Say's.[221] At the same time, Say was following Smith's line of thought when he criticized the notion that "the most useful citizen is the one who spends the most."[222] In that sense, there is continuity, however paradoxical it may appear, between Smith's (qualified) rejection of the idea that the development of commerce and luxury produces a stronger and better state, and Say's affirmation of the autonomy of economic science.

We are now in a position to answer Stigler's question: "If self-interest dominates the majority of men in all commercial undertakings, why not also in all their political undertakings?" What is implicit in the question is that, in order to be consistent, Smith should have subscribed to the interest doctrine: he should have assumed that all human behavior is driven by self-interest and that "all legislation with economic effects is the calculated

---

[217] "On mit du savoir et de l'esprit à soutenir ce paradoxe en prose; on l'habilla en beaux vers." Ibid.
[218] "*Sachez surtout que le luxe enrichit / Un grand état, s'il en perd un petit.*" Voltaire, *Dictionnaire philosophique*, edited by J. Benda and R. Naves, Paris: Garnier, 1954 [Paris, 1764], article "Luxe."
[219] Say, *Treatise on Political Economy*, III.v.
[220] "Il fallait commencer par connaître la nature et les sources de cette richesse, et Montesquieu ne s'en formait aucune idée." Ibid., p. 33/23.
[221] See Winch, *Riches and Poverty*, pp. 76–80.
[222] Say, *Treatise on Political Economy*, p. 407. "Que le plus utile citoyen était celui qui dépensait le plus." *Traité d'économie politique*, p. 459.

achievement of interested economic classes."[223] As we have seen, in Smith's analysis, self-interested behavior is a very specific and historically determined type of behavior. It is tied to the development of commerce and to our desire to seek the approbation of others. The self-interested behavior of *individuals* can be harnessed towards the public good. This applies both to commercial transactions and to the delivery of public services. In that sense, it is wrong to assume that the invisible hand cannot apply to "political undertakings." At the same time, in Smith's harmony-of-interests scheme, it is difficult to see how the interest of *groups* can be harnessed toward the public good. Instead of presenting legislation as "the calculated achievement of interested economic classes," Smith analyzes it as the result of a public debate about the public interest. Driven by our propensity to persuade, this debate is based on information that is complete or incomplete, knowledge that is adequate or inadequate, good faith that is present or absent. From this point of view, Stigler is right to notice that, according to Smith, "reforms must be effected, if effected they can be, by moral suasion."[224] It is clear that, for Stigler, "moral suasion" is a rather weak and uncertain way of getting things done: self-interest would be a much stronger foundation for political reform. Yet, in Smith's system, "moral suasion" and self-interested commerce are both based on the same fundamental principle of human nature: the principle of sympathy. As Kalyvas and Katznelson have shown, for Smith, commercial transactions and political discourse are forms of persuasion.[225] From a modern economist's point of view, Smith is inconsistent or disappointing because he declines to use self-interest as an explanation for political behavior. From a historian's point of view, this is an anachronistic reading of Smith that presupposes the modern dichotomy between politics and economics. At the same time, the economists' point of view captures an essential feature of Smith's theory: the fact that Smith deliberately rejected the "interest doctrine" that used self-interest as an explanation of all human behavior, including political behavior. Or, to put it more precisely, Smith did not deny that self-interest (as it is understood in reason of State theory) was a valid explanation for the behavior of politicians. But this type of self-interest was, in his view, almost always adverse to the public good. For Smith, self-interest could have beneficial consequences only when an institutional mechanism was in place to enforce an identity between individual interest and the interest of the public. Yet precisely, Smith was extremely skeptical regarding the

---

[223] Stigler, "Smith's Travels on the Ship of State", p. 268.   [224] Ibid., p. 274.
[225] Andreas Kalyvas and Ira Katznelson, "The Rhetoric of the Market: Adam Smith on Recognition, Speech, and Exchange," *Review of Politics* 63:3 (2001), pp. 549–579.

possibility of enforcing such an identity of interests between the statesman and society as a whole. The cause of Smith's skepticism is to be found in his republican leanings, which led him to reject reason of State theory and the countervailing passions doctrine. For Smith, trying to persuade a statesman to work for the public interest for reasons of self-interest is futile. The only reason Smith gives to legislators for following his advice is that it serves the public interest.

Conclusion

Much of the ambiguity regarding the first principles of economic science can be traced to the fact that Smith, along with Rousseau, was putting forward a complex response to what Hume called "the selfish hypothesis": the idea (associated with Mandeville and the Epicurean/Augustinian tradition) that self-interest was a general explanatory principle for human behavior. Smith's response was a refutation of Mandeville that integrated many aspects of Mandeville's doctrine. As a consequence, assessing the exact place of the "selfish hypothesis" in Smith's doctrine has long been a matter of controversy. A crucial historical moment in that respect was the *Adam Smith problem*: the polemic that occurred from the 1870s to the 1890s regarding the role of the self-interest principle in Smith's doctrine.[1] One could think of the Adam Smith problem as the moment when the relationship between economic science and the "selfish hypothesis" presented itself as an exegetical problem: is it legitimate to read Smith as the first proponent of the idea that self-interest is the first principle of economics?

The Adam Smith problem has many similarities with the *Homeric problem*, a controversy that was started by the publication of F.A. Wolf's *Prolegomena ad Homerum* in 1795.[2] By pointing to narrative and stylistic inconsistencies in *The Iliad* and *The Odyssey*, Wolf had questioned the existence of a single author called Homer, and hypothesized that "Homer's" works had been written by many different authors. The Homeric problem was thus a clash between a "one Homer theory" and a "many Homers theory." The use of a philological approach to discuss the consistency of an author had long been restricted to ancient authors: by the middle of the nineteenth century, modern authors also became the object of philological investigations, and

---

[1] The best overview of the Adam Smith problem is August Oncken's article, "The Consistency of Adam Smith," *Economic Journal* 7:27 (1897), pp. 443–450.

[2] F.A. Wolf, *Prolegomena to Homer*, translated by Anthony Grafton, Glenn W. Most, and James E.G. Zetzel, Princeton: Princeton University Press, 1985 [*Prolegomena ad Homerum*, Halis Saxonum: a libraria Orphanotrophei, 1794–1795].

the consistency of Adam Smith thus became a pertinent question. In the Adam Smith problem, the issue was of course not the historical existence of Adam Smith. Nonetheless, as in the Homeric problem, there was a conflict between a "one Adam Smith theory" and a "two Adam Smiths theory." After generating countless books and articles, the Homeric problem is no longer taken seriously as a philological problem. The same can be said of the Adam Smith problem: the editors of the Glasgow edition of the works and correspondence of Adam Smith present it as a "pseudo-problem based on ignorance and misunderstanding."[3] However, because, in a broad sense, the Adam Smith problem has to do with the overall consistency of Smith's work, it never seems to go away entirely. As Knud Haakonssen puts it in his recent edition of *The Theory of Moral Sentiments*, "it has taken an immense amount of debate to set '*das Adam Smith problem*' aside and it is still good for another round."[4]

A leading proponent of the "two Adam Smiths theory" was Lujo Brentano, a professor of economics at the University of Leipzig. Brentano argued that there had been a "revolution" in Smith's "fundamental views"[5] between *The Theory of Moral Sentiments* and *The Wealth of Nations*. He contrasted the explicit rejection of the "selfish hypothesis" by Smith in Book VII of *The Theory of Moral Sentiments*[6] with what he saw as the endorsement of the same hypothesis in *The Wealth of Nations*. Brentano's explanation for this change of views was the influence of Helvétius, whom Smith had met in Paris:

In the "Investigations into the Wealth of Nations," on the contrary, he holds entirely to the views of the book of Helvetius upon the nature of man, and regards selfishness as the only motive of human action. The consequences of this dogma of selfishness permeate almost all parts of his work.[7]

In an article summarizing the Adam Smith problem, August Oncken noted that "the same view which we find in Brentano . . . is at the foundation of the writings of Hildebrand, Knies, and others."[8] In other words, the

---

[3] D.D. Raphael and A.L. Macfie, introduction to *The Theory of Moral Sentiments*, *The Glasgow Edition of the Works and Correspondence of Adam Smith*, vol. 1, Oxford: Oxford University Press, 1976, p. 20.

[4] Knud Haakonssen, introduction to *The Theory of Moral Sentiments*, Cambridge: Cambridge University Press, 2002, p. xxiv.

[5] Lujo Brentano, *The Relation of Labor to the Law of Today*, New York: G.P. Putnam's Sons, 1891 [*Das Arbeitsverhaltniss gemass dem heutigen Recht*, Leipzig: Duncker & Humblot, 1877], p. 64.

[6] "That whole account of human nature, however, which deduces all sentiments and affections from self-love, which has made so much noise in the world . . . seems to me to have arisen from some confused misapprehension of the system of sympathy." Smith, *The Theory of Moral Sentiments*, VII.iii.1.4.

[7] Brentano, *The Relation of Labor to the Law of Today*, p. 64.

[8] Oncken, "The Consistency of Adam Smith", p. 445.

proponents of the "two Adam Smiths theory" were all members of the "German historical school,"[9] a group of economists who were critical of the systematic nature of economic theory as it had developed since Adam Smith. In particular, Hildebrand criticized Smith for believing in eternal economic laws based on the assumption of self-interest:

The Smithian system represented itself as a general theory of human econ-omy, but it was only an expression of a money economy just become pre-eminent . . . Economics was treated by the entire Smithian school as a natural sci-ence of commerce, in which the individual was assumed to be a purely selfish force, active like any natural force in a constant direction and which, given similar con-ditions, will produce the same results. For this reason its laws and regularities were called both in Germany and in England natural economic laws, and attributed eternal duration to them, like other natural laws.[10]

The Adam Smith problem presented itself as a philological problem (how do we account for the apparent contradictions between *The Theory of Moral Sentiments* and *The Wealth of Nations*?). What was at stake, however, was a more fundamental issue. The proponents of the "two Adam Smiths the-ory" stressed the inconsistency of Adam Smith because they took a polem-ical stance against the Ricardian orthodoxy, which used self-interest as the first principle of economic theory. When Edwin R.A. Seligman re-viewed Sidgwick's *Scope and Methods of Economic Science* in 1886, he wrote: "Sidgwick finds the pith of the argument of the German school in the assumption that economic man is not actuated by the motives of self-interest,"[11] and he explained that Sidgwick sided with the orthodox school in upholding the assumption of self-interested behavior. In an earlier ar-ticle reviewing Sidgwick's *Principles of Political Economy*, Seligman had argued that the fundamental difference between the orthodox school and the German historical school did not lie with the choice between deductive and historical methods. It had to do with differing assumptions regard-ing the first principles of human behavior. The orthodox school posited

---

[9] Lujo Brentano is usually associated with the "younger historical school," while Bruno Hildebrand and Karl Knies belong to the "older historical school."

[10] Bruno Hildebrand, *Die Nationalökonomie der Gegenwart und Zukunft*, Frankfurt: Literarische Anstalt, 1848, p. v, quoted in Keith Tribe, "Historical Schools of Economics: German and English," Working Paper no. 2002/02, Department of Economics, Keele University, p. 7.

[11] Edwin R.A. Seligman, review of *The Scope and Method of Economic Science. An address delivered to the economic science and statistics section of the British Association at Aberdeen, 10 September, 1885*, by Henry Sidgwick (London: Macmillan, 1885), in *Political Science Quarterly* 1:1 (1886), p. 144. A supporter of the German Historical School, Seligman was the founder of the Columbia Economics Department, and a co-founder of the American Economic Association. See Joseph Dorfman, "The Role of the German Historical School in American Economic Thought," *American Economic Review* 45:2 (1955), pp. 17–28.

self-interest as the sole principle of human behavior, while the historical school allowed for a multiplicity of motives:

The one posits the "universal spirit of self-interest" as the sole factor in evolving the "immutable" laws of the "science which belongs to no nation, which is of no country"; the other lays stress on the multiplicity of motives which cannot be jumbled together in the phrase "desire for wealth," on the importance of legal systems and historical causes in molding economic facts and economic tendencies, on the close connections between ethics and economics as sister moral sciences.[12]

The context of the Adam Smith problem was a debate on the axioms of economic science. For the members of the German historical school, who formulated the Adam Smith problem, it was important to show that the founding father of economic science had not consistently held the view that self-interest was the engine of human behavior: at the beginning, he was a follower of Hutcheson and Hume (who both rejected the "selfish hypothesis"); after living in France for three years, he became corrupted by the neo-Epicureanism of Helvétius, who held that self-interest is the only motive of human actions.

Oncken's own take on the Adam Smith problem was informed by recently published works: the *Catalogue of the Library of Adam Smith*, by James Bonar (1894), the *Life of Adam Smith*, by John Rae (1895) and the first publication of Smith's *Lectures on Justice, Police, Revenue and Arms* by Edwin Cannan (1896). On the basis of this new information, Oncken was able to show that the interpretation of Smith as a follower of Helvétius was untenable, and he argued for the consistency of Adam Smith. However, Oncken's "one Adam Smith theory" depended on a crucial distinction. According to Oncken, Smith's system did assume multiple motives for human behavior, but a distinction had to be made between economic behavior (which was driven by self-interest alone) and other forms of behavior (which were driven by other motives). As Oncken puts it, "self-love is not the root of *all*, but only of economic actions."[13] In other words, the dividing line was not between Smith as a disciple of Hutcheson and Smith as a disciple of Helvétius. It was between Smith as a moral philosopher and Smith as an economist.

Even though it is philologically untenable, Brentano's reading of Smith as a disciple of Helvétius is understandable, at least for two reasons. First, in the nineteenth century, the orthodox school of economics relied on Bentham,

---

[12] Edwin R.A. Seligman, review of *The Principles of Political Economy*, by Henry Sidgwick (London: Macmillan, 1883), in *The Index. A Weekly Paper*, Boston, August 16, 1883, p. 75.
[13] Oncken, "The Consistency of Adam Smith," p. 447.

rather than Smith, for its psychological assumptions. In that sense, the psychological underpinnings of economic theory were neo-Epicurean, and, beyond Bentham, they could be traced back to Helvétius. As John Stuart Mill puts it in an article on Bentham, "the greatest service rendered by him to the philosophy of universal human nature, is, perhaps, his illustration of what he terms 'interest-begotten prejudice' – the common tendency of man to make a duty and a virtue of following his self-interest."[14] Mill adds that "the idea was given him by Helvetius, whose book, '*De l'Esprit*', is one continued and most acute commentary on it."[15] Because Smith was still considered the founder of economic science, the natural tendency was to perform a neo-Epicurean reading of *The Wealth of Nations*. Second, Epicurean principles do have a place in Smith's moral philosophy. In Book VI of *The Theory of Moral Sentiments*, Smith analyzes the virtue of prudence (the cardinal virtue for Epicureans). He defines it as "the care of the health, of the fortune, of the rank and reputation of the individual."[16] The prudent man is characterized by the "steadiness of his industry and frugality," and by his ability to sacrifice "the ease and enjoyment of the present moment for the probable expectation of the still greater ease and enjoyment of a more distant but more lasting period of time."[17] It has often been noticed that there is a good deal of overlap between this prudent man and the man driven by the desire to better his condition that Smith describes in *The Wealth of Nations* and in Book I of *The Theory of Moral Sentiments*: in both cases, the concern for one's reputation is tied to a strategy of postponed gratification. The important point here is that Smith characterizes this type of prudence as "that of the Epicurean."[18]

Of the behavior of the prudent man, Smith says in Book V that it commands "a certain cold esteem."[19] In Book I, the same type of behavior is criticized from a Stoic point of view, with arguments that are strongly reminiscent of Rousseau's *Second Discourse*: "It is the vanity, not the ease, or the

---

[14] John Stuart Mill, "Bentham," *London and Westminster Review*, August 1838, revised in *Dissertations and Discussions*, London: John Parker, 1859, vol. 1, p. 382. Henry Sidgwick expresses a similar view: "Still the premises of Bentham are all clearly given by Helvetius; and the task which the former took up is that which the latter clearly marks out for the moralist. Indeed, if we imagine the effect of *L'Esprit* on the mind of an eager young law-student, we seem to have the whole intellectual career of Bentham implicitly contained in a 'pensée de jeunesse.'

"Helvetius puts with a highly effective simplicity, from which Hume was precluded by his more subtle and complex psychological analysis, these two doctrines: first, that every human being 'en tout temps, en tout lieu' seeks his own interest, and judges of things and persons according as they promote it; and secondly, that, as the public is made up of individuals, the qualities that naturally and normally gain public esteem and are called virtues are those useful to the public." "Bentham and Benthamism in Politics and Ethics," *Fortnightly Review* 21 (1877), p. 638.

[15] Mill, "Bentham," p. 383.   [16] Smith, *The Theory of Moral Sentiments*, VI.i.5.

[17] Ibid., VI.i.11.   [18] Ibid., VI.i.15.   [19] Ibid., VI.i.14.

pleasure, which interests us."²⁰ In other words, it is wrong to assume, as the Epicureans do, that the search for pleasure explains our behavior. Smith, as he often does, argues on both sides of the issue. In the end, however, it is the Stoic perspective that includes and integrates the Epicurean perspective, and not the reverse. Smith's response to the "selfish hypothesis" is very similar to Rousseau's. Like Rousseau, Smith acknowledges that the description of human behavior one finds in Mandeville and La Rochefoucauld is in many ways accurate. As Mandeville puts it, "the true object of pride or vainglory is the opinion of others,"²¹ and this concern for the opinion of others drives most of what we do in society. At the same time, Smith and Rousseau are highly suspicious of a theory that would use the "selfish hypothesis" to explain everything. The challenge is therefore to construct a theory that will preserve Mandeville's description of human behavior while using assumptions other than the search for one's pleasure, or interest. The demonstration is both psychological and historical. For Rousseau, human behavior in modern commercial society is driven by *amour-propre*, a passion that has little to do with natural selfishness, and much to do with reason, reflection, and our ability to identify with the feelings of others. For Smith, the driving force of human behavior in modern commercial society is *vanity*, a passion that does not originate in self-love (in the Stoic sense of concern for one's preservation) but rather in sympathy and the desire for sympathy. The historical dimension of the demonstration lies in the fact that both *amour-propre* and *vanity* are made possible by the development of commerce and the division of labor.

The consistency of Smith's system lies in the principle of sympathy, which is the foundation of the desire to better our condition. The apparent inconsistencies have come from various attempts to reconstruct Smith's system on the basis of neo-Epicurean, hedonistic principles. The fact that these attempts never seem to go away testifies to the staying power of the "selfish hypothesis," and to its "highly effective simplicity."²² In contrast, Smith's anthropology, like Rousseau's, is complex and peculiar, because it uses neo-Stoic assumptions to account for forms of behavior that La Rochefoucauld, Bayle, and Mandeville had explained from an Epicurean/Augustinian point of view. This is what makes the status of self-interest so ambiguous in Smith's doctrine. On the one hand, self-interest is far removed from the status of a first principle in *The Wealth of Nations*. Appealing to self-interest is the way

---

²⁰ Ibid., I.iii.2.1.
²¹ Bernard Mandeville, *The Fable of the Bees*, edited by F.B. Kaye, Oxford: Oxford University Press, 1924 [sixth edition, London: J. Tonson, 1732], vol. 2, p. 64.
²² Sidgwick, "Bentham and Benthamism in Politics and Ethics," p. 638.

to persuade someone to engage in a transaction. The principle behind the transaction is not self-interest but the propensity to barter and trade, which is itself based on reason and speech, and the propensity to persuade. Finally, the propensity to persuade is itself based on the principle of sympathy. This scheme is very close to Rousseau's analysis of *amour-propre*, which is based on "reason and reflection," and on our ability to identify with the feelings of others. According to Rousseau, in modern commercial society, calculations of interest are a means to an end: maximizing our standing in the eyes of others. Both Smith and Rousseau understand the pursuit of self-interest in a very restricted sense: self-interest requires an explicit transaction, the use of rational calculation, and a social organization that makes the transaction possible. In that sense, self-interest is far from being a general explanatory principle.

On the other hand, a fundamental point in Rousseau's satire of modern commercial society is that *amour-propre* has become a nearly universal motive of human behavior. Smith is ambivalent about Rousseau's satire: he endorses it and he criticizes it at the same time. What he does not question in Rousseau's description is the fact that vanity (or the desire to better one's condition) has become the preponderant motive. While the urge for immediate gratification was dominant in earlier stages of economic development, the dominant strategy in modern commercial society consists in postponing gratification in order to obtain the admiration of others through the accumulation of wealth. In that sense, self-interest, to the extent that it is tied to the desire to better our condition, is to be found in the vast majority of human enterprises. Smith's psychological analysis of economic behavior is paradoxically grounded in a doctrine that is fundamentally critical of modern commercial society.

Smith's analysis is focused on showing exactly under what conditions the pursuit of self-interest will contribute to the public good. Smith thinks of the connection between individual interest and the public interest within a harmonic scheme, distinct from the countervailing passions scheme that was prevalent at the time. There is harmony between partial interests and the public interest to the extent that partial interests are "small" enough to be harnessed by adequate institutional mechanisms. Whenever someone's actions have "large" consequences, it is impossible to enforce an identity of interests between the general and the particular. In that case, the only way of attending to the public interest is by rising above one's particular point of view in order to take a more general point of view.

Jean-Baptiste Say's affirmation of the autonomy of economics with respect to politics in his 1803 *Treatise on Political Economy* can be understood in two different ways. On the one hand, it is a way of keeping a prudent distance from the republican interpretations of *The Wealth of Nations*. On the other hand, it can be seen as an expression of Say's republican views. One of Say's principal beliefs was the need to educate the statesman and the citizens in order to achieve a more enlightened understanding of the public good. On this point, Say agreed with Smith and Rousseau, who questioned the rationality of reason of State theory, and rejected the notion that the statesman would work for the public good for reasons of self-interest. In that sense, the autonomy of economic science is an unintended consequence of Adam Smith's republican principles.

Bibliography

PRIMARY SOURCES

Abbadie, Jacques, *Traité de la vérité de la religion chrétienne*, Rotterdam: Reinier Leers, 1684

Aristotle, *Nicomachean Ethics*, translated by H. Rackham, Cambridge, MA: Harvard University Press, 1926

Arnauld, Antoine, *Réflexions philosophiques et théologiques sur le nouveau système de la nature et de la grâce*, in *Œuvres de Messire Antoine Arnauld*, vol. 39, Paris: Sigismond d'Arnay, 1781 [Cologne: N. Schouten, 1685–1686 (3 vols.)]

Augustine, *Confessions*, translated by Albert C. Outler, Philadelphia: Westminster Press, 1955

The City of God, translated by John O'Meara, London: Penguin Books, 1984

Bayle, Pierre, *Pensées diverses écrites à un docteur de Sorbonne à l'occasion de la comète qui parut au mois de décembre 1680*, in *Œuvres diverses*, vol. 3, The Hague: P. Husson, F. Boucquet et al., 1727 [Rotterdam: Reinier Leers, 1682]

Continuation des pensées diverses, in *Œuvres diverses*, vol. 3, The Hague: P. Husson, F. Boucquet et al., 1727 [Rotterdam: Reinier Leers, 1704]

Dictionnaire historique et critique, Amsterdam: P. Brunel, 1740 [Rotterdam: Reinier Leers, 1697]

Bentham, Jeremy, *An Introduction to the Principles of Morals and Legislation*, edited by J.H. Burns and H.L.A. Hart, Oxford: Clarendon Press, 1996 [London, 1789]

Bernier, François, *Abrégé de la philosophie de Gassendi*, Corpus des œuvres de philosophie en langue française (7 vols.), Paris: Fayard, 1992 [Lyon: Anisson, Posuel et Rigaud, 1684]

Bonnet, Charles, *Contemplation de la nature*, in *Œuvres*, vol. 4, Neuchâtel: S. Fauche, 1781 [Amsterdam, 1764]

Bossuet, Jacques Bénigne, *Divers écrits, ou Mémoires sur le livre intitulé: Explication des maximes des saints, etc.* in *Œuvres*, vol. 28, Versailles: Lebel, 1817 [Paris: J. Anisson, 1698]

Relation sur le quiétisme, in *Œuvres*, vol. 29, Versailles: Lebel, 1817 [Lyon: J. Anisson, 1698]

Réponse à quatre lettres de Monseigneur l'archevêque duc de Cambrai, in *Œuvres*, vol. 29, Versailles: Lebel, 1817 [Paris: J. Anisson, 1698]

Brentano, Lujo, *The Relation of Labor to the Law of Today*, New York: G.P. Putnam's Sons, 1891 [*Das Arbeitsverhaltniss gemass dem heutigen Recht*, Leipzig: Duncker & Humblot, 1877]

Butler, Joseph, *Fifteen Sermons Preached at the Rolls Chapel*, sixth edition, London: Rivington, 1792 [London: Knapton, 1726]

"Fifteen Sermons," in *British Moralists, 1650–1800*, edited by D.D. Raphael, Oxford: Clarendon Press, 1969

Cicero, *De Officiis*, translated by Walter Miller, Cambridge, MA: Harvard University Press, 1913

Condorcet, Jean-Antoine-Nicolas de Caritat, marquis de, *Esquisse d'un tableau historique de l'esprit humain*, Paris: Boivin, 1933 [Paris: Agasse, 1794]

Sketch for a Historical Picture of the Progress of the Human Mind, translated by June Barraclough, London: Weidenfeld and Nicolson, 1955

Defoe, Daniel, *Colonel Jack*, London, 1723

Dufresnoy, Nicolas Lenglet, *L'Histoire justifiée contre les romans*, Amsterdam, 1735

Edgeworth, Francis Y., *Mathematical Psychics. An Essay on the Application of Mathematics to the Moral Sciences*, London: C. Kegan Paul, 1881

Encyclopédie ou dictionnaire raisonné des sciences, des arts et des métiers, Paris, 1751–1772 (17 vols.)

Epictetus, *Discourses*, translated by George Long, London: George Bell, 1909

Epicurus, *Letter to Menoeceus*, in *The Epicurus Reader*, translated and edited by Brad Inwood and L.P. Gerson, Indianapolis: Hackett, 1994

Esprit, Jacques, *La Fausseté des vertus humaines*, Paris: Desprez, 1677–1678 (2 vols.)

Faujas de Saint-Fond, Barthélémy, *Travels in England, Scotland and the Hebrides, undertaken for the purpose of examining the state of the arts, the sciences, natural history and manners, in Great Britain*, London: James Ridgway, 1799 [Paris: H.-J. Jansen, 1797]

Fénelon, François de Salignac de la Mothe, *Explication des maximes des saints*, Paris: Blond, 1911 [Paris: B. Aubouin, 1697]

The Maxims of the Saints Explained, Concerning the Interiour Life, by the Lord Archbishop of Cambrai, London: H. Rhodes, 1698

Instruction pastorale de Mgr l'archevesque duc de Cambray au clergé et au peuple de son diocèse, en forme de dialogue, Cambrai: N.J. Douilliez, 1714 (2 vols.)

Œuvres, Versailles: Lebel, 1822–1824 (20 vols.)

Œuvres complètes, Paris: Méquignon Jr. and J. Leroux, 1848–1852 (10 vols.)

Ferguson, Adam, *An Essay on the History of Civil Society*, edited by Fania Oz-Salzberger, Cambridge: Cambridge University Press, 1995 [Edinburgh: Kincaid & Bell, 1767]

Gassendi, Pierre, *Animadversiones in Decimum Librum Diogenis Laertii, qui est de vita, moribus, placitisque Epicuri*, in *Greek and Roman Philosophy*, vol. 19, New York: Garland Publishing, 1987 [Lyon: Guillaume Barbier, 1649, 3 vols.]

Helvétius, Claude Adrien, *De l'Esprit*, Paris: Durand 1758 (2 vols.)

Essays on the Mind, London: Albion Press, 1810

De l'Homme. De ses facultés intellectuelles, et de son éducation, London: Société Typographique, 1773

A Treatise on Man, translated by W. Hooper, New York: Burt Franklin, 1969 (2 vols.)

Hildebrand, Bruno, *Die Nationalökonomie der Gegenwart und Zukunft*, Frankfurt: Literarische Anstalt, 1848

Hobbes, Thomas, *Leviathan*, edited by Edwin Curley, with selected variants from the Latin edition of 1668, Indianapolis: Hackett, 1994 [London: Andrew Crooke, 1651]

Holbach, Paul Henri Thiry, baron d', *Système de la nature, ou des lois du monde physique et du monde moral*, Geneva: Slatkine Reprints, 1973 (2 vols.) [London, 1770]

Hume, David, *A Treatise of Human nature, being an attempt to introduce the experimental method of reasoning into moral subjects*, Oxford: Clarendon Press, 1975 [London: John Noon, 1739]

Enquiry Concerning the Principles of Morals, edited by J.B. Schneewind, Indianapolis: Hackett, 1983 [1777 edition; first edition 1751]

Political Essays, edited by Knud Haakonssen, Cambridge: Cambridge University Press, 1994 [*Political Discourses*, Edinburgh: A. Kincaid and A. Donaldson, 1752]

Hutcheson, Francis, *An Inquiry into the original of our Ideas of Beauty and Virtue, in two treatises, in which the principles of the late Earl of Shaftesbury are explained and defended, against the author of The Fable of the Bee*, in *Collected Works*, vol. 1, Hildesheim: Georg Olms, 1990 [London: J. Darby, 1725]

A System of Moral Philosophy in three books, in *Collected Works*, vols. 5 and 6, Hildesheim: Georg Olms, 1990 [Glasgow: Robert Foulis, 1755]

La Rochefoucauld, François, duc de, *Maximes*, edited by Jean Lafond, Paris: Gallimard, 1976 [fifth edition, Paris: Barbin, 1678; first edition 1665]

The Maxims, translated by Louis Kronenberger, New York: Stackpole, 1936

Locke, John, *An Essay Concerning Human Understanding*, edited by Peter Harold Nidditch, Oxford: Clarendon Press, 1975 [London, 1689]

Second Treatise of Government, edited by C.B. Macpherson, Indianapolis: Hackett, 1980 [London, 1690]

Malebranche, Nicolas, *De la Recherche de la vérité*, in *Œuvres complètes de Malebranche*, vols. 1 and 2, Paris: Vrin, 1962 [Paris: Pralard, 1674]

Traité de morale, in *Œuvres complètes de Malebranche*, vol. 11, Paris: Vrin, 1966 [Rotterdam: Reinier Leers, 1684].

Mandeville, Bernard, *Letter to Dion*, Liverpool: University Press of Liverpool, 1954 [London: J. Roberts, 1732]

The Fable of the Bees, edited by F.B. Kaye, Oxford: Clarendon Press, 1924 (2 vols.) [sixth edition, London: J. Tonson, 1732]

Melon, Jean-François, *Essai politique sur le commerce*, Rouen(?), 1734

Mill, John Stuart, *Dissertations and Discussions*, London: John Parker, 1859

Mirabeau, Victor Riqueti, marquis de, *L'Ami des hommes, ou traité de la population*, Avignon, 1756

Mirabeau, Victor Riqueti, marquis de, and Quesnay, François, *Philosophie rurale, ou économie générale et politique de l'agriculture, réduite à l'ordre immuable des lois physiques et morales qui assurent la prospérité des empires*, Amsterdam: Libraires Associés, 1764

Montaigne, Michel Eyquem de, *Essays*, translated by Donald Frame, Stanford: Stanford University Press, 1965

    Les Essais, edited by Pierre Villey and V.-L. Saulnier, Paris: PUF, 1992 (3 vols.) [Paris, 1598]

Charles-Louis de Montesquieu, *Persian Letters*, translated by J. Robert Loy, New York: Meridian Books, 1961

    Lettres persanes, in *Œuvres complètes*, Paris: Seuil, 1964 [Paris, 1721]

    De L'Esprit des lois, in *Œuvres complètes*, Paris: Seuil, 1964 [Geneva, 1748]

    The Spirit of the Laws, translated and edited by Anne M. Cohler, Basia Carolyn Miller, and Harold Samuel Stone, Cambridge: Cambridge University Press, 1989

Nicole, Pierre, *Essais de morale*, edited by Laurent Thirouin, Paris: PUF, 1999 [Paris: Desprez, 1675]

    Moral Essays, London: Manship, 1696

Nietzsche, Friedrich, *On the Genealogy of Morals*, translated by Walter Kaufmann, New York: Vintage Books, 1989 [*Zur Genealogie der Moral*, 1887]

Ovid, *Metamorphoses*, translated by Frank Justus Miller, Cambridge, MA: Harvard University Press, 1916 (2 vols.)

Pascal, Blaise, *Pensées*, in *Œuvres complètes*, edited by Louis Lafuma, Paris: Seuil, 1963 [Paris: Desprez, 1670]

    Pensées, translated by A.J. Krailsheimer, London: Penguin Books, 1966

    Pensées, edited by Philippe Sellier, Paris: Bordas, 1991

    Écrits sur la grâce, in *Œuvres complètes*, edited by Jean Mesnard, vol. 3, Paris: Desclée de Brouwer, 1991

Quesnay, François, and Dupont de Nemours, Pierre-Samuel (eds.), *Physiocratie, ou Constitution naturelle du gouvernement le plus avantageux au genre humain*, Leyden, 1767–1768 (2 vols.)

Robinet, Jean-Baptiste, *De la nature*, Amsterdam: Van Harrevelt, 1761

Rohan, Henri de, *De l'intérêt des princes et des États de la chrétienté*, edited by Christian Lazzeri, Paris: PUF, 1995 [Paris, 1638]

Rollin, Charles, *Histoire ancienne des Egyptiens, des Carthaginois, des Assyriens, des Babyloniens, des Grecs*, Paris: Veuve Etienne, 1731–1738 (13 vols.)

    Œuvres complètes, Paris: Didot, 1821–1831 (30 vols.)

Rousseau, Jean-Jacques, *Œuvres complètes*, edited by Bernard Gagnebin and Marcel Raymond, Paris: Gallimard, Bibliothèque de la Pléiade, 1959–1969 (4 vols.)

    Émile, translated by Allan Bloom, New York: Basic Books, 1979

    The Collected Writings of Rousseau, edited by Roger D. Masters and Christopher Kelly, Hanover, NH: University Press of New England, 1990–2001 (9 vols.)

Say, Jean-Baptiste, *Olbie, ou Essai pour reformer les mœurs d'une nation*, Paris: Deterville, 1799

    A Treatise on Political Economy, Philadelphia: Grigg & Elliot 1832

    Traité d'économie politique, Paris: Guillaumin, 1841 [Paris: Deterville, 1803]

Seligman, Edwin R.A., "Review of *Principles of Political Economy*, by Henry Sidgwick," *The Index. A Weekly Paper*, Boston, August 16, 1883, pp. 75–76
"Review of *The Scope and Method of Economic Science*, by Henry Sidgwick," *Political Science Quarterly* 1:1 (1886), pp. 143–145
Shaftesbury, Anthony Ashley Cooper, Third Earl of, *An Inquiry Concerning Virtue*, in *Characteristics of Men, Manners, Opinions, Times*, Anglistica & Americana Series no. 123, vol. 2, Hildesheim: Georg Olms, 1978 [London: A. Bell, E. Castle, and S. Buckley, 1699]
Sensus Communis, viz. An Essay on the Freedom of Wit and Humor, in *Characteristics of Men, Manners, Opinions, Times*, Anglistica & Americana Series no. 123, vol. 1, Hildesheim: Georg Olms, 1978 [London: Egbert Sanger, 1709]
Characteristics of Men, Manners, Opinions, Times, Anglistica & Americana Series no. 123 Hildesheim: Georg Olms, 1978 (3 vols.) [London, 1711]
Sidgwick, Henry, "Bentham and Benthamism in Politics and Ethics," *Fortnightly Review* 21 (1877), pp. 627–652
Principles of Political Economy, London: Macmillan, 1883
The Scope and Method of Economic Science. An address delivered to the economic science and statistics section of the British Association at Aberdeen, 10 September, 1885, London: Macmillan, 1885
The Methods of Ethics, seventh edition, London: Macmillan, 1907 [London, 1874]
Smith, Adam, *The Glasgow Edition of the Works and Correspondence of Adam Smith*, Oxford: Clarendon Press, 1976–1983 (6 vols.)
Steuart, Sir James, *An Inquiry into the Principles of Political Economy, Being an Essay on the Science of Domestic Policy in Free Nations*, Edinburgh: Oliver & Boyd, 1966 (2 vols.) [London: A. Millar and T. Cadell, 1767]
Vauvenargues, Luc de Clapiers, marquis de, *Réflexions et maximes*, in *Introduction à la connaissance de l'esprit humain*, Paris: Briasson, 1747
Voltaire, *Lettres philosophiques*, Paris: Hachette, 1915–1917 [Paris, 1734]
Dictionnaire philosophique, edited by J. Benda and R. Naves, Paris: Garnier, 1954 [Paris, 1764]
Wolf, Friedrich August, *Prolegomena ad Homerum*, Halis Saxonum: a libraria Orphanotrophei, 1794–1795
Prolegomena to Homer, translated by Anthony Grafton, Glenn W. Most, and James E.G. Zetzel, Princeton: Princeton University Press, 1985

SECONDARY SOURCES

Adam Smith, 1776–1926. Lectures to Commemorate the Sesquicentennial of the Publication of "The Wealth of Nations", New York: Augustus M. Kelley, 1966 [reprint of original 1928 edition]
Arrow, Kenneth, and Hahn, F.H., *General Competitive Analysis*, San Francisco: Holden Day, 1971
Becker, Gary, *The Economic Approach to Human Behavior*, Chicago: University of Chicago Press, 1976

"The Economic Approach to Human Behavior," in *Rational Choice*, edited by
Jon Elster, New York: New York University Press, 1986, pp. 108–122

Becker, Gary, and Stigler, George J., "De Gustibus Non Est Disputandum,"
American Economic Review 67:2 (1977), pp. 76–90

Bénichou, Paul, *Morales du grand siècle*, Paris: Gallimard, 1948

Bloch, Olivier-René, *La philosophie de Gassendi*, The Hague: Nijhoff, 1971

Bobzien, Susanne, *Determinism and Freedom in Stoic Philosophy*, Oxford:
Clarendon Press, 1998

Bonar, James, *A Catalogue of the Library of Adam Smith*, New York: Augustus
M. Kelley, Reprints of Economic Classics series, 1966 [1894]

Philosophy and Political Economy in Some of Their Historical Relations, New
Brunswick, NJ: Transaction Books 1992 [New York: Macmillan 1893]

Bourdieu, Pierre, *Outline of a Theory of Practice*, translated by Richard Nice,
Cambridge: Cambridge University Press, 1977 [*Esquisse d'une théorie de la
pratique*, Geneva: Droz, 1972]

Campbell, T.D., *Adam Smith's Science of Morals*, London: Allen & Unwin, 1971

Dagen, Jean, *Entre Épicure et Vauvenargues. Principes et formes de la pensée morale*,
Paris: Champion, 1999

Dickey, Laurence, "Historicizing the 'Adam Smith Problem': Conceptual, Historiographical, and Textual Issues," *Journal of Modern History* 58 (1986),
pp. 579–609

Dorfman, Joseph, "The Role of the German Historical School in American Economic Thought," *American Economic Review* 45:2 (1955), pp. 17–28

Dumont, Louis, *From Mandeville to Marx. The Genesis and Triumph of Economic
Ideology*, Chicago: University of Chicago Press, 1977

Dupuy, Jean-Pierre, "De l'émancipation de l'économie: retour sur 'le problème
d'Adam Smith'," *L'Année sociologique* 37 (1987), pp. 311–342

Eden, Kathy, *Hermeneutics and the Rhetorical Tradition*, New Haven: Yale University Press, 1997

Elias, Norbert, *The Court Society*, New York: Pantheon Books, 1983

Elster, Jon, *Ulysses and the Sirens: Studies in Rationality and Irrationality*, Cambridge:
Cambridge University Press, 1979

Sour Grapes: Studies in the Subversion of Rationality, Cambridge: Cambridge
University Press, 1983

"The Nature and Scope of Rational-Choice Explanations," in *Actions and Events:
Perspectives on the Philosophy of Donald Davidson*, edited by Ernest LePore and
Brian P. McLaughlin, Oxford: Blackwell, 1985, pp. 60–72.

Nuts and Bolts for the Social Sciences, Cambridge: Cambridge University Press,
1989

Strong Feelings: Emotion, Addiction and Human Behavior, Cambridge, MA: MIT
Press, 1999

Ulysses Unbound: Studies in Rationality, Precommitment, and Constraints,
Cambridge: Cambridge University Press, 2000

Force, Pierre, "What Is a Man Worth? Ethics and Economics in Molière and
Rousseau," *Romanic Review* 1 (1989), pp. 18–29

Molière ou Le Prix des choses. Morale, économie et comédie, Paris: Nathan, 1994
"Self-Love, Identification, and the Origin of Political Economy," in *Exploring the Conversible World: Text and Sociability from the Classical Age to the Enlightenment*, edited by Elena Russo, *Yale French Studies* 92 (1997), pp. 46–64
Force, Pierre, and Morgan, David (eds.), *De la morale à l'économie politique. Dialogue franco-américain sur les moralistes français*, Pau: Publications de l'Université de Pau, 1996
Frankfurt, Harry G., "Freedom of the Will and the Concept of Reason," *Journal of Philosophy* 68:1 (1971), pp. 5–20
Necessity, Volition and Love, Cambridge: Cambridge University Press, 1999
Fuchs, Hans-Jürgen, *Entfremdung und Narzißmus. Semantische Untersuchungen zur Geschichte der "Selbstbezogenheit" als Vorgeschichte von französisch "amour-propre"*, Stuttgart: Metzler, 1977
Gadamer, Hans-Georg, *Truth and Method*, translation revised by Joel Weinsheimer and Donald G. Marshall, New York: Crossroad, 1992
Goldschmidt, Victor, *Anthropologie et politique. Les principes du système de Rousseau*, Paris: Vrin, 1974
Griswold, Charles, *Adam Smith and the Virtues of Enlightenment*, Cambridge: Cambridge University Press, 1999
Gunn, J.A.W., "Interest Will Not Lie: A Seventeenth Century Political Maxim," *Journal of the History of Ideas* 29:4 (1968), pp. 551–564
Haakonssen, Knud, *The Science of a Legislator. The Natural Jurisprudence of David Hume and Adam Smith*, Cambridge: Cambridge University Press, 1981
Haakonssen, Knud (ed.), *Adam Smith*, Aldershot: Dartmouth Publishing Company, 1998
Hadot, Pierre, and Davidson, Arnold, *Philosophy as a Way of Life. Spiritual Exercises from Socrates to Foucault*, Oxford: Blackwell, 1995
Harpham, Edward J., "Liberalism, Civic Humanism, and the Case of Adam Smith," *American Political Science Review* 78 (1984), pp. 764–774
Hasbach, Wilhelm, "Larochefoucault und Mandeville," in *Jahrbuch für Gesetzgebung und Volkswirtschaft im Deutschen Reich*, Leipzig, 1890, pp. 1–43
Untersuchungen über Adam Smith und die Entwicklung der Politischen Ökonomie, Leipzig, 1891
Hausman, Daniel M., *The Inexact and Separate Science of Economics*, Cambridge: Cambridge University Press, 1992
Hausman, Daniel M., and McPherson, Michael S., *Economic Analysis and Moral Philosophy*, Cambridge: Cambridge University Press, 1996
Havens, George Remington, *Voltaire's Marginalia on the Pages of Rousseau. A Comparative Study of Ideas*, Columbus: Ohio State University Press, 1933
Hayek, Friedrich A., "Dr. Bernard Mandeville," *Proceedings of the British Academy* 52 (1966), pp. 125–141
Studies in Philosophy, Politics and Economics, London: Routledge & Kegan Paul, 1967

Heath, Eugene, "The Commerce of Sympathy: Adam Smith on the Emergence of Morals," *Journal of the History of Philosophy* 33:3 (July 1995), pp. 447–466

Hirschman, Albert O., "Against Parsimony: Three Easy Ways of Complicating Some Categories of Economic Discourse," in *Rival Views of Market Society*, Cambridge, MA: Harvard University Press, 1992 [1986], pp. 142–160

"The Concept of Interest: From Euphemism to Tautology," in *Rival Views of Market Society*, Cambridge, MA: Harvard University Press, 1992 [1986], pp. 35–55

The Passions and the Interests. Political Arguments for Capitalism before its Triumph, Princeton: Princeton University Press, 1997 [1977]

Hollander, Samuel, "Adam Smith and the Self-Interest Axiom," *Journal of Law and Economics* 20 (1977), pp. 133–152

Hont, Istvan, and Ignatieff, Michael, "Needs and Justice in the 'Wealth of Nations'," in *Wealth and Virtue. The Shaping of Political Economy in the Scottish Enlightenment*, edited by Istvan Hont and Michael Ignatieff, Cambridge: Cambridge University Press, 1983, pp. 1–44

Horne, Thomas A., *The Social Thought of Bernard Mandeville. Virtue and Commerce in Eighteenth-Century England*, New York: Columbia University Press, 1978

Hundert, E.J., *The Enlightenment's Fable. Bernard Mandeville and the Discovery of Society*, Cambridge: Cambridge University Press, 1994

Ignatieff, Michael, *The Needs of Strangers*, London: Chatto & Windus, 1984

"Smith, Rousseau and the Republic of Needs," in *Scotland and Europe, 1200–1850*, edited by T.C. Smout, Edinburgh: J. Donald, 1986, pp. 187–206

Ingrao, Bruna, and Israel, Giorgio, *The Invisible Hand. Economic Equilibrium in the History of Science*, Cambridge, MA: MIT Press, 1990

James, E.D., *Pierre Nicole, Jansenist and Humanist*, The Hague: Nijhoff, 1972

"Faith, Sincerity and Morality: Mandeville and Bayle," in *Mandeville Studies. New Explorations in the Art and Thought of Dr. Bernard Mandeville*, edited by Irwin Primer, The Hague: Nijhoff, 1975, pp. 43–65

Kalyvas, Andreas, and Katznelson, Ira, "The Rhetoric of the Market: Adam Smith on Recognition, Speech, and Exchange," *Review of Politics* 63:3 (2001), pp. 549–579

Kerkhof, Bert, "A Fatal Attraction? Smith's *Theory of Moral Sentiments* and Mandeville's *Fable*," *History of Political Thought* 16:2 (Summer 1995), pp. 219–233

Lafond, Jean, *La Rochefoucauld. Augustinisme et littérature*, third edition, Paris: Klincksieck, 1986 [1977]

"De la morale à l'économie politique, ou de La Rochefoucauld et des moralistes jansénistes à Adam Smith par Malebranche et Mandeville," in *De la morale à l'économie politique. Dialogue franco-américain sur les moralistes français*, edited by Pierre Force and David Morgan, Pau: Publications de l'Université de Pau, 1996, pp. 187–196

L'Homme et son image. Morales et littérature de Montaigne à Mandeville, Paris: Champion, 1996

Larrère, Catherine, *L'Invention de l'économie au XVIIIe siècle. Du droit naturel à la physiocratie*, Paris: PUF, 1992

Lewis, Thomas J., "Persuasion, Domination and Exchange: Adam Smith on the Political Consequences of Markets," *Canadian Journal of Political Science* 33:2 (2000), pp. 273–289

Lovejoy, Arthur O., *Reflections on Human Nature*, Baltimore: Johns Hopkins University Press, 1961

Macfie, Alec L., *The Individual in Society. Papers on Adam Smith*, London: Allen & Unwin, 1967

"The Invisible Hand of Jupiter," *Journal of the History of Ideas* 32:4 (1971), pp. 595–599

Mansfield, Harvey C., "Self-Interest Rightly Understood," *Political Theory* 23:1 (February 1995), pp. 48–66

Marshall, David, *The Figure of Theater. Shaftesbury, Defoe, Adam Smith, and George Eliot*, New York: Columbia University Press, 1986

The Surprising Effects of Sympathy: Marivaux, Diderot, Rousseau, and Mary Shelley, Chicago: University of Chicago Press, 1988

McKenna, Antony, *De Pascal à Voltaire. Le rôle des Pensées de Pascal dans l'histoire des idées de 1670 à 1734*, Oxford: The Voltaire Foundation, 1990 (2 vols.)

"Bayle, moraliste augustinien," in *De la morale à l'économie politique. Dialogue franco-américain sur les moralistes français*, edited by Pierre Force and David Morgan, Pau: Publications de l'Université de Pau, 1996, pp. 175–186

McKenna, Antony, and Jehasse, Jean (eds.), *Religion et politique. Les avatars de l'augustinisme*, Saint-Etienne: Publications de l'Université de Saint-Etienne, 1998

Meek, Ronald L., *Social Science and the Ignoble Savage*, Cambridge: Cambridge University Press, 1976

Mizuta, Hiroshi, *Adam Smith's Library. A Supplement to Bonar's Catalogue with a Checklist of the Whole Library*, Cambridge: Cambridge University Press, 1967

Morel, Jean, "Recherches sur les sources du discours de l'inégalité," *Annales Jean-Jacques Rousseau*, vol. 5, Geneva, 1909, pp. 119–198

Morrow, Glenn R., *The Ethical and Economic Theories of Adam Smith*, Cornell Studies in Philosophy no. 13, New York: Longmans, Green and Co., 1923

Neuendorff, Hartmut, *Der Begriff des Interesse*, Frankfurt: Suhrkamp, 1973

Nicholls, David, "The Invisible Hand: Providence and the Market," in *The Values of the Enterprise Culture: The Moral Debate*, edited by Paul Heelas and Paul Morris, London, New York: Routledge, 1992, pp. 217–236

Nozick, Robert, "Invisible Hand Explanations," *American Economic Review* 84:2 (May 1994), pp. 314–318

Nuchelmans, Gabriël, "On the Fourfold Root of the *Argumentum ad Hominem*," in *Empirical Logic and Public Debate*, Amsterdam, 1993, pp. 37–47

Oncken, August, "The Consistency of Adam Smith," *Economic Journal* 7:27 (1897), pp. 443–450

Pack, Spencer J., "Theological (and Hence Economic) Implications of Adam Smith's 'Principles which Lead and Direct Philosophical Inquiries'," *History of Political Economy* 27:2 (1995), pp. 289–307

Parfit, Derek, *Reasons and Persons*, Oxford: Clarendon Press, 1984

Perelman, Michael, "Adam Smith and Dependent Social Relations," *History of Political Economy* 21:3 (1989), pp. 503–520

Perrot, Jean-Claude, *Une histoire intellectuelle de l'économie politique*, Paris: Editions de l'Ecole des Hautes Etudes en Sciences Sociales, 1992

Phillipson, Nicholas, "Adam Smith as a Civic Moralist," in *Wealth and Virtue. The Shaping of Political Economy in the Scottish Enlightenment*, edited by Istvan Hont and Michael Ignatieff, Cambridge: Cambridge University Press, 1983, pp. 179–202

Pocock, J.G.A., *The Machiavellian Moment. Florentine Political Thought and the Atlantic Republican Tradition*, Princeton: Princeton University Press, 1975

"Cambridge Paradigms and Scotch Philosophers," in *Wealth and Virtue. The Shaping of Political Economy in the Scottish Enlightenment*, edited by Istvan Hont and Michael Ignatieff, Cambridge: Cambridge University Press, 1983, pp. 235–252

Pribram, Karl, *A History of Economic Reasoning*, Baltimore: Johns Hopkins University Press, 1983

Primer, Irwin (ed.), *Mandeville Studies. New Explorations in the Art and Thought of Dr. Bernard Mandeville*, International Archives of the History of Ideas 81, The Hague: Nijhoff, 1975

Raphael, D.D., *Adam Smith*, Oxford: Oxford University Press, 1985

Raphael, D.D. (ed.), *British Moralists 1650–1800*, Oxford: Clarendon Press, 1969

Recktenwald, Horst Claus, *Das Selbstinteresse – Zentrales Axiom der ökonomischen Wissenschaft*, Stuttgart: Steiner-Verlag-Wiesbaden, 1986

Robertson, John, "The Scottish Enlightenment at the Limits of the Civic Tradition," in *Wealth and Virtue. The Shaping of Political Economy in the Scottish Enlightenment*, edited by Istvan Hont and Michael Ignatieff, Cambridge: Cambridge University Press, 1983, pp. 137–178

Rohou, Jean, *Le XVIIe siècle, une révolution de la condition humaine*, Paris: Seuil, 2002

Rosenberg, Nathan, "Some Institutional Aspects of the *Wealth of Nations*," *Journal of Political Economy* 68:6 (1960), pp. 557–570

Rothschild, Emma, "Adam Smith and the Invisible Hand," *American Economic Review* 84:2 (May 1994), pp. 319–322

Economic Sentiments. Adam Smith, Condorcet, and the Enlightenment, Cambridge, MA: Harvard University Press, 2001

Sauvé Meyer, Susan, "Fate, Fatalism, and Agency in Stoicism," *Social Philosophy and Policy* 16:2 (1999), pp. 250–273

Scarre, Geoffrey, "Epicurus as a Forerunner of Utilitarianism," *Utilitas* 6:2 (November 1994), pp. 219–232

Schatz, Albert, "Bernard de Mandeville. Contribution à l'étude des origines du libéralisme économique," *Vierteljahrschrift für Social- und Wirtschaftgeschichte*, Leipzig, 1903, pp. 434–480

Schmitt, Carl, *The Concept of the Political*, Chicago: University of Chicago Press, 1996

Sellier, Philippe, "La Rochefoucauld, Pascal, saint Augustin," *Revue d'histoire littéraire de la France* (May–August 1969), pp. 551–575

   Pascal et saint Augustin, second edition, Paris: Albin Michel, 1995 [Paris: Armand Colin, 1970]

   "La Rochefoucauld ou l'anamorphose des grands hommes," in *De la morale à l'économie politique. Dialogue franco-américain sur les moralistes français*, edited by Pierre Force and David Morgan, Pau: Publications de l'Université de Pau, 1996, pp. 145–153

   Port-Royal et la littérature, vols. 1 and 2, Paris: Champion, 1999–2000

Sen, Amartya, "Rational Fools: A Critique of the Behavioral Foundations of Economic Theory," *Philosophy and Public Affairs* 6 (1977), pp. 317–344

   On Ethics and Economics, Oxford: Blackwell, 1987

Sewall, Richard B., "Rousseau's Second Discourse in England from 1755 to 1762," *Philological Quarterly* 17:2 (April 1938), pp. 97–112

Shovlin, John, "Luxury, Political Economy, and the Rise of Commercial Society in Eighteenth-Century France," doctoral dissertation, University of Chicago, 1998

Silver, Allan, " 'Two Different Sorts of Commerce' – Friendship and Strangership in Civil Society," in *Public and Private in Thought and Practice*, edited by Jeff Weintraub and Krishan Kumar, Chicago: University of Chicago Press, 1998, pp. 43–74

Skinner, Quentin, *Reason and Rhetoric in the Philosophy of Hobbes*, Cambridge: Cambridge University Press, 1996

Stark, Oded, *Altruism and Beyond. An Economic Analysis of Transfers and Exchanges within Families and Groups*, Cambridge: Cambridge University Press, 1995

Stigler, George J., "Smith's Travels on the Ship of State," *History of Political Economy* 3 (1971), pp. 265–277.

   "Preface" in *The Wealth of Nations*, Chicago: University of Chicago Press, 1976, pp. xi–xiv

   "The Successes and Failures of Professor Smith," Selected Papers no. 50, Graduate School of Business, University of Chicago, 1976

Stigler, George J., and Becker, Gary S., "De Gustibus Non Est Disputandum," *American Economic Review* 67:2 (1977), pp. 76–90

Suttle, Bruce B., "The Passion of Self-Interest: The Development of the Idea and its Changing Status", *American Journal of Economics and Sociology* 46:4 (October 1987), pp. 459–472

Talmon, J.-L., "Rohan and Interest of State," in *Staatsräson: Studien zur Geschichte eines politischen Begriffs*, edited by Roman Schnur, Berlin: Duncker & Humblot, 1975

Teichgraeber, Richard, " 'Less Abused than I had Reason to Expect': The Reception of *The Wealth of Nations* in Britain, 1776–90," *Historical Journal* 30:2 (1987), pp. 337–366

Thirouin, Laurent, *Le Hasard et les règles. Le modèle du jeu dans la pensée de Pascal*, Paris: Vrin, 1991

Tribe, Keith, *Genealogies of Capitalism*, London: Macmillan, 1981
"Historical Schools of Economics: German and English," Working Paper no. 2002/02, Department of Economics, Keele University

Veblen, Thorstein, "The Preconceptions of Economic Science (I)," *Quarterly Journal of Economics* 13:2 (1899), pp. 121–150
"The Preconceptions of Economic Science (II)," *Quarterly Journal of Economics* 13:4 (1899), pp. 396–426

Viner, Jacob, "Guide to John Rae's *Life of Adam Smith*," in *Life of Adam Smith*, Reprints of Economic Classics series, New York: Augustus M. Kelley, 1965, pp. 1–145
The Role of Providence in the Social Order. An Essay in Intellectual History, Princeton: Princeton University Press, 1972

Vivenza, Gloria, *Adam Smith and the Classics. The Classical Heritage in Adam Smith's Thought*, Oxford: Oxford University Press, 2001

Walsh, Vivian, "Rationality as Self-Interest versus Rationality as Present Aims," *American Economic Review* 84:2 (1994), pp. 401–405
Rationality, Allocation, and Reproduction, Oxford: Clarendon Press, 1996

Waszek, Norbert, "Two Concepts of Morality: A Distinction of Adam Smith's Ethics and its Stoic Origin," *Journal of the History of Ideas* 45 (1984), pp. 591–606

Whatmore, Richard, *Republicanism and the French Revolution. An Intellectual History of Jean Baptiste Say's Political Economy*, Oxford: Oxford University Press, 2000

Winch, Donald, *Adam Smith's Politics. An Essay in Historiographic Revision*, Cambridge: Cambridge University Press, 1978
"Adam Smith's 'Enduring Particular Result': A Political and Cosmopolitan Perspective," in *Wealth and Virtue. The Shaping of Political Economy in the Scottish Enlightenment*, edited by Istvan Hont and Michael Ignatieff, Cambridge: Cambridge University Press, 1983, pp. 253–269
"Adam Smith: Scottish Moral Philosopher as Political Economist," *Historical Journal* 35:1 (1992), pp. 91–113
Riches and Poverty. An Intellectual History of Political Economy in Britain, 1750–1834, Cambridge: Cambridge University Press, 1996

Index

Abbadie, Jacques 59, 116, 183
Alexander the Great 143
Almquist, Katherine ix
amour de soi see love of oneself
amour-propre see self-love
Aristotle 49, 169
Arnauld, Antoine 191
Arnauld d'Andilly, Robert 183
Arrow, Kenneth 7
Augustine and Augustinianism 52–53, 57–58,
 60, 61, 71, 84, 112–114, 118, 150, 153, 187,
 188
autonomy (of economic science) *see* economic
 science, autonomy of

Bayle, Pierre 53–54, 60–61, 101, 118, 148–150, 192,
 261
Becker, Gary 8, 91–96, 99
benevolence 10, 93, 194–200
Bénichou, Paul 180
Bentham, Jeremy 92–94, 102, 170, 259
Bernier, François 49–51, 59–60
"bettering one's condition" 75, 126, 133, 161, 179,
 202, 232, 246, 253, 261 *see also* vanity
Bloch, Olivier-René 63
Bloom, Allan 6
Bonar, James 2, 259
Bonnet, Charles 72–73
Bossuet, Jacques Bénigne 184–190
Bourdieu, Pierre 173, 178
Brentano, Lujo 257
Butler, Joseph 65, 81–82, 192–193,
 200

Caesar, Gaius Julius 143
Calvin, John 148, 187
Campbell, T.D. 16, 68, 229
Camus, Jean-Pierre 64
Cannan, Edwin 259
Carlyle, Alexander 227
Carthage 226, 251

Catholic Church 1, 138, 187
Charles VIII of France 210
Chicago Group on Modern France viii
Cicero 49, 83
civic humanism *see* republicanism
Collins, John D. viii
commerce 77, 126–130, 151–153, 172–175,
 208–213, 215–225, 239, 241–251, 261
Condorcet, Jean-Antoine-Nicolas de Caritat,
 marquis de 3, 248–249
consequences, unintended *see* unintended
 consequences
contrarieties (in human nature) 55–56, 79, 120
countervailing passions 135, 145, 146–150, 160,
 211, 223, 225–241, 242, 249

Davidson, Arnold 23
Defoe, Daniel 72
Descartes, René 85
d'Holbach *see* Holbach
Dickey, Laurence 162
Diderot, Denis 89
disinterestedness 5, 38, 174, 194, 197, 198, 218
Dorfman, Joseph 258
Dumont, Louis 2
Dupuy, Jean-Pierre 165

economic science, autonomy of 5, 171, 178, 180,
 200–204, 205–207, 237, 251–255, 262
economy
 of greatness 73–75, 107, 179
 of nature 67–69, 72–73, 232, 237
Eden, Kathy viii, 68
Edgeworth, Francis Y. 7, 11, 169–170, 200,
 201–204
egoism 6, 11, 200–204
Elias, Norbert 176–179
Elster, Jon viii, 10, 13, 85, 91, 97–98, 104–105,
 108–113
Encyclopédie 89, 206, 224
envy 143, 164–167

276

IDEAS IN CONTEXT

Edited by QUENTIN SKINNER (*General Editor*),
LORRAINE DASTON, DOROTHY ROSS and JAMES TULLY